Havana

Scott Doggett
David Stanley

LONELY PLANET PUBLICATIONS
Melbourne • Oakland • London • Paris

Havana
1st edition – March 2001

Published by
Lonely Planet Publications Pty Ltd ABN 36 005 607 983
90 Maribyrnong St, Footscray, Victoria 3011, Australia

Lonely Planet Offices
Australia Locked Bag 1, Footscray, Victoria 3011
USA 150 Linden St, Oakland, CA 94607
UK 10a Spring Place, London NW5 3BH
France 1 rue du Dahomey, 75011 Paris

Photographs
All of the images in this guide are available for licensing from
Lonely Planet Images.
email: lpi@lonelyplanet.com.au

Front cover photograph
Classic American car, Havana (Mason Florence)

Title page photograph
Havana map section (Alfredo Maiquez)

ISBN 1 86450 229 0

text & maps © Lonely Planet 2001
photos © photographers as indicated 2001

Printed by the Bookmaker International Ltd
Printed in China

Contents

INTRODUCTION 9

FACTS ABOUT HAVANA 11

History 11
Geography 26
Climate 27
Ecology & Environment . . 28
Flora & Fauna 28
Government & Politics . . 31
Economy 32
Population & People 36
Arts 39
Society & Conduct 49
Religion 50
Language 52

FACTS FOR THE VISITOR 53

When to Go 53
Orientation 53
Maps 54
Responsible Tourism 54
Tourist Offices 55
Documents 57
Embassies & Consulates . . 62
Customs 63
Money 64
Post & Communications . . 67
Internet Resources 69
Books 70
Films 72
CD ROM 72
Newspapers & Magazines 73
Radio & TV 74
Photography & Video . . . 75
Time 75
Electricity 76
Weights & Measures 76
Laundry 76
Toilets 76
Luggage Storage 76
Health 76
Women Travelers 79
Gay & Lesbian Travelers . . 80
Disabled Travelers 80
Havana for Children . . . 81
Helpful Organizations . . . 81
Libraries 81
Cultural Centers 81
Dangers & Annoyances . . 82
Emergencies 83
Business Hours 83
Public Holidays 84
Special Events 84
Work 85

GETTING THERE & AWAY 86

Air 86
Bus 91
Train 92
Taxi 93
Boat 93
Organized Tours 93

GETTING AROUND 96

The Airport 96
Bus 97
Train 98
Car 98
Taxi 101
Walking 101
Bicycle 101
Boat 102
Organized Tours 102
Travel Agencies 103

THINGS TO SEE & DO 104

La Habana Vieja 105
Centro Habana 116
Eastern Forts 121
Vedado 124
Playa & Marianao 133
Parque Lenin Area 135
Activities 137
Courses 138

PLACES TO STAY 140

La Habana Vieja 142
Centro Habana 143
Vedado 145
Playa & Marianao 147
Parque Lenin Area 150

PLACES TO EAT   151

La Habana Vieja 153   Eastern Forts 161   Playa & Marianao 166
Centro Habana 157   Vedado 161   Parque Lenin Area   168

ENTERTAINMENT   169

Bars 170   Cinemas 176   Classical 178
Folk Dance & Music . . . 172   Theater 176   Spectator Sports 178
Cabaret 173   Rock 177
Dance Clubs 175   Jazz 178

SHOPPING   179

What to Buy 179   Where to Shop 181

EXCURSIONS   185

Museo Hemingway 185   Guanabacoa 188   Cojímar Area 189
Regla 187   Casablanca 189   Playas del Este 190

LANGUAGE   193

GLOSSARY   199

INDEX   202

HAVANA MAP SECTION   209

Havana (Map 1). 210   Playa & Marianao   Regla, Guanabacoa,
La Habana Vieja & Centro   (Map 4) 220   Casablanca &
Habana (Map 2). 212   Parque Lenin Area   Cojímar Area (Map 6) . . 224
Vedado (Map 3). 218   (Map 5) 222   Playas del Este (Map 7). . 226
                                                                    Map Legend. 228

The Authors

Scott Doggett

Scott's interest in Latin America dates from 1983 when, as a recent graduate of the University of California at Berkeley, he moved to El Salvador to work as a photojournalist for the Associated Press. His initial career was followed by postgraduate work at Stanford University; reporting for United Press International in Los Angeles, Pakistan and Afghanistan; and seven years (1989–1996) as a staff editor for the *Los Angeles Times* (he currently writes about business and technology for the newspaper). In 1996, Scott coauthored and coedited (with his future wife, journalist Annette Haddad) the award-winning anthology *Travelers' Tales: Brazil*. Scott is the author of Lonely Planet's *Panama*, *Las Vegas* and *Yucatán* guidebooks and coauthor of *Mexico* and *Dominican Republic & Haiti*. He has also written guidebooks to Amsterdam and Los Angeles. Scott can be reached at sdoggett@aol.com when he's not on the road or on deadline, but please don't email him questions like, 'Could you recommend a hotel in Havana?' The answers to such questions appear in this book.

FROM THE AUTHOR

It's been said again and again that behind every successful man there's a woman, and that is certainly the case with me. Annette Haddad has been my best friend and, next to my parents, my strongest advocate since she and I reported on crime in Los Angeles for UPI way back in the days of the Soviet Union, station wagons and dot matrix printers. Since then, I've gone in and out of war zones, climbed fiery mountains, swum with really big sharks and done a lot of other things I now look back on as stupid and death-wishy (though undeniably interesting). Annette was always there for me when I wasn't sure what I was doing professionally or privately. She offers good advice and perspective, and she's been a godsend in my times of crisis, of which there have been surprisingly too damn many for a man my age living in the USA. Our marriage, celebrated in a charming chapel in San Francisco's Presidio 10 years after our first date, was the best thing that ever happened to me. With profound love and appreciation, this book is dedicated to her.

A senior editor at Lonely Planet, Tom Downs is the best editor with whom I've had the privilege of working in the 15 years I've been writing. Tom was my go-to guy when crises arose during research or writing, and through it all, proved a good friend and a skillful editor. Tom kept the project on track when signs of derailment abounded.

Rachel Bernstein was the eagle-eyed editor who read every word of the manuscript I submitted and, more often than I like to say, corrected errors and caught discrepancies before they appeared in print. Rachel, bless her soul, fixed all the kinks I included in *Havana*, and under an unusually tight schedule. Rachel, I raise my glass to you for outstanding work under fire.

Many other people are involved in the production of these books. Among them are cartographers, designers, illustrators and proofreaders – all very capable, as they demonstrate with every new title and every updated book. A heartfelt *Thank you!!!* to them all.

3

David Stanley

David Stanley studied Spanish literature at schools in Canada, Mexico and Spain, and has spent much of the last three decades on the road, with visits to more than 170 countries. In the late 1970s, he worked at hotels in Cuba as a representative of a Canadian tour company. His guidebook writing experience includes authoring Lonely Planet's *Cuba*, and the Havana chapter of that book was fleshed out for this city guide. Much of the background information and practical advice of this book are the result of David's research, but much of the tone and political slant are not.

This Book

FROM THE PUBLISHER

Havana was edited by Rachel Bernstein in Lonely Planet's Oakland office. Paul Sheridan proofread every page and lent his hand during layout, Tom Downs was the senior editor and Maria Donohoe, Kate Hoffman and Mariah Bear gave much-appreciated support. Patrick 'Peaches' Phelan crafted the maps with a smile and a story, with help from Dion Good and Tessa Rottiers and the guidance of Monica Lepe and Alex Guilbert. Shelley Firth designed *Havana*, her last Lonely Planet book, and Wendy Yanagihara created the cover. Beca Lafore coordinated the illustrating while Suzanne Benton, Hugh D'Andrade, Hayden Foell, Justin Marler and Beca did the illustrating. Susan Rimerman ensured that *Havana*'s design went smoothly. Rick Gerharter contributed not only many photos, but also the boxed text, 'Meeting Gays & Lesbians in Havana.' Ken DellaPenta indexed this book. Special thanks go to the authors for their good natures and flexibility throughout the project.

Foreword

ABOUT LONELY PLANET GUIDEBOOKS

The story begins with a classic travel adventure: Tony and Maureen Wheeler's 1972 journey across Europe and Asia to Australia. Useful information about the overland trail did not exist at that time, so Tony and Maureen published the first Lonely Planet guidebook to meet a growing need.

From a kitchen table, then from a tiny office in Melbourne (Australia), Lonely Planet has become the largest independent travel publisher in the world, an international company with offices in Melbourne, Oakland (USA), London (UK) and Paris (France).

Today Lonely Planet guidebooks cover the globe. There is an ever-growing list of books, and there's information in a variety of forms and media. Some things haven't changed. The main aim is still to help make it possible for adventurous travelers to get out there – to explore and better understand the world.

At Lonely Planet we believe travelers can make a positive contribution to the countries they visit – if they respect their host communities and spend their money wisely. Since 1986 a percentage of the income from each book has been donated to aid projects and human-rights campaigns.

Updates Lonely Planet thoroughly updates each guidebook as often as possible. This usually means there are around two years between editions, although for more unusual or more stable destinations the gap can be longer. Check the imprint page (following the color map at the beginning of the book) for publication dates.

Between editions, up-to-date information is available in two free newsletters – the paper *Planet Talk* and email *Comet* (to subscribe, contact any Lonely Planet office) – and on our website at www.lonelyplanet.com. The *Upgrades* section of the website covers a number of important and volatile destinations and is regularly updated by Lonely Planet authors. *Scoop* covers news and current affairs relevant to travelers. And, lastly, the *Thorn Tree* bulletin board and *Postcards* section of the site carry unverified, but fascinating, reports from travelers.

Correspondence The process of creating new editions begins with the letters, postcards and emails received from travelers. This correspondence often includes suggestions, criticisms and comments about the current editions. Interesting excerpts are immediately passed on via newsletters and the website, and everything goes to our authors to be verified when they're researching on the road. We're keen to get more feedback from organizations or individuals who represent communities visited by travelers.

Lonely Planet gathers information for everyone who's curious about the planet – and especially for those who explore it firsthand. Through guidebooks, phrasebooks, activity guides, maps, literature, newsletters, image library, TV series and website, we act as an information exchange for a worldwide community of travelers.

Research Authors aim to gather sufficient practical information to enable travelers to make informed choices and to make the mechanics of a journey run smoothly. They also research historical and cultural background to help enrich the travel experience and allow travelers to understand and respond appropriately to cultural and environmental issues.

Authors don't stay in every hotel because that would mean spending a couple of months in each medium-size city and, no, they don't eat at every restaurant because that would mean stretching belts beyond capacity. They do visit hotels and restaurants to check standards and prices, but feedback based on readers' direct experiences can be very helpful.

Many of our authors work undercover; others aren't so secretive. None of them accept freebies in exchange for positive write-ups. And none of our guidebooks contain any advertising.

Production Authors submit their raw manuscripts and maps to offices in Australia, the USA, the UK or France. Editors and cartographers – all experienced travelers themselves – then begin the process of assembling the pieces. When the book finally hits the shops, some things are already out of date, we start getting feedback from readers and the process begins again....

WARNING & REQUEST

Things change – prices go up, schedules change, good places go bad and bad places go bankrupt – nothing stays the same. So, if you find things better or worse, recently opened or long since closed, please tell us and help make the next edition even more accurate and useful. We genuinely value all the feedback we receive. Julie Young coordinates a well-traveled team that reads and acknowledges every letter, postcard and email and ensures that every morsel of information finds its way to the appropriate authors, editors and cartographers for verification.

Everyone who writes to us will find their name in the next edition of the appropriate guidebook. They will also receive the latest issue of *Planet Talk*, our quarterly printed newsletter, or *Comet*, our monthly email newsletter. Subscriptions to both newsletters are free. The very best contributions will be rewarded with a free guidebook.

Excerpts from your correspondence may appear in new editions of Lonely Planet guidebooks, the Lonely Planet website, *Planet Talk* or *Comet*, so please let us know if you *don't* want your letter published or your name acknowledged.

Send all correspondence to the Lonely Planet office closest to you:

Australia: Locked Bag 1, Footscray, Victoria 3011
USA: 150 Linden St, Oakland, CA 94607
UK: 10a Spring Place, London NW5 3BH
France: 1 rue du Dahomey, 75011 Paris

Or email us at: talk2us@lonelyplanet.com.au

For news, views and updates, see our website: www.lonelyplanet.com

HOW TO USE A LONELY PLANET GUIDEBOOK

The best way to use a Lonely Planet guidebook is any way you choose. At Lonely Planet, we believe the most memorable travel experiences are often those that are unexpected, and the finest discoveries are those you make yourself. Guidebooks are not intended to be used as if they provided a detailed set of infallible instructions!

Contents All Lonely Planet guidebooks follow the same format. The Facts about the Country chapters or sections give background information ranging from history to weather. Facts for the Visitor gives practical information on issues like visas and health. Getting There & Away gives a brief starting point for researching travel to and from the destination. Getting Around gives an overview of the transport options available when you arrive.

The peculiar demands of each destination determine how subsequent chapters are broken up, but some things remain constant. We always start with background, then proceed to sights, places to stay, places to eat, entertainment, getting there and away, and getting around information – in that order.

Heading Hierarchy Lonely Planet headings are used in a strict hierarchical structure that can be visualized as a set of Russian dolls. Each heading (and its following text) is encompassed by any preceding heading that is higher on the hierarchical ladder.

Entry Points We do not assume guidebooks will be read from beginning to end, but that people will dip into them. The traditional entry points are the list of contents and the index. In addition, however, some books have a complete list of maps and an index map illustrating map coverage.

There may also be a color map that shows highlights. These highlights are dealt with in greater detail later in the book, along with planning questions and suggested itineraries. Each chapter covering a geographical region usually begins with a locator map and another list of highlights. Once you find something of interest in a list of highlights, turn to the index.

Maps Maps play a crucial role in Lonely Planet guidebooks and include a huge amount of information. A legend is printed on the back page. We seek to have complete consistency between maps and text, and to have every important place in the text captured on a map. Map key numbers usually start in the top left corner.

Although inclusion in a guidebook usually implies a recommendation, we cannot list every good place. Exclusion does not necessarily imply criticism. In fact, there are a number of reasons why we might exclude a place – sometimes it is simply inappropriate to encourage an influx of travelers.

Introduction

The visitor to the Caribbean's largest city encounters scenes that are simply spellbinding. La Habana Vieja, the city's unparalleled Spanish colonial quarter, is, in places, so unaltered by time that you can effortlessly imagine how it looked and felt in the days buccaneers roamed the surrounding sea and milkmen milked goats door-to-door. As you glance down a Havana street these days, it sometimes seems only the fashion of clothing has changed.

Although taxis and *triciclos* now ply Old Havana's cobblestoned streets, so too do horse-drawn carriages. And to gaze from a café in Old Havana upon the mighty forts guarding the entrance of the Bay of Havana, breakers expiring at the foot of their monstrous walls, is every bit as memorable as a red-ball sunset over the Mekong River or watching Mt Everest appear in morning's dawn.

Ironically, the economic doldrums that gripped Havana from the takeover in '59 through the end of the last century aided immensely in the city's historical salvation. During those four decades, Habaneros had to make do with what they had, too poor were they to tear down and rebuild. In other former Spanish colonial cities, wealth allowed residents to replace aging buildings with soulless concrete monstrosities. In La Habana Vieja and Centro Havana, the magnificent sun-baked structures survived long enough to receive the recent restoration work they truly deserved.

Conservation efforts have benefited from a government policy of diverting resources to the countryside and limiting growth in the capital. Since 1997, Cubans have needed official permission to move to Havana; only if suitable housing and employment are available are new residents allowed in. Although many of Havana's colonial-era houses have yet to be renovated, the heavy vehicular traffic, rampant commercialization and sprawling slums that choke many Latin American cities aren't found in the Cuban capital.

Even the US embargo that has frustrated Fidel Castro for more than 40 years has helped maintain Havana's rich colonial ambiance by limiting US consumer tourism and by barring many of the cruise ships that clog most other Caribbean ports. Havana's 2.2 million residents have yet to see the cheesy golden arches of a McDonald's appear on their streets, and none of Havana's neighborhoods has been invaded by minimalls or quickimarts.

Of course, there's much more to Havana than its baroque palaces, its aristocratic homes and its tree-filled plazas, which are as graceful today as they were back when the red-and-yellow striped flag of Spain snapped

RICHARD I'ANSON

9

in sea breezes above the city's many fortresses. The city is home to world-class cabarets (Who hasn't heard of the Tropicana?); clubs where bands play Afro-Cuban music 'round the clock; and museums – dozens of them – devoted to subjects ranging from the history of the revolution to traditional Cuban musical instruments to Spanish colonial furniture and decorations.

It should be noted at the outset that Havana, like most capital cities, has two faces: one tourists see and one they don't. In addition to being Cuba's center of government, education, medicine, research, communications, trade and tourism, Havana is also home to much of the country's industry, including chemical plants, bleach-spewing paper mills and a petroleum refinery. Many of the industries date from before the revolution and pollute without shame.

Unfortunately, Havana also suffers from deteriorating sewage systems and dwindling water supplies due to antiquated plumbing. Nearly half the housing in the city is in bad repair and thousands of Habaneros have had to be evacuated. In spite of the ongoing restoration work, which was initiated in 1999 and is being carried out by a 6000-strong army of laborers, each year dozens of buildings collapse or are demolished for safety reasons.

As a visitor you'll doubtless become aware of some of Havana's problems, but you'll also be overwhelmed by the wealth of historical monuments and the exuberant friendliness of the people. Indeed, if you arrive with good walking shoes and an adventurous spirit, you'll likely find Havana as intoxicating as a dark Cuban rum and as welcoming as an old friend.

Facts about Havana

HISTORY
Early Peoples

Well before Christopher Columbus mistook the New World for part of the Old, three distinctly different groups settled Cuba in three migratory waves that were hundreds of years apart. Archaeological evidence indicates that all three peoples migrated from eastern Venezuela or thereabouts, although at least two historians, citing cultural similarities between the migrants and Peru's mountain people, contend that the last group may have begun its journey in the Peruvian Andes.

Cuba's earliest-known inhabitants arrived around 2500 BC, using huge dugout canoes that allowed them to island hop, over a period of many years, from the southern tip of the Lesser Antilles north and west into the Greater Antilles. Most of the islands are within sight of each other and currents favor travel from south to north – two factors that greatly facilitated the Indians' movement from one island to another. But what prompted these people to leave the food-filled forests of South America for relatively inhospitable islands continues to baffle scientists.

In time a third group of arrivals spread out across most of the West Indies and absorbed or eliminated most members of the two earlier migratory groups. By 1100 AD these migrants had a distinct culture and occupied the Bahamas and all of the Greater Antilles. It was this relatively sophisticated third group – who called themselves Taínos, or 'friendly people' in their tongue – that occupied Cuba when a Genoese navigator know as Cristoforo Colombo in Italian and Cristóbal Colón in Spanish set foot on the jungle-draped island.

The Taínos

When Columbus reached Cuba in 1492, the island contained anywhere from 60,000 to 400,000 Taínos (a more accurate estimate does not exist). A large group of Taínos is known to have lived in villages in what is today Havana's Guanabacoa neighborhood; indeed, the Cuban capital takes its name from Habaguanex, a Taíno chief who lived in western Cuba 500 years ago.

The Taínos were a civilized, peaceful and community-minded people who slept in hammocks and resided in wood-and-thatch houses, which were irregularly arranged around a main plaza. Several related families often lived in a single house, no part of which was partitioned for privacy.

Had the Taínos survived their encounter with the Spaniards, it's likely they would have contributed much to the world. As it was, slave traders carried the Taínos' principal crop, cassava, as well as the Taínos' techniques for cultivating and processing the nutritious plant, to sub-Saharan Africa, where it was widely adopted. Cassava eventually reached India and Southeast Asia, where it became a staple food in areas unsuited to rice cultivation.

The Taínos also introduced the European boat people to the sweet potato, bean, peanut, squash, guava, mamey and pineapple.

Peaceful Taínos were killed off by European invaders.

A Cuban Chronology

3500 BC – first humans arrive in Cuba
250 BC – second South American group arrives
1250 AD – Taíno Indians arrive from the east
1492 – Columbus sights Cuba
1508 – Sebastián de Ocampo sails around Cuba
1512 – Diego Velázquez de Cuéllar lands at Baracoa
1514 – first seven settlements established
1515 – Santiago de Cuba named colonial capital
1518 – Hernán Cortés leaves for Mexico
1519 – Havana established at present site
1522 – first African slaves brought to Cuba
1542 – encomienda system abolished
1555 – French pirates sack Havana
1556 – Spanish captains general move to Havana
1564 – first treasure fleet departs from Havana
1589 – Havana and Santiago de Cuba fortified
1607 – Havana declared capital of Cuba
1628 – Piet Heyn captures the flota
1674 – construction of Havana city walls begins
1700 – tobacco becomes the main export
1728 – University of Havana founded
1762 – the British capture Havana
1763 – the British trade Cuba for Florida
1765 – commerce with Spain liberalized
1790 – mass importation of African slaves
1800 – sugar becomes the main export
1818 – trade with all countries allowed
1820 – slave trade ineffectively abolished
1825 – most of Latin America has independence
1837 – first Cuban railway line built
1848 – US attempts to buy Cuba from Spain
1850 – Narciso López raises Cuban flag
1854 – US tries again to buy Cuba
1865 – importation of African slaves ends
1868 to 1878 – First War of Independence
1879 – slavery converted to 'apprenticeship'
1886 – 'apprenticeship' system ends
1895 to 1898 – Second War of Independence
1898 – Americans land at Santiago de Cuba, Spanish rule ends
1898 to 1902 – US military government controls Cuba
1901 – Platt Amendment imposed on Cuba

1902 – Cuba achieves independence
1903 – US takes Guantánamo naval base
1906 – US military intervention
1917 – US military intervention
1925 – first Communist Party founded
1933 – Machado dictatorship overthrown
1934 – Platt Amendment abrogated
1940 – second constitution proclaimed
1952 – Batista military coup
1953 – rebels attack Moncada army barracks
1956 – Granma lands Castro's rebels in Oriente
1956 to 1958 – Castro organizes in Sierra Maestra
1958 – Che Guevara captures Santa Clara
1959 – Batista flees, rebels take over and pass agrarian reform law
1960 – large companies nationalized, US partial trade embargo begins
1961 – abortive Bay of Pigs invasion
1962 – Cuban Missile Crisis
1963 – Second Agrarian Reform Law
1965 – refounding of the Communist Party
1966 – Tricontinental Conference in Havana
1967 – Che Guevara killed in Bolivia
1968 – small businesses nationalized
1972 – Cuba joins Comecon trading block
1975 – first Cuban Communist Party congress; Cuban troops sent to Angola
1976 – third constitution comes into force
1979 – Non-Aligned Movement summit in Havana
1980 – 135,000 Cubans depart through Mariel
1988 – Cuban troops withdraw from Angola
1990 – Castro declares five-year austerity program
1991 – Soviet Union collapses
1993 – Cubans allowed to hold US dollars
1995 – direct foreign investment allowed, tourism becomes the main money earner
1996 – Helms-Burton Law tightens US embargo
1998 – Pope John Paul II visits Cuba
1999 – Fidel launches a law-and-order crackdown
2000 – US takes baby steps toward normalizing relations with Cuba

SEÑORES IMPERIALISTAS iNO LES TENEMOS ABSOLUTAMENTE NINGUN MIEDO i

And the Taínos introduced the rest of the world to tobacco, which they smoked as cigars (indeed, the Taíno word for tobacco was *tabaco*). Today, some of the world's finest cigars continue to originate from land once worked by these extinct people.

The Taínos are known for something else as well: Before Spanish abuses and diseases wiped them out, the Indians gave the invaders syphilis, which the white men unwittingly brought back with them to Europe and their loved ones.

Columbus Spies 'Japan'

Had the Taínos been a warring people like the cannibalistic Caribs of the Windward Islands their culture might have survived the Spanish Conquest. But the Taínos were a peaceful lot, and the Spaniards who arrived in Cuba were well armed, mean and greedy. They needed people for arduous manual labor and countless tedious chores, and it wasn't going to be them. They enslaved the Taínos and gradually killed them off with Old World diseases and abysmal treatment.

But it's hard to believe that anyone sailing with Columbus could have envisioned the holocaust their voyage would spark, in a world they didn't even know existed, when they left Spain on August 3, 1492, in search of Asia. Yes, Asia. Due to miscalculations of the Earth's circumference and the size of Asia and Europe, the flotilla's leader – the Great Explorer himself – expected to reach eastern Asia by sailing 3860km to the west. Indeed, when Columbus reached the New World, he mistook Cuba for Japan.

Land was sighted just before dawn on October 12, and later that day the expedition dropped anchor near the small Bahamian island of Guanahaní under the gaze of many bedazzled 'Indians' who paddled out to greet the strange winged ships. Certain he had reached some part of Japan, Columbus gave thanks to God for guiding him to the Indies. In God's honor he named the island San Salvador (Holy Savior) and called the welcoming people *los Indios*. Columbus then made plans to enslave them and rob them of their valuables. But finding no gold or spices on the island, the little fleet moved on, leaving the people of San Salvador alone for the time being.

In the following weeks the ships made additional landings, including one at Cuba. Surely *this* island was part of the Grand Khan's domain, Columbus thought, but again he found no treasure there, only Indians breathing smoke through tight rolls of leaves and living their lives in peace. So the Spaniards and their Italian navigator moved on, continuing their quest for wealth and invading the Western Hemisphere in the process.

Spanish Conquest

In 1514, San Cristóbal de la Havana was founded on the south coast of Cuba near the mouth of the Río Mayabeque, which today is a swampy, sparsely inhabited area. A few years later the settlement shifted to the mouth of the Río Almendares between present-day Vedado and Miramar. Only in 1519 did the town reestablish itself next to the mouth of the harbor, an area presently referred to as La Habana Vieja, or Old Havana.

Although Havana was one of the seven original towns established in Cuba by Diego Velázquez, no one ever intended for it to be the capital. The town's remote location in the far northwest made it a poor site from which to administer the center and east of the island, and it's not coincidental that almost every rebellion against authorities in Havana since the early 19th century has broken out at the eastern end of the island, where Cuba's first capital was located.

It took the Spanish conquest of Mexico and Peru to swing the pendulum in Havana's favor. The town's strategic location, at the mouth of the Gulf of Mexico facing a coastline washed by the northeast-bound Gulf Stream, made it a perfect gathering point for the annual treasure fleets. The colonial authorities also channeled trade through the town, and in 1556 Havana replaced Santiago de Cuba as seat of the Spanish captains general. The first combined *flota* sailed to Spain from here in 1564, and for the next 200 years Havana was the most important port in the Americas, the key to the vast Spanish colonial empire. In 1592 Havana was declared a city, and in 1607 the capital of the colony was officially moved here.

Salvaging Sunken Galleons

During the Spaniards' colonization of the New World in the 16th, 17th and 18th centuries, galleons left Spain carrying goods to the colonies and returned loaded with gold and silver mined in Colombia, Peru and Mexico. Many of these ships sank in the Caribbean Sea and the Gulf of Mexico, overcome by pirates or hurricanes. During these years literally thousands of ships – not only Spanish but also English, French, Dutch, pirate and African slave ships – foundered in the green-blue waters of the Caribbean and the darker waters of the Gulf.

The frequency of shipwrecks spurred the Spaniards to organize operations to recover sunken cargo. By the 17th century, Spain maintained salvage flotillas in the ports of Havana, Portobelo (Panama) and Veracruz (Mexico). These fleets awaited news of shipwrecks and then proceeded immediately to the wreck sites, where Caribbean and Bahamian divers, and later African slaves, were employed to scour sunken vessels and the sea floor around them. On many occasions great storms wiped out entire fleets, resulting in a tremendous loss of lives and cargo.

As early as the 1620s, salvagers were using bronze diving bells to increase the time they could spend underwater. The bell was submerged vertically from a ship and held air in its upper part. Divers would enter it to breathe, rest and observe. Over time, such divers became very skilled and the salvaging business became very lucrative – so lucrative that the English, who were established in Bermuda and the Bahamas, entered the salvage business in the Caribbean and the Gulf at the end of the 17th century. And pirates, as you'd expect, were always pleased to come upon a salvage operation.

After Havana was sacked by French privateers led by Jacques de Sores in 1555, the castles of La Fuerza, La Punta, and El Morro were built between 1558 and 1630. From 1674 to 1740, a strong wall was built around the city. These defenses kept out the pirates but proved ineffective when Spain became embroiled in the Seven Years' War with Britain, the strongest maritime power of the time.

On June 6, 1762, a British army under the Earl of Albemarle attacked Havana, landing at Cojímar and striking inland to Guanabacoa. From there they drove west along the northeast side of the harbor, and on July 30 they attacked El Morro from the rear. Other troops landed at La Chorrera, west of the city, and by August 13 the surrounded Spanish were forced to surrender. The British held Havana, home to roughly a quarter of Cuba's entire population, for 11 months. (The same war cost France almost all its colonies in North America, including Québec and Louisiana.)

When the Spanish regained the city a year later in exchange for Florida, they began a crash program to upgrade the city's defenses so it would never fall again. A new fortress, La Cabaña, was built along the ridge from which the British had shelled El Morro, and by the time the work was finished in 1766, Havana had become the most heavily fortified city in the New World, the 'bulwark of the Indies.' It was also during this period that construction of many of its finest buildings occurred, including Havana's cathedral and the Palace of the Captains General.

The British occupation resulted in Spain opening Havana to freer trade. In 1765 the city was granted the right to trade with seven Spanish cities instead of only Cádiz, and beginning in 1818 Havana was allowed to ship its sugar, rum, tobacco and coffee directly to any part of the world. During this time, the number of ships annually entering the port at Havana soared from several dozen to several thousand.

The Sugar Boom
After US independence from Britain in 1783, Cuba gradually replaced the British

colony of Jamaica as the main supplier of sugar to the US market, and many Cuban planters desired union with the US to guarantee the continuation of slavery and free trade. In 1791 a slave uprising in nearby Haiti eliminated the main competitor to Cuba's sugar industry, and production sharply increased due to the labor of tens of thousands of newly imported African slaves. French planters fleeing Haiti set up coffee plantations and modernized the Cuban sugar industry. By the 1820s Cuba was the world's largest producer of sugar.

Between 1810 and 1825, Mexico and all of mainland South America won their independence from Spain, leaving Cuba and Puerto Rico the only remaining Spanish colonies in the Western Hemisphere. The great liberator Simón Bolívar had wanted to free Cuba as well, but the US declared that it preferred continued Spanish rule and warned him to desist. In Cuba the Spanish authorities were supported by loyalists fleeing the former Spanish colonies as well as recent immigrants from Spain. Both *peninsulares* (Spaniards born in Spain) and *criollos* or Creoles (Spaniards born in the New World) feared that independence might lead to a slave revolt similar to Haiti's. In 1820 diplomatic pressure from Britain forced Spain to agree to halt the slave trade, although the import of African slaves continued unabated, and by the 1840s some 400,000 were present in Cuba. At this time, roughly one-quarter of the Cuban population lived in Havana.

The Slave Trade

The story of the slaves brought to the New World is one of great cruelty and heartache, as most of us are well aware. But what most people don't know is that there was an extremely active slave trade in Africa long before the Europeans arrived on the continent.

Between the seventh century and the time the Portuguese reached the West African coast in 1450, organized intercontinental slave trades had transported millions of Africans north and east to slave-holding Islamic states. A northern route carried as many as 10 million slaves across the Sahara to North Africa and to Egypt. An eastern network took another 5 million slaves north to Egypt, or across the Red Sea to Saudi Arabia and the Middle East.

After the Europeans arrived, Africans continued to control the supply of slaves, adding a transatlantic trade route to their established network. Because they had no immunity to malaria or yellow fever, the Europeans did not try to set up their own networks but instead were content to establish forts along the coast and purchase slaves from African dealers.

Due to demand from North Africa, the Middle East, Saudi Arabia and finally the New World, the slave business from the 16th century through the 18th century was a seller's market, with the Europeans taking whatever the African sellers offered.

European traders named slaves after the port where they purchased them because they generally didn't know where their bondmen had been captured. Today, the precise places of the origin of Caribbean blacks are unknown.

The notorious 'middle passage' between Africa and the New World was hell on earth. Slave ships were surprisingly small, and into their cargo holds the captains would pack 300 to 500 terrified men, women and children. The men were shackled together in pairs at the wrist and leg and provided half the space given a convict. The far smaller number of women and children had it only slightly better. Food consisted mainly of dried beans, corn and palm oil.

Outbreaks of measles, smallpox and other communicable diseases ravaged the slaves and crews aboard these insidious ships. But by far the biggest killers during the three- to six-month middle passage were scurvy and anemic dysentery. Historians have estimated that more than 200,000 slaves died in order to bring approximately 1 million to Cuba.

SEÑORES IMPERIALISTAS INO LES TENEMOS ABSOLUTAMENTE NINGUN MIEDO i

Between 1838 and 1880 the Spanish continued to modernize Cuba's sugar industry until it accounted for a third of world production. The ruthless slave-owning planters expelled small farmers from their lands and cleared the island's cedar, ebony and mahogany forests. Over half of the sugar was sold to the US, which had become Cuba's largest trading partner. In 1848 the US attempted to buy Cuba from Spain for US$100 million but was turned down.

In 1862 the British finally began enforcing the ban on slave trading enacted in 1820. Most of the slaves had arrived on US ships, and only the distraction of the US Civil War allowed the British to act without fear of major repercussions. After the importation of African slaves was effectively stopped in 1865, indentured Chinese laborers and Mexican Indians were brought in to serve as *macheteros*, who cut sugar cane. Today, the descendants of the Chinese laborers run a lively Chinatown in the center of Havana.

Wars of Independence

In 1868 Spain's reactionary policies in Cuba, especially its refusal to consider internal autonomy, finally sparked the declaration of a Cuban republic by rebels in Oriente Province. At this time eastern Cuba was an economic backwater, with most of its small sugar mills powered by oxen rather than steam. The Creole planters around Bayamo had been plotting a rebellion for some time, and when the wife of one betrayed the conspirators through her confessor, the captain general in Havana ordered their arrest, forcing them to take action.

On October 10, 1868, Carlos Manuel de Céspedes launched the uprising at his plantation, La Demajagua. Céspedes called for the abolition of slavery, but to avoid alienating the wealthy planters in the west, only after independence had been achieved, and then with compensation. Although he did not declare the immediate emancipation of the slaves, he did free his own.

At first the rebels captured much of the eastern part of the island, but the Spanish placed the cities under martial law and built a fortified ditch across the island from

Júcaro to Morón to isolate the rebel-held east. When a reactionary militia was formed in the west to support continued Spanish rule, the rebels met at Guáimaro in April 1869 and passed a constitution that declared the slaves free, though they were to continue working for their former masters for wages.

The cautious rebel council rejected General Máximo Gómez' proposal to invade western Cuba, and Céspedes was removed from office (to die in a Spanish ambush soon after). In 1874 and 1875 rebels under Gómez did manage several brief forays west, but this First War of Independence dragged on into a Ten Years' War. In February 1878 a pact was finally signed at El Zanjón in which the rebels were granted an amnesty. General Antonio Maceo and several others rejected this in the 'Protest of Baraguá,' and after an additional three months of fighting, Maceo went into exile. Some 200,000 people had died and much property had been destroyed.

Havana was spared the destruction that took place in the east. Indeed, many of the city's elegant homes were improved upon then, including the marvelous Casa de Lombillo. This was also the time that the city's wealthy occupants decided to put money into their eternal resting places and constructed the artistic Necrópolis Cristóbal Colón, replete with a huge portal in Romanesque style.

During the 1880s there was a boom in railway construction as both sugar mills and plantations grew larger. US investors snapped up bankrupt Spanish plantations and other segments of the economy for a song. Some Cuban planters and businessmen continued to call for annexation to the US as a solution to their problems, a position supported by several US presidents, beginning with Thomas Jefferson. In 1890 tariffs on most trade between the US and Cuba were removed. While fostering prosperity, this arrangement made Cuba totally dependent on sugar, as other industries could not compete with US mass production. Throughout the 19th century, Cuba's trade with the US had been larger than that with Spain, and by the end of the century US trade with Cuba was larger than US trade with the rest of Latin America combined.

Meanwhile a circle of émigrés in the US plotted a return to Cuba. Their most effective spokesman was a writer named José Martí, who had earned an international reputation as a poet, playwright and essayist. Martí spent 14 years in exile divided between Mexico and the US, and although impressed by American industriousness, he was repelled by its materialism. Aware of how the US had seized half of Mexico's national territory in 1848, in his writings he denounced the exploitation of the poor by US banking and industrial monopolies.

By 1890 the autonomy movement in Cuba had been discredited by Spanish political incompetence and inflexibility, so with interest in independence again on the increase, Martí dedicated himself almost exclusively to the movement as a writer, speaker and organizer. By 1892 the movement was strong enough for Martí to travel to Santo Domingo and engage General Máximo Gómez as military commander of the revolution. Antonio Maceo was recruited in Costa Rica, where he had set up a banana plantation.

In 1894 the US upped the stakes by declaring an abrupt increase in tariffs, shattering Cuba's sugar-based economy and destabilizing Spain's shaky colonial system. Martí and the others landed in eastern Cuba in April 1895, and on May 19, Martí, conspicuous on his white horse, was shot and killed in a brief encounter. Had he lived he would certainly have become Cuba's first president; instead, he became his country's national hero whose life and vast literary legacy have inspired Cubans ever since. See the boxed text 'José Martí' for more about this hero's life.

Unwilling to repeat the mistakes of the First War of Independence, Gómez and Maceo drove west in October 1895, reaching Las Villas in November and Matanzas Province by Christmas. Everything in their path, including sugar fields, plantations, and towns, was set on fire. By January 1896 Maceo had reached Pinar del Río, while Gómez was fighting in the vicinity of Havana. In panic,

the Spaniards sent an equally ruthless captain general, Valeriano Weyler, to Cuba. Weyler reorganized the Spanish army and built north-south lines across the country to restrict the rebels' movements. The *guajiros* (country people) were forced into fortified camps in a process known as *reconcentración*, and anyone found supporting the rebellion was liable for execution. In Pinar del Río, Weyler exerted heavy pressure on the rebels in this way, and in December 1896 Antonio Maceo was killed south of Havana trying to break out to the east.

With thousands killed, estates burned, and towns sacked, Weyler's methods brought Cuba's agricultural economy to a standstill. In June 1897 Spanish Prime Minister Antonio Cánovas, a hard-line opponent of Cuban independence, was assassinated in Spain by an anarchist with Cuban connections. The new Spanish government favored resolving the conflict by granting autonomy, and in October Weyler resigned. The Spaniards adopted a conciliatory tone, attempting to persuade the Cubans to accept the home rule under the Spanish flag that they had initially wanted, although by now the rebels would be satisfied with nothing short of full independence.

US Intervention

As Martí had feared, the US government had been biding its time, and it now seemed that the moment to seize Cuba had come. Largely to increase their circulation, the US tabloid press stoked war fever throughout 1897, printing sensational and often inaccurate articles about Spanish atrocities. When William Randolph Hearst's illustrator, Frederick Remington, asked permission to return from Havana as all was quiet, the eminent publisher replied, 'Please remain. You furnish the pictures and I'll furnish the war.' Hearst's ally in this campaign was the assistant secretary of the navy, Theodore Roosevelt.

In January 1898 the US battleship *Maine* was sent to Havana 'to protect US citizens.' The *Maine* lay at anchor off the city just west of the harbor mouth for three weeks before it mysteriously blew up, killing 266

José Martí

Cuba's national hero, José Martí, was born to Spanish immigrant parents in Havana on January 28, 1853. While still in high school, Martí became involved in anticolonial activities, and in 1869 he published a political tract and the first issue of a newspaper called *La Patria Libre*. A war of independence had broken out in Oriente the previous year, and the Spanish colonial authorities were in no mood to allow criticism. In October 1869 Martí was arrested on treason charges, and in April 1870 he was sentenced to six years of hard labor.

After several months at a Havana stone quarry, the young prisoner was exiled to the Isla de Pinos (Isla de la Juventud today) in October 1870. There he spent nine weeks before his deportation to Spain, where he was allowed to enroll in a university. In 1874 Martí graduated from law school, but both the war and his critical writings had continued, and official permission to return to Cuba was denied. Martí went to Mexico City and got a job with a newspaper in 1875. In 1877 he married a Cuban woman and obtained a teaching post in Guatemala.

The First War of Independence ended in 1878 and Martí was able to return to Cuba under a general amnesty. In Havana the authorities prevented Martí from practicing law, and in 1879 his conspiratorial activities and anticolonial statements at public debates led to his arrest and a second sentence of exile to Spain. After traveling to France, the USA, and Venezuela, Martí finally settled in New York City, where he remained until just three and a half months prior to his death.

In New York Martí served as a correspondent for the Buenos Aires newspaper *La Nación* and the Caracas paper *La Opinión Nacional*. His columns describing the North American scene made him well known throughout Latin America, and he was appointed consul of Uruguay in New York. In 1892 Martí's relentless advocacy of Cuban independence and his organizational work in New York and Florida led to his election as chief delegate of the newly formed Partido Revolucionario Cubano.

On April 11, 1895, Martí, the Dominican general Máximo Gómez, and four others landed near Baracoa in eastern Cuba to launch the Second War of Independence. They soon made contact with rebels led by Antonio Maceo, but on May 19, 1895, Martí was killed during a brief skirmish with the Spanish at Dos Ríos on the Cauto River in today's Granma Province. Deprived of their political leader, the Cubans fought on under the military leadership of Maceo and Gómez, only to have imminent victory snatched from them by US intervention three years later.

In his own time Martí was best known for essays that set out his vision of a secular republic and warned of the threat to Cuba from sporadic US imperialism (the US had annexed half of Mexico less than four decades earlier). Although history was to confirm his worst fears in this regard, it's Martí's poetry that is most appreciated today. In literary circles Martí is regarded as one of the initiators of the school of modernism in Latin American poetry. Decades after his death, lines from Martí's *Versos Sencillos* (1891) were incorporated into the best-known Cuban song of all time, 'Guajira guantanamera':

Yo soy un hombre sincero	I'm a sincere man
de donde crece la palma,	from the land of the palm tree,
y antes de morirme	And before I die
quiero echar mis versos del alma.	I wish to sing these heartfelt verses.
Con los pobres de la tierra	With the poor of the land
quiero yo mi suerte echar,	I want to share a fate,
y el arroyo de la sierra me complace	And the mountain stream pleases me
más que el mar.	more than the sea.

– David Stanley

SEÑORES IMPERIALISTAS ¡NO LES TENEMOS ABSOLUTAMENTE NINGUN MIEDO ¡

US sailors, on February 15, 1898. The Spanish claimed the explosion had been caused by an accident in the ship's ammunition store, while the Americans blamed a Spanish mine. (In 1911, to remove the navigational hazard from the harbor mouth, the *Maine* was raised and sunk in deep water.)

After the explosion on the *Maine*, pandemonium broke loose in the US, and President William McKinley offered to resolve the problem peacefully by purchasing Cuba from Spain for US$300 million, a proposition rejected by the Spanish. Meanwhile, they tried desperately to avoid a conflict with the Americans. On April 9, 1898, Spain declared a cease-fire in the civil war with the Cubans, and withdrew the *reconcentración* orders for the rural populace. These measures failed to impress the Americans, who demanded a full Spanish withdrawal, and on April 25 the US declared war on Spain.

By May 28 the US had blockaded the Spanish fleet at Santiago de Cuba Bay. On July 3 the outgunned Spanish fleet tried to break out. Although they managed to evade the chaotic US fleet, the wooden Spanish ships caught fire in a strong tailwind and ran aground. Of 2225 Spanish sailors, 1670 managed to get to shore and surrender. US losses in this non-battle were one dead and two wounded.

Meanwhile, the US tightened its siege of Santiago de Cuba, and the Spaniards surrendered on July 17, 1898. A peace treaty ending the 'Spanish-American' War was signed in Paris six months later by the Spanish and the Americans. The Cubans were not invited. An amendment known as the Teller Resolution (after Senator Henry M Teller of the US state of Colorado), passed simultaneously with the declaration of war on Spain, had committed the US to respect Cuban self-determination. Only this prevented the US from adding Cuba when they annexed Puerto Rico, Guam, and the Philippines. Cuba was placed under US military occupation instead.

Crooked Presidents

The US intervention endowed Cuba with a series of weak, corrupt and dependent governments. Cuba became an independent republic on May 20, 1902, after Tomás Estrada Palma was elected president. However, a revolt broke out when Estrada Palma's Liberal opponents accused him of employing fraud to obtain a second term. This led to a US military intervention in September 1906. A US governor named Charles Magoon held power until January 1909, when a deal was worked out specifying that the Liberals and Conservatives would alternate in power under the threat of Platt Amendment intervention. Elections were carefully managed to ensure that the results came out right.

The first Liberal president, José Miguel Gómez, initiated corruption, incompetence and discrimination against blacks, which persisted until 1959. When Afro-Cubans in Oriente demonstrated against this discrimination in 1912, some 3000 were slaughtered by government troops. That same year the US intervened militarily to stop a revolt by former slaves in Pinar del Río, and in 1917 US soldiers were back again to ensure a steady flow of sugar during WWI.

By the 1920s US companies owned two-thirds of Cuba's farmland and most of its mines. The US saw Cuba as a source of raw materials. Manufacturing in Cuba itself was crippled by high US tariffs on most Cuban goods other than raw sugar, tobacco leaves and unprocessed minerals. Yet Cuba's sugar industry boomed during the 1920s, and with Prohibition in force in the US from 1919 to 1933, tourism based on legal drinking, gambling and prostitution flourished. Signs of that booming time are evident at every turn inside the Capitolio Nacional in central Havana, which was built during the 1920s to seat the House of Representatives and the Senate. However, only a few benefited from the boom, and when commodity prices collapsed in the wake of the Great Depression, Liberal President Gerardo Machado y Morales used terror to quell the resulting unrest.

In August 1933 Machado was toppled during a spontaneous general strike. Chaos followed, and on September 4 an army sergeant named Fulgencio Batista seized power in a noncommissioned officers' coup.

Batista served as the army's chief of staff from 1934 to 1940, and in 1940 he had a democratic constitution drafted guaranteeing many rights. He was duly elected president in 1940, and during WWII he won US favor by supporting the Allied war effort. In 1944 Batista allowed free elections, but his preferred candidate lost. The next two governments, led by Presidents Ramón Grau San Martín and Carlos Prío Socarrás of the Partido Auténtico, were corrupt and inefficient. Public services hardly existed and millions of Cubans were unemployed. In 1947 Eduardo Chibás formed the Partido Ortodoxo to fight corruption, and in 1948 Batista set up the Partido de Acción Unitaria in an attempt to make a comeback.

On March 10, 1952, just three months before the scheduled election date, Batista staged a second military coup. The coup, motivated mostly by his impending defeat in the presidential election, invalidated the 1940 constitution and prevented the almost certain election of a young Ortodoxo candidate named Fidel Castro to the House of Representatives. Opposition politicians were unable to unite against the dictator, who later sought legitimacy through rigged elections in 1955 and 1958. By this time over half of Cuba's land, industry and essential services were in foreign hands, and Batista's cronies had enriched themselves with bribes.

Revolutionary Cuba

After Batista's second coup, a revolutionary circle formed in Havana, including Abel Santamaría, his sister Haydée Santamaría, Melba Hernández, Castro, and others. They decided on a dramatic gesture that would signal a general uprising throughout the country. On July 26, 1953, Castro led 119 rebels in an attack on the Moncada army barracks in Santiago de Cuba, the second most important military base in Cuba at that time. They assumed that the soldiers would be drunk due to a carnival then in progress, but the assault failed when a patrol jeep encountered Castro's motorcade by chance, costing the attackers the essential element of surprise.

After the abortive assault, 55 of the men detained by the army were cruelly tortured and executed. Castro managed to escape into the nearby foothills, where he intended to launch a guerrilla campaign. It was only through extraordinary luck that he was captured a week later by an army lieutenant named Sarría, who took him to Santiago de Cuba's main jail instead of immediately shooting him as the army chiefs had secretly ordered.

Castro's capture soon became known, and the Batista regime had no choice other than to put him on trial. Castro was a lawyer by profession and his defense summation at the trial was later edited and released as a political manifesto entitled *History Will Absolve Me*. In the end, Castro was sentenced to 15 years imprisonment on Isla de Pinos (now Isla de la Juventud).

In February 1955, Batista won a fraudulent presidential election and in an effort to win popular support he freed all political prisoners in May 1955, including Castro. Castro departed for Mexico in July 1955, but he left behind in Santiago de Cuba a Baptist schoolteacher named Frank País to organize the underground resistance of the 26th July Movement, or 'M-26-7' as it was commonly called. In December 1955, students at Havana University formed the Directorio Revolucionario (DR), which was led by José Antonio Echeverría.

In Mexico the M-26-7 trained and equipped a revolutionary force, and on December 2, 1956, Castro and 81 companions landed from the motor vessel *Granma* at Playa Las Coloradas near Niquero in Oriente. Three days later the group was decimated in an initial clash with Batista's army at Alegría de Pío, but Castro and 11 others (including an Argentine doctor named Ernesto 'Che' Guevara, Fidel's brother Raúl, and future *comandantes* Camilo Cienfuegos and Juan Almeida) escaped into the Sierra Maestra, where the M-26-7 underground leader in Manzanillo, Celia Sánchez, managed to send them supplies.

On January 17, 1957, the guerrillas scored their first success by overrunning a small army outpost on the south coast. Soon after,

From Doctor to Revolutionary to Hero

Ernesto 'Che' Guevara was born to a middle-class family in Rosario, Argentina, on June 14, 1928. His family moved to Buenos Aires in 1945, and it was there that Guevara finished medical school in 1953. He traveled widely in Latin America, both before and after graduation, and the widespread poverty he saw convinced him that he had a mission in life more important than medicine.

In December 1953 he arrived in Guatemala, where an elected government led by Jacobo Arbenz was working to solve social problems. Six months later Guevara witnessed the CIA-backed invasion that overthrew Arbenz and installed a military dictatorship, unleashing 45 years of pitiless repression.

Guevara was deported to Mexico City, where he met Fidel Castro in mid-1955, and was among the first to sign up for the *Granma* expedition to Cuba a year later. The Cubans nicknamed him 'Che' for the interjection *che* (meaning 'say!' or 'hey!') that Argentines frequently insert into their sentences. Although wounded during an initial engagement with Batista's troops, Guevara was among the small band that escaped into the Sierra Maestra.

In July 1957 Guevara was made *comandante* of a second rebel column, and in August 1958 he and his men set out on an epic trek to spread the revolution to central Cuba. In October they reached the Sierra del Escambray, where they linked up with other revolutionaries, and by December they had captured several small towns, effectively splitting Cuba in two. The Battle of Santa Clara began on December 28, and the next day they captured an armored train that Batista had sent to reinforce the city. With the capital of Las Villas Province falling to the rebels, Batista fled into exile, and on January 2, 1959, Guevara and other *barbudos* (bearded guerrillas) entered Havana.

Guevara was granted Cuban citizenship in February 1959, and soon assumed a leading role in Cuba's economic reforms as head of the Industry Department of the National Institute of Agrarian Reform (October 1959), president of the National Bank of Cuba (November 1959), and Minister of Industry (February 1960). Guevara made several trips to Europe, Asia, and Africa, arranging trade agreements and promoting Cuban interests. In time he became convinced that the poverty he had witnessed throughout Latin America could be corrected only by a continent-wide revolution.

In March 1965, Guevara withdrew from public life and secretly returned to Africa, where he helped organize left-wing rebels in the Congo. By December 1965 he was back in Cuba making preparations for a guerrilla campaign that he felt would make the Andes into a new Sierra Maestra, a revolutionary stronghold.

In November 1966 Guevara arrived in Bolivia, and there his group established a base. After the successful ambush of a Bolivian detachment in March 1967, he issued a call for 'two, three, many Vietnams.' This alarmed the US, which quickly sent military advisors to Bolivia. Soon, thousands of Bolivian troops began combing the area where Guevara's small band of guerrillas was operating. On October 8, 1967, Guevara was captured by the Bolivian army, and after consultation with military leaders in La Paz and Washington, DC, he was shot in front of US advisors. His remains were returned to Cuba in 1997 and reburied in Santa Clara.

– David Stanley

SEÑORES IMPERIALISTAS ¡NO LES TENEMOS ABSOLUTAMENTE NINGÚN MIEDO!

university students belonging to the DR attacked the Presidential Palace in Havana in an unsuccessful attempt to assassinate Batista. The attackers fought their way into the building and reached Batista's office on the 2nd floor. But Batista's troops soon surrounded the building and many of the attackers were shot trying to escape. Of the 35 students who had attacked the palace, 32 were killed.

On May 28, 1957, the M-26-7 forces overwhelmed 53 Batista soldiers at the army post in El Uvero and captured badly needed supplies. On July 30 Frank País was trapped in Santiago de Cuba and shot. Yet reinforcements from the cities continued to trickle in, and by the end of 1957 Castro was able to establish a fixed headquarters at La Plata, high up in the Sierra Maestra.

A year later Batista sent an army of 10,000 into the Sierra Maestra to liquidate Castro's 300 armed guerrillas. By August the rebels defeated this advance and captured a great quantity of arms. With the weapons and growing popular support, the rebels fought and won several decisive battles.

At 9 pm on December 31, 1958, Batista's general in Santiago de Cuba warned the dictator that the city was about to fall. Five hours later, Batista fled to the Dominican Republic, which was then ruled by fellow dictator Rafael Trujillo. (Batista took with him US$40 million in government funds and died in comfortable exile in Spain in 1973.) To prevent opportunists from stepping into the vacuum, Guevara and Cienfuegos immediately set out for Havana, which they reached on January 2.

Consolidating Power

On January 5, 1959, the Cuban presidency was assumed by Manuel Urrutia, a judge who had defended the M-26-7 prisoners during the 1953 Moncada trials. Castro entered Havana on January 8 and on February 16 he was named prime minister. Among the first acts of the revolutionary government were cuts in rent and electricity rates, and racial discrimination was made illegal.

In April 1959 Castro made a private visit to Washington to address a gathering of the National Press Club. To avoid meeting the Cuban leader, President Eisenhower made a point of leaving on a golfing holiday, and Vice President Richard Nixon received Castro at the White House. Nixon accused the Cuban leader of being a communist, something Castro had always denied. Castro later remarked that the Americans were far more concerned about possible communist infiltration into his administration than in finding out what he planned to do to reform Cuba. After their one-hour meeting, Nixon set in motion a process of anti-Castro subversion that eventually led to the Bay of Pigs.

Back in Cuba, most of 1959 was devoted to the promised agrarian reform. In May, all estates larger than 400 hectares were nationalized as part of the First Agrarian Reform, which directly affected the holdings of large US companies such as the United Fruit Company. The first half of 1959 also saw revolutionary groups supported by Cuba launch unsuccessful campaigns against undemocratic regimes in Panama, Nicaragua and the Dominican Republic. In July 1959 President Urrutia resigned after criticizing the agrarian reforms. He was replaced by Osvaldo Dorticós, an M-26-7 leader from Cienfuegos.

In the meantime Cuba's economic problems mounted as thousands of professionals, managers and technicians who didn't share Castro's vision of a new society left the country for exile in Miami. As relations with the US deteriorated due to the land seizures, Cuba made overtures to the Soviet Union to provide a balance. In February 1960, Soviet Vice Premier Anastas Mikoyan visited Cuba as the head of a trade delegation. Important contracts were signed, and the USSR agreed to send technicians to replace some of those who had left for the US.

June 1960 was a time of crisis for Cuba: Refineries on the island owned by Texaco, Standard Oil and Shell bowed to US pressure and refused to refine Soviet petroleum rather than the Venezuelan crude oil they had been purchasing from their own subsidiaries at inflated prices. Two weeks later these companies were nationalized. After this, Cuba was dependent on the USSR for its fuel and the degree of economic leverage the US could apply diminished sharply.

On July 6 President Eisenhower cut 700,000 tons from the Cuban sugar quota, but a few days later the USSR offered to buy any sugar the US rejected. This greatly strengthened Castro's position, as he could now present himself as a defender of Cuban sovereignty against US aggression.

In August 1960 the Cuban government nationalized the American-owned telephone and electricity companies and 36 sugar mills, including US$800 million in US assets. The outraged American government quickly pushed through a resolution by the Organization of American States condemning Soviet intervention in the Western Hemisphere, to which Cuba responded in September 1960 by establishing diplomatic relations with communist China.

In September 1960 the Committees for the Defense of the Revolution (CDR) were formed to consolidate grassroots support for the revolution. Later, these neighborhood bodies would play a decisive role in health, education, social and voluntary labor campaigns. Also in September, at a meeting of the United Nations in New York, Soviet Premier Nikita Khrushchev agreed to supply arms to Cuba to defend itself against émigré groups based in the US.

On October 13, 1960, most banks and 382 major Cuban-owned firms were nationalized, and the next day an Urban Reform Law nationalized rental housing. On October 19, 1960, a partial trade embargo was imposed on Cuba by Washington, to which Cuba responded five days later by nationalizing all remaining US businesses in the country. In effect, the Cold War politicians in Washington, DC, had made it easy for Castro to steer the revolution toward communism in partnership with the Soviet Union.

Conflict with the USA

By January 1961 the US embassy in Havana had become the crux of destabilization attempts against Cuba, so Castro ordered the embassy to reduce its staff from 300 to 11 – the same number then serving at the Cuban embassy in Washington. The US broke off diplomatic relations with Cuba and promptly banned US citizens from traveling to Cuba. In March 1961 President Kennedy abolished the remaining Cuban sugar quota.

On April 14, 1961, some 1400 Cuban émigrés trained by the CIA in Florida and Guatemala set sail in six ships from Puerto Cabeza, Nicaragua. The next day, planes from Nicaragua bombed Cuban airfields, but they failed to eliminate the Cuban Air Force. On April 16, during a speech honoring the seven Cuban airmen killed in the raids, Castro proclaimed the socialist nature of the Cuban revolution for the first time.

The next day the invaders landed at Playa Girón and Playa Larga in the Bahía de Cochinos (Bay of Pigs). Cuban planes immediately attacked their supply ships, sinking two and forcing the rest to withdraw,

Mission: Assassinate Fidel   Method: Exploding cigar

Result: ¿Viva Fidel?!

leaving the troops stranded on the beaches without most of their equipment. Eleven aircraft were shot down, including all of the B-26 bombers flown from Nicaragua that day. Castro took personal charge of the forces moving against the 'mercenaries,' and within 72 hours the invaders at the beachheads surrendered after about 200 of them had been killed. Eventually 1197 of the men captured at the Bay of Pigs were 'ransomed' by the US for US$53 million in food and medicine.

During his 1961 May Day speech, Fidel Castro reaffirmed that the Cuban Revolution was socialist, and on December 1, 1961, he declared that he had been a Marxist-Leninist since his university days. He claimed that he had concealed his communist beliefs to avoid damaging the chances of success of the revolution.

After their stinging defeat at the Bay of Pigs, the Americans declared a full trade embargo in June 1961, and in January 1962 managed to have Cuba expelled from the Organization of American States, followed by OAS economic sanctions.

By the middle of 1961, inventories in Cuba had been exhausted and the country was facing shortages of almost everything. Rationing began in March 1962. In April, Khrushchev decided to install missiles in Cuba to use as bargaining chips in the Soviet Union's ongoing rivalry with the US.

On October 22, 1962, President Kennedy ordered the US Navy to stop Cuba-bound Soviet ships in international waters and to carry out searches for missiles. This led to the Cuban Missile Crisis, which brought the world closer to the brink of nuclear war than it has ever been. Only after receiving a secret assurance from Kennedy that Cuba would not be invaded did Khrushchev defuse the crisis on October 28 by ordering the missiles dismantled.

Shortly after the missile crisis, the US focused on new military adventures in Vietnam and largely forgot Cuba.

Building Socialism

During the first decade of the revolution, Cuba's economy was run on a trial-and-error basis marked by inconsistency, disor-

ganization, falls in production, declining quality and growing bureaucracy. As president of the National Bank and later as minister of industries, Guevara had pushed for centralization and moral, rather than material, incentives for workers, but these proved ineffective. Inexperience and the departure of so many trained people took their toll.

In August 1963 some 10,000 medium-size farms were taken over in the Second Agrarian Reform, which fixed maximum private holdings at 65 hectares. More than two-thirds of Cuban farmland was now held by the state.

In 1968 Cuba underwent a mini Cultural Revolution, or 'Great Revolutionary Offensive,' in which some 55,000 surviving small businesses and holdings were nationalized, and self-employment and private trading were banned. Bureaucrats were assigned to agricultural work in the countryside, while military officers filled posts in government and the economy. Self-defense brigades of workers were formed in the factories and on state farms. Production sagged and the shortages became worse than ever.

Despite massive Soviet aid, the Cuban economy languished during the late 1960s, and the effort to produce 10 million tons of sugar in 1970 almost led to an economic breakdown, as the many consumer scarcities were multiplied by the overemphasis on sugar. After this failure more attention was placed on careful economic planning and the sugar harvest was increasingly mechanized.

Conditions improved slowly during the 1970s as a new generation of technicians and managers dedicated to the revolution graduated from school to replace those who had left for the US. Half of Cuba's 6000 doctors left the country during the early '60s, but by 1974 the number was back up to 9000 doctors.

In 1975 the number of provinces was increased from six (La Habana, Pinar del Río, Matanzas, Las Villas, Camagüey and Oriente) to the present 14. Also in 1975, the First Congress of the Communist Party of Cuba approved a process known as institutionalization, which installed an actual Soviet system in Cuba. A third Cuban constitution was drawn up to replace the Ley Fundamental (Fundamental Law) enacted in February 1959. This was approved by referendum in February 1976, and Fidel Castro replaced Osvaldo Dorticós as president.

Cuban Internationalism

After the US defeat at the Bay of Pigs, the Kennedy administration launched an 'Alliance for Progress,' which channeled economic aid to Latin American countries to counter Cuban attempts to export revolution. This coincided with a period when many democratic Latin American governments were being overthrown by military coups, and by 1964 the time looked ripe for a continent-wide revolution. Both Castro and Guevara began actively supporting guerrilla movements in Latin America and Africa.

In February 1973 Cuba and the US had signed a reciprocal agreement on the return of hijackers, in which both countries promised to punish anyone attempting to launch attacks on the territory of the other. On September 1, 1977, the US established an interests section in Havana, and Cuba opened one in Washington, DC. A restoration of diplomatic relations seemed to be in the offing when anti-communist hard-liner Zbigniew Brzezinski, President Carter's national security advisor, scuttled the talks. In 1982 Cuba scored points in Latin America by supporting Argentina during the Falklands War.

Communism in Crisis

By the mid-1980s the inefficiencies of Cuba's Soviet-style economy had become obvious, as quality was sacrificed to meet production quotas set by central planners, and ordinary citizens were alienated from government by the vertical command structure. In 1986 a process known as the 'rectification of errors' began, which attempted to reduce bureaucracy and allow for greater decision-making at local levels. In 1989 an anticorruption campaign reached to the highest levels, as General Arnaldo Ochoa

Sánchez, a hero of the war in Angola, was tried for complicity in drug trafficking and sentenced to death.

In the middle of the rectification process came the collapse of Eastern European communism in 1989. As trade and credits dried up, President Castro declared a five-year *período especial* (special period) austerity program in August 1990. For almost three decades Cuba had adhered closely to Soviet foreign policy, to the extent of endorsing the invasion of Czechoslovakia in 1968 and tilting toward the USSR in its conflict with China. Soviet economic subsidies, in the form of above-market prices for Cuban exports, totaled around US$5 billion a year, and the loss of this support was a disaster for Cuba.

In late 1991 Russia announced that its 11,000 military advisors and technicians in Cuba would be withdrawn. The US refused to do likewise, and thousands of US troops remain at the Guantánamo naval base in eastern Cuba. The US tightened its hold with the 1992 Torricelli Act, which forbids foreign subsidiaries of US companies from trading with Cuba and bans ships that have called at Cuban ports from docking at US ports for six months. Ninety percent of the trade banned by this law consists of food, medicine, and medical equipment.

In October 1991 at the Fourth Congress of the Cuban Communist Party in Santiago de Cuba, President Castro declared that he would remain loyal to communism and that ideological concessions could endanger the revolution. Economic reforms, however, were not ruled out. In December 1991 the National Assembly eliminated all references to Marxism-Leninism from the Cuban Constitution.

However, the strain of the special period was bringing Cuba to breaking point, and in a 1993 speech to mark the 40th anniversary of the attack on Moncada, President Castro announced that henceforth, individual Cubans would be allowed to possess US dollars. In August 1993 the constitution was amended to allow Cubans to hold foreign currency, to open dollar bank accounts, and to spend cash dollars at hard-currency stores. In September 1993 self-employment in more than 100 trades was legalized. Taxes on dollar incomes and profits were announced in August 1994, and in October farmers' markets were opened. In September 1995 a law was approved allowing foreign companies to run wholly owned businesses and possess real estate in Cuba, although the Cuban state was to continue to control the workforce. Previously only joint ventures with state-owned companies had been permitted.

These reforms led to the reemergence of class differences in Cuba, as those with dollars gained access to goods and services out of reach of those without. Many Cubans became desperate for dollars, and prostitutes known as *jineteras* (jockeys) reappeared in the tourist areas. Cuban émigrés returning for visits from the US found themselves treated like royalty for the dollars in their wallets. These reforms did relieve some of the pressure for even greater change and

gave Cuba's socialist system some breathing room.

By 1996 the post-Soviet crisis had subsided, most investors hadn't been scared away by US intimidation, and tourism was booming. Hard-liners led by Castro became concerned about the appearance of a nouveau riche and decided it was time to take back some of the concessions granted in 1993. Heavy taxes were imposed and private businesses deemed too competitive with state enterprises were closed down. The size of the police force was greatly increased in 1999 to deal with burgeoning crime. Yet putting the genie back in the bottle hasn't been easy, and communist Cuba is still looking for its place in a predominantly capitalist world.

GEOGRAPHY
Havana is perched atop the arching finger of Cuba, far to the north and west of the center of the country and beside a bay that

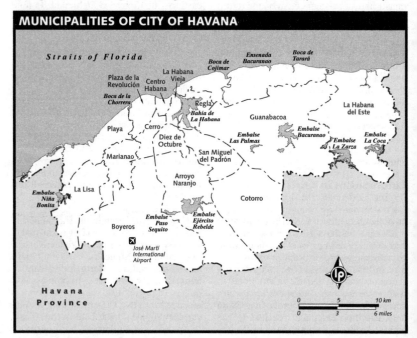

MUNICIPALITIES OF CITY OF HAVANA

faces the Atlantic Ocean and the mouth of the Gulf of Mexico (as opposed to the glorious Caribbean Sea, which laps up against the southern side of the island). On the world map, Havana is just south of the Tropic of Cancer, which puts it on the same longitudinal line as Calcutta, Hong Kong and the Hawaiian island of Kauai, give or take a degree. Yes, Havana *is* in the Tropics, but just barely.

The Cuban capital lies 150km south of its political nemisis, the great and powerful USA, separated only from the southernmost tip of Florida by a strait containing mostly northward-flowing currents. The largest land mass west of Havana is the Yucatán Peninsula of Mexico, which lies 200km away. The islands of the Bahamas appear 200km to the northeast of Havana, and most of Cuba – practically 90% of the island – stretches to the south and east of town.

On a map of Cuba, Havana appears near the western tip of the island, looking not so much like a planned development but rather more like a splatter; indeed, the contours of the city seem to follow not so much a well-executed scheme but rather the outline of a dash of spaghetti sauce. The city abuts the chilly waters of the Atlantic for approximately 50km, while the remainder of Havana borders what's left of Havana Province.

Within Havana lie more than a dozen municipalities, or neighborhoods as Habaneros prefer to call them. Near the center of the sprawling city of 2.2 million people, and also lining the lower lip of the Bahía de La Habana (Bay of Havana), is the oldest part of town, La Habana Vieja. As the city burst its pirate-thwarting walls, it spread for kilometers to the west, south and east, where all of the other municipalities now lie.

Of the municipalities, those of greatest importance to the tourist are: La Habana Vieja, with its spectacular Spanish colonial buildings and plazas, its many free and nonstop music venues, and its multitude of pleasant restaurants and bars; Centro Habana, which abuts Old Havana and contains yet more Spanish-era buildings and plazas, as well as several of the city's finest museums; and

Vedado, which flanks Centro Habana to the west and offers visitors some excellent dining options, even more historical sites, and plenty of shopping opportunities.

CLIMATE

Most people find Havana generally hot and sticky, although the climate can be quite pleasant at times. The mean average temperature during the warmest months (June to October) is 27.3°C, while during the coolest months (December to March) it's 22.5°C. The average relative humidity is 78%.

Havana's wettest months are also its hottest; the city receives an average of 10.2 rainy days a month June through August. Havana's driest months are February, March and April, when there are usually no more than four days of rain in a single month. December and January are also relatively dry months, receiving an average of six rainy days a month.

For lower highs and drier days, the best time to visit Havana is December through April. November and May are the marginal months – sometimes they are oppressively hot, wet, or both – and forget visiting Havana during the long, hot summer unless you tolerate obscenely warm weather well.

The hurricane season runs from June to November, with the worst storms usually landing in September and October. If a hurricane is brewing in the area when you're in Havana, stay away from ocean's edge and from windows that can shatter in your face. Better yet, leave the city; whether your hotel weathers hurricanes well or not, the city's electrical system usually doesn't and long power outages are common following major

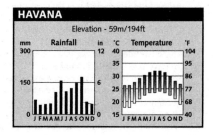

HAVANA

Elevation - 59m/194ft

Killer Storms

The hurricanes that occasionally strike Havana originate off the coast of Africa, forming as winds that rush toward a low-pressure area and swirl around it due to the rotational forces of the Earth's spin. The storms move counterclockwise across the Atlantic, fed by warm winds and moisture, building up force in their 3000km run toward Central and North America.

A hurricane builds in stages, the first of which is called a tropical disturbance. The next stage is a tropical depression. When winds exceed 64km/h, the weather system is upgraded to a tropical storm and is usually accompanied by heavy rains. The system is called a hurricane if wind speed exceeds 120km/h and intensifies around a low-pressure center, the so-called 'eye of the storm.'

Hurricane systems can range from 80km in diameter to devastating giants more than 1600km across. Their energy is prodigious – far more than the mightiest thermonuclear explosions ever unleashed on Earth. The area affected by winds of great destructive force may exceed 240km in diameter. Gale-force winds can prevail over an area twice as great.

The strength of a hurricane is rated from one to five. The mildest, a Category 1 hurricane, has winds of at least 120km/h. The strongest and rarest hurricanes, the Category 5 monsters, pack winds that exceed 250km/h; Hurricane Mitch, which killed more than 10,000 people in Central America and southeastern Mexico in late 1998, was a rare Category 5 hurricane. Hurricanes travel across the sea at varying speeds too, from as little as 10km/h to more than 50km/h.

If you're in Havana and a Category 4 or Category 5 hurricane is threatening Cuba, consider leaving the region. If you decide to chance it, at least lower your risk by moving into a hotel away from the waterfront and by avoiding the temptation to see the big waves the storm brings in. Even Category 2 hurricanes send waves over the seawall along the Malecón, flooding the ground floors of most of the buildings along the boulevard and typically drowning a few people.

For up-to-the-minute tropical-storm information, go to *The Miami Herald's* website (www.herald.com) and scan the top menu for hurricane and storm information. Another excellent place to find current tropical-storm information is the website maintained by the US National Oceanic and Atmospheric Administration (www.esdim.noaa.gov/weather_page.html).

storms. Needless to say, you also wouldn't be doing much sightseeing during a hurricane.

ECOLOGY & ENVIRONMENT

You need only look to the sky above Havana to realize that Cuba is far behind other countries in imposing strict pollution controls on some of its industries. Likewise, pollution of the Bahía de La Habana is one of the nation's biggest environmental problems. Waste-depositing industries such as chemical plants and paper mills and Havana's inadequate sewage-disposal system have taken a toll on the bay.

Food shortages of recent years have led to overfishing around the entire island. Along many reefs, fish large enough to eat have become extremely rare. Local anglers have also swept through the fish nurseries in the coastal mangroves, and lobsters, turtles or any fish fit for a tourist's table have been ruthlessly pursued.

Most of Cuba's conch shells have been sold as curios, and the black coral formations have been attacked to provide jewelry for visitors. As the marine creatures disappear, coral diseases such as yellow band, black band, and nuisance algae have multiplied on the receding reefs. Items made from turtle shells, black coral and conch shells are sold in Havana stores; please be decent and resist the urge to purchase them.

FLORA & FAUNA
Flora

Cuba is home to 650 known species of trees, and in Havana's plazas and lining the city's boulevards it's possible to see samples of some of the country's largest tree species. Indeed, some of the trees providing shade in plazas in the neighborhoods of La Habana Vieja and Centro Habana are hundreds of years old and are terrific examples of their kind. There are also hundreds of species of orchids in Cuba; eagle-eyed visitors can spot many in the trees of Havana. The national flower, incidentally, is the white *mariposa* (butterfly jasmine).

Altogether, more than 8000 species of plants are present in Cuba, over half of them endemic. The portion of Cuba covered by forests declined from 90% in 1812 to 54% in 1900 to only 14% in 1959. Of this, 43% is semideciduous forest, 31% mangroves, 12% pines, and only 1.5% tropical rainforest. The Plan Manatí, begun in 1987, resulted in the planting of some 3 billion trees of many different species all around Cuba, raising the forested area to 20% of the national territory. However, the gathering of firewood continues to impact the forests.

Semideciduous or tropical green forests are found in rocky or lower mountainous areas. Many coastlines are fringed with spiderlike mangroves that protect the shoreline from erosion and provide a habitat for small fish and birds. The most extensive mangrove swamps lie in the Ciénaga de Zapata. The largest pine forests grow in western Pinar del Río, on Isla de la Juventud, in eastern Holguín Province, and in central Guantánamo. The pine forests are especially susceptible to fire damage, and much pine reforestation has been necessary.

Cuba's most characteristic tree is the stately royal palm, or *Reistonea regia*, depicted on the country's coat of arms. It's easily distinguished by the green stalk at the top, and there are said to be 20 million royal palms in Cuba reaching up to 40m tall. The cork palm *(Microcycas calocoma)* is a living link with the Cretaceous period (between 65 and 135 million years ago). It's very rare and found mostly in the west. The *palma barrigona* (big belly palm, *Colpothrinax wrightii)* is easily distinguished by its shape.

The *jagüey* is a huge fig tree with aerial roots. The royal poinciana, or flamboyant tree, an exotic import from the Far East, has bright orange and red flowers that bloom around Christmas. The *uva caleta* (sea grape, *Coccoloba uvifera)* is a tree with grapelike fruit found along much of the coast. The *yagruma* tree is easily recognizable for its large leaves, which are green on top and white on the bottom. The agave is found in drier areas. Its long pointed stalks contain a strong fiber called sisal, or heniquen.

All three primary cultures of Cuba – Indian, African, and European – have considered sacred the *ceiba*, or *kapok* (silk-cotton tree). It's notable for its wide trunk and billowing top. Buoyant brown fibers obtained from the fruit pods of this tree can be used as stuffing in life preservers, although its flammability has led to replacement by synthetic fibers.

In Havana, it's possible to see examples of all of the species mentioned here in the Jardín Botánico Nacional, in the Parque Lenín area (see Map 5 for the garden's specific location).

A Break for Turtles

In a bid to raise a quick chunk of cash, the Cuban government, in the year 2000, asked the UN Convention on International Trade in Endangered Species if it could sell its stocks of rare hawksbill turtle shells to Japan, where some insensitive individuals use the turtle shells to make jewelry and ornaments. A 25-year-old ban on the trade of the shells was in effect at the time, and the UN group decided to maintain it. Cuba has also requested the right to catch and trade up to 500 hawksbill turtles a year from its waters, but it withdrew that proposal in the face of broad opposition. The beautiful turtles, with shells elaborately patterned with streaks of amber, yellow and brown, have lived in the oceans for more than 400 million years. But their numbers have fallen dramatically in recent decades and with governments such as Cuba's trying to cash in on their lovely shells, it's anyone's guess whether they will survive another 20 years.

¡ABSOLUTAMENTE NINGÚN MIEDO!

Those Colorful Trees

Havana is home to many gorgeous, blooming trees. Below are some you'll undoubtedly come across while strolling around town.

Mammee-Apple This native of the Antilles bears delicious fruit that is served raw and as jam. The green-brown fruit is round and the size of a baseball. The flowers have four white pedals. The tree can grow to 30m and is taller than it is wide. It blooms May through September.

Flamboyant This large, spreading, colorful tree is easily identified by its brilliant, five-petal red flowers and brown machete-resembling pods. This Madagascar native is found in gardens throughout Havana. It blooms April through August.

Mango A native of India, this spreading tree is famous for its sweet fruit, which is made into jam, candy, sodas and ice cream, and eaten raw. The tree's flowers are tiny, white and edible, although the sap can cause itching. It blooms several times a year.

Elephant's Ear This tree, which can reach 25m in height, is found in plazas around town. It takes its name from its fruit, which is brown and resembles an ear. The flowers are small, white and spherical. It blooms October through November.

Sandbox This native of the American Tropics reaches 30m, is shaped like an oak, and bears red berries, tiny brown flowers, and pods that look like little pumpkins. Careful: The fruit is poisonous. It blooms May through August, and November and December.

Star-Apple This popular cultivation tree produces sweet green apples that are said to have many health-giving properties. The tree, which can reach 25m, takes its name from star-formation seeds. The flowers are tiny and yellow. It blooms May through October.

Cashew This American Tropics native, wider than it is tall, is famous for its nut. The nut is attached to a yellow, meaty growth that looks like a piece of fruit but isn't; it is in fact quite poisonous. The flowers are red and white. It blooms April through August.

SEÑORES IMPERIALISTAS ¡NO LES TENEMOS ABSOLUTAMENTE NINGUN MIEDO!

Fauna

Havana is a big city that's been settled for many centuries. The wildlife that once lived in the area is pretty much gone. The areas in which the endemic fauna is least disturbed are the swamps of southern Matanzas, approximately 75km east of Havana; the country's mountainous areas; and the offshore islands of the five main archipelagos (although these are now being impacted by resort development).

Among the 350 species of bird found in Cuba are many varieties of crane, egret, flamingo, flycatcher, hawk, heron, hummingbird, ibis, kingbird, mockingbird, nightingale, owl, parakeet, parrot, pelican, pigeon, quail, royal thrush, sparrow, spoonbill, stork, warbler, woodpecker and wren. Prime bird-watching areas include the Península de Guanahacabibes in Pinar del Río, the Ciénaga de Zapata near the Bay of Pigs, the Sierra Maestra, the mountains behind Baracoa, and Isla de la Juventud. Egrets and cranes occasionally make an appearance in Havana, but don't count on seeing any other exotic birds in the city.

You'll be interested to know that Cuba hosts the world's smallest bird – the bee hummingbird, or *Mellisuga helenae*. The male weighs only 2g and is just a bit bigger than a grasshopper. In May or June the slightly larger female lays two jellybean-size eggs in a 4cm-wide nest. Habitat destruction has restricted these birds to remote areas such as the Ciénaga de Zapata. The June 1990 issue of *National*

Geographic contains several rare photos of the tiny creature.

GOVERNMENT & POLITICS

The Constitution of February 1976 provides for a 601-member Asamblea Nacional del Poder Popular (National Assembly of People's Power) elected every five years. In 1992 the constitution was amended to allow direct elections by universal suffrage and secret ballot (previously, the National Assembly was elected indirectly by the municipalities). Half of the candidates are nominated by mass organizations, while the other half are chosen by elected municipal delegates from among their ranks (previously, all were nominated by Communist Party committees).

Only one candidate contests each assembly seat, and a negative vote of at least 50% is required to reject a candidate, which makes the elections something of a referendum on candidates previously selected. The 1192 delegates to the 14 provincial assemblies are elected in the same way. The municipal assemblies are elected in districts, with several candidates for each seat.

The National Assembly elects the 31-member Consejo de Estado (Council of State), which has a president, first vice president, five additional vice presidents, and a secretary. This body represents the National Assembly between its twice annual meetings, and the Council's president is the head of government and state. The president nominates a 44-member Consejo de Ministros (Council of Ministers), which must be confirmed by the National Assembly. In practice, the National Assembly is a rubber-stamp parliament that never questions the policies or actions of Cuba's top leaders.

The only political party is the Partido Comunista de Cuba (PCC), which was formed in October 1965 by merging cadres from the Partido Socialista Popular (the pre-1959 Communist Party founded by Julio Antonio Mella in 1925) and veterans of the guerrilla campaign, including members of Castro's M-26-7 and the Directorio Revolucionario 13 de Marzo. The present party has 780,000 members and is led by First Secretary Fidel Castro. Every five years, party congresses elect a 150-member Central Committee, which in turn chooses the 24 members of the Political Bureau, or Politburo. Although the Politburo decides policy, it doesn't actually run the country – the members of the Council of Ministers do that.

The most important party-controlled organizations are the Confederación de Trabajadores Cubanos (CTC), a trade union confederation with 80,000 branches; the Asociación Nacional de Agricultores Pequeños (ANAP), an association of small private farmers; the Federación de Mujeres Cubanas (FMC), a women's federation founded in 1960; the 500,000-member Unión de Jóvenes Comunistas (UJC), a student group; and the Comités de Defensa de la Revolución (CDR), a neighborhood-watch organization with more than 7 million members.

Persons opposed to Cuba's current political and economic systems are not represented at any level of government. Anyone publicly expressing opinions critical of the country's leadership faces arrest, and all attempts to organize a political opposition are immediately squelched. In early 1999 new legislation instituted long prison terms for any person convicted of undermining Cuba's national independence or the state economy. Every Cuban lawyer is employed

Don't Call Him 'Loco'

Cuban President Fidel Castro does not mind being labeled a 'dictator,' but any aspersions cast on his mental health really tug at his beard, a former intelligence agent for Cuba told reporters in Paris recently. 'Investigations of Castro's mental condition, this really bothers him because it humiliates him,' said Jorge Masetti, who left Cuba a decade ago for Paris. 'They don't mind if you call him a dictator, in fact he even likes it, but if you treat him like a nut...'. Masetti didn't finish his sentence, but 'it drives him crazy' would suffice.

!ABSOLUTAMENTE NINGUN MIEDO!

by the government, and the will of the party is never challenged in court.

Moreover, a computerized list is maintained of those guilty of 'antisocial behavior' and such persons are barred from government employment, including anything related to the lucrative tourism industry or joint ventures with foreign companies. Most of the checks and balances of a modern democracy, such as opposition parties, a free press, an independent judiciary, limits of powers, autonomous trade unions and other powerful organizations, are absent in Cuba today. Nevertheless, it's possible that a majority of Cubans sincerely support their charismatic leader and the revolution, although this has never been tested in an election in which the opposition was allowed to participate.

Although little is likely to change as long as Castro is at the helm, what will happen after he goes is anybody's guess. Castro's prestige within Cuba is overwhelming, and he has held firmly to communist orthodoxy as a means of defending Cuba's socialist system. His successors are unlikely to be as inflexible. Fidel's brother and designated successor, Raúl Castro, serves as first vice president and minister of the Revolutionary Armed Forces. Raúl has a reputation for being less doctrinaire than his brother. National Assembly President Ricardo Alarcón has also positioned himself as a centrist. Vice President Carlos Lage is the regime's leading reformer. In May 1999 Roberto Robaina was replaced as foreign minister by Fidel's personal secretary, Felipe Pérez Roque, largely because Robaina was considered too moderate.

Cuba's best-known dissident (and political prisoner) is Vladimiro Roca, a former air force fighter pilot and son of the late communist leader Blas Roca. Roca and three colleagues were arrested in July 1997 for holding press conferences with foreign journalists, warning foreign investors against complicity with the regime, calling for an election boycott, and criticizing the one-party state. The four were found guilty of 'enemy propaganda' and were sentenced to four to five years in prison. They turned down the opportunity to go into exile and have promised to redouble their efforts to build a peaceful opposition as soon as they are released.

Cuba is divided into 169 municipalities, including the Special Municipality of Isla de la Juventud (2398 sq km), and 14 provinces: the City of Havana (727 sq km), Havana Province (5731 sq km), Pinar del Río (10,925 sq km), Matanzas (11,978 sq km), Villa Clara (8662 sq km), Cienfuegos (4178 sq km), Sancti Spíritus (6744 sq km), Ciego de Ávila (6910 sq km), Camagüey (15,990 sq km), Las Tunas (6589 sq km), Holguín (9301 sq km), Granma (8372 sq km), Santiago de Cuba (6170 sq km), and Guantánamo (6186 sq km). The municipal assemblies are elected by universal suffrage every 2½ years, and these in turn elect their own executive committees. Isla de la Juventud is run by the central government.

ECONOMY

Until recently Cuba had a centrally planned economy, administered by the state, according to policy guidelines laid down by the Communist Party of Cuba. All economic activities except small farming were government operated, and all employees worked for the state. There was no direct taxation because resources could be assigned any way the state planners saw fit. State enterprises were not required to make a profit and prices were arbitrary. Full employment was guaranteed and labor productivity was low.

Things began to change in July 1992, when direct foreign investment in joint ventures and other forms of economic association with state enterprises became easier. Joint ventures with the government had been possible since 1982, and the first such agreement was signed in 1988 (joint ventures with private individuals in Cuba are banned). Most joint ventures are with companies from Spain, Canada, Italy, France, the United Kingdom and Mexico (in order of the number of associations), and currently 350 joint ventures worth US$2.6 billion are operating (compared with only 20 joint ventures in 1991).

Castillo de la Real Fuerza, the oldest extant colonial fortress in the Americas

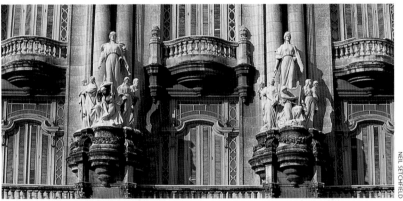

The magnificent Gran Teatro de La Habana, home to the Ballet Nacional de Cuba

A lovely day for a bike ride…or a rest

RICHARD I'ANSON

CHARLOTTE HINDLE

RICHARD I'ANSON

Fans, a fountain of lions and weathered facades

Havana's architecture, 'music set in stone'

View over Centro Habana

Paseo del Prado, 'very Latin, very Spanish, very agreeable'

Dominoes, serious business in Centro Habana

Enterprises created in this way operate on a for-profit basis and are independent of government control, except that state enterprises have first option to supply raw materials and purchase the products. All Cuban workers are hired and paid in Cuban pesos by the Cuban partner, even though the foreign company is required to pay their wages to the Cuban government in dollars. Despite this, labor costs are much lower than in other countries due to Cuba's low wage scales. Joint ventures may export their own products, and the repatriation of profits and capital is guaranteed. Profits are taxed at 30%, and the local payroll is subject to an 11% tax, payable in hard currency. Foreigners who spend more than 180 days a year in Cuba must pay Cuban income tax.

Since September 1993 Cuban nationals have been allowed to set up personal or family businesses, and private trading by individual Cubans has had an impact in the retail, catering, and accommodations fields. In fact, the government had no choice but to allow self-employment when it was forced to lay off excess workers to avoid financial collapse, bringing unemployment back to Cuba.

To avoid the reemergence of a capitalist class, private entrepreneurs are not allowed to employ staff, though many get around this by claiming their workers are co-owners or relatives. In 1999 there were 130,000 licensed *cuentapropistas* (self-employed workers) in Cuba, down from 210,000 in 1997, due to punitive taxation. Since 1996 personal income taxes of between 10% and 50% have been collected on all hard-currency earnings (gifts from abroad and pensions are exempt). The Cuban government has imposed ruinously high taxation and cumbersome licensing regulations on

The Ration Card

The ration card or *libreta* was created in 1962 to provide a basic social safety net for the population and to reduce speculation. During the relatively affluent '70s and '80s, with Soviet subsidized products pouring in, it seemed that the card might be on the way out, but the economic crisis of the '90s has ensured its survival.

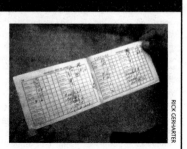

RICK GERHARTER

The basic 30-product monthly food basket allotted to every Cuban includes 2.5kg of rice, 1.5kg each of refined and brown sugar, 1kg of fish, .5kg of beans, 28g of coffee, 270g of salt, and 14 eggs.

Another 29 products are distributed irregularly on a per family basis, including soap, detergent, vegetable oil, cornmeal, food paste, crackers, tinned tomatoes, fruit and vegetables, and a small quantity of meat once or twice a year. Everyone gets one bread roll a day, and children up to the age of seven get a liter of fresh or canned milk a day, plus regular allotments of chicken, beef, and soy-based yogurt. Pensioners, pregnant women, and those with certain chronic diseases also receive milk rations.

Rationed goods are sold at government stores, called *bodegas*, at subsidized peso prices that haven't changed for years. The same items sold freely without ration cards at farmers' markets cost 20 times more. Maintaining the ration system is a serious drain on state finances, but without it many Cubans would suffer real hardship in a society where the circulation of two unequal currencies has created tangible class differences. As it is, the monthly ration is only a supplement that must be topped up elsewhere somehow.

– David Stanley

SEÑORES IMPERIALISTAS ¡NO LES TENEMOS ABSOLUTAMENTE NINGÚN MIEDO!

all forms of private business to protect inefficient state enterprises, and advertising is also restricted. Laws relating to private enterprise in Cuba change frequently without notice, making any sort of business planning impossible.

Cubans employed by the government or in joint ventures take home an average monthly wage of 200 pesos, or US$10 at the semi-official market rate of exchange. Although housing, transportation, health, and education are heavily subsidized by the Cuban state, life on official wages is extremely difficult. Every Cuban has a ration book used to purchase basic foodstuffs at state-operated stores or *bodegas*, but these supplies are insufficient and must be supplemented by groceries purchased for much higher prices at farmers' markets.

Little Loss of Control

Although foreign companies, such as the Spanish hotel chain Sol Meliá, can forge ventures with the Cuban government, Cuban laws forbid workers from freely organizing and still prevent firms from owning, but not managing, property. Chances are you are (or will be) staying at one of Havana's hotels. It might interest you to know that Cuba's government siphons off approximately 95% of hotel employees' salaries and forbids companies from doling out individual financial incentives, although Sol Meliá in 2000 was given the go-ahead to give its top employees free shampoo and soap. Not exactly the big bonus or the 10% raise top employees most everywhere else hope for. It might also interest you to know that tips left for waiters are (reluctantly) turned over to the restaurant's manager; waiters throughout Havana, and the rest of Cuba as well, don't get to keep their tips as a matter of practice. It's one of the many ways Castro tries to keep capitalism to a minimum in Cuba – and why so many Cubans risk drowning in the Straits of Florida to reach the Land of Opportunity.

¡ABSOLUTAMENTE NINGÚN MIEDO!

Cuba's rich natural resources, excellent climate, and favorable geographical position should ensure it a high standard of living, if the country can find a way to develop peacefully without official obstruction from foreign embargoes and state monopolies. After shrinking 35% between 1989 and 1993, the gross domestic product (GDP) increased 0.7% in 1994, 2.5% in 1995, 7.8% in 1996, 2.5% in 1997, 1.2% in 1998 and 6.2% in 1999, indicating that the Cuban economy is regaining the ground it lost in the early '90s.

Agriculture

Prior to the revolution, 47% of arable or grazing land was held by only 1% of landowners, and 8% of farms occupied 70% of the land. On October 10, 1958, while still fighting in the Sierra Maestra, the rebel army declared that small holdings worked by tenant farmers, sharecroppers and squatters would become their property. The First Agrarian Reform Law of May 1959 nationalized landed estates *(latifundios)* of more than 400 hectares, and the Second Agrarian Reform Law of August 1963 expropriated all holdings larger than 65 hectares. The confiscated areas were converted into state farms *(granjas estatales)*, which until 1992 accounted for 75% of farmland (compared to 33% today).

By 1989, 40% of Cuba's food and 80% of its fertilizers and pesticides were imported from the Soviet bloc, and the collapse of that trade in 1991 caused real problems. In 1993 the first Basic Units of Cooperative Production (or UBPC, in Spanish) were created to grow more food for the population. Underutilized sections of state farms were turned over to city people, and today around 42% of Cuba's cultivable land is farmed by the cooperatives. Presently some 2705 self-supporting cooperatives of this kind are operating, each with several hundred participants. However, 70% of the UBPCs are unprofitable because of interference in their operations by the central government.

The balance of Cuba's land has long been divided into private farms, worked by about

70,000 small-scale farmers *(campesinos)*, many of them former tenant farmers who were given title after 1959. Private farms are most common in Pinar del Río and Guantánamo Provinces, followed by Sancti Spíritus, Holguín, and Granma. Over half the private farms belong to Agricultural Production Cooperatives (CPAs in Spanish) established in 1977. Since October 1994, private farmers have been allowed to sell their surplus crops (above official production quotas) in public markets, called *mercados agropecuarios*, for personal profit. A high percentage of state and cooperative land is devoted to sugar production, while small private farmers often specialize in tobacco, coffee, and food production. Although private farms account for only 20% of Cuba's farmland, they produce 40% of Cuba's food.

The main agricultural product is sugar, and until the early 1990s Cuba produced about 7 million metric tonnes per annum, a level surpassed only by Brazil. Today most cane is cut by mechanical harvesters. Fuel shortages in the early 1990s led to a partial return to manual harvesting, and by 1998 production had fallen to just 3.2 million tons, the lowest level in 50 years. The government will have to spend millions of dollars modernizing Cuba's 156 dilapidated sugar mills and close the most uneconomic of them down if the industry is to recover. Sugar still accounts for about 70% of Cuba's export revenue; it's shipped mostly to Russia and China either crude, refined, or as molasses. The molasses can be made into rum, the cane-juice froth into fertilizer, and the crushed fibers into cardboard or construction material. Most mills are now fueled by burning spent fibers. The harvesting season for cane is January to May.

Other crops include tobacco, coffee, rice, corn, sweet potatoes, beans, and tropical fruit such as oranges, grapefruit, bananas, mangoes, and pineapples. Cuba's citrus plantations were created to supply the Soviet Union, and the fruit produced is too low quality to be sold on most Western markets. Cuba's 5 million cattle are all state-owned, but 80% of the 3 million pigs are owned by private farmers, cooperatives, or

Sugarcane's Story

Sugarcane originated on the island of New Guinea in the South Pacific and was widely used in ancient India. The Arabs brought the plant to medieval Spain, and the first Spanish explorers carried it to the New World. This perennial grass plant of the genus *Saccharum* has a noded stalk containing a sweet juice that can be released by pressing. Sugar, molasses, rum, alcohol, fertilizer, fuel, and livestock feed are only the main products of this useful plant.

Sugarcane is initially propagated from cuttings, and one planting can harvest three annual crops. After the third harvest, the stumps are removed and the field is replanted. The soil must be well drained to avoid root rot, and chemical fertilizers are used. The fields are weeded by hand until the cane is high enough to form a canopy (mature cane is over 3m high). About 2000mm of rainfall is required during the growing season, and cane is harvested in the dry season (January to May). Sugarcane is susceptible to various diseases and pests, and much effort is expended breeding resistant hybrid varieties with ever higher sugar contents.

– David Stanley

work centers. The Zebu (Brahma) breed of cow, resistant to heat but a low milk producer, has been crossed with Holstein bulls imported from Canada to produce an acclimatized breed that is also a good milk producer. Since 1990 the Cuban dairy herd has been downsized 50% due to curtailed fodder imports from Eastern Europe, slashing milk production by 75%.

Tourism

Cuba's tourist industry is the fastest growing in the world, and it's now the country's largest single source of foreign exchange. In 1998 Cuba earned US$1.9 billion from tourism, though the imports required to support the industry meant that only 30 cents out of every US dollar spent by a tourist actually stayed in Cuba. Prior to the revolution Cuba was the leading tourist destination in the Caribbean; destinations such as Jamaica became popular only after the US embargo was imposed in 1961. International tourism returned to Cuba in 1975, when Canadians on package tours started arriving in large numbers, and since 1990 tourism has become a top priority. Varadero is now the largest tourist resort in the Caribbean.

Yet with 2 million foreign tourists in 2000, Cuba is still far from inundated. Much smaller countries, such as the Bahamas and Puerto Rico, receive four times as many visitors. To look at it another way, the Bahamas get 14 tourists a year for every local resident, while Cuba gets one tourist a year for every eight Cubans. That's partly why the Cubans are still so sincerely friendly. Canada sends the most tourists to Cuba, followed by Italy, Spain, Germany, France, Britain, and Mexico. Cuba is the top Caribbean destination for Canadian tourists. Over half of Cuba's visitors are from Europe, a quarter from North America, and 18% from Latin America. Tourism is increasing at the astonishing rate of 20% a year, and the number of beds in Cuban resort hotels is doubling every decade.

The Cuban government runs international tourism as a state monopoly, and private competition is either strictly controlled (and heavily taxed) or banned. Resort development follows the usual socialist model of huge industrial complexes closely controlled by a central authority. The massive resorts are no-go zones for ordinary Cubans, and foreign guests' freedom is also effectively curtailed through the use of all-inclusive packages designed to tie the dollar-machine tourists to their hotels. Foreign tour companies and the hotel chains happily cooperate in all of this by pushing prepaid tour packages, which guarantee easy profits. Independent travel, which might mean lower yields for the tour companies and revenue leakage to the private sector inside Cuba, is downplayed. Symptomatic of this policy is the official

requirement for an advance hotel reservation prior to arrival in Cuba.

Virtually all hotels are state owned, although foreign companies may hold management contracts on terms dictated by Havana. Even the horse carriages that take tourists on rides through the resorts are owned by the government, the drivers mere employees. People selling handicrafts at street markets or inside the hotels must pay substantial licensing fees. For example, handicraft vendors at the beach resorts pay US$40 a month for their license, plus 50% of their profits. Around 140,000 Cubans have jobs directly related to tourism, and these prized positions are used to reward government supporters. The names of persons with a history of 'antisocial' activities are recorded on a computerized blacklist of people banned from participation in the industry. Government spokespersons justify the above by arguing that income from tourism is essential to maintaining the unquestioned social benefits provided by the state to all Cubans.

POPULATION & PEOPLE

Cuba has more than 11 million inhabitants. The largest cities are Havana (2.2 million), Santiago de Cuba (440,000), Camagüey (300,000), Holguín (240,000), Guantánamo (208,000), and Santa Clara (200,000). Others, in descending order, include Bayamo, Cienfuegos, Pinar del Río, Las Tunas, Matanzas, Manzanillo, Ciego de Ávila and Sancti Spíritus. The most heavily populated regions of the country are around Havana, between Cienfuego and Santa Clara, and Oriente. Since May 1998, Cubans have required official permission to migrate to Havana.

Cuba's native Indians were almost entirely wiped out during the first half century of Spanish rule. To replace them as laborers the Spanish imported African slaves, over 800,000 of whom were brought to Cuba from West Africa during Spanish rule. Most belonged to the Yoruba and Bantu tribes, and some of their original traditions survive today in the various Afro-Cuban religions. The African population was strengthened between 1919 and 1926, when a quarter million black laborers were recruited from Jamaica and Haiti to work on the plantations.

Prior to 1959 there was much discrimination against blacks both socially and in employment, but this was officially banned after the revolution. Mixed marriages have become commonplace, and the proportion of blacks and mixed race people is increasing gradually due to improved health services and a higher percentage of white emigrants. While the overwhelming majority of Cuban-Americans are light-skinned, a majority of the population of Cuba itself has some black ancestry. Officially, the present population is 66% white, 12% black, and 22% mixed, although other sources estimate the proportion of mixed blood Cubans to be much higher. The percentage of blacks in the population is noticeably higher in eastern Cuba.

Almost all Cuban whites are of Spanish origin, and their numbers were increased by an influx of a million immigrants from Spain and the Canary Islands between 1900 and 1929.

Some 125,000 Cantonese men were brought to Cuba as laborers between 1847 and 1874, but after their eight-year contracts expired most left due to poor conditions. Another 30,000 Cantonese men arrived during the 1920s. Most of those who stayed married Cuban women and the Chinese element is now highly diffuse, although a small Chinatown does exist in Havana.

Housing

Soon after the revolution, rents on housing were reduced 50%, and since 1962 rent payments have been limited to 10% of family income. The Urban Reform Law of October 1960 converted rent payments into mortgage payments on a five- to 20-year basis, making owners out of renters. Almost half a million Cuban families acquired title to their homes or lands this way. The sale of such housing is prohibited, but units can be traded among owners. Today a large majority of Cubans own their own homes and pay no property taxes, which explains how

they're able to get by on salaries of around US$10 a month.

Prefabricated apartment blocks have been built throughout the country, often in rural areas or in modern housing developments outside the cities. By chance, this process has saved the historic centers of cities like Havana from being knocked down by developers, although much prerevolution housing is poorly maintained.

Since the revolution, efforts have been made to reverse the developing world's trend of concentrating development in the main cities, and the government has worked to improve conditions in the countryside. Thus there has been little new construction in Havana since 1959. Soon after the revolution, the miserable slums that had once encircled the city were demolished, and a series of new satellite cities of modern apartment buildings was erected, the most notable of which are Habana del Este and Alamar, on the coast just east of Havana.

Education

The greatest successes of the revolution have been in the fields of health and education. Prior to the revolution a quarter of adult Cubans were illiterate and another million were semiliterate. Ten thousand teachers were unemployed, and 70% of the rural population had no schools. After 1959 all private schools were nationalized and education became free and universal. Former military garrisons were also turned into schools.

In 1961 all schools were closed for eight months, and some 100,000 students and teachers were sent to rural areas to teach reading and writing, resulting in Cuba's present literacy rate of 94.5%. This campaign brought tens of thousands of city youth into contact with the country people, breaking down racial barriers and instilling revolutionary spirit. The early literacy campaigns were followed up with continuing programs to ensure that nearly every adult attained a sixth-grade (age 12) education level. Today education is compulsory up to the 12th grade (age 18). The school year is from September to June.

A special effort has been made to build schools in rural areas that previously had been totally neglected. Since 1970 many 'secondary schools in the countryside' have been constructed, especially on Isla de la Juventud. At these schools, agricultural work is combined with study, making it financially possible for this developing country to offer a high school education to every child. At the hundreds of such schools, students divide their time between classes and work in the fields, allowing the facilities to be utilized in two shifts. Room and board are free.

In fact, education is free from kindergarten through university, and schools are accessible to virtually all children. Schoolbooks are provided at no charge – when there are any. University students often have a hard time supporting themselves on the scant government aid they receive, and upon graduation they must perform two years of social service work in their fields at a low rate of pay before accepting permanent positions in their professions.

Since 1959 the focus of education has shifted from the liberal arts to technical and professional training, with the intention of reducing class differentiation and promoting manual labor. There are 46 centers of higher education, with a total of 22,000 professors, 20% of whom hold doctorates, and some 574,000 persons have graduated with professional degrees since 1959. In all, 300,000 teachers instruct 3 million students.

Yet while the educational system has taught Cubans many practical skills, it has been less successful in teaching people to make individual decisions, and this is reflected in the low efficiency of some sectors of the state economy. And just as an American family's wealth often determines the type of education the children receive, a Cuban family's political background often influences whether the children will be able to go to university (the offspring of anyone blacklisted for 'antistate activities' would be at a serious disadvantage).

Also, while Castro likes to boast that Cuba has the finest educational system in the world, a close look at it makes one wonder. A part-time waitress working in one of Havana's restaurants in 2000 said she was enrolled in one of her country's most popular vocational schools, gastronomy. Its popularity was due to the fact that waiters can earn more than doctors, engineers and lawyers – if they withhold some of the tips they are supposed to turn in to the government. And how long is the gastronomy course? Four years! There's something wrong with a system that requires a person to spend four years in school to become a waitress.

Public Health

In the year 2000, the World Health Organization ranked Cuba's public health system as the 39th best of the 191 systems it ranked worldwide. By comparison, WHO ranked France No 1, Spain No 7, the UK No 18, Australia No 32 and the USA No 37. Since 1959, life expectancy in Cuba has increased from 55 years to 68.4. This and a declining birthrate, the free availability of contraception and abortion, and continuing outward migration have led to a progressive aging of the population. About 80% of married women use birth control. It's estimated that by the year 2025 a quarter of Cubans will be over 60 years of age, as those born during the baby boom of the 1960s reach retirement age.

Since 1959 hundreds of hospitals, polyclinics (half hospital/half clinic), and clinics have been built, and tens of thousands of doctors and nurses have been trained to replace those who left for the US. In 1960 a rural health system was created and medical graduates are now required to do a two-year internship in the countryside after graduation. In 1958 there was only one rural hospital, but by 1975 the number had increased to 58. Between 1958 and 1975, Cuba's public health budget increased by 20 times. In 1999, 39% of Cuba's budget was devoted to public health and education, and another 15% to social assistance and security. Some 421 clinics and 267 hospitals are spread throughout the land. In addition, between 1960 and 1990 over 26,000 Cuban doctors provided medical assistance to

Human Rights in Cuba

The Cuban government is often criticized over its human rights record, and it's a fact that many individuals who would be considered 'prisoners of conscience' in the Western context are presently being held in Cuban jails simply for voicing opinions critical of Cuba's present leadership or for attempting to organize political opposition. The Cuban Commission for Human Rights and National Reconciliation, an independent rights group, reported in 2000 that it knew of 314 political prisoners incarcerated in Cuba.

But the freedom to express an opinion in Cuba – or rather the inability to do it without severe repercussions – goes far beyond standing on a street corner and criticizing Fidel Castro or his administration. In reality, you, José Cubano, are either part of the program or you're against it: If, for example, you question the political teachings given you at all levels of education in Cuba, your 'lack of patriotism' will be noted and you might likely find it difficult to get a desirable job when you finish your studies. Examples like this abound in Cuba.

On the day this was written (June 9, 2000), Reuters news service moved a story about eight Cubans aboard a boat off the coast of Florida who attempted to set themselves on fire and threatened to eat rat poison, saying they would rather die than fail in their voyage to the United States. Such dramas play out almost weekly in the 150km-wide Straits of Florida, which separate Cuba from the USA. Cubans who manage to set foot in the United States are allowed to stay there.

Speak with any Cuban at length about freedom in Cuba – in a setting where your conversation can't be overheard by Cuban secret police, who make a point of mingling in tourist haunts to catch 'dissidents' (anyone who disagrees with Castro on anything) – and you'll soon realize that even one passing remark about life in Cuba can cost a Cuban a job, access to basic services, and future prospects in Cuban society.

Havana is a terrific tourist destination, made all the more interesting because Cuba is the only communist nation in the Western Hemisphere. But it's not a place you'd want to live – at least, not if you're Cuban. If you wonder about that statement, ponder this: Each year the US Interests Section, the de facto US embassy in Havana, holds a lottery to give Cubans a chance at immigration visas. The US allows 20,000 Cubans to immigrate to the US annually, of which the lottery provides about 15,000. Each year more than 500,000 Cubans – or about 5% of the island's population – place their names in the lottery.

SEÑORES IMPERIALISTAS ¡NO LES TENEMOS ABSOLUTAMENTE NINGÚN MIEDO!

countries in Africa, Asia and Latin America. Today some 1700 Cuban doctors serve in 40 countries.

Retirement

Cuban women can retire at the age of 55, Cuban men at the age of 60 (men working in difficult jobs, such as mining, can also retire at 55). Those who wish to continue working are free to do so and receive a salary supplement as compensation. Pensions vary according to the length of service, and are a percentage of a person's salary. Elderly persons without families to support them are accommodated free of charge in *hogares de ancianos*.

ARTS

Since the revolution there has been a conscious effort to promote Cuban culture, which had previously been suffocated by foreign commercial culture. In Havana alone, dozens of art schools were created, museums opened, and theater groups formed. Musicians were guaranteed a salary, and a national film industry was established. To balance the influence of North American mass culture, Cuba's unique African culture was revalued and Afro-Cuban folklore ensembles were granted subsidies. The National Ballet of Cuba has received international acclaim. The Consejo Nacional de Cultura (National Cultural Council) coordinates activities in the fields of music, art, drama, and dance. Cuban artists and writers enjoy many privileges as members of the party-controlled Unión Nacional de Escritores y Artistas de Cuba (UNEAC), and expulsion from this body is the artistic equivalent of being sent to Siberia.

Dance & Theater

The rumba is a dance style of Afro-Cuban origin in which the rhythm is provided by drums, maracas, and a singer. It can be seen in bars and restaurants in La Habana Vieja any time of day (see the Entertainment chapter for details). Never a specific genre in its original setting, the term 'rumba' originally referred to any of the lively and often erotic dances of former slaves. Underscoring it all are the Afro-Cuban rituals of *Santería* (an Afro-Cuban religion) in which African deities *(orishas)* have merged with Catholic saints. Rhythms played on *batá* drums evoke ghosts who take possession of the dancers in certain rituals. Varieties of Cuban rumba include the slower *yambú*, the faster *guaguancó*, and the acrobatic *columbia*. The latter originated as a devil dance of the Náñigo rite, and today it's performed only by solo males.

During the late 1920s, the rumba spread to New York, where the original percussion-and-vocal form was corrupted by placing greater emphasis on the tune through the addition of horns and strings to the lineup. The three-step ballroom rumba subsequently propagated by Hollywood has little to do with the original Cuban dance. Within two decades this big-band rumba had developed into mambo under the influence of Afro-Cuban jazz. In mambo, the two fast side steps and one slower forward step of ballroom rumba are replaced by a step back, a step forward, and a close. The chachachá was invented in the early '50s specifically to appeal to white dancers: not too fast, easy to learn, and with simple lyrics to the songs.

Unlike the rumba, the *habanera* developed within Cuba's Spanish population and spread to Europe during the late 19th century. The habanera is a slow to moderate dance for couples in which the feet barely leave the floor and provocative gestures of the eyes, head, hips, and limbs mirror the music. The high-pitched singing is reminiscent of flamenco. Around 1910 the habanera was developed into the tango in Argentina; the slow, romantic Cuban *bolero* also emerged from this milieu.

Danzón also has upper-class roots, compared to the more popular rumba. It's an urban orchestral dance that began as an offshoot of Spanish *contradanzas* picked up by domestic servants during the colonial era. On a signal the dancers suddenly stop and wait a few beats before starting again. Danzón was in style from 1880 until 1940, and it had a lasting influence on Cuban popular music.

In the *danza tajona*, often performed for tourists, the dancers weave ribbons around a pole and then unwind the ribbons at great speed. Shows at Cuban hotels frequently feature a conga as the band comes down and leads a snake of dancing bodies around the floor. The conga originated as a dance for African slaves who could only take short steps due to the shackles on their feet. These days its one-two-three-kick is an irresistible icebreaker.

Cuba has a widely acclaimed ballet, which performs at the Gran Teatro de La Habana (see the Entertainment chapter for details). If you've never had the opportunity to see a Russian ballet, you might like to know that many of Cuba's dancers trained at the foremost ballet schools in Russia.

You can generally find some type of live musical event at Havana's Grand Theater every Friday, Saturday and Sunday. Lighter fare can be found at other theaters around town.

Music

Cuban music is a happy combination of forceful African rhythms and Spanish poetic melody that ethnomusicologist Fernando Ortíz termed 'a love affair between the African drum and the Spanish guitar.' Cuba is a living model of cross-cultural fertilization, and during the '60s and '70s the process came full circle as Cuban arrangements inspired new trends in West African pop music. Similarities in sound between the dance bands of Cuba and Francophone Africa are no coincidence. In fact, musicians on four continents have long drawn energy and inspiration from Cuban rhythms, and salsa artists from New York to Puerto Rico continue to play predominantly Cuban music. The drumming and strumming you frequently hear on Cuban city streets and country lanes has deep cultural roots, and Cuba's rumba revolution continues to shake the world.

Most contemporary popular music in Cuba is based on *son*, the Cuban equivalent of American country music. Son lyrics consist of rhyming eight-syllable *décima* verses. The form originated in the hills of Oriente in the late 19th century and was popularized with the advent of radio in the 1920s. At that time son was played by a

Cuban Musical Instruments

During slavery in the USA, drumming was prohibited, but in Cuba the opposite was true. When Cuban popular music began to diversify and spread in the early 20th century, Cuban musicians had a whole range of instruments at their disposal.

The strong rhythms in Cuban music are usually provided by the *tumbadora* (conga), a tall barrel-like drum held together by metal hoops. The *bongó* is a pair of small round drums joined by a piece of wood. The *batá* is a conical two-head drum of varying size used in Afro-Cuban religious rituals. Folk dances are often accompanied by a single-skinned drum of Congolese origin called a *joca*.

The gourd-shaped rattle called the *maraca* is one of the only Cuban musical instruments of pre-Hispanic origin. *Chequeré* rattles (a gourd covered with beads) are used in Afro-Cuban religious rituals. The *maruga* is a metal shaker. The *güiro* is an elongated gourd rasped with a stick, although there are also tin güiros. The *cata*, or *guagua*, is a wooden tube beaten with sticks. No band would be complete without *claves*, two wooden sticks tapped together to set the beat.

The *tres* is a small folk guitar with three sets of steel double strings. The similar *cuatro* has four sets of double strings. Cuban folk groups often include a West African hand piano or *marímbula*, a wooden box with five metal keys. The only wind instrument in Cuban folk music is the *botija*, a clay jug with a short narrow neck bearing an opening on the side for blowing. Musicians vary the pitch of the tones by moving a hand along the neck of the jug. During carnival a small five-note horn called a *corneta china* produces a sharp sound like the bagpipe. Modern instruments commonly used in Cuba include the bass, clarinet, guitar, saxophone, trombone and trumpet.

Cuba is the only country outside Europe with a tradition of street organs. During the 19th century, refugees from Haiti brought the French mechanical organ to eastern Cuba, where Hispano-Cuban sones, boleros, and danzones soon replaced waltzes and mazurkas in the repertoire. The Cubans made the European organ dynamic by adding a second crank that the operator uses to vary the speed at which the boards pass through the machine. Five or six percussionists joined an organ grinder to form an orchestra playing popular Cuban dance music under the control of the organ grinder, who can innovate stops or breaks.

– David Stanley

SEÑORES IMPERIALISTAS ¡NO LES TENEMOS ABSOLUTAMENTE NINGÚN MIEDO!

sexteto of guitar, *tres* (a Cuban guitar with three sets of double strings), double bass, bongó, two singers who played the *claves* (two sticks tapped together to set the beat) and maracas. A decade later a cornet was added to form a *septeto*, or *sonora*. During the '40s and '50s, horn and drum sections were added to the son ensembles to create big bands that played rumba, mambo, and chachachá. *Charanga* is the same but with flutes and fiddles added to the mix.

In the '60s and '70s, Cuban son and other Latin rhythms stirring in New York combined to create a loosely defined style related to jazz called salsa. Cuban exiles such as Celia Cruz embraced salsa as a substitute for their lost roots, and catchy salsa tunes were soon blaring from radios and jukeboxes all across Latin America. The phenomenal commercial success of New York salsa has displaced more authentic Cuban sounds in the glitzy American music marketplace, but the real thing awaits rediscovery in Cuba.

The most famous Cuban song is 'Guajira Guantanamera,' composed in 1928 by Joseíto Fernández (1908–79). In the late 1950s Cuban musician Hector Angulo added lyrics from the *Versos Sencillos* of José Martí, and this version was popularized by American folk singer Pete Seeger at a 1963 Carnegie Hall concert in solidarity with Cuba. Also during the '60s, the late Carlos Puebla sang songs in praise of the revolution (including the famous 'Hasta Siempre, Comandante Che Guevara').

Nueva trova has its origins in the late 1960s when guitar players Pablo Milanés, Silvio Rodríguez, and Noel Nicola began expressing their view of life in poetic form. From 1972 to 1986 some 500 troubadours from all around Cuba were brought together in an official Nueva Trova Movement that organized events and festivals. Cuban folk singers are allowed some latitude in their social criticism, and the lyrics are a type of social poetry favoring equality and even change.

Classical Music In the realm of classical music, pianist Ignacio Cervantes (1847–1905) composed a series of romantic *Danzas Cubanas* based on Afro-Cuban and Creole traditions. Later the ethnomusicological research of Fernando Ortíz (1881–1969) allowed composers Amadeo Roldán (1900–39) and Alejandro García Caturla (1906–40) to write orchestral works based on Afro-Cuban themes. Caturla also set the poems of Alejo Carpentier and Nicolás Guillén to music. Eliseo Grenet (1893–1950) and Ernesto Lecuona (1895–1963) made liberal use of Afro-Cuban rhythms in *zarzuelas* (operettas) such as Lecuona's *María la O* (1930), based on the classic Cuban theme of the biracial woman betrayed by a white man (available in Cuba on compact disc).

Popular Music During the 1920s, groups such as the Sexteto Nacional de Ignacio Piñeiro, Sexteto Boloña, and Sexteto Matancero popularized son in the US. The first big Cuban hit of those years was 'El Manicero' ('The Peanut Vendor'), played by Don Azpiazu and his Havana Casino Orchestra in New York in 1930. Antonio Arcaño y sus Maravillas adapted the danzón to mambo rhythms after 1938. The same period was the heyday of the Septeto Anacaona, comprised of seven sisters, one of the few women's bands of the time.

In 1927 the famous trumpeter Félix Chappottín began playing with the Sexteto Habanero, which had formed in 1920. The blind tres player Arsenio Rodríguez took over the band in 1940 and expanded the horn section under the influence of the American big-band sound. The three or four trumpets extended the expressive possibilities, while a piano reinforced the melody and a *tumbadora* (tall drum) kept the beat. A prolific composer, Rodríguez reinforced the African element in Cuban music through his lyrics and rhythms. In 1950 he moved to New York and formed another group, while Chappottín and Miguelito Cuní took over the band in Cuba. Harry Belafonte has referred to Rodríguez as the father of salsa.

Born in Spain but raised in Cuba, Xavier Cugat (1900–90) was the first Cuban musician to achieve mass popularity in the US.

Xavier Cugat and His Gigolos were already providing music for Hollywood before Cugat became bandleader of New York's Waldorf Astoria Orchestra in 1933. Although his smooth arrangements of Latin American dance music were a great mainstream success, Cugat's rumbas were not really Cuban.

During the '40s, Frank 'Machito' Grillo (1912–84) made his mark in New York by mixing jazz with Afro-Cuban music. During a long career Machito passed effortlessly from mambo to chachachá and salsa as tastes evolved. It was violinist Enrique Jorrín (1926–87) and his Orquesta América who really popularized chachachá in New York with 'La Engañadora,' recorded in 1953. Drummer and singer Chano Pozo (1915–48) brought Cuban jazz to the fore with numbers like 'Manteca.' He was murdered by another Cuban in Harlem.

During the '50s, piano player Dámaso Pérez Prado (1916–83) was known as the 'King of the Mambo.' As early as 1943 Prado was preparing arrangements for the Orquesta Casino de la Playa in Cuba, and by 1950 he was leader of his own mambo band in Mexico City. Although highly commercialized, Prado's torrid trumpets, swinging organs, and pervasive beat in hits such as 'Cherry Pink and Apple Blossom White' (1955) and 'Patricia' (1958) anticipated American rock and roll.

A more bona fide mambo bandleader and singer was Benny Moré (1919–63), 'El Bárbaro del Ritmo' (The Barbarian of Rhythm). Throughout the '40s Moré sang with various groups in Havana, Mexico City, and Panama, including those of Pérez Prado and Miguel Matamoros (1894–1971), who penned 'Son de la Loma' and 'Lágrimas Negras.' Back in Cuba in 1953, Moré formed a Banda Gigante comprised of 21 black musicians like himself. Benny's band and velvet voice were without rivals in their time, though his bohemian lifestyle and heavy drinking led to an early death from liver disease.

The year 1950 saw the introduction of television and long-playing records to Cuba, and by this time radios and cinemas were widespread. The large dance orchestras

'El Bárbaro del Ritmo,' Benny Moré

mentioned above were sustained by this media, while groups such as Cuarteto D'Aida and Los Zafiros, and female singers such as Paulina Álvarez (the 'Empress of Danzonete'), María de los Ángeles Santana, Esther Borja, Celeste Mendoza (the 'Queen of Guaguancó'), Juana Bacallao (the 'Mistress of Irreverence') and María Teresa Vera (also a guitarist and bandleader) became popular nightclub performers as tourism from the US boomed. The star vocalists of the '50s were Rita Montaner (died 1958) and Bola de Nieve (1911–71) who sang romantic ballads a la Nat King Cole.

After the 1959 revolution, Afro-Cuban music was revalued, and during the '60s Pello el Afrocán popularized a fast drum dance called the *mozambique*. The Ballet Folklórico Cutumbá, founded at Santiago de Cuba in 1961, and the Havana-based Conjunto Folklórico Nacional continue to perform Afro-Cuban dances.

Charanga bands still active in Cuba today include the Septeto Nacional de Ignacio Piñeiro (first formed in 1927 and reestablished in 1985), the Orquesta Aragón (founded in 1939), and the Orquesta Ritmo Oriental (formed in the '50s). In 1969 Juan Formell (born 1942), a veteran of Elio Revé's Orquesta Revé, founded Orquesta

Los Van Van and transformed the traditional charanga lineup by adding modern instruments such as the electric guitar, electric bass, and drum battery. Van Van's percussionist Changuito invented a new rhythm called *songo*. The repertoires of the Orquesta Original de Manzanillo and Conjunto Rumbavana are also excellent examples of musicians' abilities to adapt son to changing conditions.

Cuba's top jazz band is Irakere, founded in Havana in 1973 by pianist Jesús 'Chucho' Valdés. Irakere's Afro-Cuban drumming doesn't obscure the group's deep son roots. NG La Banda, a band formed in 1988 of the *nueva generación*, mixes Cuban tradition with jazz and rap in a complex style called *timba*. Riding on the same wave are Charanga Habanera, Moncada, and Paulito y Su Elite. Other notables include jazz pianist Gonzalo Rubalcaba, Pachito Alonso y sus Kini Kini, Juan Carlos Alfonso y el Dan Den, Isaac Delgado, and Adalberto Álvarez y Su Son.

One of the best contemporary son bands is Grupo Sierra Maestra, founded in 1980. Their lineup comprises a lead singer, three guitar-type instruments, trumpet, bass, bongó, percussion, piano, and various acoustic instruments. The Familia Valera Miranda plays son dance music around Oriente at weddings, birthday parties, and receptions. Cuarteto Patria, formed in Santiago de Cuba in 1940, continues to play traditional son and bolero under the leadership of Eliades Ochoa. Also from 1940, Cañambú performs son with singer Arístides Ruiz Boza. Síntesis is a Yoruba rock group.

Los Muñequitos de Matanzas play authentic contemporary rumba employing only percussion and voice. Folkloyuma is a traditional rumba *cabildo* (fraternity) formed in Santiago de Cuba in 1964. The Conjunto Clave y Guaguancó also plays real rumba, as does singer Lázaro Ros.

Celina González (born 1928) lives in Havana and sings with the band Campo Alegre led by her son Reutilio Domínguez. Her *música guajira* combines the music of Cuban country folk of Spanish descent or *guajiros* with the Afro-Cuban tradition

(Celina herself is a devotee of the Yoruba goddess Changó, or Santa Bárbara). The late Merceditas Valdez sang traditional Yoruba songs to the batá drumming of Jesús Pérez.

While in Havana, you'd be foolish to miss a performance by any of the artists or groups mentioned above. Remember too that Cuban restaurant and hotel musicians playing mostly to create atmosphere are usually quite talented and experienced performers, and they often have a few tricks up their sleeves. When you get tired of 'Guantanamera' and 'Bésame mucho,' request something unusual *(algo insólito)* and you'll probably get a surprise.

CDs & Recordings Quality recordings of Cuban music are readily available in Havana on compact discs produced by the state record company Egrem (Empresa de Grabaciones y Ediciones Musicales) for Artex (Promociones Artísticas y Literarias); see the Shopping chapter for store names and locations.

A good introduction to Cuban music is provided on the Egrem-Artex series *Antología de la Música Cubana*, especially volumes 1 and 2, and *Joyas de la Música Cubana*, particularly volume 3, sold at most hotel shops. The sampler *Fiesta Cubana Guajiras* is also outstanding. (All Egrem-Artex CDs are marked 'Made in Canada,' so you should have no problem taking them home if you're from the US.)

Internationally, *Buena Vista Social Club* has become the classic recording of Cuban son, which had been neglected in recent years due to the salsa craze. In a six-day flurry of sessions in 1996, US guitarist Ry Cooder brought together some little-known masters of Cuban music, such as veteran pianist Rubén González, vocalist Ibrahim Ferrer, guitarist Eliades Ochoa and singer/guitarist Compay Segundo to assemble a formidable collection. German director Wim Wenders made *Buena Vista Social Club* into a splendid film.

In 1998 Estudios Abdala SA (☎ 24-4000), Calle 32 No 318, Miramar, opened in Havana as a joint venture between singer Silvio Rodríguez and the Corporación

Buena Vista Social Club's **Compay Segundo**

Cimex. Here foreign musicians and producers can book the studio's state-of-the-art facilities for recording sessions at below market prices.

Literature

The real lives of Cuban writers have often mirrored their country's long struggle for freedom, independence, and social justice. The lyric poet José María de Heredia y Heredia (1803–39), from Santiago de Cuba, was forced into exile by the Spanish colonial authorities soon after graduating from law school. In Mexico he wrote *En el Teocali de Cholula,* followed a few years later by the *Ode to Niagara,* among the earliest examples of Spanish romanticism.

The self-educated mixed-race poet Gabriel de la Concepción Valdés (1809–44), better known as 'Plácido,' wrote romantic verses that were popularized as songs. Plácido is best remembered for his involvement in an abortive slave uprising at Matanzas that led to his death before a Spanish firing squad.

Cuba's greatest 19th-century novelist, Cirilo Villaverde y de la Paz (1812–94), also struggled against Spanish colonial rule and was imprisoned in 1848. Later he fought alongside General Narciso López and spent many years in exile in the US. His most celebrated work is *Cecilia Valdés,* the story of a slave trader's son who falls in love with a beautiful biracial woman who eventually turns out to be his illegitimate sister. No book has ever come closer to capturing the emotions of slavery in Cuba and the class differences stifling colonial society, and the novel's violent ending foreshadowed the actual fate of colonialism itself. Years later composer Gonzalo Roig used the story in a zarzuela of the same name.

Cuba's most famous and influential writer is José Martí (1853–95), the revolutionary leader who died in one of the initial clashes of the Second War of Independence. Martí's collected works comprise 25 volumes of poems, plays, and essays written in an uncomplicated style accessible to most readers. In 1871 Martí was deported to Spain for his revolutionary writings, and he spent most of his life in exile, including long stays in New York, where he served as correspondent for several leading South American newspapers. His last book of poetry, *Versos Sencillos,* is considered his best, while *Los Estados Unidos* is a collection of essays reflecting his ambivalent feelings toward the US. (See the 'José Martí' boxed text, earlier.)

During the 1930s the biracial poet Nicolás Guillén (1902–89) played a leading role in the Afro-Cuban movement transforming Cuban literature, music, and dance. Some of the onomatopoetic verses in Guillén's *Sóngoro Cosongo* (1931) can be recited to the beat of a drum. His works championed social and racial equality, and as a journalist covering the Spanish Civil War he supported the Republican side and became a communist. He spent the Batista years in exile, and *La Paloma de Vuelo Popular* and *Elegías* (both published in 1958) protest the repression and US domination of the time. After 1959 Guillén returned to Cuba and in 1961 he helped found the Unión Nacional de Escritores y Artistas Cubanos (National Union of Cuban Writers and Artists). His prolific writings made him the poet laureate and cultural ambassador of the revolution.

The career of historical novelist Alejo Carpentier (1904–80) partly parallels that of Guillén. In 1927 Carpentier was imprisoned by the Machado regime, and he subsequently spent most of the years until 1959 in exile in France and Venezuela. After his return to Cuba he served as head of the national publishing company, professor of literature at the University of Havana, and Cuban cultural attaché to France. Carpentier's first novel, *Ecué-Yamba-O* (1933), deals with Afro-Cuban culture. In the surrealistic novel *El Reino de Este Mundo* (1949), Carpentier explores Haiti's African roots through the life of the tyrannical Henri Christophe. *El Siglo de las Luces* (1962) is set in the Caribbean during the French revolution, while *El Recurso del Método* (1974) is a caricature of the Machado dictatorship. *Concierto Barroco* (1974) is considered Carpentier's masterpiece, a 93-page novel in which a wealthy Mexican and his black servant travel to Europe for the carnival season, and through a Vivaldi opera they rediscover their common Latin American identity.

Other contemporary Cuban writers of note include: Dulce María Loynaz (1902–97), a lyric poet indifferent to the politics of her time; José Lezama Lima (1910–76), whose controversial novel *Paradiso* (1966) explores same-sex relationships; Guillermo Cabrera Infante (born 1929), author of the innovative novel *Tres Tristes Tigres* (1967) about cultural decadence during the Batista era; Edmundo Desnoes (born 1930), best known for *Memorias del Subdesarrollo* (1965), an existential novel about failure; Miguel Barnet (born 1940), master of the testimonial novel; and Leonardo Padura Fuentes (born 1956), author of the socially critical novel *Máscaras* (1995).

Apart from the influence of the writers just mentioned, Cuba has had an important impact on Latin American literature through competitions organized by the Casa de las Américas. Among others, Colombia's Nobel Prize winner Gabriel García Márquez has had a long and cordial relationship with revolutionary Cuba.

For a good anthology of Cuban writing in English translation, ask your bookseller to order a copy of *Dream with No Name: Contemporary Fiction from Cuba* edited by Juana Ponce de León and Esteban Ríos Rivera. Cuba's strong storytelling tradition is well represented in this collection of short stories by 11 well-known and lesser-known writers.

Painting

Little is known about Cuban painting before José Nicolás de la Escalera (1734–1804), who worked in the second half of the 18th century. The early-19th-century painter Vicente Escobar (1762–1834) can be considered part of the *costumbrista* movement that produced realistic images of everyday life.

In 1818 the French painter Jean Baptiste Vermay (1786–1833), decorator of El Templete on Havana's Plaza de Armas, became the first director of the Academy of San Alejandro, which was destined to decisively influence Cuban art right into the 1920s. In 1878 the Cuban painter Miguel Melero (1836–1907) took over direction of the academy.

Two trends are evident in 19th-century academic landscape painting: romanticism, as exemplified by Esteban Chartrand (1840–83) and José Joaquín Tejada (1867–1943); and realism, as represented by Valentín Sanz Carta (1849–98) and Guillermo Collazo (1850–96).

In the early years of the 20th century, many Cuban painters visited Europe, where they learned new techniques and were exposed to contemporary trends. By 1925 many were back in Cuba, abandoning academic art and producing the type of avant-garde paintings that had sensationalized Europe several decades earlier. Artists such as Eduardo Abela (1889–1965), Víctor Manuel García (1897–1969), Marcelo Pogolotti (1902–88), and Roberto Diago (1920–57) saw Cuba through fresh eyes and produced paintings reminiscent of Picasso and Gauguin.

During the 1940s and '50s Cuban painting became ever more individualistic as artists sought to express their Cuban identity in their own way. By this time the European forms of expression had been fully absorbed, and although the paintings and stained glass windows of René Portocarrero (1912–85) bear a resemblance to those of Marc Chagall, they are original works of great expressive power. Amelia Peláez (1896–1968) adorned Havana buildings with colorful ceramic murals. Other outstanding figures from this period include Wilfredo Lam (1902–82) and Marianao Rodríguez (1912–90). Cuba's leading contemporary artist, Manuel Mendive (born 1944), incorporates Afro-Cuban mythology into his work.

With the revolution, Cuban artists gained a new social role as articulators of a rediscovered national identity. Historical subjects taken from Cuba's 19th-century wars of independence became popular, and there was a return to realism. Many Cuban artists, however, continued to experiment freely with new means of expression. Posters and billboard art were adopted as a means of directly communicating with common people in a simple and often compelling way. The political art one sees along Cuban roads and highways has an esthetic value quite apart from its messages. In the '60s Raúl Martínez (born 1927) elevated poster painting to a high art form with a series of political paintings of Castro, Guevara, Martí, and others. Salvador González Escalona has carried the process forward by painting the façades of buildings along Havana's Callejón de Hamel in brilliant colors rich with Santería symbolism.

Architecture

Little remains of the architecture of Cuba's Indian population, although a reconstructed Arawak village called Villa Guamá exists as a tourist resort near the Bay of Pigs. The traditional thatched farmhouse of Cuba, the *bohío*, is derived from an indigenous dwelling.

Many architectural styles adopted in Cuba – including renaissance, baroque, and neoclassical – originated in Europe. Only a handful of 16th-century renaissance structures survive in Cuba. These include the Casa de Diego Velázquez in Santiago de Cuba and the Parroquia de San Juan Bautista in Remedios. The Spanish colony left behind mostly baroque buildings, and among the many superb 18th-century churches are the Catedral de San Cristóbal de La Habana; the Iglesia de Nuestra Señora del Rosario near Havana; the Iglesia de Nuestra Señora de la Soledad and the Iglesia de Nuestra Señora de la Merced, both at Camagüey; and the Iglesia Parroquial Mayor de San Salvador at Bayamo.

There are many impressive 18th-century baroque palaces in Havana, including the Palacio de los Capitanes Generales, the Palacio del Segundo Cabo, and the Casa de la Obra Pía; see the Things to See & Do chapter for details. Trinidad, in the Province of Sancti Spíritus, also has numerous baroque buildings, including the Palacio Brunet. A fine example of 18th-century baroque military architecture is the Fortaleza de San Carlos de la Cabaña in Havana.

The 19th century was mostly an era of neoclassical construction, the earliest and finest representatives of which are El Templete in Havana and a few palaces such as Casa Cantero in Trinidad. Also built in this style were churches such as the Catedral de San Carlos Borromeo in Matanzas and the Catedral de la Purísima Concepción in Cienfuegos, and grand theaters such as the Teatro Sauto in Matanzas, the Teatro Tomás Terry in Cienfuegos, and the Teatro Principal in Camagüey. Neoclassical construction continued into the 20th century with the Universidad de La Habana and neoclassical colonnades along streets and squares throughout the country.

There are few neo-Gothic buildings in Cuba, the Iglesia del Santo Angel Custodio in Havana being a notable exception. The early 20th century produced a number of distinguished neobaroque buildings, such as the Centro Gallego and the Ministerio de Relaciones Exteriores, both in Havana. The Moorish-style Palacio de Valle in Cienfuegos also dates from this time.

Contemporary architecture in Cuba is both functional and striking. An early example of a large modern building intended to impress is the Palacio de las Convenciones (1979) in Havana's Cubanacán District. The Estadio Panamericano near

Havana is an additional example along those lines. One of the finest examples of a modern building that incorporates the remains of an earlier construction is Restaurante Las Ruinas at Parque Lenin near Havana.

Film

Cinemas are popular in Cuba as they are in most countries, and there is no shortage of cinemas in Havana (see the Entertainment chapter for names and locations). Unfortunately for fans of nostalgia, classic Cuban films are seldom shown anymore. Instead, most Cubans are treated to films they prefer – Hollywood movies made long ago. Though they'd really rather watch Hollywood's latest releases, that isn't possible under the US embargo.

Cuba's national movie company is the Instituto Cubano del Arte e Industria Cinematográficos (Cuban Institute of Cinematographic Art and Industry, www .cinecubano.cu), or ICAIC, with its Havana headquarters beside the Cine Charles Chaplin, Calle 23 No 1155, Vedado. Every December since 1979 the Festival Internacional del Nuevo Cine Latinoamericano has brought filmmakers from across the Americas to Havana. Many Latin American students attend an important film school near San Antonio de los Baños, south of Havana.

An early priority of ICAIC, founded just a few months after the 1959 revolution, was the documentary. And one of the most successful practitioners of this genre was San-

Sara Gómez Yera

tiago Álvarez (1919–98), with *Hanoi, Martes 13* (1967), *Hasta la Victoria Siempre* (1967), *79 Primaveras* (1969), *Despegue a las 18:00* (1969), *La Guerra Olvidada* (1969), *¿Como, Por Qué y Para Qué Se Asesina un General?* (1971), and *Mi hermano Fidel* (1977). His six-minute film *Now* (1965), a visual account of the US Civil Rights struggle set to the music of Lena Horne's rendition of *Hava Nagila*, is considered the world's first music video.

Manuel Octavio Gómez's 1971 film *Los Días de Agua* tells the true story of Antoñica Izquierdo, a humble Pinar del Río woman who in 1936 discovered the miraculous curative powers of water. As politicians and hucksters try to exploit the near hysteria surrounding the saint, we sense the unrest that eventually led to the revolution.

Cuba's most acclaimed director of recent years was Tomás Gutiérrez Alea (1928–96), whose *Fresa y Chocolate* won the jury's special prize at the 1994 Berlin Film Festival. This humorous film about an uncomfortable liaison between a straight young Cuban and a gay man, which eventually develops into friendship, is a poignant plea for human tolerance and understanding. Earlier films by Gutiérrez Alea include *La Muerte de un Burócrata* (1966), a critique of bureaucratic muddling; *Memorias del Subdesarrollo* (1968), about an intellectual landlord who decides to stay in Havana after his family leaves for Miami in 1961; *La Última Cena* (1976), a portrayal of religious hypocrisy during the slaveholding era; *Los Sobrevivientes* (1979), a frivolous look at the effect of the revolution on the bourgeoisie; and *Cartas del Parque* (1988), the touching tale of two lovers who correspond through an intermediary. Gutiérrez Alea's last film, *Guantanamera* (1995), is a hilarious spoof on the Cuban undertaking industry.

Sara Gómez Yera's tragic death in 1974 didn't prevent the release of her *De Cierta Maniera*, which was completed in 1977 by Gutiérrez Alea and Julio García Espinosa. *One Way or Another* (the English title) examines the phenomenon of machismo in a poor Cuban barrio in a masterful juxtaposition of socialist ideals with often antisocial

Latin realities. Pastor Vega's *El Retrato de Teresa* (1979) dealt with the same subject and evoked considerable discussion in Cuba.

Another important Cuban director is Humberto Solás (born 1941), whose 1969 film *Lucía* is the story of three women of the same name who lived in different eras; Marjorie Rosen of *Ms.* magazine called it 'one of the wittiest, most sympathetic statements on the inequality suffered by women.' In 1976 Solás' *Cantata a Chile* won the main prize at the Karlovy Vary Film Festival. His *Un Hombre de Éxito* (1986) recounts 30 years in the lives of two brothers divided by ideology.

Other directors of note include Daniel Díaz Torres, who parodies civil servants in *Alicia en el Pueblo de Maravillas* (1990); Gerardo Chijona, whose *Adorables Mentiras* (1992) traces two unsuccessful individuals who adopt false identities to escape humdrum lives; and Julio García Espinosa, who made *Reina y Rey* (1994), about a widow and her dog 'Rey,' who offers to house-sit when her wealthy employer flees to Miami in the '60s. Cuba's leading animator is Juan Padrón (born 1947), whose cartoon character Elpidio Valdés raises his machete to fight for the independence of Cuba.

SOCIETY & CONDUCT

Like Spaniards, most Cubans are extremely courteous and polite toward guests, and will try to please you if at all possible. Because of this, their statements sometimes gloss over reality, their promises may be wishful thinking and their appointments are often not kept. This characteristic can be extremely annoying to those unaccustomed to Latin American ways.

A first line of defense is to avoid suggesting the answer in your question. If things don't work out exactly as you expected or desired, have an alternative plan ready and avoid getting angry. It's far better to display a sense of humor than to make a fool of yourself by showing your temper. If a situation is really intolerable, just try to get around it or avoid it. Attempting to correct what you see as a problem inherent in the system or culture, or telling Cubans how they should correct it, is an utter waste of time. Oftentimes the more people working on a problem the longer it will take to get anything done.

Generally, Cubans will pick up on your attitude instantly, and if you come across as patient and friendly, you'll always get a friendly response. If you look the other way and avoid eye contact, they'll do exactly the same. It's rare for a Cuban to be indifferent toward travelers, as happens frequently in North America and Europe.

Dos & Don'ts

When doing any sort of business with individual Cubans, respect them by keeping a low profile. Many will be breaking the law by engaging in private business transactions with you, and they'll be the ones who will face the consequences if anything goes wrong. This applies mostly to traveling in cheap 'pirate' taxis, but it can also apply at unlicensed private restaurants and guest houses or when changing money on the street. For example, keep your voice down, and don't count your dollars in plain sight of other Cubans. If in a private taxi, get the money ready during the trip and hand it over to the driver just as you are approaching your destination. Don't force the driver to sit and wait while you dig for money in a place that may be crawling with police.

Don't try to generate political discussions in hotel lobbies, bars, tour buses, or other public places where those nearby may understand only a small part of what is being said – you could end up seriously embarrassing someone without even realizing it. Bystanders may only hear 'Fidel Castro' or 'communism' – words Cubans themselves do not utter casually. An equivalent situation in a US context might be having a stranger quiz you about abortion in a public place. Remember that the Cubans understand their political situation far better than you do, so rather than tell them what you think, ask them to explain what they feel is good or bad about their system. Always keep in mind that any state employee – including all tourism workers – overheard making comments critical of the system to tourists would be out of a job.

Treatment of Animals

The Cuban blood sport most offensive to English-speaking visitors is cock fighting, which is commonly practiced in rural areas and is quite legal. Cock fights are often staged in circular cock pits, called *vallas*, for Spanish-speaking tourists, usually at a type of model Cuban farm where country-style lunches are served to tourist groups. You won't find it in Havana.

Another unsavory activity associated with tourism is the hunting of exotic African animals, such as antelopes, in special 'reserves' set aside for this purpose. Dog fights are arranged by local Cubans, usually without tourists being involved. Neither of these 'sports' can be found in Havana either, thank God.

The horses pulling carriages along Havana streets certainly would rather be chewing hay in a meadow somewhere and pontificating subjects such as, *Which is better, green hay or dry?* But the fate of these horses is no joke: The horses are literally worked to death because it's officially prohibited to slaughter them.

It must also be said that some traditional Santería sacrifices involve cruelty to chickens, goats and other animals. Some people believe that those people who sacrifice animals are destined to be sacrificed in a heaven where animals rule and humans are merely pets, beasts of burden or strays. (OK, maybe only one person believes it.)

RELIGION

Prior to the revolution, 85% of Cubans were nominal Roman Catholics, although only 10% were regular churchgoers. Today 40% of Cubans are baptized Catholics but just 400,000 regularly attend mass at Cuba's 688 Catholic churches. In 1959 there were about 700 Catholic priests in Cuba, a majority of them from Spain. Some 140 of the Spaniards were expelled for reactionary political activities, and another 400 left voluntarily. The rest were allowed to continue their work unhindered. The Nationalization of Education Law of June 1961 transferred control of Catholic and other private schools to the government. In 1966 some foreign priests were allowed to return to Cuba, and church services were never prohibited.

Cuban Catholicism had always been the religion of the affluent, and Cuban Protestants were usually poorer. Protestant churches enjoyed fewer privileges before the revolution, so they had less to lose. Many of those who left Cuba after the revolution were Catholics, thus the ratio of Protestants in the population has grown. Since 1992 the number of Protestant churches has almost doubled to 1666, with 54 denominations and over 300,000 members. The largest Protestant denomination has always been the Baptists, currently numbering around 70,000. The Catholics are found mostly in the cities while numerous small Protestant congregations are scattered throughout the country. While 136 of the 281 Catholic priests are foreign-born, the vast majority of Protestant pastors are Cuban.

Government policy toward the church remains basically live and let live. A July 1992 constitutional amendment guarantees freedom of religion in Cuba, although the separation of church and state is complete. The Pope's visit in January 1998 lent respectability to Catholicism and led to a surge in church attendance. Religious processions outside church buildings are now permitted, as are Catholic publications. Although church spokespersons are often forthright in their social criticisms, they are careful to avoid involvement in politics. The policy of the Catholic church seems to be one of gradually reestablishing its influence while outliving the regime.

The religious beliefs of former African slaves have merged with Catholic iconography and doctrines in a number of Afro-Cuban cults, including Santería, that combine African deities with Catholic saints. Adherents of the Afro-Cuban religions regard Catholicism as the form of Santería followed by descendants of the Spanish tribe from Europe. There are probably more followers of Santería than of pure Catholicism. The Afro-Cuban religions have long been tolerated in Cuba, and in recent years Santería has even been encouraged as an indigenous folk religion with a cultural role to play.

Migene González-Wippler, author of *Santería: The Religion*, reports that Fidel himself is believed to be a practicing santero and the son of Elegguá. If true, this would be nothing unusual, as it's said that every Cuban president since independence has been initiated into Santería. Former dictators Machado and Batista were considered sons of Changó.

Afro-Cuban Religions

Slaves brought from West Africa between the 16th and 19th centuries carried with them a system of animistic beliefs that they managed to hide behind a Catholic veneer. The slave owners were poor missionaries, and they kept tribes together in order to pit one group against another. Tribes such as Arará, Lucumí and Congo are organized in *cabildos* (associations). Abakuá is a secret society made up of male members known as *ñáñigos*. Initiates address each other as *ambia, asere, boncó,* and *monina,* and say *'qué bolá?'* instead of the usual *'qué tal?'* or *'como está?'* Such phrases are common in contemporary Havana slang.

In Cuba today there may be more followers of the Afro-Cuban religions than practicing Roman Catholics. The largest Afro-Cuban religion is an amalgam of Catholic and Yoruba beliefs known as *Santería,* or *Regla de Ocha.* In Santería, Catholic saints and apparitions of the Virgin are associated with Yoruba deities, or *orishas.* Unlike the Catholic saints, however, the orishas do not represent perfection, and they have many human frailties. The concepts of original sin and a final judgment are unknown. Ancestral spirits are worshipped.

Among the major orishas is the androgynous creator god Obatalá, who is always dressed in white and associated with Christ or Nuestra Señora de la Merced. Obatalá's wife, Odudúa, goddess of the underworld, is also associated with the Virgin. Obatalá's son, Elegguá (St Anthony), is the god of destiny. Yemayá, the goddess of the ocean and mother of all orishas, is identified by the color blue and associated with Nuestra Señora de Regla. Changó, the Yoruba god of fire and war, lives in the tops of royal palm trees and controls lightning. His color is red and he's associated with Santa Bárbara. His son Aggayú Solá, god of land and protector of travelers, is associated with San Cristóbal (St Christopher). Ochún, wife of Changó and companion of Yemayá, is the goddess of love and rivers. She's a very powerful orisha and is associated with Cuba's patron saint, the Virgin de la Caridad del Cobre (whose color is yellow). Ogún is associated with John the Baptist. Babalú Ayé (St Lazarus) is the orisha of disease.

The rites of Santería are controlled by a male priest called a *babalawo,* or *babalao,* of whom there are estimated to be 4000 in Cuba. A babalawo is often consulted for advice, to cure sicknesses or to grant protection, and offerings are placed before a small shrine in his home. Although the figures of Catholic saints mounted on the shrines represent a variety of orishas, the real power resides in stones draped with colored bead necklaces. The stones are believed to harbor the spirits of the orishas, and they must be fed with food, herbs and blood. Animals such as chickens, doves and goats are often sacrificed during rituals.

Cubans are surprisingly open about Santería, and travelers are welcome to inspect household shrines and attend ceremonies. It's unlikely anyone will be offended if you ask them about Santería; in fact, they'll probably be pleased that you're interested in Cuban culture. Many hotels stage special Santería shows for visitors, and cult objects are often sold in hotel shops. If you attend a Santería ceremony at a private residence, you'll be expected to leave a few dollars for the saint (and babalawo) on the altar. Ask about special Santería services if you happen to be in Cuba on December 4 (the day of Santa Bárbara) or December 17 (the day of San Lázaro); celebrations begin the night before.

– David Stanley

SEÑORES IMPERIALISTAS ¡NO LES TENEMOS ABSOLUTAMENTE NINGUN MIEDO!

LANGUAGE

Spanish is spoken by most Cubans, and some knowledge of it is a great help. In Havana, you can expect hotel and restaurant employees to understand basic English, but average Joe Cubano won't know more than a handful of English words or phrases. An hour or so spent learning some common Spanish words and phrases will make your time in Havana more enjoyable. For information and a small Spanish-English glossary of useful terms, turn to the Language chapter toward the back of the book.

Facts for the Visitor

WHEN TO GO

Winter (December through April) is the best time to visit Havana. That's when the weather is most pleasant and the likelihood of rain is at its lowest. Also, hurricanes don't strike during this time of year – at least, one hasn't done so in memory.

Not surprisingly, winter is also the busiest time in Havana, with hotels often filled to capacity. Arriving during winter without a hotel reservation is risky if you're hoping to stay in one. Also, if you make your reservation from abroad, you might be able to get a greatly reduced room rate. But if you arrive at a hotel unannounced, you'll almost certainly be quoted a high rate.

Avoid visiting Havana from June through October. This is Havana's hurricane season. Moreover, these are Havana's hottest months – when high temperatures and high relative humidity combine to make visitors extra-sticky and miserable. July and August can be simply unbearable, especially if there's no breeze coming off the ocean to quell the Hades-like heat.

If visiting Havana when few tourists are there is your No 1 priority, try to visit during May, June or November. These aren't the best months weather-wise, but they are Havana's slowest months for tourism.

ORIENTATION

Havana is bordered to the north by the Atlantic Ocean and to the east, west and south by the remainder of Havana Province. The city is divided into 15 municipalities: La Habana Vieja, Centro Habana, Plaza de la Revolución, Playa, La Lisa, Marianao, Cerro, Diez de Octubre, Boyeros, Arroyo Naranjo, San Miguel del Padrón, Cotorro, Regla, Guanabacoa and La Habana del Este.

La Habana Vieja, or Old Havana, sits on the west side of Bahía de La Habana (Bay of Havana) in an area once bounded by 17th-century city walls that ran along present Av de Bélgica and Av de las Misiones. In 1863 these walls were demolished and the city spilled west into an area now called Centro Habana, bisected by busy San Rafael.

West of Centro Habana lies Vedado, the 20th-century hotel and entertainment district that developed after independence in 1902. Near Plaza de la Revolución and between Vedado and Nuevo Vedado, a huge government complex was erected in the 1950s. West of the Río Almendares are Miramar, Marianao and Playa, Havana's most fashionable residential suburbs prior to the 1959 revolution.

Between 1955 and 1958, a 733m tunnel was drilled between La Habana Vieja and La Habana del Este under the harbor mouth, and since 1959 much high-rise construction has taken place in La Habana del Este, Cojímar (a former fishing village) and Alamar, northeast of the harbor. South of La Habana del Este's endless blocks of flats are the old colonial towns of Guanabacoa, San Francisco de Paula, and Santa María del Rosario. On the east side of the harbor are the old towns of Regla and Casablanca.

The bulk of Havana's working-class population lives south of Centro Habana and the harbor in industrial areas such as Cerro,

---

Think Feet!

If you see Havana as it ought to be seen – on foot – you'll want to be sure to bring with you at least one pair of well-used walking shoes and pack plenty of blister protection. Even if you think your shoes are broken in, don't assume you won't get any blisters. Instead, be prepared. At the very least, pack lots of large adhesive bandages, a roll of athletic tape and a tube of ointment. Soft flannel padding, such as Dr Scholl's Moleskin Plus, helps prevent blisters. There's nothing like a large, ruptured blister to take the pleasure out of a leisurely stroll through Old Havana.

FACTS FOR THE VISITOR

Diez de Octubre and San Miguel del Padrón. South of that is Boyeros, with the golf course, zoo and international airport, and Arroyo Naranjo with Parque Lenin.

Visitors spend most of their time in La Habana Vieja, Centro Habana and Vedado, and they should become familiar with important street names: Obispo, which cuts through the center of La Habana Vieja; Paseo de Martí (also known as Paseo del Prado), an elegant 19th-century promenade in Centro Habana; Av de Italia (or Galiano), Centro Habana's main shopping street for Cubans; Malecón (or Av de Maceo), Havana's broad coastal boulevard; and Calle 23 (or La Rampa), the heart of Vedado's hotel district.

Confusingly, many main avenues around Havana have two names in everyday use – a new name that appears on street signs and in this book, and an old name still commonly used by local residents and provided in parentheses below:

Agramonte (Zulueta)

Aponte (Someruelos)

Av Carlos Manuel de Céspedes (Av del Puerto)

Av de Bélgica (Egido and Monserrate)

Av de España (Vives)

Av de Italia (Galiano)

Av de la Independencia (Av de Rancho Boyeros)

Av de las Misiones (Monserrate)

Av de México (Cristina)

Av Salvador Allende (Carlos III)

Av Simón Bolívar (Reina)

Brasil (Teniente Rey)

Calle 23 (La Rampa)

Calle G (Av de los Presidentes)

Capdevila (Cárcel)

Enrique Barnet (Estrella)

Leonor Pérez (Paula)

Malecón (Av de Maceo)

Máximo Gómez (Monte)

Padre Varela (Belascoaín)

Paseo de Martí (Paseo del Prado)

San Martín (San José)

Throughout this book the listings are in geographical order, beginning with La Habana Vieja, Centro Habana and Vedado – the neighborhoods of greatest interest to Havana's visitors.

MAPS

The maps within these pages contain most of the sites mentioned in the text – and those sites represent Havana's most important – eliminating the need to spend money on more maps of the city. However, if you simply must buy more Havana maps, seek out *Ciudad de La Habana*, published by Ediciones Geo. It's a fairly large foldout map that contains Havana's major neighborhoods, their streets in easy-to-read print, and an elaborate index.

The same company also publishes *La Habana*, which is more difficult to read due to the low quality of ink and printer used. Still, it's the next-best map of Havana if *Ciudad de La Habana* isn't available. Both of these maps, as well as several maps of Old Havana, can be found in hotel gift shops, bookstores and at the international airport (departures lounge always, other areas of the airport only occasionally).

Tienda El Navegante (☎ 57-1038, fax 66-6763), Mercaderes No 115, between Obispo and Obrapía, has maps of many parts of Cuba, and sells Cuban nautical charts for US$16 each. It's open 8 am to noon and 1 to 5 pm weekdays, 8 am to 1 pm Saturday.

RESPONSIBLE TOURISM

Cubans must adhere to a different set of rules than foreigners, and visitors should avoid getting them in trouble. For example, Cubans assumed by the police to be hustlers could be punished if seen with you. Places frequented by tourists are closely watched by secret police and should be avoided while in the company of Cuban friends.

Visitors also should refrain from purchasing environmentally unfriendly souvenirs. Curios made from seashells, black coral and turtle shell should be avoided. To be completely safe, don't buy anything that incorporates coral, shells or the local fauna at all. One should even refrain from collecting these items off the beach.

TOURIST OFFICES
Local Tourist Offices

There are many tourist offices, travel agencies and visitor-assistance counters in Havana, most located inside larger hotels. Indeed, chances are you'll find a desk in the lobby of your hotel staffed with a person who can answer touristy questions about Havana, book tours for you and hook you up with a rental car (if you're seeing only Havana, you certainly won't need a rental car).

In La Habana Vieja, Havana's helpful tourist information office, Infotur (☎ 33-3333, 63-6095), Obispo No 358, at San Ignacio, sells locally published maps and guidebooks and can book a variety of excursions and activities at competitive rates. The staff speaks English and is usually good about answering questions. Infotur's office is open 8:30 am to 5:30 pm daily.

For information on special events, try the Buró de Convenciones de Cuba (☎ 31-3600, fax 33-4261), Calle M, between Calles 17 and 19, below the Edificio Focsa and diagonally opposite Hotel Victoria in Vedado. It's open 8 am to 5 pm weekdays, 8 am to noon Saturday.

The state-run travel agencies Cubatur, Havanatur and Rumbos book accommodations, rental vehicles, sightseeing tours, flights and so on. Don't bother comparing prices among these three; prices for tours, etc, are identical to prevent competition among them and, God forbid, possible capitalism. One or more of these agencies has a representative in every hotel; see the Getting Around chapter for specific locations and telephone numbers.

Islazul, Intur and Campismo Popular are reservations offices for peso-paying Cubans. Don't bother going inside them as there's usually a long wait (compared to generally no wait at the foreigner-served agencies) and these agencies aren't set up to handle foreigners and, therefore, occasionally do them a disservice.

Tourist Offices Abroad

Cuba has an extensive network of tourism promotion offices overseas. We provide a

---

Floss It

For the cost of a crummy cigar, you can buy a vacation-saving item. It's called dental floss, and its uses are innumerable. Got a fishhook but no line? Four words: green waxed dental floss. Need to secure a mosquito net? Reach for dental floss. Forgot to pack a clothesline? You're in luck if you've packed dental floss. Tear in your jeans, rip in your pack? A little dental floss and a sewing needle and life goes on.

Dental floss comes in 50m and 100m lengths and is sold in nifty little cases complete with built-in cutters. It's cheap, it's light, it's strong and it's outrageously useful. Some say dental floss can even remove decay-causing material from between teeth and under gums. Now in cinnamon, mint and grape flavors. No kidding.

¡ABSOLUTAMENTE NINGUN MIEDO!

---

complete list of these below, and it's well worth dropping in or giving them a call as you make your plans.

The Ministry of Tourism's informative Spanish-language website can be visited at www.cubatravel.cu. Other Cuban travel companies with offices around the world include Cubana Airlines and the government hotel corporation Grupo Cubanacán, both potential sources of useful information (addresses below).

Argentina
Oficina de Turismo de Cuba (☎ 54-1-326-7810, fax 54-1-326-3325), Paraguay No 631, 2do piso A, Buenos Aires

Canada
Bureau de Tourisme de Cuba (☎ 1-514-875-8004, fax 1-514-875-8006), 440 Boulevard René Lévesque Ouest, suite 1105, Montréal, Québec H2Z 1V7

Cuban Tourist Board (☎ 1-416-362-0700, fax 1-416-362-6799), 55 Queen St E, suite 705, Toronto, Ontario M5C 1R6

France
Office de Tourisme de Cuba (☎ 33-1-45-38-90-10, fax 33-1-45-38-99-30), 280 Boulevard Raspail, 75014 Paris

Germany
Cubanisches Fremdenverkehrsamt
(☎ 49-69-288-322, fax 49-69-296-664), An der
Hauptwache 7, 60313 Frankfurt/Main

Italy
Ufficio di Promozione e Informazione Turistica
di Cuba (☎ 39-2-6698-1463, fax 39-2-6738-0725),
Via General Fara 30, terzo piano, Milano 20124

Mexico
Oficina de Turismo de Cuba (☎ 52-5-255-5897,
fax 52-5-255-5866), Goethe No 16, Colonia
Anzures, Delegación Miguel Hidalgo,
Mexico, DF

Spain
Oficina de Promoción e Información Turística
de Cuba (☎ 34-91-411-3097, fax 34-91-564-5804),
Paseo de La Habana No 54, Madrid 28036

Switzerland
Cuban Tourist Board (☎ 41-31-302-9830,
fax 41-31-302-2111), Gesellschaftstrasse No 8,
3012 Bern

UK
Cuban Tourist Board (☎ 44-20-7240 6655,
fax 44-20-7836 9265), 154 Shaftesbury Ave,
London WC2H 8JT

Cubanacán Offices

The hotel corporation Grupo Cubanacán
(www.cubanacan.cu) has offices worldwide
that provide information about their hotels
and sell Cuban travel videos, but it doesn't
book tours or reserve rooms.

Brazil
Cubasol do Brasil (☎ 55-11-256-8521,
fax 55-11-259-0987), Rue 7 de Abril,
404-8vo Andar-CJ-81, Centro São Paulo,
SP CEP-01044-000

Canada
Cubanacán (☎ 1-416-601-0343,
fax 1-416-601-0346), 372 Bay St, suite 1902,
Toronto, Ontario M5H 2W9

France
Cubanacán International (☎ 33-1-5369-0101,
fax 33-1-5369-0143), 7 rue Pérignon, 75014 Paris

Italy
Cubanacán (☎ 39-2-6671-1219, fax 39-2-6671-
0839), Vía Pirelli 27, 8th floor, 20124 Milano

Mexico
Cubanacán (☎ 52-5-211-1553, fax 52-5-286-4982),
Av Nuevo León No 159, 4to piso, Colonia
Hipódromo Condesa, Delegación Cuauhtemoc,
06100 Mexico, DF

Netherlands
Cubanacán (☎ 31-70-390-5152,
fax 31-70-319-3452), Visseringlaan 24,
2288 ER Rijswijk

Spain
Ibernacán Internacional (☎ 34-91-359-8543,
fax 34-91-359-8637), Calle Doctor Fleming 31,
9-D, Madrid 28036

UK
Cubanacán (☎ 44-20-7537 7909,
fax 44-20-7537 7747), Skylines Unit 49,
Limeharbour, Docklands, London E14 9TS

Cubana Offices

Cuba's national airline, Cubana de Aviación, has offices in many of the world's
large cities. In addition to the locations
listed below, there are offices in Barcelona,
Bogotá, Buenos Aires, Caracas, Fort de
France, Frankfurt, Guayaquil, Las Palmas,
Lima, Lisbon, Montevideo, Moscow, Nassau, Panama City, Quito, Rio de Janeiro,
Rome, San José de Costa Rica, Santiago de
Chile, Santiago de Compostela, and São
Paulo. These are often good sources of
brochures and other visitor information,
and Cubana de Aviación staff will be able
to give you the names of travel agencies
around the world that routinely sell its
tickets.

Belgium
(☎ 32-2-640-2050, fax 32-2-640-0810), Av Louise
363, 1050 Bruxelles

Canada
(☎ 1-514-871-1222, fax 1-514-871-1227), 1 Place
Ville Marie, suite 1535, Montréal, Québec H3B
3N6
(☎ 1-416-967-2822, fax 1-416-967-2824), 1240
Bay St, suite 800, Toronto, Ontario M5R 2A7

Dominican Republic
(☎ 1-809-227-2040, fax 1-809-227-2044), Av
Tiradentes y 27 de febrero, Plaza Merengue,
local 209, Santo Domingo

France
(☎ 33-1-5363-2323, fax 33-1-53-63-23-29), 41
Boulevard du Montparnasse, 75006 Paris

Germany
(☎ 49-69-9130-9820, fax 49-69-9130-9840), An
der Hauptwache 7, 60313 Frankfurt/Main

Italy
(☎ 39-6-474-1104, fax 39-6-474-6836), Via
Barberini 86, 4to piano, 00187 Roma

Jamaica
  (☎ 1-876-978-3410, fax 1-876-978-3406), 22
  Trafalgar Rd, 2nd floor, suite 11, Kingston 10
Mexico
  (☎ 52-5-250-6355, fax 52-5-255-0835),
  Temístocles 246, Colonia Polanco, CP 11560
  Mexico, DF
  (☎/fax 52-98-86-0192), Av Yaxchilán No 23,
  Cancún, Quintana Roo
Spain
  (☎ 34-91-758-9750, fax 34-91-541-6642),
  Princesa 25, Edificio Hexágono, 28008 Madrid
UK
  (☎ 44-20-7734 1165, fax 44-20-7437 0681),
  49 Conduit St, London W1R 9FB

DOCUMENTS
Passports & Tourist Cards

Every visitor needs a passport valid at least
six months ahead and a *tarjeta de turista*
(tourist card). Those booking a package
tour will receive the card together with their
other travel documents. Those going 'air
only' can usually buy the tourist card from
the travel agency or airline office that sells
them their plane ticket. Some agents in the
UK (and perhaps elsewhere) will claim they
are unable to issue the card unless three to
five hotel nights have been booked through
them. In general, Cuban embassies don't
issue tourist cards or provide tourist information. If you wish to apply for a visa or
tourist card at a Cuban consulate, call ahead
and ask if you must make an appointment.

If necessary, you can also buy the card
upon arrival at Havana's José Martí International Airport (but not at other airports).
Everyone, even babies, must have a card.
The cards cost around US$15 when ob-
tained through a travel agency or airline, or
about twice that when purchased at a consulate or airport. The passport number
entered on the tourist card must correspond
to the number of the passport you'll use to
travel, so don't fill in the card until you're
already at the airport. If you get a new passport for any reason, you'll also need a new
card.

When you arrive, check that immigration
stamps the correct date on your tourist card.
It allows a stay of four weeks, and this can
be extended for another four weeks without

Through Cuba's Door

The immigration control booths at Havana's
international airport are identical copies of
those maintained by the former East German
government until 1989. You step into a tiny
cubicle and pass your documents through a
narrow slit to an officer seated behind bullet-
proof glass. This person looks directly at you
to compare your face with the mug shot in
your passport, then everything disappears
onto a table below your line of vision.

Your details are punched into an unseen
computer and you get your airline ticket
back. If everything else checks out, you'll see
the officer bend forward to stamp your
tourist card (and perhaps also your passport
with a tiny stamp that doesn't mention
Cuba). Then all your remaining documents
are pushed back through the slit and a buzzer
sounds, allowing you to push open the back
door and step out into the real world.

FACTS FOR THE VISITOR

difficulty upon payment of a US$25 fee.
Once inside Cuba, you'll seldom have to
show the card unless you try to extend your
stay at an immigration office. Thus it can be
safely stowed away with your airline ticket
in your money belt (don't leave it in your
passport, as it could fall out). Replacing a
lost tourist card in Cuba also costs US$25,
and you won't be allowed to leave the
country until you've paid. Transit passengers spending fewer than 72 hours in Cuba
may not need a tourist card (verify this with
your airline).

Be sure to write the name of a likely
hotel in the 'Address in Cuba' space on your
tourist card: Don't leave that line blank.
Also don't list the cheapest hotel in town, as
this will prompt the official to ask to see
your hotel voucher; if you're searching for a
name for that line, write 'Hotel Nacional' or
'Hotel Havana Libre.' Officially, you're supposed to have a hotel reservation for at least
three nights' accommodations (not necessarily consecutive nights) upon arrival in
Cuba, and Cuban immigration could hang

onto your passport until you've made the necessary reservations at the airport tour desk.

The only object of this exercise is to make a little money by obliging you to stay at an expensive state-owned hotel, and considering the difficulty in booking Cuban hotel rooms on an individual basis from outside the country, this requirement is a real nuisance. Probably the question won't come up, but it can, and obvious backpackers, Americans arriving from Mexico, and people of color are the most likely to be asked to show their vouchers.

Quite a few travelers have reported being delayed at the airport for hours waiting for the tour desk person to show up, and then having to quibble over which hotel they wanted to stay in. Some said they would never return to Cuba after the experience. If it happens to you, stay calm and friendly, and try to get reservations at the hotel you wanted anyway. Never say you intend to stay in a *casa particular* (private room), as this is the very thing they are trying to discourage.

Tourist Card Extensions

A one-month extension of your tourist card is easily arranged, though expect a long line (and long wait) to reach the official who can issue you the extension. The correct procedure is to go to an immigration office and show the officials your tourist card and passport. Upon receiving the US$25 fee, immigration will give you an extension. (See also Visa Extensions, later.)

Visas

Anyone wishing to prearrange a stay of longer than four weeks must apply for an official visa at a consulate. But rather than enter such a process, it's much easier simply to arrive in Cuba with a tourist card and extend your stay for another four weeks once there. Visas are required of business travelers and journalists on assignment, and applications should be made through a consulate at least three weeks in advance (longer if you apply through a consulate in a country other than your own). Visitors with

visas or anyone who has stayed in Cuba longer than 90 days must apply for an exit permit from an immigration office. Those planning to stay in Cuba more than three months must have an HIV test; those who test positive are denied a visa.

In the UK, the Cuban Consulate in London issues tourist cards (£15 and no photos) in one day upon presentation of a photocopy of the information pages of the passport and a booking note from a travel agent (your agent can also supply the card for the same price or less with no questions asked). Official visas (£32 plus two photos) take two weeks to issue, and the name of an official contact in Cuba is necessary (£13 additional charge for any fax or telex sent in connection with the visa).

Visa Extensions A one-month extension of your tourist card is easily arranged. The correct procedure is to go to an immigration office and show the officials your tourist card and passport. Upon receiving the US$25 fee, immigration will give you an extension. Some travel agencies and tour desks are authorized to grant visa extensions. After two months you must leave Cuba, though it's okay to come back the next day and start on another two months. (See also Tourist Card Extensions, earlier.)

Entry Permits for Cubans & Naturalized Citizens

Naturalized citizens of other countries who were born in Cuba require an *autorización de entrada* (entry permit) issued by a Cuban embassy or consulate. In 1995 a travel document called Vigencia de Viaje was introduced for Cuban residents abroad. It allows the holder to visit Cuba as many times as he or she likes over a two-year period. Persons hostile to the revolution or with a criminal record are not eligible. Current information is available at all Cuban diplomatic offices.

The Cuban government does not recognize dual citizenship. All persons born in Cuba are considered Cuban citizens unless they have formally renounced their Cuban citizenship at a Cuban diplomatic mission and the renunciation has been accepted.

Cuban Americans with questions about dual nationality can contact the Office of Overseas Citizens Services, Department of State, Washington, DC 20520.

Mexican Tourist Cards

Travelers (other than Mexicans) making a return trip to Cuba from Mexico or continuing to Mexico from Cuba must have a Mexican tourist card or visa; otherwise, they could be refused entry to Cuba. Mexican tourist cards are issued free of charge by Mexican consulates and tourist offices around the world, and those making a roundtrip to Cuba via Mexico should obtain two cards, one for each journey through Mexico. However, this is not true if you are traveling on a special charter. Your travel agent or airline will be able to provide advice.

Licenses for US Visitors

In 1961 the US government imposed an order limiting the ability of its own citizens to visit Cuba (see the Conflict with the USA section in Facts about Havana). As of late 2000, the US continued to bar normal tourist travel to Cuba from the US. The US government has, though, made it easier to visit Cuba for reasons of business investigation, and cultural, academic, sport and other 'people-to-people' exchanges. Also, 'fully hosted' Americans (those visiting at someone else's expense) are allowed to travel to Cuba, as long as they don't spend money there. Obtaining a license to travel to Cuba legally has never been easier (see Obtaining a License, later).

For its part, the Cuban government has never prohibited Americans from visiting Cuba, and it continues to receive US passport holders under exactly the same terms as any other visitor. (As a matter of fact, the US doesn't prohibit anyone from visiting Cuba. However, with the exceptions mentioned above, the US government prohibits Americans and US residents from spending any money there, which essentially amounts to a prohibition on travel.)

Unofficially, Americans can easily go to Cuba via Canada, Mexico, the Bahamas or

Jamaica, and estimates of the number of Americans sneaking into Cuba each year range from 20,000 to 50,000. American travel agents are prohibited from handling tourism arrangements, so most Americans must work through a foreign travel agency. Travel agents in those countries routinely arrange Cuban tourist cards, flight reservations, and accommodations packages (see the Getting There & Away chapter).

The immigration officials in Cuba know very well that a Cuban stamp in a US passport can create problems. However, before handing over your passport to the Cuban immigration officer, do request that the officer not stamp it. The officer will instead stamp your tourist card on a separate visa form that is collected as you leave Cuba. If you don't ask, you'll probably get a tiny stamp on page 16 or the last page in the

Should Americans Visit Cuba?

In conjunction with the US embargo against Cuba, the US government has prohibited its people from spending money in Cuba. This restriction has, for almost four decades, effectively prevented US citizens from visiting their neighbor, although the enforcement of this law has fluctuated with the political climate in the US.

The Helms-Burton Bill, which was signed into law by President Clinton on March 12, 1996, imposes without judicial review fines of up to US$50,000 on US citizens who visit Cuba at their own expense without US government permission. It also allows for confiscation of their property. In addition, under the Trading with the Enemy Act, they may also face up to US$250,000 in fines and up to 10 years in prison. Although individuals who go to Cuba on a personal holiday are generally not prosecuted, those organizing such travel for others have been.

The author and publisher of this guide accept no responsibility for repercussions suffered by US citizens who decide to circumvent these restrictions.

¡ABSOLUTAMENTE NINGÚN MIEDO!

shape of a plane, barn, moon, or some other strange symbol that doesn't mention Cuba.

The US government has an 'Interests Section' in Havana, but American visitors are advised to avoid all contact with this heavily guarded office unless they have official US government permission to be in Cuba. Unofficial US visitors should be especially careful not to lose their passport while in Cuba, as this would put them in a very difficult position.

Obtaining a License The US Treasury Department's Washington DC–based Office of Foreign Assets Control issues general licenses to visit Cuba under the following four categories of travel: '(a) official business of the US government, foreign governments, and certain intergovernmental organizations; (b) journalistic activity engaged in by full-time journalists and their supporting broadcast or technical personnel; (c) professional research by full-time professionals and attendance at professional meetings or conferences; and (d) amateur or semi-professional athletic competition.'

OFAC also issues specific licenses to 'accredited US academic institutions' to authorize travel transactions related to certain educational activities by students or employees affiliated with the institution. Such licenses are valid for multiple trips over a two-year period. Specific licenses may also be issued (in some instances with extended validity permitting multiple trips) for educational activities that do not take place under the auspices of an accredited US academic institution. Religious organizations are also eligible for multiple trip, two-year specific licenses authorizing travel transactions by their representatives in connection with a program of religious activities in Cuba.

Other travel categories for which specific licenses may be issued (in some instances with extended validity permitting multiple trips) include but are not limited to: free-lance journalism; activities of recognized human rights organizations and other humanitarian projects that directly benefit the Cuban people; certain public performances, clinics, workshops, exhibitions and athletic and other competitions; certain non-commercial activities of private foundations or research or educational institutions; and travel-related transactions involving informational materials, donations of food or exportations of goods licensed by the Department of Commerce.

Americans whose travel to Cuba is fully hosted by a non-American entity and who won't be spending any money in Cuba may also be allowed to visit Cuba, as are Americans who have close relatives in Cuba and who want to go to Cuba specifically to visit those relatives. (OFAC's definition of 'close relative' is very broad and includes in-laws and cousins.) Neither general nor specific permits are ever issued for the purpose of business travel or tourism, so don't specify either as your reason for seeking a license.

These regulations are subject to change. To be certain the information here has not changed, we suggest that you contact OFAC (☎ 202-622-2480, www.ustreas.gov/ofac), Office of Foreign Assets Control, US Department of the Treasury, 1500 Pennsylvania Ave NW, Annex Building, 2nd floor, Washington, DC 20220. Travel arrangements for those eligible for a license can be made by US companies that have received OFAC's blessing to provide travel services to Cuba. A list of these companies appears in the Getting There & Away chapter. Be advised that license holders are allowed to spend only US$100 per person per day in Cuba, and a maximum of US$500 in a single year.

US Import Limitations Under the Trading with the Enemy Act, goods originating in Cuba are prohibited from entering the US. Cuban cigars, rum, books and so on will be confiscated by US customs, and the officials can create additional problems if they feel so inclined. Possession of Cuban goods inside the US is also banned. Theoretically, one can receive a US$50,000 fine and 10 years in prison for attempting to smuggle Cuban goods into the US.

American travelers who choose to go to Cuba (and wish to avoid unnecessary hassles with the US border guards) should get rid of everything related to their trip to Cuba – including used airline tickets, baggage tags, travel documents, receipts and souvenirs – before returning to the US. If transiting Canada, Mexico or the Bahamas, use two or more of your birth certificate, driver's license and voter's registration card to enter those countries, none of which require a passport of US citizens. If the Cubans don't stamp your passport, there will be no official record of your trip. If you make a collect or operator-assisted telephone call from Cuba to the US, there could be a record of that, so use a prepaid Cuban telephone card.

If US customs asks you directly if you have been to Cuba, you could say that you've only been to Toronto, Cancún, Nassau or Montego Bay, in which case you'll probably be waved on even if it's pretty obvious from your body language that you're lying. Have the name of a likely hotel ready in case they ask where you stayed. If you admit you've been to Cuba, you'll probably receive a stern lecture from the official, your baggage will be searched, and your details will be noted officially, after which you'll be told to go and that will be the end of it.

In the past few years, around 40 people have been assessed civil fines of US$500 to US$1500 for the type of 'offense' described in this section, and 10 have been criminally prosecuted for traveling to Cuba. Most of those cases involved people who were trying to profit personally from the situation by organizing trips for other Americans (including US yachties who carried passengers to Cuba).

More than 200,000 US citizens a year travel to Cuba – as many as 50,000 unofficially – with no consequences. However, as long as these regulations remain in place, visiting Cuba certainly qualifies as soft adventure travel for Americans.

Onward Tickets

Everyone entering Cuba must have a return- or onward-travel plane ticket. This is always checked by immigration. It's unwise to arrive with an 'open' ticket as you may be given only a five-day or one-week stay in Cuba. If you're allowed to change the return date without penalty and you aren't sure how long you really want to stay, plan to visit for one month. Then if you wish to stay longer you can extend both your visa and reservation at the same time. Individuals not on a package tour could also be asked to show US$50 for every day they plan to spend in Cuba, though this seldom happens.

Travel Insurance & Driver's License

Emergency medical care is free in Cuba, and outpatient treatment at special clinics designed for foreigners is reasonably priced. Travel health insurance will pay off only if you require prolonged hospitalization or an emergency medical evacuation to your home country (make sure that's covered). Many plans only reimburse expenses above those already covered by your regular group insurance and are invalid if you don't have another policy.

Either your regular driver's license or an international driving permit is sufficient to rent a car in Cuba.

Hostel Card & Student, Youth & Seniors' Cards

There are no youth hostels in Havana (or anywhere else in Cuba), so a Hosteling International card won't prove useful.

We're not aware of any discounts or special privileges accruing from student, youth or seniors' cards in Cuba. You might be allowed free or reduced entry to a museum by showing a student card, but such treatment is usually as a personal favor granted by the museum staff rather than any official policy (before 1990 all museums were free to everyone).

International Health Card

If you're coming from a country plagued by cholera or yellow fever, be prepared upon arrival to show Cuban authorities an International Certificate of Vaccination against these diseases. From the perspective of all Cuban immigration authorities, anyone traveling from South America needs a vaccination certificate. Same deal with Africa. If you're traveling from either continent, play it safe and obtain an International Certificate of Vaccination showing you've been vaccinated against cholera or yellow fever or both.

Photocopies

The best 'travel insurance' available is a photocopy of your passport data pages and visa page, birth certificate, credit cards, travel insurance policy, airline tickets, driver's license, and other documents, and a list of all your traveler's check numbers with the phone number you'd need to call should they be lost. Leave one set of copies with someone at home and carry another with you, separate from the originals.

It's also a good idea to store details of your vital travel documents in Lonely Planet's free online Travel Vault in case you lose the photocopies or can't be bothered with them. Your password-protected Travel Vault is accessible online anywhere in the world – create an account for yourself at www.ekno.lonelyplanet.com.

Yacht Entry Procedures

No prior visas or reservations are required of those traveling by yacht, but you'll have to purchase US$20 tourist cards upon arrival if you plan to stay longer than 72 hours. Private yachts bound for Cuba should try to make radio contact with the Cuban port authorities over channel 16 or 68 (VHF) or the National Coastal Network over 2760 HF (SSB) before crossing the 12-mile limit. Say *llamando seguridad marítima* (calling maritime security) and quote the name of the port. If you're approaching Havana, call the Marina Hemingway over channel 72 and they'll arrange everything.

If you receive no answer, continue sailing toward your port of entry with your yellow quarantine flag flying below the Cuban courtesy flag. Repeat the message at regular intervals, and eventually a Cuban official will answer and ask for information about your boat. All you need to do from then on is follow the instructions.

Required documents include the passports of everyone on board; the ownership papers, title, and registration certificate of the vessel; and the zarpe (clearance document) from your last port with Cuba listed as your destination. For maximum flexibility, ask for 30 days even if you expect to be in Cuban waters for only a week. At any Cuban port the officials may bring along a small dog to sniff for drugs.

Much more information about all these matters is contained in *The Cruising Guide to Cuba* by Simon Charles, mentioned in the Books section, later in this chapter.

EMBASSIES & CONSULATES
Cuban Embassies & Consulates

Australia
Cuban Consulate-General (☎ 61-2-9311-4611, fax 61-2-9311-1255), PO Box 1412, Maroubra, NSW 2035

Belgium
Cuban Embassy (☎ 32-2-343-0020, fax 32-2-343-9195), Robert Jonesstraat 77, 1180 Brussels

Canada
Cuban Embassy (☎ 1-613-563-0141, fax 1-613-563-0068), 338 Main St, Ottawa, Ontario K1S 1E3
Cuban Consulate-General (☎ 1-416-234-8181, fax 1-416-234-2754), 5353 Dundas St W, suite 401, Etobicoke, Ontario M9B 6H8
Cuban Consulate-General and Trade Commission (☎ 1-514-843-8897, fax 1-514-982-9034), 1415 Ave des Pins Ouest, Montréal, Québec H3B 1B2

France
Cuban Embassy (☎ 33-1-45-67-55-35, fax 33-1-45-66-80-92), 16 Rue de Presles, 75015 Paris

Germany
Cuban Embassy (☎ 49-30-9161-1810), Stavanger Strasse 20, 10439 Berlin
Cuban Consulate (☎ 49-228-3090), Kennedy Allee 22, 53175 Bonn

Mexico
Cuban Embassy (☎ 52-5-280-8039, fax 52-5-280-0839), Presidente Masarik 554, Colonia Polanco, 11560 Mexico, DF

Netherlands
Cuban Embassy (☎ 31-70-360-6061, fax 31-70-364-7586), Mauritskade 49, 2514 HG Den Haag
Cuban Consulate (☎ 31-10-206-7333, fax 31-10-206-7335), Stationsplein 45, 3013 AK Rotterdam

Spain
  Consulado de Cuba (☎ 34-91-401-6941,
  fax 34-91-402-1948), Conde Peñalver No 38,
  piso 6, 28006 Madrid

UK
  Cuban Embassy (☎ 44-20-7240 2488,
  fax 44-20-7836 2602), 167 High Holborn,
  London WC1V 6PA

USA
  Cuban Interests Office (☎ 1-202-797-8609/8518,
  fax 1-202-986-7283), 2639 16th St NW,
  Washington, DC 20009

Embassies in Cuba

Austria (☎ 24-2394; 9 am to noon weekdays),
  Calle 4 No 101, at Av 1, Miramar

Belgium (☎ 24-2410; 9 am to 2 pm weekdays),
  Av 5 No 7408, at Av 76, Miramar

Canada (☎ 24-2516; 8:30 am to 5 pm Monday,
  Tuesday, Thursday, and Friday, 8:30 am to 2 pm
  Wednesday; also represents Australia),
  Calle 30 No 518, at Av 7, Miramar

Denmark (☎ 33-8128; 8 am to 4 pm weekdays),
  Paseo de Martí No 20, 4th floor,
  Centro Habana

France (☎ 24-2132; 8:30 am to noon weekdays),
  Calle 14 No 312, between 3 and 5, Miramar

Germany (☎ 33-2569; 9 am to noon weekdays),
  Calle 13 No 652, at B, Vedado

Italy (☎ 33-3334; 10 am to 1 pm weekdays),
  Paseo No 606, between 25 and 27, Vedado

Japan (☎ 33-3454; 8 am to 3 pm weekdays),
  Calle N No 62, at Calle 15 behind Servi-Cupet,
  Vedado

Mexico (☎ 24-2383; 9 am to noon weekdays),
  Calle 12 No 518, at 7, Miramar

Netherlands (☎ 24-2512; 8:30 to 11:30 am weekdays), Calle 8 No 307, between 3 and 5,
  Miramar

Spain (☎ 33-8029; 9 am to 1 pm weekdays),
  Capdevila No 51, at Agramonte, Centro Habana

Sweden (☎ 24-2563; 9 am to noon weekdays),
  Av 31 No 1411, between 14 and 18, Miramar

Switzerland (☎ 24-2611; 9:15 am to 1 pm weekdays), Av 5 No 2005, between 20 and 22,
  Miramar

UK (☎ 24-1771; 8:30 am to noon weekdays),
  Calle 34 No 708, at Av 7, Miramar

USA (☎ 33-4401; 8:30 am to 5 pm weekdays),
  Interests Section, Calzada, between L and M,
  Vedado

CUSTOMS

Cuban customs regulations allow visitors to bring along their personal belongings (including clothes, shoes, toilet articles, photography equipment, binoculars, musical instrument, tape recorder, radio, personal computer, tent, fishing rod, tennis racket, nonmotorized bicycle, canoe or kayak under 5m long, surfboard, and other sporting gear), gifts up to a value of US$100, and 10kg of medicine (excluding veterinary or blood-based medicines). In addition, those over the age of 18 may import 3 liters of wine or other alcoholic beverages, plus a choice of either 200 cigarettes, 50 cigars, or 250g of cut tobacco.

Unused items that do not fit into the categories mentioned above are subject to a 100% customs duty to a maximum of

Those Unhelpful Embassies

As a tourist, it's important to realize what your own embassy – the embassy of the country of which you are a citizen – can and can't do.

Generally speaking, it won't be much help in emergencies if the trouble you're in is remotely your own fault. Remember that you are bound by the laws of the country you are in. Your embassy will not be sympathetic if you end up in jail after committing a crime locally, even if such actions are legal in your own country.

In genuine emergencies you might get some assistance, but only if other channels have been exhausted. For example, if you need to get home urgently, a free ticket home is exceedingly unlikely – the embassy would expect you to have insurance. If you have all your money and documents stolen, it might assist in getting a new passport, but a loan for onward travel is out of the question.

Embassies used to keep letters for travelers or have a small reading room with home newspapers, but these days most embassies have stopped the mail holding service, and even newspapers tend to be out of date.

!ABSOLUTAMENTE NINGÚN MIEDO¡

US$1000. For information on importing consumer goods worth over US$1000 and not for personal use, contact a Cuban consulate. Exporting more than US$5000 per person in cash from Cuba is prohibited. Those carrying larger amounts of cash should fill out a *declaración de valor* (customs declaration) upon arrival, in which case they will be allowed to export up to the amount imported and declared.

Items one cannot bring into Cuba include narcotics, explosives, obscene publications and prerecorded video cassettes. The import of weapons, ammunition, telecommunications equipment, flora and fauna specimens, live animals, biological or pharmaceutical goods of animal origin and unprocessed food (including all fresh fruit, meat or vegetables) is restricted. Canned, processed and dried food is usually no problem.

MONEY

The US dollar was Cuba's only currency until 1934, when the first peso notes were issued. Notes marked 'República de Cuba' were used from 1934 to 1949, when the present 'Banco Nacional de Cuba' notes came into circulation. In 1993 the dollar was brought back for all serious business, and three currencies now circulate in Cuba.

The Cuban peso or moneda nacional, divided into 100 centavos, is officially linked to the US dollar at a one-to-one rate, but its actual value hovers around 20 to one – a rate that has been maintained since 1995 (in 1993 it fell as low as 150 to the dollar). Although this seems like a bargain, it doesn't mean much since there's little to buy with pesos. A more powerful currency is the US dollar, which will buy just about anything.

In 1994 the peso convertible was introduced, and it really does have exactly the same value as the dollar. However, since US dollars are more widely accepted than moneda nacional and pesos convertibles, don't exchange your dollars for them.

The best type of money to bring with you to Cuba is US dollars in cash. Traveler's checks cost you commissions at both the buying and selling ends, cashing them takes time, and smaller hotels don't accept them.

Many Cuban cashiers are paranoid about getting stuck with counterfeit American currency, and you'll often be asked to show your passport when you spend a US$50 or US$100 bill. Your passport number and the serial number of the bank note will then be entered in a ledger.

Currency

The Cuban peso comes in notes of one, three, five, 10, 20, 50, and 100 pesos, and coins of one, two, five, 20, and 40 centavos, and one and three pesos. Each note has a distinct color. The five-centavo coin is called a medio, the 20-centavo coin a peseta. The three-peso coin bearing the likeness of Ernesto 'Che' Guevara makes a nice souvenir.

The convertible peso comes in multicolored notes of one, three, five, 10, 20, 50, and 100 pesos, and there are also special coins marked 'Intur' of the same size and value as US coins (five, 10, 25, and 50 cents and one peso). American coins also circulate.

Banks

In La Habana Vieja, the Banco Financiero Internacional, Oficios and Brasil, near the Monasterio de San Francisco de Asís, is open 8 am to 3 pm weekdays. Also in the old town is the Banco de Crédito y Comercio, Aguiar No 310, just off Obispo. It's open 8:30 am to 1:30 pm weekdays.

In Vedado, the Banco de Crédito y Comercio in the Airline Building, Calle 23, between Calle P and Malecón, changes traveler's checks for 2.5% commission, and makes cash advances on credit cards. It's open 8:30 am to 3 pm weekdays.

The Banco Financiero Internacional, inside Vedado's Hotel Habana Libre, with a street entrance off Calle 25, charges 3% commission to change traveler's checks. It'll give cash advances on Visa and MasterCard. It's open 8 am to 3 pm weekdays. A small exchange window here is open 9 am to 7 pm Monday to Saturday, 9 am to 2 pm Sunday.

May Day celebration in the Parque de la Fraternidad against the backdrop of the Capitolio Nacional

The life of a cigar, from its origin to its much-appreciated finale

Old American cars taxi around town.

Ceremony and street vendors blend into the mix of sights and smells.

Island icons of hope: Che Guevara, José Martí and La Milagrosa

The Banco Metropolitano, Línea and Calle M in Vedado, has an ATM outside. It's open 8:30 am to 3 pm Monday to Saturday. The Banco Financiero Internacional branch at Línea and Calle O has lengthy lines. It's open 8:30 am to 3 pm weekdays.

Out near the Hotel Meliá Cohiba is the Banco de Crédito y Comercio, Línea No 705, at Paseo, opposite Cine Trianón. It's open 8:30 am to 3 pm weekdays. A Cadeca kiosk (see below) is adjacent.

Exchanging Money

Dollar traveler's checks can be changed into cash dollars at hotel exchange desks and banks for 2.5% to 5% commission. Traveler's checks in most other hard currencies can also be changed into cash dollars at any bank.

In 1995 the government opened a chain of exchange offices called Casas de Cambio, or 'Cadeca,' which change dollars and pesos back and forth at the free-market rate, thereby effectively ending the black market. You'll often see lines of Cubans in front of Cadeca offices waiting to buy dollars. If you're selling dollars you can skip the queue and walk straight in. Otherwise, someone near the door may offer to buy your dollars at the same rate you'd receive inside, a common practice though technically illegal.

Traveler's Checks & Credit Cards Until recently traveler's checks and credit cards issued by US companies such as American Express, Citibank and Diners Club, or any traveler's checks that cleared through New York, were not negotiable in Cuba. However, at last report the Banco Financiero Internacional was happily cashing American Express traveler's checks. US-issued credit cards are still not being accepted in Cuba. MasterCard and Visa credit cards issued by non-US banks have always been accepted, as have Thomas Cook and Visa traveler's checks expressed in US dollars, provided they were not issued by a US bank.

Travelers have complained about double billing by government restaurants and suggest you keep your card in sight at all times. Cuban businesses often add a sur-

charge of 2% to 5% to your bill if you pay by credit card. Always ask beforehand if you think you might like to pay by credit card, and at the smaller hotels don't be surprised if your card isn't accepted in the morning even when the clerk the night before had said it would be fine.

Expect a 2.5% commission to be charged when you change traveler's checks into cash US dollars at the Banco de Crédito y Comercio, formerly called the Banco Nacional de Cuba. The Banco Financiero Internacional takes 3% and the Caja de Ahorros 3.5%. Hotel receptionists often deduct 4% commission. Larger Cadeca offices will also cash traveler's checks for 3% commission and give cash advances, worth remembering as they're open much longer hours than the banks.

There's often no commission to change foreign cash into cash US dollars, but the rate of exchange may be low (ask). Don't write in the place, date or payee when signing a traveler's check as it might be refused. Getting a refund for checks lost in Cuba is difficult, and all you can do is report the loss by phone and wait until you reach another country.

ATMs The banks are in the process of installing ATMs at main branches, but at last report these weren't set up to accept Visa or MasterCard.

International Transfers

An easy way to transfer money to Cuba is by credit card via Transcard (☎ 416-296-0738 to hear a recording). In emergencies, relatives, friends or business associates abroad could send money to you through Antillas Express (☎ 514-385-9449, 514-385-9221, fax 514-385-9062), 9632 Charton Ave, Montréal, PQ H2B 2C5, Canada. Antillas promises delivery in less than four days to Havana, or five days elsewhere in Cuba, for a commission of US$10 to US$85, depending on the amount. You can use the same system to send cash to Cuban relatives or friends.

Whenever transferring money related to travel to Cuba, beware of the long reach of the US government. We heard from an Australian reader who had to transfer US$2600 from Australia to the Havanatur office in the UK to pay for a trip to Cuba. Because the amount was in US dollars it went via New York, where the bank's computer picked up Havanatur on the transfer and diverted the payment to the Office of Foreign Assets Control of the US Department of the Treasury, which confiscated the entire amount. This explains why some travel agencies ask US clients to pay their deposit by certified check delivered via courier.

Costs

Generally speaking, Havana hotel rooms aren't cheap. Expect to pay US$45 a night for a decent room, considerably more for a room at one of the city's fancier places. Room prices are seasonally lower from April to June and September to mid-December, the least expensive months to visit. (See the Places to Stay chapter.)

Meals vary a great deal in quality and price, but if you follow the suggestions made in the Places to Eat chapter you'll get good value for your money. Expect to pay US$25 to US$40 a day on food if you like to eat well (alcohol not included). Generally speaking, Cuban food is better known for being filling than it is for being delicious. However, the city's tastiest restaurants are mentioned in the Places to Eat chapter.

Transportation in Havana is one of the best deals around. You can take a taxi from La Habana Vieja to most anywhere in Centro Habana or Vedado for US$5 or less, and vice versa. Taxis are metered, so you won't be ripped off. However, if you step into a taxi and the meter isn't operating or it's been removed, agree on a price before you pull away from the curb.

Triciclo peddling is an arduous exercise, and triciclo peddlers deserve every penny they get, nine times out of ten. But because they aren't metered, if you don't agree on a price before you go on a ride, you can be in for a jolt when you arrive. And most people find it difficult to tell a triciclo peddler that US$20 for a 10-block ride is excessive when the driver is sweating from scalp to foot (a 10-block triciclo or taxi ride usually costs about US$1.50).

Tipping & Bribes

Until 1993, tipping was discouraged, but it's now pervasive. Bus and taxi drivers, guides, waiters and housekeepers all expect to be tipped by foreigners. A 10% tip is generally appreciated. Anything more is considered generous.

People who deserve a US$1 tip include museum staff who give you a complete tour, hotel guards who watch your rental car all night, helpful bus drivers, or anyone in the service industry who does you a favor beyond the call of duty.

Tax and service charges may or may not be included in the bill at restaurants. Some private paladares don't mention it on their menus but will add 10% to 20% to your bill. Usually this amount is simply extra income for the restaurant: If you ask if you can keep the bill they'll quickly write out another for the total sum without the 'tax' amount being itemized. In these cases, you shouldn't leave any tip at all and don't go back.

Don't offer money to persons in official positions as a way of obtaining preferential treatment because, unlike the rest of Latin America, governmental corruption is rare in Cuba and you may only make matters worse. If the police are interested in you, it isn't because they want to be paid off. It might be because you have been mistaken for someone else or that you were seen associating with someone the authorities believe is up to no good. Don't assume the worst. In Havana, the police have been instructed to treat tourists with respect.

Taxes & Refunds
Except in restaurants, no additional taxes or service charges will be added to your bills in Cuba. This could change, however, as new taxes are being introduced all the time. Small private tourism businesses are heavily taxed, and of course these taxes are passed along to you indirectly.

Refunds are a delicate matter in Havana, given the poverty in which most Habaneros live. For example, if you want to return an item to a store, the store owner, thrilled to have received your business, will be reluctant to give it up. In most cases, a customer will get money back only after a bit of pleading.

Hotels in Havana rarely give full refunds. If you book in advance, you'll be told of a cancellation penalty. If you arrive in Havana and are lucky enough to find a room off the street, you'll likely be asked to pay in advance and told that if you cut your stay short, you'll be docked 10% or more of the payment.

POST & COMMUNICATIONS
Postal Rates
Postcards cost US$0.50 to all countries. Letters are US$0.65 to the Americas, US$0.75 to Europe, and US$0.85 to all other countries. Postage stamps (sellos) are sold for pesos at some post offices, and for dollars at hotels and tourist post offices. Some tourist post offices will try to sell you more stamps than you need. You can sidestep this scam by buying only the prepaid US$0.50 postcards, including international postage, available at most hotel shops.

Sending & Receiving Mail
Cuban mailboxes are blue. The mail service is no worse than in any other Latin American country, and even the US Postal Service delivers postcards mailed from Cuba.

In La Habana Vieja, dollar post offices are at Oficios No 102 on Plaza de San Fran-

cisco de Asís, and in Centro Habana in the Gran Teatro on Paseo de Martí, at the Capitolio end of the building. The Unidad de Filatelia, Obispo No 518, has stamps for collectors. It's open 9 am to 7 pm daily. In Vedado it's Filatelia Especializada, Calle 27, off Calle L, which also has a photocopy machine. It's open 8 am to 7 pm daily.

Post offices serving mostly the local population are at the Estación Central de Ferrocarril (Central Train Station), Av de Bélgica and Arsenal, in La Habana Vieja; on Calle 23, at Calle C, in Vedado, open 8 to 11:30 am and 2 to 6 pm weekdays, 8 to 11:30 am Saturday; and in the Ministry of Communications building, Av de la Independencia, between Plaza de la Revolución and the bus station, open 8 am to 6 pm Monday to Saturday. The ministry building also contains the Museo Postal Cubano, with a philatelic shop, open 9 am to 5 pm weekdays. Admission costs US$1.

Stamp collectors can buy, sell and trade philatelic materials at the regular meetings of the Club Filatélico, San Martín No 1172, between Infanta and Basarrata. It's open 1 to 4 pm Wednesday and Saturday, 9 am to 1 pm Sunday.

For important business mail, DHL Express offers a courier service from Cuba that utilizes the regular daily flights to Mexico. If you'll be spending a long time in Cuba and need to receive mail, a DHL office may be able to help.

DHL Worldwide Express courier service is available at Aerocaribbean (☎ 33-4543, fax 33-5016), Calle 23 No 64, at Calle P, in the Airline Building in Vedado. The main DHL office (☎ 33-4351), Calzada No 818, between Calles 2 and 4, near the Hotel Meliá Cohiba, is open 8:30 am to 5 pm weekdays.

Telephone
To call Havana from abroad, dial your international access code (which varies from country to country), Cuba's country code (53), Havana's city code (7), and the local number.

To get a line to call out of the country, dial Cuba's international access code ☎ 119, the country code, the area code, and the number. To place a call through the operator, dial ☎ 00 for domestic calls or ☎ 09 for international calls.

Throughout Cuba, the information number is ☎ 113. To get the local operator dial ☎ 110. For the international operator, it's ☎ 180. Emergency numbers include ☎ 115 to call the fire department, ☎ 116 to call the police, and ☎ 185 to call an ambulance. Remember, however, that they'll speak only Spanish.

In 1996 a Brazilian partner of the Empresa de Telecomunicaciones de Cuba SA, or 'Etecsa,' began installing the network of blue card telephones now found throughout the country. These are very convenient and inexpensive to use for both local and international calls. Magnetic telephone cards are sold at many hotels and dollar stores, plus all post offices and telephone centers. It's wise to buy the lowest denomination card (US$10), as it's easy to forget to remove your card from the phone when you're finished.

Direct-dial international telephone calls cost US$2.50 a minute to North America, US$3.25 a minute to Mexico and the Caribbean, US$4.25 a minute to South America, or US$5.50 a minute to the rest of the world. With a card, you only pay for the time you're actually connected, with no minimum; the amount left on your card is displayed in a small window on the phone. The cards tick off time left in increments of 10 seconds.

If you place a call through your hotel receptionist from the phone in your room, it will be much more expensive. You must tell the number to the receptionist who will dial it for you, and you could be charged for the first minute even if no one answers. Some hotels offer direct dialing from room phones, using the code 88 (plus the country and city codes) for international calls or 86 (plus the city code) for calls within Cuba. Another option is to call home and quickly provide a number at which your party can call you back. Collect calls are not possible from public telephones in Cuba. You can call collect only by dialing the international operator at ☎ 180 from a private phone.

Even if you're not a guest, it's possible to place calls from most of the upscale hotels. Simply tell a receptionist that you'd like to place a call and nine times out of ten you'll be asked the number and steered to a private call box, where you will receive the operator-assisted call. This is not an inexpensive way to place calls, but it eliminates street noise from the conversation.

Email & Internet Access

Except for guests staying at the ritzy Meliá Havana Hotel, non-Cubans are able to access the Internet from only one site in Havana – a so-called press room inside the Capitolio Nacional, the mural-filled marble building that served as the seat of the Cuban Congress from 1929 until the revolution 30 years later.

Any foreigner wanting to surf the Internet or check email must reserve a time to use one of the two sluggish computers in the press room. A day's notice is generally sufficient. The rental cost is US$5 an hour, and the machines share a printer (US $0.50 page). The state-run service is available 9 am to 7:30 pm weekdays.

To reach the press room free of charge, tell the ticket-taker at the entrance of the centrally located capital building that you're there for the Internet. (Just say, *Internet, por favor.*) Otherwise, you'll be charged a $3 admission fee. If you ask, *Donde esta la sala de prensa?* you'll be directed to the press room, which is seldom used by members of the press.

The Cuban government permits only five of the dozens of hotels in Havana to offer email service to their guests, and in most cases it is tightly restricted. Only at the Melia Havana, for example, can guests access the Internet and send and receive email using their own email addresses. The cost is US$10 an hour and the service is available 8 to 8 daily.

At the four other hotels – the Golden Tulip, the Havana Libre, the Nacional and the Meliá Cohiba – guests are allowed to send and receive email using only the hotels' email addresses. In all instances, incoming email to guests at these hotels needs to include the guest's name and room number. The system does not prevent hotel workers from reading and possibly copying guests' email.

If you bring a laptop to Havana, it is possible to call your Internet service provider from your hotel room. Americans: The Cuban phone jack is the same as the US phone jack (no adapter is needed). However, there are no local access numbers for non-Cuban ISPs, such as AOL and CompuServe; connecting costs as much as making an overseas telephone call. And in Havana, overseas calls placed from hotels are expensive.

INTERNET RESOURCES

The World Wide Web is a rich resource for travelers. You can research your trip, hunt down bargain air fares, book hotels, check on weather conditions, or chat with locals and other travelers about the best places to visit – or avoid.

There's no better place to start your web explorations than the Lonely Planet website (www.lonelyplanet.com). Here you'll find succinct summaries on traveling to most places on earth, postcards from other travelers, and the Thorn Tree bulletin board, where you can ask questions before you go or dispense advice when you get back. You can also find travel news and updates to many of our most popular guidebooks, and the subWWWay section links you to the most useful travel resources elsewhere on the web.

Cuba-Related Sites

Granma Internacional (www.granma.cu), the official newspaper of the Communist Party of Cuba, offers the latest news from Cuba in five languages.

CubaNet (www.cubanet.org) is an exile-operated Miami site that provides quite different information about Cuba and offers links to additional Cuba-related sites.

Global Exchange (www.globalexchange .org) provides excellent information on US-Cuban relations, and offers 'reality tours' to Cuba, Spanish language courses in Havana, serious dance courses, and links to Cuba-friendly support groups.

Signing On in Havana

There are dozens of hotels in Havana, but only five that offered Internet and/or email service at the time of writing:

- Melia Havana, full Internet access and email service for guests only, $10 per hour with a $3 minimum, ground-floor business center, open 8 am to 8 pm daily

- Golden Tulip, email only using hotel's email address, available to guests and nonguests alike, $17.50 per hour, 2nd-floor business center, open 8 am to 8 pm weekdays, 8 am to 4 pm weekends

- Hotel Nacional, email only using hotel's email address, available to guests only, $10 per hour, 6th-floor business center, open 8:30 am to 6 pm weekdays, 8:30 am to 4:30 pm weekends

- Havana Libre, email only using hotel's email address, free to guests, nonguests pay $2 per email sent and $1 per email received, 20th-floor business center, open 7 to 11 am daily

- Melia Cohiba, email only using hotel's email address, available to guests and nonguests, $15 per hour, ground-floor business center, open 8 am to 8 pm Monday through Saturday

¡ABSOLUTAMENTE NINGUN MIEDO!

Cuban Culture (www.cubanculture.com) offers a good mix of general facts and detailed information on Cuban music, dance, painting, literature, film, photography, architecture, famous people and more.

The fascinating subject of Santería is well covered on OrishaNet (www.orishanet.com).

You can listen to Cuban music on the site of an American recording company, Bembé Records (www.bembe.com).

Precise information on special events is available from the Cuban Convention Bureau (www.buroconv.cubaweb.cu).

Since 1996 CubaWeb (www.cubaweb.cu) has provided a fairly comprehensive index of Cuba-based websites, although sometimes you can't get it to load. For another

Cuba website index, click on SmallShop (www.smallshop.com/cubawebsites.htm). A third website index based at the University of Texas (lanic.utexas.edu/la/ca/cuba) offers lots of intriguing links.

Cuba's Internet service provider, Ceniai (www2.cuba.cu), provides a directory of email addresses, links and an unusual free fax service. They also run the cybercafe at Havana's Capitolio.

BOOKS

Most books are published in different editions by different publishers in different countries. As a result, a book might be a hardcover rarity in one country but readily available in paperback in another. Fortunately, bookstores and libraries can search by title or author, so the staff of your local bookstore or library is best placed to advise you on the availability of the following recommendations.

Lonely Planet

If you intend to see more of Cuba than Havana, by all means pick up a copy of *Cuba*, by Lonely Planet author David Stanley. David tells you what you want to know about Cuba in 528 succinct pages; most other authors of Cuba guides have shown an inability to self-edit.

If you will be combining your trip to Havana with visits to other Caribbean islands, check out *Eastern Caribbean*, by Glenda Bendure and Ned Friary, a practical guide to the Windward and Leeward Islands.

Bahamas, Turks & Caicos and *Jamaica*, both by Christopher P Baker; *Mexico*, by John Noble, Michele Matter, Nancy Keller, Daniel C Schechter, James Lyon and Scott Doggett; and *Dominican Republic & Haiti*, by Scott Doggett and Leah Gordon, should prove useful to travelers passing through those countries.

Scuba divers should pick up a copy of the Lonely Planet Pisces guide, *Diving & Snorkeling Cuba*, by Diana Williams, which describes 61 dive sites from the underwater valleys of Isla de la Juventud to the wrecks off Varadero.

Guidebooks

Yachties will want to order *The Cruising Guide to Cuba*, by Simon Charles. This handy little volume includes sketch maps of all of the main anchorages and lots of practical tips for both yacht owners and charterers. Only a foolish mariner would sail into Cuban waters without it. It is published by Cruising Guide Publications (☎ 727-733-5322, 800-330-9542, fax 727-734-8179), Box 1017, Dunedin, FL 34697-1017, USA.

Travel

Pico Iyer includes some amusing impressions of Cuba in his travelogue *Falling Off the Map: Some Lonely Places of the World* (1994). Iyer's first novel, *Cuba and the Night* (1996), is also set here.

In *The Reader's Companion to Cuba* (1997), editors Alan Ryan and Christa Malone have gathered together some of the finest writing about Cuba by 23 famous travelers, including John Muir, Frederic Remington, Graham Greene, Mark Kurlansky, and Carlo Gébler.

Trading with the Enemy: A Yankee Travels Through Castro's Cuba (1996), by Tom Miller, is a rich feast of Cuban lore gleaned during eight months of perceptive travel. It may just be the best travel book about Cuba ever written.

Jerzy Adamuszek claims that in 1994 he became the first person to cycle around Cuba without official permission, and his humorous (and ironic) book *Cuba Is Not Only Varadero* (1997) is the result.

Stephen Smith's *The Land of Miracles* (1998) is another intriguing travelogue, this one by a British writer who toured Cuba in an old American car. His encounters with inept émigrés in the Everglades and Santería devotees in Cuba stir our imagination, but most of all, Smith wants to meet Fidel.

In *Ay, Cuba!: A Socio-Erotic Journey* (1999), by Andrei Codrescu, a Romanian writer visits 'the laboratory of pre–postcommunism' and finds important differences between the island nation and how his own homeland was in 1989.

Australian photographer Tania Jovanovic has put together a lively photographic essay called *Cuba: Que Bola!* (1999). Cuba's peeling paint, ghostly limousines, musical rhythms, and Santería rites are all skillfully portrayed in Jovanovic's images.

History & Politics

Cuba, or The Pursuit of Freedom (1971; updated in 1998), by Hugh Thomas, is a monumental 1696-page history of Cuba from 1762 to 1962. Though hostile to the revolution, it's a valuable reference source on almost everything that happened during that period. Leslie Bethell's *Cuba: A Short History* (1993) is a readable summary of events that took place between 1750 and 1992.

Herbert L Matthews, the *New York Times* editorial writer who interviewed Fidel Castro in the Sierra Maestra in 1957, sympathetically evaluates personalities, motivations, and achievements in *Revolution in Cuba* (1975; out of print). Matthews writes that 'the coverage of the Castro Revolution in the American news media has been one of the greatest failures in the history of American journalism.' Matthews' own writings were truly a candle in the darkness.

Castro: A Biography of Fidel Castro (1986; out of print), by Peter B Bourne, is a primary source for understanding the Castro era. *Face to Face with Fidel Castro* (1993), the transcript of an interview that Castro granted Nicaraguan writer Tomás Borge, presents Castro's opinions on a wide range of topics. In *My Early Years* (1998), Castro himself reflects on his childhood, youth and student activism.

Two outstanding biographies of 'El Che' are *Che Guevara: A Revolutionary Life* (1997), by Jon Lee Anderson, and *Compañero: The Life and Death of Che Guevara* (1998), by Jorge G Castañeda. *Che in Africa* (1999), by William Gálvez, tells the little-known story of Guevara's 1965 guerrilla campaign in the Congo. Guevara himself wrote a number of books, including *Guerrilla Warfare* (1960), *Reminiscences of the Cuban Revolutionary War* (1963) and *Socialism and Man in Cuba* (1965).

Thomas G Paterson's *Contesting Castro* (1995) is a detailed look at American-Cuban relations during the 1950s, with important clues as to what went wrong. For a view of the American economic embargo, see *Cruel and Unusual Punishment: The US Blockade of Cuba* (1993), by Mary Murray. Jane Franklin's *Cuba and the United States: A Chronological History* (1997) provides a day-by-day record of developments between 1959 and 1995.

Cuba: Talking About Revolution (1997) is a provocative discussion of the Cuban situation between Cuban intellectual Juan Antonio Blanco and American aid worker Medea Benjamin. Blanco sees the American obsession with Cuba as an inevitable result of Cuba's continuing defiance of American authority, which must be punished as a warning to others.

General

Dreaming in Cuban (1993), by Cristina García, is an intriguing novel about the real and imaginary worlds affecting relationships in a Cuban family. The characters are torn between differing outlooks in a compelling tale strongly influenced by Afro-Cuban religious beliefs. Migene González-Wippler's *Santería: La Religion* (1999) is a treasure trove of trivia on the subject.

Graham Greene's *Our Man in Havana* (1958) is an entertaining story about a British vacuum cleaner salesman who enlists in the British secret service to earn money to support his daughter's expensive tastes. To justify his stipend, he pretends to recruit subagents and sends in bogus reports that mysteriously begin to come true. Another classic is Hemingway's *The Old Man and the Sea* (1952), the simple but powerful story of a Cuban fisherman's fight with a great fish.

Cuba: Five Hundred Years of Images (1992), by Jorge Guillermo, is a *National Geographic*–style assessment of Cuba's colonial history. The color photography by Brynn Bruyn conveys the flavor of the period. *National Geographic* magazine ·itself published remarkably equitable feature articles on Cuba in its January 1977, August 1989, August 1991, and June 1999 issues.

Cuba: World Bibliographical Series, Volume 75 (1996), by Jean Stubbs, contains critical reviews of 900 important books about Cuba.

Cookbooks

There are at least three interesting cookbooks involving Cuban cuisine. *Cuban Flavor: Typical Creole Cuisine Recipes* (1999), by Nitza Villapol, contains not only dozens of recipes, but color photos showing how many of the meals ought to be presented. It's written in English and can often be found in Havana's bookstores.

Old Havana Cookbook (1999) contains recipes in Spanish and English compiled by the editors of Hippocrene Books. The publisher is in New York, but the book can occasionally be found in Havana.

Afro-Cuban Cuisine: Its Myths and Legends (1998), by Natalia Bolívar Aróstegui and Carmen González Díaz de Villegas, is a fascinating book that contains descriptions of traditional Cuban meals in addition to legends surrounding their origins. It's in English, available in Havana's bookstores.

Also often found in Havana is a pocket-size guide entitled *My Cuban Cocktail Recipe Book* (1997), by Ramón Pedreira Rodríguez, which describes in English how to make scores of drinks that probably taste as delicious as their names sound, among them Rainbow, Golden Sands, Kiss, White Witch and South Coast.

Specialist Publishers

An optimum source of books in English about Cuba is Ocean Press (☎ 61-3-9372-2683, fax 61-3-9372-1765, ocean_press@msn.com.au), GPO Box 3279, Melbourne, Victoria 3001, Australia. In the US its 35 Cuba-related titles can be ordered by contacting Ocean Press (☎ 201-617-7247, fax 201-617-0203), Box 834, Hoboken, NJ 07030, USA.

Another excellent resource is Pathfinder (☎ 212-741-0690, fax 212-727-0150), 410 West St, New York, NY 10014, USA. It publishes numerous autobiographical books by Che Guevara and Fidel Castro.

The Center for Cuban Studies (☎ 212-242-0559, www.cubaupdate.org), 124 W 23rd St, New York, NY 10011, USA, carries many titles looking at the subject of Cuban-American relations.

FILMS

Joseph Mankiewicz's 1955 version of the musical *Guys and Dolls* has a scene with gamblers Frank Sinatra and Marlon Brando vying for the attention of Jean Simmons in prerevolutionary Havana.

In 1964 Soviet director Mikhail Kalatozov made what has become the classic of the revolution, *I Am Cuba.* Shot in Spanish, the film was dubbed into Russian, and it's now available with English subtitles. The cinematography is exhilarating, and if you can see only one film about Cuba, this should be it.

Sydney Pollack's 1990 film *Havana* is set in the last days of the Batista regime, as high-stakes American gambler Robert Redford falls in love with the wife of an imprisoned revolutionary. Panned by the critics as a takeoff on Casablanca, this tantalizing glimpse of a turning point in Cuban history will delight anyone who has ever been to Havana.

Randa Haines' *Dance With Me* (1998) contrasts dancing styles in the tale of a Cuban émigré who opens another world for competition ballroom dancer Vanessa Williams. It's a charming introduction to Cuban dancing. German director Wim Wenders does something similar for Cuban music in *Buena Vista Social Club* (1999), which documents a group of aging Cuban musicians who have taken traditional Cuban music to the world.

CD ROM

At US$40, the CD ROM *Che por siempre,* sold at the Museo de la Revolución in Havana and elsewhere, is an exceptional purchase. It includes 500 pages of text, including Che's Bolivian diary, speeches, maps, photos, 30 minutes of video, and another 30 minutes of sounds and song, including the original version of Carlos Puebla's song *Hasta Siempre, Comandante Che Guevara.*

NEWSPAPERS & MAGAZINES
Government Publications

All media is operated by the government. The national newspaper *Granma* is the official organ of the Communist Party of Cuba, published Tuesday to Saturday. The paper was founded in 1963 through the merger of two former papers, *Revolución* and *Hoy*, and was named for the motor vessel *Granma*, which carried Fidel Castro's band from Mexico to Cuba in 1956 (the name of the boat itself means 'grandmother'). Many other former daily newspapers are now published only weekly due to paper shortages. Even *Granma* itself sells out quickly, so get in line whenever you see it being sold. Even if you can't read Spanish, it makes a good souvenir and the cultural listings are easy to decipher.

Granma Internacional (US$0.50), a weekly summary of the Cuban press, is published in Spanish, English, French, Portuguese and German. It's possible to subscribe by sending a check or money order for US$40 to *Granma Internacional*, Apartado 6260, CP 10699 Havana, Cuba; or you can fax them at 537-33-5176. In the US, Pathfinder Books (☎ 212-741-0690) takes *Granma* subscriptions for US$40 a year.

Other Havana newspapers include *Trabajadores*, the organ of the Central de Trabajadores de Cuba (published Monday); *Juventud Rebelde* (Wednesday to Sunday); *Tribuna de La Habana* (Sunday); and *El Habanero* (Tuesday and Friday). Among the many provincial weekly newspapers are *Guerrillero* (Pinar del Río), *Girón* (Matanzas), *5 de Septiembre* (Cienfuegos), *Vanguardia* (Santa Clara), *Adelante* (Camagüey), *Ahora* (Holguín), *Sierra Maestra* (Santiago de Cuba) and *Victoria* (Isla de la Juventud).

Bohemia (☎ 81-1431, fax 33-5511), Av de la Independencia No 575, at San Pedro, Plaza de la Revolución, 10696 Havana, is a Cuban newsmagazine published weekly in Spanish.

Cuba's monthly business magazine is *Business Tips on Cuba* (☎ 24-1797, fax 24-1799, www.tips.cu). It's packed with useful information on investment opportunities in Cuba, and there are simultaneous editions in English, French, Spanish, Italian, German, Portuguese and Russian.

The tourism magazine *Prisma* is published every other month in English and Spanish by Prensa Latina (www.prensa-latina.cu). The monthly lifestyle magazine *Habanera* also carries summaries in English. Copies of these are available at airport kiosks and the main hotels.

Foreign Publications

For information on Cuba, read the *CUBA Update*, published quarterly by the Center for Cuban Studies (☎ 212-242-0559, fax 212-242-1937), 124 W 23rd St, New York, NY 10011, USA. It costs US$35 a year to US addresses (or US$50 with membership included). The center's stated goal is 'contributing to a normalization of relations between Cuba and the US.'

Target Research puts out the monthly *CubaNews* (☎ 202-543-5076, fax 301-421-9810, www.cubanews.com), 611 Pennsylvania Ave SE, No 341, Washington, DC 20003, USA, a surprisingly evenhanded and comprehensive monthly report on the Cuban economy formerly published by the *Miami Herald*. As the US$399 annual subscription rate indicates, it's aimed mostly at top executives who need reliable information on which to base critical business decisions. A detailed index of previous issues is sent to subscribers twice a year.

RICK GERHARTER

Cuba's official news source, *Granma*

Similar but less expensive is Jim Hitchie's monthly *Cuban Investment Letter* (☎ 604-929-9694, fax 604-929-3694, jhitchie@direct.ca), Box 30003, North Vancouver, BC V7H 2Y8, Canada. It provides detailed business news and valuable tips on investment opportunities. The US$125 annual subscription includes frequent emailed summaries of wire service reports on Cuba.

Another excellent source of political and economic news about Cuba is the monthly *Cuban Review* (☎ 31-20-615-1122, fax 31-20-615-1120, cubanreview@globalreflexion.org), Box 59262, 1040 KG Amsterdam, Netherlands. Subscriptions for individuals are 35 euros a year. Most of the stories are written by Cuban journalists working in the official media, but it's fairly balanced and informative.

RADIO & TV

National TV programming dates from the 1950s, and today there are two Havana-based national channels, Tele Rebelde (on the air 6:30 to 8:30 am and 7 pm to midnight weekdays, 7 to 9 am and 4 pm to 1 am Saturday, and 1 pm to midnight Sunday) and CubaVision (noon to 1 pm and 6 pm to midnight weekdays, 4:30 pm to 1:30 am Saturday, and 10 am to midnight Sunday). Local TV stations such as CH-TV in Havana are broadcast over the same channels from 6 to 7 pm before the national programs come on the air.

Tele Rebelde specializes in news and sports, and sometimes carries programs produced by CNN or other foreign networks. CubaVision features movies, soap operas, and documentaries. Both channels broadcast a 30-minute news report at 12:30 and 8 pm weekdays and at 1 and 8 pm weekends, although foreigners will find it boring due to the emphasis on industrial and agricultural production reports. Many visitors will be grateful to note that at least there isn't any advertising.

There are cable television sets in most of Havana's hotel rooms, typically showing CNN, HBO and Deutsche Welle.

Havana's most famous radio station may be Radio Reloj (950 kHz AM and 101.5 MHz FM), which gives the time each minute 24 hours a day. It's a good station for Spanish-language news, and on weekends there are in-depth reports.

Radio Rebelde (640 kHz and 710 kHz AM, and 96.7 MHz FM) also provides news and interviews, along with other varied programming. Its call-in contests are extremely popular. Radio Progreso (640 kHz AM and 90.3 MHz FM) is also immensely popular for its afternoon soap operas and humorous programs.

Radio Metropolitana (910 kHz AM and 98.3 MHz FM) caters to middle-age listeners with 1950s music and traditional boleros. Cadena Habana (1140 kHz AM and 99.9 MHz FM) is similar.

Radio Ciudad de la Habana (820 kHz AM and 94.9 MHz FM) is more youth oriented, with Cuban music during the day and foreign pop in the evening.

Instrumental classical music is the usual fare at Radio Enciclopedia (1290 kHz AM and 94.1 MHz FM) and Radio Musical Nacional (590 kHz AM and 99.1 MHz FM).

Cuba's Two-Channel Government

Although tourists can watch CNN, HBO and at least one south Florida television station in their Havana hotel rooms, the average Cuban is not allowed to own a satellite dish or an antenna that could receive foreign programs. Havana police, armed with binoculars, are quick to spot and destroy unauthorized TV antennas. As a result, Habaneros are able to watch only two state-run stations, one of which seems to broadcast Fidel Castro's every move. Ironically, the situation is not unlike the 1950s, when Fulgencio Batista's police forbade listening to Radio Rebelde (Rebel Radio) from the Sierra Maestra.

SEÑORES IMPERIALISTAS ¡No LES TENEMOS ABSOLUTAMENTE NINGUN MIEDO!

From 3 to 9 pm, Habana Radio (106.9 MHz FM) offers cultural information relating to La Habana Vieja.

Finally, you can listen to programming in English, French and Spanish over Radio Taíno (1290 kHz AM and 93.3 MHz FM), Cuba's national tourism station. Radio Taíno often provides a good introduction to Cuban music and culture. A special youth program broadcast nightly from 5 to 7 pm provides up-to-the-minute information on live performances around town, airs interviews with well-known musicians, and plays great salsa music.

PHOTOGRAPHY & VIDEO
Film & Equipment
Kodak color print film is readily available in Havana, costing as much as US$7.70 for a roll of 24 or US$8.90 for a roll of 36. You can buy film at most hotel and tourist shops, but it's much cheaper at any of the many Photo Service branches around town. Photo Service also develops color print film, sells the most common camera batteries, and has a small selection of other materials. Rather than hoping to find film, batteries, and lens-cleaning tissue in Havana, however, it's better to bring your own supplies with you from home.

Video Systems
Travel videos are sold in various formats in Havana, so it's important that you know what format your VCR back home requires. As a general rule, you'll need NTSC for North America, PAL for Britain, Germany, Japan, and Australia, and SECAM for France. In Cuba, the NTSC system is in common use.

Technical Tips
Your greatest potential disappointment when you get your processed photographs of your trip is a washed-out look. This is due to overexposure. The bright tropical light can fool even the most sophisticated light-metering systems.

To avoid this problem, consider purchasing a polarizing filter. A polarizing filter is primarily used to darken a pale blue sky and to remove reflections from glass and water surfaces. No serious photographer would visit an island without one. The filter is mounted on your lens and can be rotated within a ring. Its position determines the effectiveness of the polarizer. At a right angle to the sun, the effect is greatest, heightening the contrasts so that the subject is clearly visible – removing, for example, the glare off the ocean and bringing the sailboat you're aiming at into sharp focus.

If you intend to take most of your photos outside during daylight hours, consider purchasing a 'slow' film, which will provide the best color rendition. Fujichrome Velvia is the pro's choice among slide films, followed closely by Kodachrome 25 and 64. For print film, avoid film with an ISO higher than 100.

Restrictions
Taking photos of military facilities, soldiers and factories is not permitted. Photography inside museums used to be prohibited, but now that museums charge admission, many allow it. It's always wise to ask first.

Photographing People
Most Cubans love to have their pictures taken and will happily pose if you ask '*¿Puedo tomar una foto?*' (Can I take a photo?). Be prepared to have your subjects quickly write out their names and addresses on a piece of paper with the request that you mail them prints, which is fun to do. Only museum attendants ask money for the right to take photos.

Airport Security
It's a good idea to avoid sending your film through airport X-ray machines. While most modern machines won't damage your film, there's no point in taking the chance. Most security personnel will hand inspect your film if you ask them to, removing the necessity of having it X-rayed. Don't forget to have your camera hand-inspected if it has film inside.

TIME
Havana is five hours behind GMT/UTC, the equivalent of Eastern Standard Time in the

USA and Canada. If it's noon in Havana it will be 6 pm in continental Western Europe, 5 pm in Britain, 11 am in Mexico City, 9 am in California and 5 am in New Zealand.

Havana is on daylight saving time from April to September, during which Havana is only four hours behind GMT/UTC. In other words, clocks are turned an hour back at the beginning of October and an hour forward in late March.

ELECTRICITY
Voltage & Cycle
The most common electrical voltage in Havana is 110 volts, 60 cycles, the same as in North America. Confusingly, however, some of the newer hotels operate on 220 volts, and in some hotel rooms one outlet will supply 220 volts and another, 110 volts. It's usually the outlet supplying the air conditioner that is 220 volts, but always check carefully before plugging in any electrical appliance. If you can't live without your hair drier or electric shaver, bring along a transformer to convert to the other voltage, just in case.

Plugs & Sockets
North American–style plugs and outlets are the norm, although in some hotels you'll still see the two-round-holes type. Generally, if your plug has anything other than two flat parallel prongs, you'll also need to bring a plug adapter, as none is available in Havana.

WEIGHTS & MEASURES
Cuba uses the metric system. Occasionally one hears references to American and old Spanish measurements, such as an American gallon (3.785 liters), an arroba (25 Spanish pounds or 11.5kg), a caballería (13.4 hecares), a besana (0.625 acres), a cordel (a tenth of an acre or 0.04 hectares), a quintal (100 Spanish pounds or 46kg) and a vara (one yard).

LAUNDRY
There are no coin laundries in Havana, but most hotels offer a laundry service at reasonable cost. In many places, it's easier to use the sink in your room to wash small

clothes and then hang them in the shower to dry. In Havana, however, the humidity is so high that clothes often become mildewy before they dry if not hung in direct sunlight.

TOILETS
Be advised that many restaurants do not have toilets for patrons. When they do, the men's room has a sign reading *hombres* or *señores*, the women's room a sign reading *mujeres* or *señoras*. Service attendants can be found in the bathrooms of many upscale restaurants and hotels. They spend their days beside small plates, hoping for tips to augment their meager wages.

LUGGAGE STORAGE
There are no lockers at Havana's international airport nor at its bus and train stations. Most of the upscale hotels will let you store your stuff for at least several hours – if you ask while extending a tip (a couple of dollars will suffice). Several hours might not sound like much time, but if you've arrived in town without a hotel reservation and are finding it difficult to find a room, you might want to drop off your bags at an upscale hotel, explain that you're looking for less-expensive lodging and continue your search. Then, when you find a room, come back and claim your bags. This tactic might seem cumbersome, but it's a whole lot less cumbersome than hauling your luggage around town.

HEALTH
Compared with the rest of Latin America, the medical facilities available to both travelers and local residents here are excellent. Hospital emergency departments are open around the clock, and first visits to the doctor, at both hotel infirmaries and public hospitals, are usually free of charge.

Travel health depends greatly on your predeparture preparations, your day-to-day health care while traveling, and how you handle any medical problem or emergency that does develop. While the list of potential dangers that follows can be disconcerting, few travelers to Havana experience more than upset stomachs and sunburn. We provide this information for reference in case of need, although for most visitors it will constitute only entertaining poolside reading.

Predeparture Preparations

Immunizations Vaccinations provide protection against diseases you might meet along the way. The only immunizations currently necessary to enter Cuba are for yellow fever and cholera, and only if you're coming from a country where there's an epidemic of either disease.

Most travelers from developed countries will have been immunized against various diseases during childhood, but your doctor may still recommend booster shots against tetanus and measles. You should also be immunized against hepatitis.

Other Preparations Make sure you're healthy before you start traveling. If you wear glasses, take a spare pair and your prescription, as losing your glasses can be a real dilemma. If you require a specific medication, take an adequate supply, as it probably won't be available locally.

Basic Rules

Care in what you eat and drink is the most important health rule; stomach upsets are the most likely travel health problem, but the majority of these upsets will be relatively minor. Don't become paranoid; after all, trying the local food is part of the experience of travel.

Water The water in Havana cannot be trusted. Drink only bottled water there (ie, no tap water), and be sure to ask for it without ice. Bottled water or soft drinks are safe and readily available at hotel shops. Take care with fruit juice, particularly if water may have been added. Tea or coffee should be OK, since the water should have been boiled.

Food Thoroughly cooked food is safest, but not if it has been left to cool or if it has been reheated. Shellfish such as mussels, oysters and clams should be avoided unless they're

Medical Kit Check List

Following is a list of items you should consider including in your medical kit – consult your pharmacist for brands available in your country.

❑ **Aspirin or paracetamol** (acetaminophen in the USA) – for pain or fever

❑ **Antihistamine** – for allergies, eg, hay fever; to ease the itch from insect bites or stings; and to prevent motion sickness

❑ **Cold and flu tablets, throat lozenges and nasal decongestant**

❑ **Multivitamins** – consider for long trips, when dietary vitamin intake may be inadequate

❑ **Antibiotics** – consider including these if you're traveling well off the beaten track; see your doctor, as they must be prescribed, and carry the prescription with you

❑ **Loperamide or diphenoxylate** – 'blockers' for diarrhea

❑ **Prochlorperazine or metaclopramide** – for nausea and vomiting

❑ **Rehydration mixture** – to prevent dehydration, which may occur, for example, during bouts of diarrhea; particularly important when traveling with children

❑ **Insect repellent, sunscreen, lip balm and eye drops**

❑ **Calamine lotion, sting relief spray or aloe vera** – to ease irritation from sunburn and insect bites or stings

❑ **Antifungal cream or powder** – for fungal skin infections and thrush

❑ **Antiseptic (such as povidone-iodine)** – for cuts and grazes

❑ **Bandages, Band-Aids (plasters) and other wound dressings**

❑ **Water purification tablets or iodine**

❑ **Scissors, tweezers and a thermometer** – note that mercury thermometers are prohibited by airlines

❑ **Sterile kit** – in case you need injections in a country with medical hygiene problems; discuss with your doctor

served in a high-class restaurant, as should undercooked meat, particularly in the form of mince or ground beef. Steaming does not make bad shellfish safe for eating.

Climatic & Geographical Considerations

Sunburn You can get sunburned surprisingly quickly in Havana, even on a cloudy day. Use a sunscreen with a minimum sun protection factor of 15. A hat provides added protection, and you should consider using zinc cream or some other barrier cream for your nose and lips. Calamine lotion or aloe gel are good for mild sunburn.

Prickly Heat Prickly heat is an itchy rash caused by excessive perspiration trapped under the skin. It usually strikes people who have just arrived in Havana from a cooler country and whose pores have not yet opened sufficiently to cope with greater sweating. Keeping cool by bathing often, using a mild talcum powder, and even resorting to air-conditioning may help until you acclimatize.

Diseases of Poor Sanitation

Diarrhea Despite all your precautions you may still have a mild bout of traveler's diarrhea, but a few rushed toilet trips with no other symptoms is not indicative of a serious problem. Moderate diarrhea, involving half a dozen loose bowel movements in a day, is more of a nuisance.

Dehydration is the main danger with any diarrhea – children dehydrate particularly quickly. Fluid replacement remains the mainstay of management. Weak black tea with a little sugar, soda water, or soft drinks allowed to go flat and diluted 50% with bottled water are all good.

Lomotil or Imodium can be used to bring relief from the symptoms, although they do not actually cure the problem. Use these drugs only when absolutely necessary – that is, if you must travel. Antibiotics may be needed for diarrhea that lasts for more than five days, or that is severe, or for watery diarrhea with fever and lethargy or with blood and mucus (gut-paralyzing drugs like

Imodium or Lomotil should be avoided in this situation). Alcohol must be avoided during treatment and for 48 hours afterward.

Hepatitis Hepatitis A is spread by contaminated food or water. The symptoms are fever, chills, headache, fatigue, feelings of weakness and aches and pains, followed by loss of appetite, nausea, vomiting, abdominal pain, dark urine, light-colored feces, jaundiced skin and possible yellowing of the whites of the eyes. If you come down with hepatitis A, you should seek medical advice, but in general there is not much you can do apart from resting, drinking lots of fluids, eating lightly and avoiding fatty foods.

Hepatitis B is spread through contact with infected blood, blood products or bodily fluids – especially through sexual contact, unsterilized needles and blood transfusions. The symptoms of type B are much the same as type A, except that they are more severe and may lead to irreparable liver damage or even liver cancer. Although there is no treatment for hepatitis B, an effective prophylactic vaccine is readily available in most countries.

Typhoid Typhoid fever is another gut infection that travels the fecal-oral route – contaminated water and food are responsible. In its early stages typhoid resembles many other illnesses, and in the second week a high fever and slow pulse continue and a few pink spots may appear on the body; trembling, delirium, weakness, weight loss and dehydration are other symptoms. If there are no further complications, the fever and other symptoms will slowly diminish during the third week. Still, medical help is essential since pneumonia (acute infection of the lungs) or peritonitis (perforated bowel) are common complications, and typhoid is very infectious. Keep the victim cool and hydrated.

Diseases Spread by Animals & People

Tetanus This potentially fatal disease is found throughout the Tropics. It's difficult to treat, but is preventable with immunization. Tetanus occurs when a wound becomes infected by a germ that lives in the feces of animals or people. Clean all cuts, punctures or animal bites. Tetanus is also known as lockjaw, and the first symptom may be discomfort in swallowing, or stiffening of the jaw and neck; this is followed by painful convulsions of the jaw and whole body.

Sexually Transmitted Diseases
STDs are spread through sexual contact with an infected partner. Abstinence is the only 100% preventative, but using condoms is also effective. Gonorrhea and syphilis are common STDs; sores, blisters or rashes around the genitals, discharges, or pain when urinating are common symptoms. Symptoms may be less marked or not observed at all in women. Syphilis symptoms eventually disappear completely, but the disease continues and can cause severe problems in later years. The treatment of gonorrhea and syphilis is by antibiotics. There is no cure for herpes, which causes blisters, or for HIV.

HIV/AIDS Authorities in Havana report a low incidence rate of HIV, the human immunodeficiency virus, and AIDS, acquired immune deficiency syndrome (*SIDA* in Spanish). However, the risk of catching this virus, transmitted by bodily fluids, from a prostitute is quite high, and in Havana many of the women one meets in tourist areas also sell sex.

Apart from abstinence, the most effective defense against HIV is to practice safer sex using condoms and dams, and to not share hypodermic needles with anybody. The Chinese condoms (preservativos) available in most Cuban pharmacies are of low quality and unreliable; foreigners should bring their own.

Because it's impossible to detect the HIV status of an otherwise healthy-looking person without a blood test, the golden rule must be 'safer sex or no sex.'

Women's Health
Poor diet, lowered resistance due to the use of antibiotics, and contraceptive pills can all lead to vaginal infections when traveling in hot climates. Wearing skirts or loose-fitting trousers and cotton underwear will help to prevent infections.

Yeast infections, characterized by a rash, itch and discharge, can be treated with a diluted vinegar or lemon-juice douche, or with yogurt. Trichomoniasis is a more serious infection; symptoms are a discharge and a burning sensation when urinating. Sexual partners must also be treated. If a vinegar-water douche is not effective, seek medical attention.

WOMEN TRAVELERS
Women in Havana are the object of great attention from local men, regardless of whether they are foreign or Cuban. That is particularly true of unaccompanied women, who should be prepared to receive plenty of direct comments and animal sounds directed at them. Although this behavior would be considered sexual harassment in an Anglo-Saxon setting, in Latin America it's considered a form of flattery. A Cuban woman responds to it by ignoring it, unless she found something attractive about the source of the attention.

A supplementary book that may be useful is *Handbook for Women Travelers*, by Maggie & Jemma Moss. There are other books devoted to this topic as well; ask at your local bookstore. Any practical advice for women from women travelers is much appreciated.

Attitudes Toward Women
Generally, women travelers will find Havana safe and pleasant to visit. This is not to say that machismo is a thing of the past. On the contrary, it is very much alive and practiced. Local men occasionally make flirtatious comments, whistle and hiss at single women – both Cuban and foreign – although the extent of this behavior is much less prevalent than elsewhere in Latin America. Women traveling together are not exempt from this attention. Cuban women usually deal with this by looking away and completely ignoring the man, which works reasonably well for gringas, too. Women

who firmly ignore unwanted verbal advances are often treated with respect.

Women who speak Spanish find that it is easier to deal with traveling and with the persistent (and often well-meant) questions: 'Where are you from? How old are you? What do you study/do for work? Are you married/do you have a boyfriend?' The subjects vary little. Some single women claim to be married or have steady boyfriends. Some wear a wedding ring and carry a photo of their 'husband.' A useful phrase in Spanish is *¡No me molestes!* (Don't bother me!), but only use it if someone is truly bothering you. It's a forceful expression that isn't always warranted.

Safety Precautions

Traveling with another woman gives you some measure of psychological support, at the very least. Traveling with a man tends to minimize the attention that Cuban men direct toward you.

Rape is a threat worldwide. To reduce your risk of it, avoid dark streets at night if traveling alone and don't get into a car or wander off with someone if you feel any sense of danger. Other suggestions include carrying a metal whistle (in your hand, not in your backpack). This produces a piercing blast and will startle off most would-be rapists long enough for a woman to get away.

GAY & LESBIAN TRAVELERS

The Cuban view of homosexuality has changed since the early 1960s, when openly gay men were forced into labor camps for 'rehabilitation.' Homosexuality is now more or less accepted, although same-sex couples would be wise to keep public displays of affection to a minimum.

A few gay and lesbian gathering spots have been established, but a straight person probably wouldn't recognize these places as such unless it were pointed out to them. Gay bars and clubs don't really exist on a permanent basis. To connect with private parties, called 'fiestas de diez pesos' (for the cost of admission), one just has to meet the right people in order to be invited. See the boxed text 'Meeting Gays & Lesbians in Havana' in the Entertainment chapter for more information.

DISABLED TRAVELERS

Havana is a tough city for blind folks and people in wheelchairs. Most of the city's curbs have not been modified to facilitate wheelchairs, sidewalks are usually in fair condition when they exist at all, and extra-wide stalls are rarely found in public bathrooms. Braille, in hotel elevators or anywhere else, is still years away; same with street lights that beep to inform the sightless that the traffic signal has changed.

Most hotels in Havana were not designed with disabled travelers in mind and adequate steps to correct the oversight haven't been taken. The Hotel Deauville, for example, has only stairs leading to its lobby and there is no secondary entrance. Among the wheelchair-friendly hotels in town are the Santa Isabel, Ambos Mundo and the Florida in La Habana Vieja; the Golden Tulip Parque Central, the Inglaterra and the Plaza in Centro Habana; and the hotels Riviera, Meliá Cohiba and the Habana Libre in Vedado.

Organizations

There are a number of organizations and tour providers around the world that specialize in the needs of disabled travelers.

In Australia, try Independent Travelers (☎ 08-232-2555), at 167 Gilles St, Adelaide, SA 5000.

In the UK, try RADAR (☎ 020-7250-3222) 250 City Rd, London, or Mobility International (☎ 020-7403-5688).

In the USA, try Mobility International USA (☎ 541-343-1284, fax 541-343-6812), a program that advises disabled travelers on mobility issues and runs an educational exchange program. Write them at PO Box 10767, Eugene, OR 97440.

Also in the USA, you can try the Society for the Advancement of Travel for the Handicapped (SATH; ☎ 212-447-7284), 347 5th Ave No 610, New York, NY 10016.

Twin Peaks Press (☎ 360-694-2462, 800-637-2256) publishes several useful handbooks for disabled travelers, including *Travel for the Disabled* and *Directory of Travel Agencies for the Disabled*. Write to them at PO Box 129, Vancouver, WA 98666, USA.

HAVANA FOR CHILDREN

Havana's chief attraction is its old section, which is best explored on foot. Let's be honest, Havana is no Disneyland: Havana is wandering the streets of a city, admiring the architecture, the museums, the many music venues. The city just isn't a lot of fun for children.

But with a policeman at every corner and crimes against foreign children virtually unheard of in Havana, it's as good a city as any to which to bring youngsters. Their biggest danger is by motorized vehicles; don't give your toddler the opportunity to wander out into a street.

Most tour companies offer reduced prices for children under the age of 12, provided they share the accommodations of their parents. Only a token amount is charged for children under the age of two. Families can often get a room for the double price if the children are young. Note that electrical safety in the room may be poor; parents should inspect appliances and wiring.

HELPFUL ORGANIZATIONS

The following groups work to foster better relations between Cuba and their respective countries. Most publish newsletters, hold social or cultural evenings and organize educational tours to Cuba. They're well worth contacting if your interests go beyond a beach holiday.

Australia
Australia-Cuba Friendship Society (☎ 61-3-9857-9249, fax 61-3-9857-6598), PO Box 1051, Collingwood, Victoria 3066

Canada
Canadian-Cuban Friendship Association (☎ 1-416-742-6931, fax 1-416-744-6143, www.lefca.com/ccfatoronto), PO Box 743, Station F, Toronto, Ontario M4Y 2N6

France
Association Cuba Si (☎ 33-1-4515-1143, fax 33-1-4515-1144), 20 Rue Denis-Papin, 94200 Ivry-sur-Seine

Italy
Associazione di Amicizia Italia-Cuba (☎ 39-02-8646-3483), Via Foscolo 3, 20121 Milano

New Zealand
Cuban Friendship Society (☎/fax 64-3-365-6055, 100250.1511@compuserve.com), 3 Oakdale St, Christchurch (10035.3205@compuserve.com), PO Box 6716, Wellesley St, Auckland (helenr@clear.net.nz), PO Box 104, Raglan, Hamilton

UK
Cuba Solidarity Campaign (☎ 44-20-7263 6452, fax 44-20-7561 0191, www.cuba-solidarity.org.uk), c/o Red Rose Club, 129 Seven Sisters Rd, London N7 7QG

USA
Center for Cuban Studies (☎ 1-212-242-0559, fax 1-212-242-1937, www.cubaupdate.org), 124 W 23rd St, New York, NY 10011
Global Exchange (☎ 1-415-255-7296, fax 1-415-255-7498, www.globalexchange.org), 2017 Mission St, room 303, San Francisco, CA 94110
USA/Cuba-Infomed (☎ 1-408-243-4359, fax 1-408-243-1229, www.igc.org/cubasoli), PO Box 450, Santa Clara, CA 95052

LIBRARIES

The main city library is the Biblioteca Pública Provincial Rubén M Villena, Obispo No 59, at Baratillo. It's open 8 am to 9 pm weekdays, 9 am to 4 pm Saturday.

The Biblioteca Nacional José Martí, Av de la Independencia, on the Plaza de la Revolución, is also open to the public, but you must leave your bags in a cloak room. Its hours are 8 am to 5:45 pm Monday to Saturday.

CULTURAL CENTERS

Cultural events frequently take place at the Fundación Alejo Carpentier (☎ 61-3667), Empedrado No 215, not far from the Plaza de la Catedral. It's open from 8:30 am to 4:30 pm weekdays. The foundation is housed within the baroque former palace of the Condessa de la Reunión, which was contructed in the 1820s. Carpentier set his famous novel *El Siglo de las Luces* (published in English as *Explosion in a Cathedral*) in this building.

Also ask about cultural activities at the Instituto Cubano de Amistad con los Pueblos (☎ 55-2395), Paseo No 406, between Calles 17 and 19, in Vedado. It's open 11 am to 11 pm daily. Many cultural and musical events unfold in this elegant mansion constructed in 1926, which also contains a restaurant, bar, and good cigar shop.

French-speaking visitors may wish to visit the Alliance Française (☎ 33-3370), Calle G No 407, between Calles 17 and 19, in Vedado. French films are shown free of charge on video in the library at 11 am Monday, 3 pm Wednesday, and 5 pm Friday. This is a good place to meet Cubans interested in French culture. The Alliance also organizes French courses for local students.

The Casa de las Américas (☎ 55-2707), Calles 3 and G, in Vedado, organizes conferences and exhibitions relating to the music, literature and art of Latin America. Each year the Casa hosts one of the Spanish-speaking world's most prestigious literary contests, with awards in the categories of novel, short story, poetry, essay, narrative, Brazilian literature, and Caribbean literature in English or Creole. An international seminar on Afro-Cuban culture is held here in August. Literary events take place at the Casa quite frequently.

Many important festivals and weekly events are held at the Casa de la Cultura de Plaza (☎ 31-2003), Calzada No 909, at Calle 8 in Vedado.

DANGERS & ANNOYANCES

Havana is an amazingly safe city, and the heavy police presence on the streets can be reassuring. You can walk through neighborhoods in Havana in the middle of the night that you might not enter midday in other capital cities – but that's not to say that we advise it.

Generally, your greatest threat in Havana is yourself. Hustlers play on greed to con people into buying crappy cigars with fancy labels. Beware of people who say they've got a friend inside a cigar factory…and they can sell you fine Cuban cigars cheap. It's the oldest con in Cuba. If something sounds too good to be true, assume that it is.

Prostitutes play on lust, and Havana's working girls can inspire lots of lust. (Male prostitutes are virtually unheard of in Havana.) Bear in mind the health threats associated with casual sexual encounters and that condoms offer limited protection. A condom won't protect its users from genital herpes or other diseases that require only skin-to-skin contact.

Havana's hustlers and beggars generally approach tourists saying 'Where are you from?' or 'Where are you going?' They try to quickly establish a rapport with you and, when they feel the time is right, mention their friend at the cigar factory or tell you a hard-luck story and ask for money. Your best tactic with these people is to communicate quickly that you don't want to talk to them. A polite but firm 'I don't talk with strangers' will usually do the trick.

Beware of people who approach you on the street asking 'What are you looking for?' If you name a site, expect a chipper, 'I can take you there' reply and expect your new acquaintance to start leading the way. If you allow this person to lead you even 10m, you can be sure he'll ask to be paid for his services. A firm I'm not looking for anything, thank you will politely convey to him that you'd like to be left alone.

Waiters and clerks in Havana have been known to overcharge patrons. If your money is important to you, take the time to count your change.

Discrimination

Visitors of non-European descent are more likely to attract the attention of the authorities than is a white person. Tourists of African, Asian and Arab origin have a better chance of being asked to show additional documentation at the airport or of receiving that borderline traffic ticket. Latin visitors with a somewhat Cuban appearance may have to show their passports to enter hotels and other places from which ordinary Cubans are barred.

Cubans of African descent are far more likely to be hassled by the police than are other Cubans. Generally, the lighter a person's skin color in Havana, the better their prospects of being left alone – on the street and in professional life.

Mixed-race couples, especially black/white mixes, face constant problems if they're traveling independently, as the black partner will be taken for a prostitute. Lonely Planet received the following email from a British reader:

I am Caucasian and I'm traveling with my girlfriend who is English and of Jamaican descent. Unfortunately many Cubans assume that she is a *jinetera*, prostitute, who's hanging around with a wealthy tourist! In some provinces, we are met with dirty looks of disapproval, which don't exactly help us relax. Restaurants, tours, and hotels have refused us entry and sometimes don't want to hear our explanation. The police have whistled my girlfriend over when we've been sitting on the beach. It has got to the point where she cannot walk anywhere without her passport ready.

A black traveler posted this comment on Thorn Tree on Lonely Planet's website:

I had trouble all over the place...whites being nicely treated and blacks being asked what the hell they're looking for in whatever establishments. It did get annoying having to excuse my color every day. I eventually figured out that snapping a 'Sorry?' and giving them a good look from top to bottom worked wonders.

EMERGENCIES

The English-speaking staff at Asistur (☎ 33-8527, fax 33-8087), in the Casa del Científico, Paseo de Martí No 212, can help in getting money sent from most countries (except the USA), expedite insurance claims (police report required), arrange rental cars, and book hotel rooms all across Cuba. This is a place to go if you are a victim of crime or need legal advice. The staff may also be able to help if your credit cards aren't accepted in Cuba. Asistur is open 8:30 am to 5:30 pm weekdays, Saturday 8 am to 2 pm.

The Policía Nacional Revolucionaria (☎ 82-0116) is on Picota, between Leonor Pérez and San Isidro, near the Estación Central de Ferrocarril. For an ambulance, call ☎ 40-5093 or 40-5094. The fire department is at ☎ 81-1115. Probably these folks will speak only Spanish.

Most medical problems can be addressed at the Hospital Nacional Hermanos Ameijeiras (☎ 33-5361, fax 33-5036), San Lázaro No 701, at Padre Varela, just off Malecón in Vedado. This modern 900-bed hospital specializes in plastic surgery and other cosmetic operations on foreign patients who pay in hard currency. General medical consultations are possible 8 am to 4 pm weekdays, 8 am to noon Saturday; it costs US$25. Entry is via the lower level below the parking lot off Padre Varela (ask for 'CEDA' in Section N). The hospital bed charge here is US$75 a night (US$40 for accompanying persons).

Farmacia Taquechel, Obispo No 155, next to the Hotel Ambos Mundos, sells Cuban wonder drugs such as the anticholesterol medication PPG. It's open 9:30 am to 6:30 pm daily. Two other old-fashioned pharmacies in the old town are Drogería Johnson, Obispo No 260 near Aguiar, and Drogería Sarrá, Brasil No 261 at Compostela. Both are open 8 am to 9 pm daily. The Sarrá offers service after hours through a small side window.

In Centro Habana there's a pharmacy at San Rafael No 108, behind the Hotel Inglaterra. It's open 8 am to 6 pm weekdays, 8 am to 4 pm Saturday. Farmacia La Central, on Neptuno opposite Hotel Plaza, is open 24 hours.

In Vedado try the pharmacy on Calle 23 at Calle M, which also carries homeopathic medicines. It's open 8 am to 8 pm weekdays, 8 am to 4 pm Saturday.

Most of these pharmacies cater to the Cuban public, and the range of medicines offered is limited. If they can't help you, try the Centro Camilo Cienfuegos (☎ 32-5554), Calle L No 151, at Calle 13, Vedado, which has an excellent dollar pharmacy open 8 am to 7:30 pm daily. There's no sign but it's in the modern seven-story building on the corner.

BUSINESS HOURS

Some offices are open 8:30 am to 5:30 pm Monday to Saturday with a lunch break 12:30 to 1:30 pm, although many stay open continuously 9 am to 5 pm. Offices remain closed every other Saturday. Post offices are generally open 8 am to 6 pm Monday to Saturday. Banks are usually open only 9 am to 3 pm weekdays, closing at noon on the last working day of each month. Cadeca exchange offices are generally open 9 am to 6 pm Monday to Saturday, 9 am to noon Sunday.

Shopping hours are generally 10 am to 5 pm weekdays and 10 am to 2 pm Saturday, although many places open 10 am to 5 pm Monday to Saturday and 10 am to 2 pm Sunday. Pharmacies are generally open 8 am to 8 pm. Museums usually are open 9 am to 5 pm Tuesday to Saturday and 8 am to noon Sunday. Churches are often open only for Mass, although you'll sometimes be let in the back door if you ask around.

PUBLIC HOLIDAYS

Cuba's public holidays are as follows:

January 1 (Liberation Day)

May 1 (Labor Day)

July 25, 26, and 27 (Celebration of the National Rebellion)

October 10 (Day of Cuban Culture)

December 25 (Christmas)

Liberation Day recalls January 1, 1959, when Cuba was liberated from the Batista dictatorship. The national rebellion celebrated in July honors the July 26, 1953, attack on the army barracks in Santiago de Cuba and Bayamo. The Day of Cuban Culture marks the beginning of the First War of Independence on October 10, 1868. On those days most shops, offices and museums are closed.

Other important dates not marked by public holidays but still commemorated include the following:

January 28 (birthday of José Martí)

February 24 (beginning of the 1895 War of Independence)

March 8 (International Women's Day)

March 13 (anniversary of the 1957 attack on Batista's palace)

April 4 (Children's Day)

April 16 (day of the militias)

April 19 (commemoration of the 1961 victory at the Bay of Pigs)

Second Sunday in May (Mother's Day)

May 17 (day of the agrarian reform)

Third Sunday in June (Father's Day)

July 30 (day of the martyrs of the revolution)

August 12 (day of the overthrow of the Machado dictatorship in 1933)

September 28 (anniversary of the founding of the Committees for the Defense of the Revolution in 1960)

October 8 (the day in 1967 on which Che Guevara was murdered)

October 28 (the day in 1959 on which Camilo Cienfuegos was killed in a plane crash)

November 27 (commemoration of eight medical students killed by the Spaniards in 1871)

December 2 (landing of the Granma in Oriente in 1956)

December 7 (anniversary of the death of Antonio Maceo)

Some care should be taken in planning your activities on these days, as schedules could be disrupted slightly.

SPECIAL EVENTS

Carnival is celebrated in Havana in late February and early March and features parades in front of the Capitolio or along the Malecón on Friday, Saturday and Sunday evenings.

Other special events include the following celebrations:

January
  Beginning of the month, Semana de la Cultura Trinitaria in Trinidad
  Last half of the month, FolkCuba in Vedado

February
  First two weeks, Jornadas de la Cultura Camagüeyana
  Every other year, Havana International Jazz Festival
  Last half of the month, Havana Carnival

May
  Every other year, International Guitar Festival in Havana

September
  Every other year, Havana International Theater Festival

October
  Havana Festival of Contemporary Music
  Beginning October 10, 10 'days of culture'
  throughout the country with many musical
  events
  Late October every other year, Havana Ballet
  Festival
November
  Second half of November, Festival de Raices
  Africanas in Guanabacoa
December
  International Festival of New Latin American
  Film in Havana

For detailed information on many of the
above events, consult the website of the
Cuban Convention Bureau (www.burocon
.cubaweb.cu).

WORK
The government controls the job situation
in Havana and it presently isn't allowing
non-Cubans to fill paid positions in Cuba.
However, there are a number of organizations worldwide that, in concert with the
Cuban government, have organized volunteer work. Each year, for example, teams of
workers arrive at the Campamento Julio
Antonio Mella near Caimito, 40km southwest of Havana, from around the world to
perform voluntary labor in solidarity with
Cuba.

Members of the brigades spend about
three weeks doing agricultural or construction work alongside Cuban workers. There's
also a full program of activities, including
educational and political events and visits to
factories, hospitals, trade unions and schools.
Entertainment is provided at the camp and
excursions to the beach and places of interest are organized.

Participants pay their own airfare to
Cuba, plus food, accommodations and excursion fares. For more information, contact
the following:

Amigos de Cuba (☎/fax 1-604-327-6844, brigade@
  vcn.bc.ca), PO Box 21540, 1850 Commercial
  Drive, Vancouver, BC V5N 4AO, Canada

France Amerique Latine (☎ 33-1-4588-2000),
  Service Voyages, 37 Boulevard St Jacques,
  75014 Paris, France

International Work Brigade (☎ 44-20-7263 6452,
  fax 44-20-7561-0191, www.cuba-
  solidarity.org.uk), Cuba Solidarity Campaign, c/o
  The Red Rose Club, 129 Seven Sisters Rd,
  London N7 7QG, UK

Southern Cross Brigade (☎ 61-3-9857-9249, fax
  61-3-9857-6598), PO Box 1051, Collingwood,
  Victoria 3066, Australia

Getting There & Away

AIR

The vast majority of international travelers visiting Havana arrive by air via the José Martí International Airport, which is a 20-minute drive from Central Habana. Some 30 major carriers offer regularly scheduled flights to the airport, with direct service provided between Havana and Canada, the Caribbean, Central and South America, Europe, Japan and the USA.

Domestically, Havana is served by Cuba's national airline, Cubana de Aviación. The carrier, which was founded in 1929 and operates a fleet of Russian-built aircraft, serves 11 Cuban cities as well as dozens of foreign ones. With Cubana, be prepared for spotty in-flight service, evasive reservations staff, overbooking and delays. Additional carriers offer chartered service between Havana and Cuba's other top destinations, and there is a plethora of charters flying between Cuba and the rest of the world.

Warning

The information in this chapter is particularly vulnerable to change: Prices for international travel are volatile, routes are introduced and canceled, schedules change, special deals come and go, and rules and visa requirements are amended. Airlines and governments seem to take a perverse pleasure in making price structures and regulations as complicated as possible. You should check directly with the airline or a travel agent to make sure you understand how a fare (and ticket you may buy) works. In addition, the travel industry is highly competitive and there are many lurks and perks.

The upshot of this is that you should get opinions, quotes and advice from as many airlines and travel agents as possible before you part with your hard-earned cash. The details given in this chapter should be regarded as pointers and are not a substitute for your own careful, up-to-date research.

Departure Tax

When departing José Martí International Airport, you'll be expected to pay a US$20 departure tax at a cashier's window (just after you've checked your luggage and received a boarding card). This tax must be paid in US dollars cash; traveler's checks and credit cards are not accepted. An Immigrations official will check to see that you've paid the tax before he'll allow you to proceed to the departures area.

Other Parts of Cuba

Cubana de Aviación (www.cubana.cu) has domestic flights from Havana to the following destinations:

Baracoa (several times a week, 1058km, US$108 one-way)

Bayamo (several times a week, 757km, US$66)

Camagüey (daily, 558km, US$60)

Ciego de Ávila (several times a week, 448km, US$50)

Guantánamo (most days, 933km, US$100)

Holguín (daily, 758km, US$74)

Las Tunas (most days, 681km, US$66)

Manzanillo (several times a week, 811km, US$66)

Moa (several times a week, 940km, US$80)

Nueva Gerona (several times a day, 186km, US$22)

Santiago de Cuba (several times a day, 884km, US$80)

While the great majority of Cubana flights occur without incident, the airline has a terrible safety record. Fatal incidents involving the airline include the crash of a Cubana flight at Quito, Ecuador, on August 29, 1998, in which 69 passengers died, and the crash of a Cubana flight moments after takeoff from Santiago de Cuba on July 11, 1997, killing all 44 persons on board.

In addition to Cubana, Aerocaribbean provides scheduled flights from Havana to Varadero (four times a week, US$28); Trinidad (weekly, US$68); Cayo Coco (twice a day, US$70); Camagüey (twice a week,

Air Travel Glossary

Cancellation Penalties If you have to cancel or change a discounted ticket, there are often heavy penalties involved; insurance can sometimes be taken out against these penalties. Some airlines impose penalties on regular tickets as well, particularly against 'no-show' passengers.

Courier Fares Businesses often need to send urgent documents or freight securely and quickly. Courier companies hire people to accompany the package through customs and, in return, offer a discount ticket which is sometimes a phenomenal bargain. However, you may have to surrender all your baggage allowance and take only carry-on luggage.

Full Fares Airlines traditionally offer 1st class (coded F), business class (coded J) and economy class (coded Y) tickets. These days there are so many promotional and discounted fares available that few passengers pay full economy fare.

Lost Tickets If you lose your airline ticket an airline will usually treat it like a traveler's check and, after inquiries, issue you with another one. Legally, however, an airline is entitled to treat it like cash and if you lose it then it's gone forever. Take good care of your tickets.

Onward Tickets An entry requirement for many countries is that you have a ticket out of the country. If you're unsure of your next move, the easiest solution is to buy the cheapest onward ticket to a neighbouring country or a ticket from a reliable airline which can later be refunded if you do not use it.

Open-Jaw Tickets These are return tickets where you fly out to one place but return from another. If available, this can save you backtracking to your arrival point.

Overbooking Since every flight has some passengers who fail to show up, airlines often book more passengers than they have seats. Usually excess passengers make up for the no-shows, but occasionally somebody gets 'bumped' onto the next available flight. Guess who it is most likely to be? The passengers who check in late.

Promotional Fares These are officially discounted fares, available from travel agencies or direct from the airline.

Reconfirmation If you don't reconfirm your flight at least 72 hours prior to departure, the airline may delete your name from the passenger list. Ring to find out if your airline requires reconfirmation.

Restrictions Discounted tickets often have various restrictions on them – such as needing to be paid for in advance and incurring a penalty to be altered. Others are restrictions on the minimum and maximum period you must be away.

Round-the-World Tickets RTW tickets give you a limited period (usually a year) in which to circumnavigate the globe. You can go anywhere the carrying airlines go, as long as you don't backtrack. The number of stopovers or total number of separate flights is decided before you set off and they usually cost a bit more than a basic return flight.

Transferred Tickets Airline tickets cannot be transferred from one person to another. Travelers sometimes try to sell the return half of their ticket, but officials can ask you to prove that you are the person named on the ticket. On an international flight tickets are compared with passports.

Travel Periods Ticket prices vary with the time of year. There is a low (off-peak) season and a high (peak) season, and often a low-shoulder season and a high-shoulder season as well. Usually the fare depends on your outward flight – if you depart in the high season and return in the low season, you pay the high-season fare.

US\$88); Holguín (four times a week, US\$98); Santiago (daily, US\$108); and Baracoa (weekly, US\$128). Though more expensive than Cubana, Aerocaribbean is also more likely to have seats.

The USA

There are scheduled flights from Los Angeles, New York and Miami to Havana, but only those American citizens and US residents who have the blessing of the US Treasury Department's Office of Foreign Assets Control are allowed to board (see the Obtaining a License section in Facts for the Visitor). Americans who cannot obtain a license or who do not meet the exemption criteria may choose to visit the island, at the risk of being fined by the US Treasury Department, by flying to Cuba from a third country.

At the time this book went to press, roundtrip tickets from Miami, New York and Los Angeles cost no less than US\$300, US\$600 and US\$600, respectively, with prices fluctuating somewhat with demand (expect higher fares around Christmas or if you book your tickets less than two weeks in advance). Regardless of whether you intend to travel legally or otherwise, you should first contact one of the following authorized travel agencies, because most will offer you the assistance you need to be able to meet the US government's criteria for Cuban travel:

Adventure Tours & Travel (☎ 626-395-7111), 110 S Rosemead Blvd, suite A, Pasadena, CA 91117

Agencia Via Cuba (☎ 323-587-0611), 3009 E Florence Ave, Huntington Park, CA 90255

American Express Travel Services (☎ 212-640-5945), World Financial Center, New York, NY 10285

Habana Cuba Express (☎ 908-354-2295), 1068 Elizabeth Ave, Elizabeth, NJ 07201

Island Travel & Tours (☎ 202-342-3171), 2111 Wisconsin Ave NW, suite 319, Washington, DC 20007

Machi Community Services (☎ 305-442-8022), 5791 NW Seventh St, Miami, FL 33126

Marazul Charters (☎ 305-559-3616), 771 NW 37th Ave, Miami, FL 33125

A much longer list of companies providing travel to Cuba from the USA can be found at the website of the US Treasury Department's Office of Foreign Assets Control (www.ustreas.gov/ofac). For information on some of these companies, see the Organized Tours section later in this chapter.

If you don't meet the US government's requirements for travel to Cuba and still intend to go there, your best option is to fly there via Canada, Mexico or another third country. Presently, most Americans who travel to Cuba without the US government's blessing do so from Mexico (there are convenient flights from Tijuana, Monterrey and Cancun). Many others opt for the Canadian connection, while an increasing number of Americans visit the island from Costa Rica, Jamaica and Panama.

Canada

Cubana flies to Havana twice weekly from Montréal and Toronto. Some of the flights are via Cienfuegos.

The Costa Rican airline Lacsa (Líneas Aéreas de Costa Rica) flies from Toronto to Havana twice a week year-round for about CDN\$600. All flights from Canada other than those of Cubana and Lacsa are charters.

On the Canadian charters you can expect to pay around CDN\$450 roundtrip (more at Christmas, Easter and on weekends), plus CDN\$46 for a Cuban tourist card and Canadian airport taxes. To get this price you'll have to work through a Canadian travel agent who books charter flights to Cuba. See Organized Tours, later in this chapter, for leads.

Australia & New Zealand

The most direct route to Cuba from Australia and New Zealand is via Los Angeles and Mexico. STA Travel offices in Australia (☎ 02-9361-4966), 79 Oxford St, Sydney, NSW 2010; (☎ 03-9349-2411), 222 Faraday St, Melbourne, VIC 3053; New Zealand (☎ 09-309-0458), 10 High St, Auckland; and other agents should be able to sell you a ticket as far as Mexico. You should make sure that any Mexico-Cuba ticket issued in

Australia or New Zealand is written on separate stock to avoid the risk of having the entire ticket confiscated by US immigration in Los Angeles; such a ticket is a violation of the US embargo of Cuba.

The UK

British Airways has a weekly flight to Havana from London-Gatwick. Cubana has flights to Havana from London-Gatwick three times a week, and to Cayo Largo del Sur and Varadero weekly. See the Organized Tours section, later in this chapter, for agents specializing in Cuba.

Continental Europe

Several European airlines fly to Cuba. Air Europe has flights to Havana from Madrid and Milan four times a week and it often offers very cheap specials to fill its planes. Iberia flies to Havana from Barcelona and Madrid four times a week. It also offers discount fares to Cuba via Madrid from most European capitals, with a maximum stay of three months. AOM French Airlines flies a wide-body DC-10 to Havana from Paris-Orly three times a week, with connections from Marseille, Nice, Perpignan and Toulon. Air France arrives from Paris twice a week.

Martinair has weekly Boeing 767 flights to Havana from Amsterdam. A 28-day roundtrip ticket from Holland costs f1100 to f1700, depending on the season, when booked through an agent such as Havanatour Benelux (☎ 31-10-411-2444, fax 31-10-411-4749) in Rotterdam. To get this fare, you must book at least two hotel nights through Havanatour, but the Cuban tourist card and Dutch airport tax are included. Air France and Iberia offer flights from Amsterdam to Havana for the same price or slightly less with a maximum stay of three months, but you must connect through Paris or Madrid.

In Amsterdam, Grand Travel/Flyworld (☎ 31-20-657-0000, fax 31-20-648-0477) sells Cuba tickets for slightly higher prices than does Havanatur Benelux. Amber Reisbureau (☎ 31-20-685-1155, fax 31-20-689-0406), Da Costastraat 77, 1053 ZG Amsterdam, Netherlands, will call around

Internet Bookings

With US travel agents restricted from booking travel to Cuba, a flourishing market in Internet ticket sales has developed. Although the websites involved are definitely worth visiting for current flight and price information, buyer beware. Avoid paying too much money up front unless you know with whom you're dealing (paying by credit card gives you a measure of protection). Some of these websites do not list any fixed business address, although telephone numbers are usually provided.

The Cuban Connection (www.cuba.tc) handles Nassau-Havana flights. Mundaca Travel (www.mundacatravel.com/cuba), based at Isla Mujeres, Mexico, sells Cancún-Havana flights. Tour & Marketing (www.gocuba.com) books all Cubana flights, and exact prices are posted. Many of the tour companies mentioned in this chapter also sell 'air only' tickets through their websites.

to try to find you a cheap ticket to Havana, and it also carries an excellent selection of maps of Cuba.

Cubana flies to Havana from the following continental European airports: Barcelona, Berlin-Schönefeld, Brussels, Copenhagen, Frankfurt, Istanbul, Las Palmas, Lisbon, Madrid, Manchester, Moscow-Sheremetyevo, Paris-Orly, Rome, Santiago de Compostela and Vitoria. Most operate only once or twice a week, except Havana-Paris, which runs five times a week.

Cubana's fares are often lower than those charged by western European airlines, and reduced last-minute fares are sometimes available. Also, Aeroflot flies to Havana from Moscow-Sheremetyevo.

Mexico

For Mexicans and residents of the western US, Tijuana and Cancún are the most direct gateways to Cuba. Both Cubana and Aerocaribe (the regional airline of Mexicana de Aviación) cover the 500km from Cancún to

GETTING THERE & AWAY

Havana. Cubana flies from Cancún to Havana daily, while Aerocaribe flies twice a day. Cancún itself is easily accessible on cheap charter flights, and Aerocaribe connects with Mexicana flights from cities all across the US. If space is available, you can buy same-day tickets to Havana at the Cubana and Aerocaribe offices at the Cancún airport.

In addition to the Cancún services, Mexicana has direct flights to Havana from Mexico City daily and from Mérida twice a week, with direct connections from Oaxaca, Tuxtla Gutierrez, Veracruz, and Villahermosa. Cubana flies to Havana from Mexico City twice a week.

From Tijuana, there's a weekly charter flight that leaves on Saturday and returns on Sunday. The charter is organized by Taíno Tours (☎ 52-6-684-9453), Comonfort No 1226, Loc-8 esq Fco J Mina, Zona Río, Tijuana, Baja California 22320. Taíno charters Aeromexico planes and charges about US$500 roundtrip. The charter makes one stop in Monterrey, Mexico. The company can obtain a Cuban tourist card for you. From downtown Los Angeles, Santa Ana and the Tijuana border, the Tijuana International Airport is conveniently reached by Trés Estrellas bus company.

From Mexico City to Havana, Mexicana charges US$329 one-way or US$477 return. From Cancún it costs US$166 one-way, US$257 return (add US$23 tax to these fares). For information on Mexicana flights to Cuba, call its reservations offices in Mexico City (☎ 52-5-448-0990) or Cancún (☎ 52-98-87-4444). Mexicana offices in the US are not allowed to book these flights.

Cubana (☎ 52-5-250-6355, fax 52-5-255-0835 in Mexico City; ☎/fax 52-98-86-0192 in Cancún) is a bit cheaper than Aerocaribe, for reasons that may become apparent if you fly them (see Other Parts of Cuba, earlier in this chapter). Check the Organized Tours section, later, for Mexican travel agencies.

The Caribbean

Cubana has flights to Havana from Curaçao, Fort de France, Kingston, Montego Bay,

Pointe-a-Pitre, Santo Domingo and St Martin. The Cuban charter carrier Aerocaribbean flies between Puerto Príncipe, Haiti, and Havana weekly.

Air Jamaica flies from Montego Bay to Havana three times a week, with numerous connections from the USA. Check its excellent website (www.airjamaica.com) for more information, and see Organized Tours, later in this chapter.

Eddy Tours (☎ 345-945-0871, fax 345-945-0872, perea_e@candw.ky), PO Box 31097 SMB, Grand Cayman, books three weekly flights on Aerocaribbean from Gran Cayman to Havana (US$190 return).

The Bahamas Cubana's daily Nassau-Havana flight costs US$180 for a 30-day return ticket, plus US$22 tax – a useful connection for blockade runners from the eastern US. An open-ended return flight costs US$265. The Cuban tourist card and the US$15 Nassau airport departure tax should be included in the ticket price, but ask. Nassau bookings can be made through the following companies in Nassau:

Havanatur Bahamas (☎ 242-394-7195, fax 242-356-2733), Wong Plaza, Madeira St, Nassau

Innovative Travel & Tours (☎ 242-325-0042/3337, fax 242-325-3339), Southland Shopping Center, East St, suite 3, PO Box N1629, Nassau

Majestic Travel (☎ 242-328-0908, fax 242-326-1995, www.majesticholidays.com), PO Box N1401, Nassau

Booking from the USA can be a little complicated, as Havanatur and Innovative don't accept credit cards for this transaction. You must call to find out if the dates you want are available, then wire a deposit through Western Union. After you fax the wire transfer number, they'll fax you back with confirmation of the dates. Otherwise, you could send a certified check by Federal Express. You actually receive your tickets at the Nassau airport.

Majestic Travel accepts credit card guarantees for flight and hotel reservations, but upon arrival in Nassau you must use its courtesy van to go to its head office, where you pay in cash. Allow yourself plenty of time.

Central America
Cubana flies to Havana from San José, Costa Rica, twice a week. Lacsa (Líneas Aéreas de Costa Rica) operates flights to Havana from San José, Guatemala City and San Salvador several times a week; the 30-day roundtrip excursion fare on any of these flights costs US$400.

The Cuban charter airline Aerocaribbean flies between Managua and Havana weekly. Aerocaribbean also has twice-weekly flights to Havana from Belize (US$300 return) and San Pedro Sula, Honduras (US$370 return).

South America
From Caracas, Venezuela, Aeropostal flies to Havana five times a week. Its roundtrip excursion fares for flights between Caracas and Havana cost US$275/290/351/451 for 21/30/60/90 days. Cubana also flies from Caracas to Havana four times a week. Book through Ideal Tours in Caracas (☎ 582-793-0037/1822/7458, fax 582-782-8063, ideal-tours@cantv.net).

Cubana flies to Havana from Bogotá, Quito, Guayaquil and Lima. Aeroflot also has weekly flights to Havana from Lima.

Cubana has flights to Havana from Buenos Aires three times a week, from Santiago de Chile twice a week, from Río de Janeiro and São Paulo once or twice a week and from Montevideo weekly. Recommended travel agencies include Evasión in Brazil; Havanatur in Argentina, Ecuador and Colombia; and Guamatur in Chile and Uruguay.

Airline Offices
Cubana Airlines' always-crowded head office (☎ 33-4949), Calle 23 No 64, at Infanta, at the Malecón end of the Airline Building, deals with international flights. It's open 8:30 am to 4 pm weekdays, 8:30 am to noon Saturday.

The Cubana office at the corner of Infanta and Humboldt in Vedado, open 8:15 am to 4 pm weekdays, handles domestic flights, but it's literally swamped with Cubans trying to buy tickets for pesos and should be avoided. Instead, book your domestic Cubana flights for the same price at

Sol y Son Travel Agency (☎ 33-3271, fax 33-5150) in the Airline Building, Calle 23 No 64, between Calle P and Infanta, Vedado. It's owned by Cubana, and since everyone is paying in dollars, there's no waiting. It's open 8:30 am to 7 pm weekdays, 8:30 am to noon Saturday.

Other airline offices, listed below, are either in the Airline Building or at the Hotel Habana Libre, Calles 23 and L, also in Vedado:

Aerocaribbean (☎ 33-4543, fax 33-5016), Airline Building

Aerocaribe (☎ 33-3621, fax 33-3871, www.aerocaribe.com.mx), Airline Building

Aeroflot-Russian Airlines (☎ 33-3200, fax 33-3288, www.aeroflot.com), Airline Building

Aeropostal (☎ 55-4000, fax 55-4128, www.aeropostal.com), Hotel Habana Libre

Air Europa (☎ 66-6918, fax 66-6917, www.air-europa.com), Hotel Habana Libre

Air France (☎ 66-2642, fax 66-2634, www.airfrance.com), Hotel Habana Libre

Air Jamaica (☎ 66-2247, fax 66-2449, www.airjamaica.com), Hotel Habana Libre

AOM French Airlines (☎ 33-4098, fax 33-3783, www.flyaom.com), Airline Building

Condor (represented by LTU; ☎ 33-3524, www.condor.de), Airline Building

COPA (☎ 33-1758, fax 33-3951), Airline Building

Grupo Taca (☎ 33-3114, fax 33-3728, www.grupotaca.com) represents Aviateca, Lacsa, Mica and Taca, Hotel Habana Libre

Iberia (☎ 33-5041, fax 33-5061, www.iberia.com), Airline Building

LTU International Airways (☎ 33-3524, fax 33-3590, www.ltu.com), Airline Building

Mexicana de Aviación (☎ 33-3531, fax 33-3077, www.mexicana.com.mx), Airline Building

TAAG (☎ 33-3527, fax 33-3049), Airline Building

Tame Línea Aérea del Ecuador (☎ 33-0012, fax 33-4126, www.tameairlines.com), Airline Building

BUS
Astro buses to all parts of Cuba depart from the bus station (☎ 79-2456), Av de la Independencia and Calle 19 de Mayo, near the Plaza de la Revolución in Vedado. Dollar

tickets are readily available at the office marked 'Venta de Boletines USD' (☎ 70-3397), down the hall to the right of the main entrance. It's open 7 am to 9 pm daily. Tickets on regular Astro buses from here cost US$7 to Pinar del Río, US$10 to Varadero, US$12 to Santa Clara, US$14 to Cienfuegos, US$21 to Trinidad, or US$35 to Santiago de Cuba. Four tickets (seats) on each bus are available for dollar sales, and you can usually get one on any Astro bus the same day.

You also have the option of using the deluxe Víazul buses, which operate on four routes. The Víazul bus to Pinar del Río (US$11) and Viñales (3 hours, US$12) departs Havana at 9 am on alternate days. Víazul buses to Varadero (3 hours, US$8) leave daily at 8 am and 4 pm. To Cienfuegos (US$20) and Trinidad (5½ hours, US$25), they leave at 8:15 am on alternate days. The bus to Santiago de Cuba (15 hours, US$51) leaves Havana at 3 pm twice a week and travels via Santa Clara (US$18), Sancti Spíritus (US$23), Ciego de Ávila (US$27), Camagüey (US$33), Las Tunas (US$39), Holguín (US$44) and Bayamo (US$44).

Tickets for Víazul services are sold immediately prior to departure by the Astro ticket office at the bus station, where you can also board the bus. These services actually begin from the Víazul terminal (☎ 81-1413), Calle 26 and Zoológico in Nuevo Vedado, 3km southwest of Plaza de la Revolución. Infotur (☎ 33-3333, 63-6095), Obispo No 358, will know which days the Víazul buses are operating. They also sell tickets that require you board at its originating station in Nuevo Vedado. Havana-bound, you can get off the Víazul bus from Varadero in Centro Habana right after the tunnel, but if you arrive from most other points you'll be let out at the Nuevo Vedado terminal. From here city bus No 27 will take you to Vedado or Centro Habana (ask). If the Víazul bus stops at the bus station on Av de la Independencia, get out there. Víazul is only a few dollars more expensive than Astro, but offers higher levels of service.

Any of the tour bus drivers parked near the Palacio de la Artesanía, Cuba No 64, near the cathedral, will gladly take you to Varadero in the afternoon for US$10 to US$20 per person. Just ask.

Buses to points in the Havana Province leave from Apodaca No 53, off Agramonte, near the main railway station. They go to Güines, Jaruco, Madruga, Nueva Paz, San José, San Nicolás and Santa Cruz del Norte, but expect large crowds and come early to get a peso ticket.

TRAIN

Trains to most parts of Cuba depart from the Estación Central de Ferrocarril (☎ 61-4259), Av de Bélgica and Arsenal, on the southwest side of La Habana Vieja. Foreigners must buy tickets for dollars at the Ladis office on the side of the station facing Arsenal. Go through the door next to the post office. Here you'll be given priority and offered a ticket with a seat reservation. The office is open 8 am to 8 pm daily. If this office is closed, try the Lista de Espera office west on Arsenal, at Cienfuegos, which sells tickets for trains leaving immediately. It's open 7 am to 7 pm daily. Rail services include the following:

Bayamo (train No 3 daily at 8:25 pm, 744km, 14 hours, US$26)

Camagüey (three daily, 537km, 8½ hours, US$20)

Ciego de Ávila (three daily, 435km, 6½ hours, US$16)

Cienfuegos (train No 15 daily at 1:25 pm, 254km, 10 hours, US$10)

Holguín (train No 15 daily at 2:05 pm, 747km, 15 hours, US$27)

Las Tunas (two daily, 657km, 9½ hours, US$24)

Manzanillo (train No 3 daily at 11:20 pm, 775km, 26 hours, US$28)

Matanzas (seven daily, 105km, 1½ hours, US$4)

Pinar del Río (train No 103 daily at 9:30 pm, 162km, six hours, US$6.50)

Sancti Spíritus (train No 7 daily at 10:05 am, 354km, seven hours, US$13.50)

Santa Clara (four daily, 281km, 4½ hours, US$10)

Santiago de Cuba (train No 11 daily at 7:30 pm and train No 13 at 4:40 pm, 856km, 14½ hours, US$30)

The information above is only a rough approximation of what should happen. Services are routinely delayed or canceled.

Trains to Cienfuegos, Pinar del Río and Unión de Reyes leave from the new Estación La Coubre on Desamparados, just south of the Estación Central de Ferrocarril. Ask Ladis about this.

TAXI

Small Lada taxis, operated by Cubataxi, park on Calle 19 de Mayo beside the bus station, charging US$0.35 a kilometer (US$44 to Varadero, US$54 to Pinar del Río, US$72 to Santa Clara, US$88 to Cienfuegos, US$102 to Trinidad). Up to four people can go for that price (provided they don't have too much luggage). It's worth considering in a pinch, and it's perfectly legal.

Unlicensed private taxis may offer to take you to Pinar del Río, Santa Clara or Cienfuegos for the equivalent of bus fare, and it's up to you to decide if you're willing to risk getting stranded somewhere if the driver gets caught. To use a metered tourist taxi for a long trip is prohibitively expensive (over US$100 to Varadero for the car).

BOAT

There are no scheduled ferry services from neighboring countries to Cuba. Thanks to the US embargo, which prohibits vessels calling at Cuban ports from visiting the US for six months, few cruise ships include Havana on their itineraries. Among those European cruise liners that do use the Sierra Maestra Marine Terminal, adjacent to Havana's Plaza de San Francisco de Asís, are the *Sun Dream* (British), *Tritón* (French) and *Italia Prima* (Italian).

Access by private yacht or cruiser is easy. Havana is served by the Marina Hemingway (Map 4). For more information turn to Yacht Entry Procedures in the Facts for the Visitor chapter.

ORGANIZED TOURS

Often the most convenient way to spend time in Cuba is through an organized tour, as most of your travel arrangements will be made for you and you won't have to spend much time planning your trip, since your time in the country will be 'filled up' for you.

The USA

In cooperation with Marazul Tours, (☎ 201-319-9670, fax 201-319-9009, www.marazul tours.com), Tower Plaza, 4100 Park Ave, Weehawken, NJ 07087, the Center for Cuban Studies (☎ 212-242-0559, fax 212-242-1937, www.cubaupdate.org), 124 W 23rd St, New York, NY 10011, organizes one-week special-interest tours to Cuba focusing on the environment, education, museums, African culture and other subjects. These generally cost from US$1500 to US$2000 for two weeks including airfare, double-occupancy accommodations, some meals and transportation in Cuba.

Global Exchange (☎ 415-255-7296, 800-497-1994, fax 415-255-7498, www.globalex change.org), 2017 Mission St, Room 303, San Francisco, CA 94110, operates monthly 'reality tours,' with an emphasis on understanding cultural, environmental and human rights issues. These seven- to 10-day trips cost between US$900 and US$2000 including airfare from Cancún, double-occupancy accommodations, meals, visas, transportation within Cuba and a trip leader. Tour applications should be submitted two months in advance. All feedback has been positive.

Canada

A list of tour companies offering package tours to Cuba is provided below. US citizens could call or fax these companies directly to request their brochures, although travel-industry etiquette usually prevents them from selling tickets directly to the public. Thus US citizens must work through a Canadian travel agent. Two Toronto discount travel agencies specializing in tours to Cuba are Bel Air Travel (☎ 416-699-8833, 800-465-4631, www.belairtravel.com) and Cuban-owned Sun Holidays (☎ 416-789-1010, 800-387-0571, www.sunholidays.ca). Many more advertise in the travel section of the Saturday edition of the *Toronto Star*, available at major newsstands throughout the US. Otherwise, if you are a US citizen, ask one of the tour companies below to give you the number of a large travel agency selling its tours. Also check out the companies' websites.

Air Transat Holidays
(☎ 905-405-8600, fax 905-405-8586, www.airtransatholidays.com), 5915 Airport Rd, suite 1000, Mississauga, Ontario L4V 1T1

Alba Tours
(☎ 416-746-2488, fax 416-485-2089, www.albatours.com), 130 Merton St, Toronto, Ontario M4S 1A4

Cuban Connection
(☎ 250-489-2558, fax 250-489-3121, www.cubanconnectiontours.com), 519 9th St S, Cranbrook, BC V1C 1R4

Hola Sun Holidays
(☎ 905-882-9445, 800-668-8178, fax 905-882-5184, www.holasunholidays.com), 146 W Beaver Creek Rd, Unit 8, Richmond Hill, Ontario L4B 1C2

Magna Holidays
(☎ 905-761-7330, 800-387-3717, fax 905-761-0929), 163 Buttermill Ave, Unit 3, Concord, Ontario L4K 3X8

Regent Holidays
(☎ 905-673-3343, fax 905-673-1717, www.regentholidays.com), 300-6205 Airport Rd, Building A, Mississauga, Ontario L4V 1E1

Signature Vacations
(☎ 416-967-1112, fax 416-967-0334, www.signature.ca), 111 Avenue Rd, suite 500, Toronto, Ontario M5R 3J8

Sunflight Holidays
(☎ 416-967-1510, fax 416-967-0334), 170 Attwell Drive, suite 200, Toronto, Ontario M9W 5Z5

Sunquest Vacations
(☎ 416-482-3333, fax 416-485-2089, www.sunquest.ca), 130 Merton St, Toronto, Ontario M4S 1A4

World of Vacations
(☎ 416-620-8687, 800-661-2227, www.worldofvacations.com), 191 The West Mall, 6th floor, Etobicoke, Ontario M9C 5K8

The UK & Continental Europe

Companies offering package tours and cheap flight tickets from the UK to Cuba include the following:

Interchange
(☎ 44-20-8681-3612, fax 44-20-8760-0031, interchange@interchange.uk.com), 27 Stafford Rd, Croydon, Surrey CR0 4NG

Journey Latin America
(☎ 44-161-832-1441, fax 44-161-832-1551), 2nd floor, Barton Arcade, 51–63 Deansgate, Manchester M3 2BH

Journey Latin America
(☎ 44-20-8747-3108, fax 44-20-8742-1312, www.cheapflights.co.uk/web/journeylatinamericaweb.html), 12 & 13 Heathfield Terrace, London W4 4JE

Progressive Tours
(☎ 44-20-7262-1676, fax 44-20-7724-6941), 12 Porchester Place, London W2 2BS

Regent Holidays
(☎ 44-117-921-1711, fax 44-117-925-4866, www.regent-holidays.co.uk), 15 John St, Bristol BS1 2HR

Special Places
(☎ 44-1892-661-157, fax 44-1892-665-670), 4 The White House, Beacon Rd, Crowborough, East Sussex TN6 1AB

Interchange has three-night packages to Havana costing £529 to £829 with airfare from London included. Unlike some companies that send their clients to inconveniently located properties in Miramar or at the Marina Hemingway, Interchange sells central medium-priced hotels such as the Capri and Inglaterra. Best of all, Interchange allows you to combine the convenience of a three-night hotel booking with the flexibility of making your own arrangements upon arrival for the balance of your stay. Other creative Interchange packages combine Havana with Varadero, Trinidad or Santiago de Cuba. It also books rental cars.

The following companies are based in continental Europe:

Guamá SA
(☎ 34-91-411-2048, fax 34-91-564-3918), Paseo de La Habana 28, 28036 Madrid, Spain

Havanatour Benelux
(☎ 31-10-411-2444, fax 31-10-411-4749, www.havanatour.nl), Hofplein 19, 3032 AC Rotterdam, Netherlands

Havanatur Paris
(☎ 33-1-4451-5080, fax 33-1-4265-1801), 24 rue du Quatre Septembre, 75002 Paris, France

Marsans International
(☎ 33-1-5334-4001), 4 rue du Faubourg, Montmartre, 75009 Paris, France

Meier's Weltreisen GmbH
(☎ 49-211-907-801, fax 49-211-941-7184), Parseval Strasse 7b, D-40468 Düsseldorf, Germany

Tropicana Touristik
(☎ 49-30-853-7041, fax 49-30-853-4070, www.tropicana-touristik.de), Berliner Strasse 161, D-10715 Berlin, Germany

Tropicana Touristik
(☎/fax 49-69-943397), Kant Strasse 10, D-60313 Frankfurt/Main, Germany

Viajes Cuevas de Altamira
(☎/fax 34-91-547-4292), Gran Vía No 80, Oficina 707, 28013 Madrid, Spain

Viajes Marsans
(☎ 34-91-343-3100, fax 34-91-343-3109, www.marsans.es), Av de Burgos 16D, Planta 10, 28036 Madrid, Spain

Mexico

If you live in the western USA, the shortest route to Cuba is through Mexico, and the Mexican tour companies offer lots of packages based in Havana itself. All of them can obtain your Cuban tourist card together with package tour or flight bookings, but ask how much they charge for the card, as some agencies will take advantage of you. If you book a tour, check carefully where they'll be sending you, as some Mexican companies use Miramar hotels that are inconveniently far from the city center. The following agencies also sell 'air only' tickets:

Merihabana
(☎ 52-99-26-1630, fax 52-99-26-0707), Calle 11 No 114, local 6, Colonia Itzimna, Mérida, Yucatán

Taíno Tours/Havanatur
(☎ 52-5-559-3907, fax 52-5-559-3951, www.pceditores.com/taino), Av Coyoacán No 1035, Colonia del Valle, 03100 Mexico, DF

Taíno Tours
(☎ 52-6-684-9453), Comonfort No 1226, Loc-8 esq Fco J Mina, Zona Río, Tijuana, 22320 Baja California

Viajes Acuario
(☎ 52-5-543-6963, fax 52-5-543-6950, www.acuario.com.mx), Diagonal San Antonio No 934, Colonia Del Valle, 03100 Mexico, DF

Viajes Acuario
(☎ 52-74-85-6100, fax 52-74-85-7100), Costera Miguel Alemán No 183–3, Acapulco, 39690 Guerrero

Viajes Divermex
(☎ 52-98-845-005, fax 52-98-842-325, www.cancun.com/tours/divermex), Cancún

Viñales Tours
(☎ 52-5-208-9900, fax 52-5-208-3704, www.spin.com.mx/vinales), Oaxaca No 80, Colonia Roma, 06700 Mexico, DF

Viñales Tours
(☎ 52-98-840-326, fax 52-98-840-396), Av Coba No 5, local A6, Plaza América, Super Manzana 4, Cancún, 77500 Quintana Roo

The Caribbean

Caribic Vacations (☎ 876-952-0293, fax 876-979-3421), 69 Gloucester Ave, Montego Bay, Jamaica, offers all-inclusive package tours of two, five, or seven nights from Jamaica to Havana. Caribic also sells 'air only' tickets from Kingston or Montego Bay to Havana for US$145/170 one-way/ return, plus US$10 to Holguín or Santiago de Cuba, and another US$30 for a stay of over one month. Add US$20 for a Cuban tourist card (available from Caribic) and US$21 Jamaican airport tax.

In the Dominican Republic, Emely Tours (☎ 809-687-7114, fax 809-686-0941, www .emely-tours.com), San Francisco de Macorís No 58, Santo Domingo, offers tours and business travel to Cuba.

Special Interest Tours

A specialist in language, conference, festival and cultural tours is Vacation-Culture in Cuba (☎ 514-982-3330, 888-691-0101, fax 514-982-2438, www.culturecuba.com), 5059 St Denis, Montréal, Québec H2J 2L9, Canada. It sells packages built around events such as the International Festival of New Latin American Film in Havana in December. All departures are from Montréal or Toronto, but prices are reasonable since they're quoted in low Canadian dollars.

Getting Around

THE AIRPORT

José Martí International Airport, 25km southwest of Havana via Av de la Independencia, serves the international and domestic needs of air travelers arriving and leaving the Cuban capital.

There are a number of terminals here. Terminal No 1, on the southeast side of the runway, handles only domestic Cubana flights. Opposite, on the north side of the runway, but 3km away via Av de la Independencia, is Terminal No 2, which receives Corsair flights and charters from Miami. All other international flights use Terminal No 3, an ultra-modern facility that opened in 1998 at Wajay, 2.5km west of Terminal No 2. Charter flights on Aerocaribbean, Aerogaviota, Aerotaxi, etc, to Cayo Largo del Sur and elsewhere use the Caribbean Terminal (also known as Terminal No 5), at the northwest end of the runway, 2.5km west of Terminal No 3. (Terminal No 4 hasn't been built yet.)

To/From the Airport

Foreigners arriving at Terminal No 3 are expected to take a taxi to their hotel, unless they've already paid for a bus transfer as part of a tour package. This trip should cost no more than US$20 in one of the newer tourist taxis based at the airport, or US$12 in an older yellow-and-black Lada taxi, which might have arrived to drop someone off. It's wise to agree on the price before heading into town. It may work out cheaper if you can convince a tourist taxi driver to use the meter, but don't bother trying this with a Lada taxi driver as their meters are set at artificially low rates and they'll simply decline your business.

The closest public bus stop to Terminal No 3 is that of the M-2 Metro Bus from Santiago de las Vegas to Parque de la Fraternidad on Av de la Independencia, 500m east of Terminal No 2. The tourist taxis at Terminal No 3 should charge US$3 to Terminal No 2, and you could easily walk from there to the bus stop. If you want to walk the 3km

from Terminal No 3 to Av de la Independencia, keep right as you leave the airport, watching for signs reading *Vuelos Nacionales* or *Terminal Doméstico*. You'll need pesos to pay the 20-centavo fare, and be aware that the M-2 is incredibly crowded and frequented by pickpockets. Unless you're the hardest of hard-core backpackers, you shouldn't try to follow this route upon arrival in Cuba, although you could consider getting to the airport on the M-2 if saving US$12 is a high priority. The bus loads on Av Simón Bolívar, between Industria and Amistad, on the west side of Parque de la Fraternidad in Centro Habana. If you're boarding at Parque de la Fraternidad, note

Private Rooms Runaround

Taxi drivers often offer to show new arrivals 'a few private rooms' for rent. The offer usually comes up during a pleasant conversation, during which you're told your hotel is very expensive. For much less money, the drivers say, you can stay at a private residence in downtown Havana.

What the drivers don't say is that these places are usually the homes of poor Cubans hard up for money, that a firm mattress, hot-and-cold tap water and air-conditioning are usually missing from these homes.

What you *can* expect is an old couple, in a very old home, desperate for a lodger. Times are hard. Every dollar makes a difference in these people's lives. Which is why, after a few minutes' visit, you feel terrible saying 'thank you, but no thank you.'

Unless you're on a very tight budget (private rooms usually run $25 a night) or you enjoy disappointing poverty-stricken strangers, you're better off telling your taxi driver, if the subject of private rooms comes up, that you're looking forward to staying at your hotel.

¡ABSOLUTAMENTE NINGÚN MIEDO!

that there are two lines here, one for persons who want seats *(sentados)* and another for those willing to stand *(de pie)*. Of course, the latter line moves faster, but it's best to wait for a seat, as it's a long, jam-packed trip. Try to sit near an exit door.

CHARLOTTE HINDLE

If you're arriving at Terminal No 1 on a domestic Cubana flight and notice all of the Cubans getting into a bus marked 'Aeropuerto' in front of the terminal, join them and you'll probably get a ride into town for one peso. It generally leaves about 15 minutes after the arrival of domestic Cubana flights and takes about an hour to reach town. Otherwise walk less than a kilometer to Av de la Independencia and try catching the M-2. Attempting to use the 'Aeropuerto' bus to get to the airport is a pain as it's not intended for foreigners, and the Cubana staff will pretend they don't know anything about it. Typical tourist taxi fares from Terminal No 1 are US$2 to Terminal No 2, US$5 to Terminal No 3, or US$20 to Havana. It should be easier to find a Lada or private taxi around Terminal No 1, as the police scrutiny there is less strict.

BUS

As Cuba emerges from a period of austerity, Havana's city bus service is slowly improving. Regular city buses are called *guaguas* (pronounced 'WAwas'), while the much larger Metro buses are termed *camellos* (camels) for the two humps their separate passenger compartments resemble. Within the city the fare is a flat 20 centavos in an extended bus with an accordion connection in the middle or 40 centavos in a regular bus, which you must toss into a box near the driver or pay to a conductor. Unfortunately, no bus route map is available.

There are *colas* (lines) at most *paradas* (bus stops) even though it may not appear so at first glance. To mark your place ask for *el último* (the last in line), and when the bus arrives get behind that person. This excellent system, which reduces pushing, is rigorously followed.

To take a bus to places farther from the tourist hub, such as Cojímar, Guanabo and Guanabacoa, you should try to board at the originating point of the bus (see the Excursions chapter), as the buses are often so full they don't stop at subsequent bus stops.

Since 1995 a public transportation crisis in Havana has been eased by the introduction of Metro buses. These huge 300-passenger buses are hauled by trucks, and all have the prefix M before their number:

M-1 Alamar-Vedado via Fraternidad

M-2 Fraternidad-Santiago de las Vegas

M-3 Alamar-Ciudad Deportiva

M-4 Fraternidad-San Agustín via Marianao

M-5 Vedado-San Agustín

M-6 Calvario-Vedado (corner of 21 and L)

M-7 Parque de la Fraternidad-Alberro via Cotorro

As you can see, many of the Metro buses leave from Parque de la Fraternidad on the south side of the Capitolio in Centro Habana. At the originating places of these buses there will be two lines, one for people who want a seat (the *sentados*) and another for those willing to stand (the *parados*). The second line moves faster and is best if you're going only a short distance and have no luggage.

Taking one of these enormous 'road trains' is the Cuban equivalent of riding the Moscow subway and it can be intimidating the first time. The conductors jam in as many 20-centavo passengers as they possibly can, and you can expect to be crushed. Begin moving toward the exit doors as soon as you get on, as you're not allowed to exit through the door where you boarded. This can be a real problem if you're going only one or two stops and can't reach the exit, so it's suggested that you use a Metro Bus only if you're going a considerable distance. Be aware of pickpockets who may spot you at the bus stop and get on right behind. Before boarding, empty your pockets into a handbag you can clutch in front of you. If the bus looks impossibly crowded, just step back and wait for the next; they run every 10 minutes and the next one may be less crowded. At most stops there is a line, so ask for *el último* (see earlier).

To go from Centro Habana to Vedado, catch the M-1 on Agramonte beside the Museo Nacional Palacio de Bellas Artes and stay on until the last stop, which is on Calle G, near the monument to José Miguel Gómez.

Tourist Bus

The Vaivén Bus Turístico is an 18-seat tourist shuttle that operates 9 am to 9 pm daily. The US$4 day pass allows unlimited stops along the 23-stop route between Hotel Palco at the Palacio de las Convenciones in Miramar and El Morro castle. Although operated by Rumbos, the service is very poorly publicized, and its brochures and timetables are hard to find. The yellow-and-purple Vaivén buses often park near El Floridita, just off Parque Central in Centro Habana. Otherwise ask at the Neptuno-Tritón, Chateau Miramar, Riviera, Melía Cohiba, Habana Libre, Capri and Deauville hotels, all of which are on or near its route. If you see a Rumbos tour desk, ask there.

To/From the Bus Terminal

The crowded M-2 Metro Bus from Santiago de las Vegas stops outside the bus station and runs directly to Parque de la Fraternidad near the Capitolio. In the other direction ask someone where to get out, as the southbound M-2 stops a block over from the bus station.

TRAIN

Cristina Station (☎ 78-4971), Av de México and Arroyo, Cuatro Caminos, lies south of Centro Habana and about a kilometer southwest of the Estación Central de Ferrocarril. It handles local trains within the city limits. At last report there were four trains a day to Boyeros; these could be used to reach Parque Lenin (Galápago de Oro Station) and airport Terminal No 1. Thursday to Sunday, one train a day leaves Cristina Station for ExpoCuba around noon. Trains to Batabanó leave twice a day (2½ hours), and four trains a day go to Wajay (1 hour). In July and August only, there's a train from here to Guanabo three times a day except Monday (1½ hours). Cristina was the first train station built in Havana, and it's worth checking out if you're spending some time in Havana and want to get around cheaply.

The Estación 19 de Noviembre (☎ 81-4431), Tulipán, in Nuevo Vedado, has trains to a couple of points in the Havana Province, including six to San Antonio de los Baños (1 hour). There's railcar service to ExpoCuba (40 minutes) at 9 am Thursday to Sunday.

CAR

With all the inexpensive taxis in Havana, there's little reason to rent a car unless you intend to drive well beyond the city's limits. But if you decide to rent a car you'll find no shortage of car rental offices in Havana.

Havanautos (☎ 24-0646) has an office open 24 hours a day at José Martí International Airport and desks at the Habana Libre, Nacional, Riviera, Sevilla, Tritón and Vista al Mar hotels. Its branch at the Servi-Cupet station on Malecón near Calle 15, near the Monumento a las Victimas del *Maine*, is more helpful than some of the hotel outlets. It's open 8 am to 8 pm daily.

The main Transtur office (☎ 33-4038) is next to the Hotel Capri, Calle 21, between Calles N and O in Vedado, and there are desks at the Ambos Mundos, Copacabana, Deauville, Inglaterra, Nacional, Neptuno, Panamericano, Plaza, Riviera and Sevilla hotels. Another Transtur office is on Calle 25, between Calles L and K, near the Hotel Habana Libre. Transtur also has an office in the Sierra Maestra Marine Terminal on Plaza de San Francisco de Asís. Transtur and

Havanautos offices in Havana tend to have only expensive cars, not the cheaper models you can find in other cities.

Micar specializes in budget compact cars. Its main office (☎ 24-2444) is opposite the Servi-Cupet gas station near the Hotel Meliá Cohiba and is open 24 hours. Micar also has a desk at the Cubalse Fiat dealership, Malecón and Príncipe, not far from the main Vedado hotel district. It's open 8:30 am to 5 pm weekdays, 8:30 am to noon Saturday. It has some of the cheapest rental cars in Havana, but you must go personally as the phone doesn't work. If you're willing to rent for 11 days, you could get a Fiat for only US$35 a day, plus US$5 insurance.

Cubacar (☎ 33-4661) is at the Hotel Meliá Cohiba, accessible from outside the building. Other Cubacar branches are at Hotel El Comodoro in Miramar and at the Marina Hemingway. Its cheapest Suzuki Sidekick starts at US$61 a day, plus US$10 insurance (minimum three-day rental). Vía Rent a Car (☎ 24-9232) is at Hotel El Bosque in Kohly.

Panautos (☎ 55-3255), at Línea and Malecón, rents diesel-powered Citroëns for US$81 a day, plus US$15 for insurance. The price is reduced in the low season or if you rent for a week. Panautos' other locations are at the Víazul bus terminal (☎ 66-6226) in Nuevo Vedado and at the corner of Calle 42 and Av 3 (☎ 22-7684) in Miramar.

Chauffeur-driven limousines are available from Rex Rent a Car (☎ 33-7788, fax 33-7789), at Línea and Malecón, for US$325 a day with 150km. Rex also leases Volvo 940s to business people for US$45 a day all-inclusive on an annual basis.

Cubacar, Havanautos, Micar, Panautos, Transtur and Vía all have offices downstairs on the arrivals level in Terminal No 3 at José Martí International Airport.

There are four Servi-Cupet gas stations in Vedado: Calle L at Calle 17; Malecón and Calle 15; Malecón and Paseo, near the Riviera and Meliá Cohiba hotels; and on Av de la Independencia (northbound lane) south of Plaza de la Revolución. All are open 24 hours a day.

Municipal parking attendants watch over the vehicles parked on Trocadero in front of the Hotel Sevilla, charging US$0.25 an hour, or US$1 7 am to 7 pm or 7 pm to 7 am (US$2 if you overlap periods). Exactly the same system is used at the parking lot of the Hotel Nacional in Vedado. Guarded parking is also available at the Parque El Curita, Av de Italia and Av Simón Bolívar in Centro Habana (US$1 a day). More of the same is at the corner of Industria and Dragones, between the Partagás cigar factory and Hotel New York.

Road Rules

As is the case in most of the rest of the Americas and continental Europe, driving is on the right-hand side of the road. The speed limit for cars is 20km/hour in driveways and parking lots, 40km/hour around schools, 50km/hour in urban areas, 60km/hour on dirt roads, in tunnels and under bridges, 90km/hour on paved highways, and 100km/hour on the freeway. Immediately slow down to 40km/hour if you see police on the highway or a red sign reading 'Punto de Control PNR'; otherwise, you face a US$10 fine. Also slow down at junctions or anywhere with crowds of people beside the road, as this is where the police hang out. Low-beam headlights must be used in towns, within 150m of an approaching vehicle or within 50m of a vehicle being overtaken. The use of seat belts is optional.

Road signs are similar to those used in Europe. A circular white sign with a red border indicates a road closed to vehicles in both directions, whereas a horizontal white bar across a red circle means simply 'no entry.' A red-bordered white circle containing two vehicles means no passing (a black-bordered white circle with a diagonal line between the two vehicles means you may pass again). A yellow diamond indicates that you have priority at a crossroads; otherwise, the vehicle approaching from the right has priority if the roads are of equal importance. A blue circle with a red diagonal bar means parking is prohibited.

Rental

Most cars are rented with unlimited kilometers and the only extras will be insurance, gasoline and parking. The basic rate usually goes down if you keep the car for seven days or more. The minimum rental period with unlimited kilometers is often three days. All told, you could end up spending nearly US$100 a day for a car you could get for half that amount in the US.

At the beginning of the rental period you'll be charged for the first tank of gas at US$0.90 a liter; a small car generally holds 32 liters, a jeep 42 liters, and a large car 55 liters. This fuel must be paid for in cash, not by credit card. If the fuel needle isn't all the way on full, ask them to fill it up or give you a discount. When you bring the vehicle back, there are no refunds for any gas remaining in the tank. Check the vehicle carefully before accepting it, making sure there's a jack, wrench and spare tire.

The rental fee must be paid in advance either in cash or by credit card, and a refundable US$200 to US$250 deposit is required (credit card imprint accepted). Delivery charges (that is, if you want to drop off the car at a different place from where you picked it up) vary according to the category of the vehicle, but are generally reasonable (for example, US$10 from Havana to either Varadero or Pinar del Río). Don't lose your copy of the rental agreement; if you do, you'll have to take the car back to the office where you originally obtained it and pay a US$50 penalty.

Your home driver's license or an international driving permit is sufficient to rent a car anywhere in Cuba, but you must be at least 21 years of age. Drivers under 25 pay a one-time US$5 fee. A one-time fee of US$15 is usually charged for each additional driver. Some agencies will also provide a chauffeur at an extra US$40 a day, in which case you don't need to pay insurance or post a cash deposit.

Cars can be picked up and delivered at most airports, and during the peak tourist season (December to April) it's wise to reserve a car through your travel agent overseas if you're sure you want one. With tourism to Cuba growing by leaps and bounds, the demand for vehicles has outstripped the supply, and you'll often be told there's nothing available. Most of the rental cars in Cuba, incidentally, are beaten up. Don't expect to drive off in a well-maintained car or you're likely to drive off disappointed.

Reservations are only accepted 15 days in advance, and without a reservation you may have to sit and wait until a car is returned to the agency. Additionally, it's common that prepaid reservations not be honored. We've also heard from people who prebooked from abroad only to have to sit at the airport for hours before being presented with a lemon (in this case, another tourist probably got the car by paying a bribe to someone at the agency). Keep your fingers crossed and have an alternative plan ready just in case it happens to you.

Insurance Two rental insurance plans are available. Plan 'A' (US$10 to US$12 a day) covers accidents but not theft; plan 'B' (US$15 daily) covers all risks except the loss of the radio and spare tire. Under both plans you're still responsible for the first US$200 to US$350 in damage or loss, so plan 'A' is quite sufficient. If you do have an accident, you must get a copy of the *denuncia* (police report) to be eligible for the insurance coverage, a process that can take all day. If the police determine that you are the party responsible for the accident, you will lose your deposit. The insurance premium must be paid directly in cash (credit cards and credit card insurance are not accepted). If the insurance is declined, a cash deposit of US$3000 or more must be posted.

Precautions To avoid being stuck with an unwelcome charge when you return the car, you should take precautions against small parts being stolen, such as the windshield wipers, rear-view mirrors, radio antenna and so on (all the more reason not to rent a car in Cuba). Most large hotels have guarded parking lots where you pay US$1 to US$2 a night; alternately, you can tip the hotel security guard a similar amount to protect your car. Some hotels charge US$1 for parking, but their parking attendants still expect an additional US$1 tip!

If the car breaks down on the road, contact the car rental company or at least try to get the vehicle to a tourist hotel. Never abandon the vehicle, as you'll be responsible for any stolen parts. If you notice a mechanical defect in the offing, take the car to any branch of the rental company and ask for a replacement vehicle. Cubans are masters of improvised repairs and passersby will invariably stop to help; please be polite if you decide to decline their assistance.

TAXI

Metered tourist taxis are readily available at all of the upscale hotels, with the air-conditioned Nissan taxis charging higher tariffs than the non–air-conditioned Ladas. The cheapest official taxis are operated by Panataxi (☎ 55-5555), costing US$1 flagfall, then US$0.45 a kilometer. Tourist taxis charge US$0.80 a kilometer and can be ordered from Turistaxi (☎ 33-5539), Habanataxi (☎ 41-9600), and Transgaviota (☎ 20-4650). Taxi OK (☎ 24-9518) is based in Miramar. Drivers of the tourist taxis are government employees who work for a peso salary.

The cheapest taxis are the older yellow-and-black Ladas, which are state-owned but rented out to private operators for US$150 a month. Many operate under the banner of Cubataxi or Panataxi. They won't wish to use their meters, as these are set at an unrealistically low rate, but you can bargain over the fare. They're not supposed to pick up passengers within 100m of a tourist hotel.

Private pirate taxis with yellow license plates are a bit cheaper, but you must agree on the fare before getting into the car and carry exact change. Many park in the middle of the street opposite the Capitolio in Centro Habana. Classic dollar taxis, including a few from the 1920s and '30s, often park in front of the Hotel Inglaterra.

Bicitaxi

Two-seater *bicitaxis* will take you anywhere around Centro Habana for US$2, after bargaining. It's a lot more than a Cuban would pay, but cheaper and more fun than a tourist

taxi. Those bicitaxis licensed to carry only Cubans may wish to go via a roundabout route through the back streets to avoid police controls, but they may be cheaper than other bicitaxis since they don't pay taxes in dollars. Many bicitaxis park along Av de Italia, and you can always try to use them (if the driver gets caught breaking the rules, it's his problem not yours).

WALKING

The most interesting parts of Havana – La Habana Vieja and Centro Habana – are best toured on foot. Indeed, one of the great joys of the city is wandering the old sections of Havana, admiring the splendid architecture, poking your head into shops and museums and imbibing at the many bars where live music is often played. So be prepared to do a lot of walking – bring good walking shoes, sunglasses and a good sun hat, plenty of sunscreen and loose-fitting, light-colored clothes.

Due to the large number of police on the streets of the city, security generally is not a problem day or night. However, as in all cities, it's prudent to leave your flashy jewelry at home. If you look like a million dollars as you stroll through Havana, you're more likely to attract the attention of thieves than if you don't look like you're wearing or carrying a fortune.

BICYCLE

As of 2000, there were no bicycle rental businesses in Havana. It might still be possible to rent a bicycle privately from a local resident, especially if you're staying in a private room. Always use the ubiquitous bicycle *parqueos* and lock the bike securely. Parts for Chinese-made bicycles can be purchased at La Lucha, Máximo Gómez No 767, toward Estación Cristina at Cuatro Caminos (see Train, earlier).

Travelers arriving by plane can easily bring their bikes. You could take apart your bike and put it in a bike box, but it's much easier to simply wheel it up to the check-in desk, where it should be treated as a piece of baggage (except on Cubana de Aviación, where you'll be charged for the full weight

GETTING AROUND

of the bicycle). You might have to remove the pedals and turn the handlebars sideways so that it takes up less space in the aircraft's hold; check all of this with the airline well in advance, preferably before you buy your ticket.

Be sure to bring a strong lock, as bicycle theft is rampant. There are plenty of bicycle parking facilities in the towns where you can safely leave your cycle for a one-peso fee. A numbered tag will be wired to your bicycle and you keep the corresponding token. Most hotels will allow you to store your bicycle in your room. A kickstand is advisable, as smart establishments object to having bicycles leaning against their walls.

BOAT
Passenger ferries shuttle across the harbor to Regla and Casablanca, leaving every 10 or 15 minutes from Muelle Luz, at San Pedro and Santa Clara, on the southeast side of La Habana Vieja. The fare is a flat 10 centavos.

ORGANIZED TOURS
Infotur (☎ 33-3333, 63-6095), Obispo No 358, in La Habana Vieja (open 9:30 am to 7 pm daily), and Rumbos (☎ 66-9713, 24-9626), at Linea at Calle M in Vedado (open 8:30 am to 7 pm daily), offer a four-hour city tour for US$15. Its visits to Tropicana Nightclub cost US$65 and up, including a quarter of a bottle of rum and a soft drink to mix it with, plus US$5 for transfers. Other organized day tours are to the Jardín Botánico Nacional (US$25), Playas del Este (US$10), Soroa (US$29), Cayo Levisa (US$65), the Boca de Guamá crocodile farm (US$44), Trinidad (US$125) and Cayo Largo del Sur (US$119). Its overnight trip to Viñales costs US$79/129/179 for one/two/three nights with breakfast and dinner and excursions to rum and cigar factories, plus US$10 single supplement if you're traveling alone. The one-night trip to Cienfuegos costs US$115 all-inclusive, leaving Havana on Tuesday, Thursday and Saturday. Infotur and Rumbos also sell air tours to Cayo Largo del Sur, starting at US$170 for one night with airport transfers at both ends, flights, meals, drinks and an excursion to Cayo Rico. Additional nights on Cayo Largo del Sur are US$60 each, with a US$15 single supplement.

Havanatur (☎ 33-1758), Calles 23 and M, below the Hotel Habana Libre, Vedado, offers identical excursions for the same prices (remember, there isn't supposed to be competition in a communist state; Cubatur, mentioned below, also offers the tours described above at the same cost). The Havanatur office is open 8:30 am to 8 pm daily. All of the companies mentioned here routinely cancel their trips when not enough people sign up, so it's a good idea to ask which tour has the best chance of actually taking place.

Cubatur (☎ 66-2077), also on Calle 23 below the Hotel Habana Libre, offers excursions to Colonial Havana (US$15, these are terrible and best avoided), the Museo Hemingway (US$15), Parque Lenin and the Jardín Botánico Nacional (US$16), Tropicana (US$55 to US$75, depending on the seat), Playas del Este (US$20, including lunch), Las Terrazas (US$38), Viñales (US$44) and Varadero (US$45, including lunch). Cubatur is open 8 am to 8 pm daily.

A Tour Best Avoided

In the lobby of every hotel in Havana there sits behind a desk a pleasant woman advertising guided walking tours of La Habana Vieja. Beware! The poor tourists who take the tour are led from one generally mediocre shop to the other and told little or nothing about the history of Old Havana or the splendid architecture that surrounds them.

Indeed, the friendly guides generally aren't even able to talk intelligently about the fans and perfumes and other items of questionable value sold at the shops on their beat. You're much better served using the self-guided walking tours provided in the Things to See & Do chapter. And leave those cruddy walking tours to those poor souls wandering Havana without this book.

¡ABSOLUTAMENTE NINGUN MIEDO!

TRAVEL AGENCIES

The travel agency of Habaguanex, San Cristóbal Agencia de Viajes (☎ 33-9585, fax 33-9586, reservas@sancrist.get.cma.net), Oficios No 110, between Lamparilla and Amargura, on Plaza de San Francisco de Asís, can reserve any hotel in Cuba. Habaguanex operates all of La Habana Vieja's classic hotels and its income is used to finance restoration work in the old city. The office is open 9 am to 6 pm Monday to Saturday, 9:30 am to 1 pm Sunday.

Havanatur (☎ 33-1758), inside the Airline Building on Calle 23, between Calle P and Infanta in Vedado, is a full-service travel agency specializing in airline tickets. Like all Havanatur offices, you can book excursions here, but unlike most it does a superior job of issuing airline tickets with minimum aggravation. It's open 8:15 am to 5:30 pm weekdays. On the outside of the same building is a travel agency owned by Cubana Airlines, Sol y Son (☎ 33-3271, fax 33-5150), Calle 23 No 64. It's the best place in town to book Cubana flights. It's open 8:30 am to 7 pm weekdays, 8:30 am to noon Saturday.

Agencia de Viajes Horizontes (☎ 66-2004, fax 33-4585), Calle 23 No 156, between Calles N and O, reserves Horizontes hotels throughout Cuba. It's open 8:30 am to 12:30 pm and 1:30 to 5:30 pm weekdays, 8:30 am to 1 pm Saturday.

Cubatur (☎ 66-2077), Calle 23, below the Hotel Habana Libre, can reserve hotel rooms anywhere in Cuba. This agency pulls a lot of weight and finds rooms where others cannot (until the early 1990s Cubatur ran every tourist hotel in Cuba). It's open 8 am to 8 pm daily.

Cubamar (☎ 66-2523, fax 33-3111), Paseo No 306, at Calle 15 in Vedado, is the international travel agency of Campismo Popular. It specializes in youth tourism at seaside or mountain resorts such as El Abra at Playa Jibacoa and Aguas Claras in Pinar del Río. The reservations office is open 8:30 am to 5 pm weekdays, 8:30 am to noon Saturday.

Marsub (☎ 33-3055, fax 33-3481, marsub@ ceniai.inf.cu), Calle B No 310, at Calle 15 in Vedado, specializes in scuba diving. The bulk of its business is prearranged, but you may be able to book one of its tours even after you arrive in Havana.

Things to See & Do

Havana consists of various neighborhoods, none more historical or fascinating than La Habana Vieja. A virtual living museum, Old Havana is undergoing extensive restoration, but it already stands as the finest former Spanish colonial city anywhere in the Western Hemisphere.

Flanking La Habana Vieja to the west is Centro Habana, home to the former national capitol, numerous palaces of bygone years, two famous cigar factories, the nation's museums of fine art, history and music, and dozens of other significant sights.

Along Centro Habana's western border is Vedado, *the* sin city of US swingers during the 1940s and '50s. Run by the American Mafia back then, Vedado was once synonymous with cheap sex, wild parties and glamorous casinos. Many of Havana's finest hotels are in Vedado in buildings once owned and operated by the Mob.

Southwest of Vedado are the neighborhoods of Playa and Marianao. It was here that wealthy Americans built elegant vacation homes prior to the Cuban Revolution and where today these homes – long since 'redistributed' to the masses – can still be appreciated facing broad, tree-lined boulevards. Also here are the national aquarium and the world-renowned Tropicana nightclub and cabaret.

Other areas of Havana of particular tourist interest are the Plaza de la Revolución and the Parque Lenin. The plaza is a gigantic square ringed by concrete-slab buildings of apparent Soviet design where Cuba's leaders tend to matters of state. The plaza was home to huge political rallies during the '60s and most Cubans now view it as Ground Zero of the ongoing revolution.

Parque Lenin, containing 670 hectares of parkland, is Havana's largest recreational area. Nearby (and nearly as big, at 600 hectares) is the Jardín Botánico Nacional, containing myriad gardens that spotlight Cuba's many plant species. A short drive away is the Parque-Zoológico Nacional, with an invigorating drive-through lion den.

Havana at Its Best

Just as beauty is in the eye of the beholder, city highlights are a very subjective matter. Here is the author's list of personal favorites for Havana:

Old Havana No question about it, La Habana Vieja is Havana's top attraction. The best way to see the former Spanish colonial city is on foot, at a leisurely pace. Following the suggested walking tour provided in these pages is a great way to appreciate this historic yet vibrant neighborhood.

Eastern Forts Touring the Fortaleza de San Carlos de la Cabaña, the largest fortress in the Americas, and the nearby castle are absolute musts. The sites are fantastic, and a cold beverage at Bar El Mirador, with its terrific view back on Old Havana, helps galvanize a long-lasting memory.

Cabaret Scene The world-famous Tropicana nightclub in Marianao district bills itself as 'a paradise under the stars,' which is a bit of a stretch. But the Carnival-born shows at this cabaret and the Cabaret Parisién in the Hotel Nacional make for a night of wide-eyed amusement.

Cuban Cuisine The cuisine in the Cuban capital is generally uninspiring. Still, there are a handful of restaurants in town that are memorable for their food and their ambiance. Among them: Paladar El Hurón Azul in Vedado, El Aljibe in Miramar and El Rancho Palco in Cubanacán.

Museum Marveling Quick, before the Revolution ends, tour the Museo de la Revolución to learn more about the Revolution's origins, its exploits and its enemies. Other worthwhile museums include: Museo Nacional Palacio de Bellas Artes, Museo de Arte Colonial and Museo de la Ciudad.

SEÑORES IMPERIALISTAS NO LES TENEMOS ABSOLUTAMENTE NINGUN MIEDO !

Although not a neighborhood at all, Havana's Eastern Forts (the Castillo de los Tres Santos Reyes Magnos del Morro and the Fortaleza de San Carlos de la Cabaña) should not be overlooked and are discussed in this chapter. Also addressed in these pages is a cemetery like few others, the Necrópolis Cristóbal Colón, which is intriguing on various levels.

Within these neighborhoods and special sites you'll find Havana's best attractions – from the largest Spanish colonial fort built in the Americas to cabaret shows that are second to none. Here in Havana you'll have the opportunity to at once experience a colonial-contemporary time warp *and* an at-times-bizarre clash of US-style capitalism and Soviet-age communism.

In Havana, the visitor often has the feeling that great history is being made all around, at the same time that tremendous efforts are being made to protect the past. Perhaps nowhere else at the start of the third millennium is the extent of this dichotomy as tangible as it is in Cuba's celebrated capital.

LA HABANA VIEJA (MAP 2)
The 142 hectares that comprise Old Havana are not merely a protected area containing 16th-century buildings, they also contain the finest buildings erected in the area over a 500-year period dating from the 16th century. Moreover, in recent years great effort has been made to renovate the entire neighborhood. There's still plenty of crumbling plaster and peeling paint, but there's also a wealth of Spanish tiles, inlay, ironwork and so on – and it can now be said that their presentation is actually improving with age.

Fact is, the Cuban economy these days rests on two pillars: tourism, which is Cuba's biggest hard-currency earner, and money sent by Cuban exiles in Miami to relatives living on the island (US$1 billion annually, or more than Cuba's entire sugar crop!). To bring Cuba up to the level of tourism found elsewhere in the Caribbean, the government has undertaken a fabulous renovation campaign that, in 2000, was being carried out by a 6000-strong force of restorers.

Everywhere one looks in Havana today, old, sagging buildings are being propped up, retrofitted, repaired and hand painted. And nowhere in town is the restoration effort mightier than in La Habana Vieja, which is home to many hundreds of structures dating from the 16th, 17th and 18th centuries.

This neighborhood, with its crooked, labyrinthine and exceedingly narrow cobblestoned streets, is home to approximately 70,000 Cubans. To wander these historic streets not only gives a taste of how life must have been when pirates roamed the sea and slave ships sailed into Bahía de La Habana, but also is a terrific way to see how the Habaneros of the here and now lead their lives.

During the 16th and 17th centuries, the wealth of the New World – gold seized from native peoples from Peru to Mexico – passed through Havana before crossing the Atlantic to Spain. The city's merchants made fortunes and spent them on the magnificent buildings you see today. Now visitors can marvel at the architecture *and* mingle with a people as hopeful and joyous as any on earth.

To really know Old Havana is to know her grand old *casas*, her plazas and her people. To do this one must proceed slowly. Take the time to stroll the streets once crowded with carriages, mules and carts. Settle frequently into a seat at a café or bar to draw in leisurely the sounds of singers and flirters and the sights of boys playing stickball and young women sashaying down nonexistent sidewalks. Catch a cool sea breeze and drift on it awhile.

La Habana Vieja Walking Tour
Colonial Havana contains far too many museums, memorials, art galleries, churches, castles and other historical monuments to see in a day. And for the reasons just mentioned, don't even try. For an introduction to the city, you could walk the following loops through La Habana Vieja and Centro Habana in a day without spending too much time at any one place, and then go back on subsequent days to do some deeper investigating at a leisurely pace. Expect most of

Party at the Cathedral

One Saturday a month, the Plaza de la Catedral is closed off for a spectacular **Noche Plaza** with 100 of Cuba's finest singers, dancers and other entertainers performing on a stage directly in front of the cathedral. The staff at Infotur and the Restaurante El Patio generally know the date of the next such extravaganza. Admission is US$10/25 without/with dinner. Forget New York. Forget Paris, Rio and Sydney. This is also *the* place to spend New Year's Eve.

¡ABSOLUTAMENTE NINGÚN MIEDO!

framing a theatrical baroque façade designed in the style of Italian architect Francesco Borromini. Novelist Alejo Carpentier called it 'music set in stone.' Author Richard Henry Dana, describing the cathedral in 1859, wrote:

The Cathedral, in its exterior, is a plain and quaint old structure, with a tower at each angle of the front; but within, it is sumptuous. There is a floor of variegated marble, obstructed by no seats or screens, tall pillars and rich frescoed walls, and delicate masonry of various colored stone, the prevailing tint being yellow, and a high altar of porphyry. There is a look of the great days of Old Spain about it; and you think that knights and nobles worshipped here and enriched it from their spoils and conquests.

One hundred and fifty years later, the murals to which Dana referred – three large original frescoes by the renowned painter Giusseppe Perovani – are in dire need of restoration, but the overwhelming ambiance inside the cathedral hasn't changed. Be sure to peek inside the often-overlooked chapel just off the altar. It contains a fine marble

the printed information and verbal guidance along the way to be in Spanish only. Regardless, this city offers such a delicious cultural banquet that you're certain to come away sated.

An excellent place to begin a walk through Old Havana is the **Catedral de San Cristóbal de La Habana**, whose two unequal towers dominate the Plaza de la Catedral,

NEIL SETCHFIELD

Plaza de la Catedral de San Cristóbal de La Habana

sculpture of Jesus and an enormous wooden procession cross dating from 1914, and portraits of priests long since returned to Him.

When the Jesuits began construction of the church in 1748, Havana was still under the ecclesiastical control of Santiago de Cuba. Work continued despite the expulsion of the Jesuits from Cuba in 1767, and when the building was finished in 1787 the diocese of Havana was created. A year later the city became a bishop's seat, elevating the church to a cathedral. Legend has it that the cathedral contained a dramatic funeral monument dedicated to Christopher Columbus, in which were the great explorer's remains. It's said that the monument was shipped to Spain in 1898, where it remains in Seville's cathedral. However, it should be noted that officials in Santa Domingo on the neighboring island of Hispaniola contend that they possess Columbus's remains – and they spent an astronomical US$200 million on a monument to the admiral (all that money for a *monument* on an island that's home to the poorest people in the Western Hemisphere). Not to be forgotten, Italy also claims to possess the remains of His Worldliness. It's fair to say that no one knows for certain where the explorer's last journey on earth ultimately took him.

The opening hours of the cathedral are also a bit of a mystery. In theory, you can wander within the cathedral 10:30 am to 4 pm Monday to Saturday, 9 am to noon Sunday. In practice, the building is usually securely locked. However, it's always possible to enter just before Mass at 8 pm Tuesday and Thursday, 5:30 pm Saturday and 10:30 am Sunday.

Prior to the Pope's visit in 1998, a tourist market filled the square in front of the cathedral. Today, that market is a block east on Calle Tacón, running from one end of the pedestrian street to the other. Avid shoppers won't want to overlook the market, but the high-quality goods there are grossly outnumbered by low-quality ones.

Many other noble buildings face the Plaza de la Catedral, among them the **Palacio de los Marqueses de Aguas Claras** (completed in 1760), San Ignacio No 54, at

Empedrado, which is now Restaurante El Patio. (El Patio is perhaps the most popular restaurant in Havana, serving international and Cuban cuisine and every kind of Cuban drink. Live music can be heard here 24 hours a day.)

The former palace is most notable for its Andalucian patio, so be sure to wander past the outdoor tables and take a look inside. If you need to use a bathroom, you'll find two open to the public inside the courtyard of El Patio. The palace-turned-restaurant, with its shady verandas, nonstop *musica viva* and its seats overlooking a lovely plaza, is one of those places in which you should try to relax and soak up the ambiance. By the way, the Cuba Libres (rum and Coke) served at El Patio are among the very best in town. Most bars and restaurants in Havana use cheap white rum in their mixed drinks. El Patio uses only dark, 3-year-old Havana Club rum.

Around the corner is La Bodeguita del Medio, a (grossly overrated and totally passable) bar-restaurant that's famous because Ernest Hemingway once drank there. The establishment, which has done all that it can to exploit the author's having had one and possibly more drinks there, claims EH used to come in for its *mojitos*. Amazingly, La Bodeguita del Medio makes the absolute worst mojitos in town, but thousands of tourists a year walk in, plunk down US$4 and drink one. For more information on El Patio and La B del M, see the Places to Eat chapter.

On Calle Empedrado a few doors down from La Bodeguita del Medio, is the **Fundación Alejo Carpentier**, also known as the Centro de Promoción Cultural. The foundation consists of an early 19th-century apartment building in which Cuba's late, great writer Alejo Carpentier (1904–80) once worked. His reputation in Cuba was made all the better when, in his later years, this son of a French man and Russian woman went from writing compelling short stories to helping the communist government crank out propaganda to indoctrinate the masses. The room in which Carpentier worked contains a display of his early works and some of his personal effects. It's open

8:30 am to 4:30 pm weekdays. Admission to the display is free.

The **Centro de Arte Contemporáneo Wilfredo Lam**, San Ignacio No 22, across the street from the cathedral, until the late 1990s proudly displayed the works of Cuba's leading modern painter, but today his works are scattered about town and, oddly, none is shown in the center named after him (the museum inside the Castillo Real de la Fuerza, just a 5-minute walk away, is usually a good place to find samples of Lam's art on display, and the Museo Nacional Palacio de Bellas Artes, in Centro Habana, always has some of his work on exhibit). Today, the center displays mostly artworks by little-known Latin artists, and the exhibits change regularly (as does the quality of the works on exhibit here). A Cuban of Chinese and African ancestry, Lam (1902–1982) was strongly influenced by Pablo Picasso (1881–1973), whom he met in Paris in 1936 and under whom he studied for a brief time. If you happen to see one of Lam's paintings, you'll no doubt recognize the influence the Spanish painter and sculptor had on him. The center is open 10 am to 5 pm Monday to Saturday. Admission is US$2. If you're short on time, don't bother with this site.

Elsewhere on the square is the **Casa de Lombillo** (completed in 1618, updated in 1741). The Casa is one of the oldest houses in Havana and is named after one of its 18th-century owners, the Count of Lombillo, who made his fortune in the slave trade. It's primarily notable for the exquisite arches of its verandas, which are supported by stately Toscana-style columns. The interior is memorable for its wonderful baroque arches and graceful use of space containing numerous interior balconies, which are still apparent even as the building undergoes a major renovation. During the mid-19th century this bygone palace served as Havana's main post office (it was the city's first) and until mid-2000 a stone mask mailbox in one of the outside walls was still in use. In late 2000, the Casa de Lombillo had been gutted and, according to construction workers, it will reopen as a museum

devoted to colonial days. Efforts were being made to return the once-magnificent structure to its original appearance.

Next to the Casa de Lombillo is the **Palacio del Marqués de Arcos** (completed in 1746), which in late 2000 had also been gutted and was in the midst of a ground-to-ceiling renovation. The work was scheduled to last until 2002, and if it is still occurring when you visit ask the security guard if you can enter and take a look around. (It's assumed you would tip him a dollar or two when you leave; if you don't speak Spanish, just approach the man with US$2 in one hand and with the other point toward the interior of the building, and he'll gladly let you in.) The former residence is a perfect example of a typical Spanish-American colonial mansion, with a spacious main room with a wide staircase hugging two walls as it winds to the 2nd floor. The formal entrance is on Calle Mercaderes, although one might mistakenly assume that the front faces the square. That's because the rear of the structure (the side facing Cathedral Square) is very stately, with five arcades on Doric columns on the ground floor and lovely porticoes above the arcades and overlooking the square.

According to the chief restorer, the building will reopen as the Hotel Casa del Marqués de Arcos. (It will, no doubt, be one of the city's finest hotels and an excellent place to stay on New Year's Eve, as Plaza de la Catedral is the main place of celebration for Habaneros at the start of every year. If you book a room here, be sure to request a room overlooking the square.) If you're in the plaza, be sure to walk around (or through) the former palace to Calle Mercaderes where, in late 2000, the sculptor Andrés Carrillo was creating a large and impressive mural, comprised of millions of tiny colored rocks, that portrays the Palacio del Marqués de Arcos as it might have looked in the 19th century, with gentlemen and ladies in formal wear entering the building as if on their way to a ball. The mural is named **Mural Artístico-Histórico**, and we can only hope that the person who christened the mural didn't spend lots of time thinking up a clever name for it. Also, notice that Calle Mercaderes is made of the original cut-granite blocks with only occasional patches of asphalt. Go ahead and say it: *They don't make roads like this anymore!*

The **Museo de Arte Colonial**, San Ignacio No 61, on the south side of the Plaza de la Catedral, displays colonial furniture and decorative arts in the former Palacio de los Condes de Casa Bayona (Palace of the Counts of Casa Bayona; completed in 1720). Among the finer exhibits are pieces of china with scenes of colonial Cuba, a collection of ornamental flowers, and many colonial-era dining room sets. To wander the rooms of the Palacio de los Condes de Casa Bayona today is to get an accurate picture of the interiors of 18th- and 19th-century Havana mansions. The former palace is itself a beauty, with a fine garden courtyard, cozy apartments and cool patios; don't let the relatively drab exterior fool you (unlike its neighbors, this former palace has no porticoes and appears rather plain from the square). The museum is open 9:30 am to 7 pm daily. Admission is US$2.

Just up Callejón del Chorro from the southwest corner of Plaza de la Catedral is the **Taller Experimental de Gráfica**, where you can see original prints being made and purchase any you like. There is no cost to enter, and some of the modern graphics created here show talent at work. The workshop also accepts serious students interested in mastering the art of engraving. Tuition costs US$250/500 for one/three months. You'll work as an intern during the Taller's open hours, 9 am to 4 pm weekdays. Nearby is the **Galería Victor Manuel**, where visitors discover Havana's top shop for art and handicrafts (see the Shopping chapter for details).

Continue one block south on San Ignacio and turn left on O'Reilly. Two blocks ahead is the **Plaza de Armas**, the seat of authority and power in Cuba for 400 years. A square has existed on this site since 1582, although the present Plaza de Armas dates only from 1792. In the center of the plaza, which is lined with royal palms and a dozen booksellers selling secondhand tomes from

shelves they painstakingly erect every morning except Sunday, is a marble statue (1955) of Carlos Manuel de Céspedes, the man who set Cuba on the road to independence in 1868. Plaza de Armas (Parade Ground) takes its name from the late 16th century, when the governor of the Castillo Real de la Fuerza used the site to conduct military exercises. Less than a century later the same site was an important place of leisure, as it is for Habaneros today. During the mid-19th century, writers described the parklike square as a favorite bandstand for local musicians, with the streets around the square filled every night with carriages used by ladies and their suitors. These days it's very pleasant to sit on a bench in the plaza listening to the typical Cuban music drifting across the square from La Mina café.

The baroque **Palacio de los Capitanes Generales**, on the west side of the Plaza de Armas, is one of Cuba's most majestic buildings. Construction began on the site of an old parochial church in 1776, and from 1791 until 1898 this was the residence of the Spanish captains general. From 1899 until 1902, the US military governors were based here, after which the building became the presidential palace. In 1920 the president moved to the building now housing the Museo de la Revolución and this palace became the city hall. The municipal authorities moved out in 1967 and since 1968 it has been home to the **Museo de la Ciudad**, which is very worthy of your time. The rooms are richly decorated and contain *lots*

A Cobblewood Road?

In front of the entrance of the Palacio de los Capitanes Generales take a good look at the street. No, those aren't cobblestones, although they do resemble the naturally rounded stones often used to pave roads centuries ago. Indeed, the stretch of road in front of the palace-turned-museum is the only one in Cuba made from round wooden disks.

¡ABSOLUTAMENTE NINGUN MIEDO!

of personal artifacts dating from the colonial era, as well as plenty of military uniforms, beautifully crafted saddles, and no shortage of cannon balls. There's a white marble statue of Christopher Columbus (1862) in the gardened courtyard, which is quite enchanting on a cloudy afternoon. Also displayed here (and nowhere else in Havana) are carriages that might have carried gentry around the Plaza de Armas a century and a half ago. War buffs will appreciate the several rooms dedicated to Cuba's wars of independence from 1868 until 1959. The museum is open 9:30 am to 6:30 pm daily. Admission costs US$3, photos US$2 and video camera rental is US$10. The guided tour (US$1 extra) visits a few rooms not accessible on your own.

Ask about the special one-day pass valid at 10 museums in the old town (excluding the museum in the Castillo de la Real Fuerza). The pass costs US$9 and offers a small savings if you already know your way around town and want to see inside everything in a day.

The baroque **Palacio del Segundo Cabo** (completed in 1772), O'Reilly No 4, at the northwest corner of the Plaza de Armas, is the former headquarters of the Spanish vice-governor. For a time the building served as a post office, then during the 20th century it variously served as the palace of the Senate, the nation's Supreme Court, the National Academy of Arts and Letters, and, for a brief period, it was the seat of the Cuban Geographical Society. Today most of the building is used by the Cuban Book Institute. There's a seldom-visited restaurant in a courtyard that courtyard buffs shouldn't miss, and there's a no-name bookstore just inside the entrance of the former palace that sells a fairly wide variety of books about Cuban culture and Cuban attractions. Most titles are in Spanish, but a good number are in English. The store is open 10 am to 5:30 pm daily.

On the northeast side of the Plaza de Armas is the oldest extant colonial fortress in the Americas, the **Castillo de la Real Fuerza**, built between 1558 and 1577 on the site of an earlier fort destroyed by French

privateers in 1555. The west tower is crowned by a copy of a locally famous bronze weathervane called **La Giraldilla**; the original was cast in Havana in 1632 by Jerónimo Martínez Pinzón and popularly believed to be of Doña Inés de Bobadilla, the wife of gold explorer Hernando de Soto, awaiting his return. (In 1539 de Soto set out on a three-year expedition from Florida to Oklahoma on which he reached the Mississippi River but found no gold. He fell ill and died while trying to return to Cuba.) The original Giraldilla (the name comes from the Spanish verb *girar*, meaning 'to rotate') is in the Museo de la Ciudad, and the figure also appears on the Havana Club rum label. The Spanish captains general resided in the castle for 200 years until they finally got around to constructing a palace of their own across the square. The castle is ringed by an impressive moat and its walls, like those of forts facing the Caribbean from Panama City to Santo Domingo, are made of blocks of coral. Today, La Fuerza shelters the **Museo de la Cerámica Artística Cubana** downstairs and a bar, snack stand, souvenir shop and restrooms upstairs. The museum contains some terrific contemporary artworks by Teresita Gomez, Roberto Fernandez, Mariano Rodriguez and many other respected Cuban artists. Contemporary-art lovers will want to see the castle for the museum alone. Upstairs you get a great view of the harbor entrance. (Photographers: If you're looking for an establishing shot of the marketplace on Calle Tacón, you'll find that the castle's roof/upper story offers an excellent vantage point.) It's open 9 am to 5 pm daily. Admission costs US$1. Signs are in Spanish only.

In 1519, the Villa de San Cristóbal de la Habana was founded on the spot marked by **El Templete** (Small Temple), a neoclassical Doric chapel erected on the east side of the Plaza de Armas in 1828. The island's first Mass was held below a ceiba tree similar to the one presently in front of the building, and inside the chapel are three large paintings of the event by the French painter Jean Baptiste Vermay (1786–1833), at least two of which have been painstakingly restored. However, don't be surprised if you see only two of the three paintings. The largest is seemingly always 'in restoration.' Admission is US$1, and worth every cent. Adjacent to El Templete is the late–18th-century **Palacio de los Condes de Santovenia**, today the five-star, 27-room Hotel Santa Isabel. The former stately palace of the counts of Santovenia dates from at least 1784 and was converted into the luxurious hotel in 1867. (A little dirt here: The excellently located and classy hotel is particularly popular with men, typically Germans, who make annual pilgrimages to Cuban prostitutes, because the hotel staff admits the women as long as they're accompanied by foreigners. The prostitutes' entry into this fine hotel is discreet and generally limited to the wee hours.)

Nearby is the **Museo Nacional de Historia Natural**, Obispo No 61, which contains examples of Cuba's flora and fauna. This museum is nothing special, but kids tend to enjoy it. Admission costs US$3. The museum is open 9:30 am to 6:30 pm Tuesday through Sunday. Next door to the museum is the **Biblioteca Pública Provincial Rubén M Villena**, a public library, which you might find interesting. Its hours are 9 am to 9 pm weekdays, and 9 am to 5:30 pm Saturday.

Several more old palaces and museums are in the first block of Oficios, off the middle of the south side of the Plaza de Armas. The 17th-century Casa del Obispo, Oficios No 8, a former residence of clerics and later a pawnshop (Monte de Piedad), now contains the **Museo Numismático**. It displays the largest Cuban coin and medal collection, with items dating from the 16th century to the present; signs are in Spanish only. The not-so-impressive museum is open 9 am to 5 pm Tuesday to Friday, 10 am to 4 pm Saturday, 9 am to 1 pm Sunday. Admission is free. The equally unimpressive **Casa de los Árabes** (House of the Arabs), in the 18th-century Colegio San Ambrosio, Oficios No 14, houses a forgettable museum of objects relating to Islamic culture consisting chiefly of poor displays of none-too-valuable daggers, swords, clothing, carpets, saddles, furniture and ceramic sculptures from Arab countries. It's open 9:30 am to 6 pm daily. Admission costs US$1.

Across the street from the Casa de los Árabes is the **Museo del Automóvil**, Oficios No 13. If you've seen any other major automobile collections, such as those found in Los Angeles and Las Vegas in the US, where many millions of dollars' worth of classic and historic vehicles are exhibited in fancy display cases like oversize precious stones, you won't be blown away by this dusty warehouse of a museum. On the other hand, Havana's public car show is the *only* place you'll find the green 1960 Chevrolet Bel Air that Che Guevara rode in in the days immediately following Batista's ouster. Other notable vehicles on view here include a 1930 La Salle Model 340, a 1926 Willy's Overland Whippet 96, a variety of Fords from 1918 on, a horse-drawn fire engine dating from 1894 and the 1918 Ford Model T truck that belonged to Castro's father. The museum is open 9 am to 7 pm daily. Admission costs US$1. Incidentally, records indicate the first car driven in Havana putted around the city back in December of 1898.

From the Plaza de Armas, head west along Obispo. At No 113 you'll find a museum containing resplendent silverware, antique watches, antique fountain pens, an exquisite marble bathtub, several 19th-century safes, a beautifully engraved revolver, sabres from the early 20th century, an assortment of walking sticks and a small gallery devoted to the works of Oswaldo Guayasamín, a locally famous Ecuadorian painter who lived and worked in Havana for a number of years. On this book's map of La Habana Vieja, this museum, which calls itself Museo de la Ciudad despite the fact there's an official and truly more representative City Museum a few blocks away, is called '**Museo de la Ciudad No 2**.' It's open 9:30 am to 6:30 pm daily. Admission costs US$1. Incidentally, the house at Obispo No 117–119, just a couple of doors down, is one of the oldest in the city, dating from around 1648. Notable are its several Moorish-style ceilings (it's now an antiquarian bookstore and the Oficina del Historiador de la Ciudad).

During the 1930s, Ernest Hemingway frequently stayed at the classy five-story **Hotel Ambos Mundos**, Obispo No 153, at the corner of Mercaderes. For US$2, between 10 am and 5 pm daily, anyone can visit room No 511, where Hemingway began writing *For Whom the Bell Tolls*. Is it worth US$2 to see the room? Not really, unless you're a big Hemingway fan. (In 1939, Papa moved to Finca la Vigía in San Francisco de Paula, 15km southeast of Havana, today the site of the Museo Hemingway. There you can get a much better feel for the man through his belongings and the way he arranged them; see the Excursions chapter.) If you decide to pay a visit to room No 511, you might as well take the elevator to the top floor, where you'll find an open-sided bar with sweeping vistas. This seldom-visited bar is a particularly fine place to be with someone you love during a downpour, as the pitter-patter of a million droplets falling on the bar's glass roof, with tropical decor and comfy seating, makes for a very romantic atmosphere. It's also a superb place to curl up with a book.

Across Obispo from the hotel is a plaque marking the spot where the Universidad de La Habana was from 1728 to 1902, and a few doors west on Obispo is the **Farmacia Taquechel**, a 19th-century pharmacy that was being restored to its beautiful original state at the time this book went to press.

Just south of the Hotel Ambos Mundo on Calle Mercaderes is **La Casa del Habano**, Mercaderes No 120, which displays cigar paraphernalia and has a salesroom. You'll see plenty of cigar stores in Havana, but this one is nicer than most. Continue south a block on Mercaderes to Obrapia and turn right to get to the **Casa de la Obra Pía** (House of Charity), Obrapía No 158. This typical Havana aristocratic residence was originally built in the first half of the 17th century and rebuilt in 1780 soon after the British occupation. It takes its name from the fact that its original owner, a man with the enviable name of Martin Calvo de la Puerta, was known for lending economic support to five orphans a year during a period of many years. Baroque decoration covers the exterior façade, and between the two inner courtyards is a wonderfully refreshing room. At 1480 meters square, this grandiose home was the largest in the neighborhood at the time it was erected. It's open 10:30 am to 5:30 pm Tuesday to Saturday, 9:30 am to 12:30 pm Sunday. Admission costs US$1; photos are an additional US$2.

Across the street at Obrapía No 157 is the **Casa de África**. It houses artifacts presented to President Castro during his 1977 Africa tour. Objects from no fewer than 26 countries are presented for your viewing pleasure. Also on display are objects relating to Santería (the Afro-Cuban religion), formerly in the collection of ethnographer Fernando Ortíz. The Casa de África is open 9:30 am to 7:30 pm daily. Admission to the collection costs US$2.

On the corner of Mercaderes and Obrapía is a bronze statue of the Venezuelan liberator Simón Bolívar, to whom a two-story museum, **Museo de Simón Bolívar**, is dedicated at Mercaderes No 160. Downstairs, there are panels containing text in English, French and Spanish that describe the man's history and his many accomplishments. Upstairs, there are a couple of reproductions of his sword, a coin minted in his honor, and paintings of him by contemporary painters (at least one of which any sane person would classify as 'weird' or 'disturbing'). Most of the museum actually contains very little to do with Mr Bolívar. Instead, the majority of the rooms are devoted to works by lesser-known Cuban contemporary artists. This rather peculiar museum is open 10:30 am to 5:30 pm Tuesday to Saturday, 9:30 am to 12:30 pm Sunday. Admission is US$1 and the price is a bit high at that. The **Casa de México Benito Juárez**, Obrapía No 116, at Mercaderes, exhibits Mexican folk art in an 18th-century palace. Consistent with the Bolívar museum, there's not a whole lot about Mr Juárez at the museum bearing his name. It's open 10:30 am to 5:30 pm Tuesday to Saturday, 9 am to 1 pm Sunday. Admission costs US$1.

Just east on Obrapía, at No 11, is the **Casa Oswaldo Guayasamín**, the workshop and home of the noted Ecuadorian painter who lived in Havana for many years before he passed away in March 1999. Samples of his work are displayed on the 2nd floor of the two-story home. Most are large portraits of Fidel Castro that the artist gave to the Cuban leader. Castro generously returned the works to Guayasamín's home-turned-museum so that all the world could appreciate them. The artist's bedroom is just as he left it, with his clothes hanging in a closet or tucked in a dresser. His bathroom is also just as he left it – you can see his toothbrushes on a rack over the sink. You may look at the bathroom, but there are no public bathrooms here. Only Guayasamín admirers would truly appreciate this place. Downstairs, as of 2000, are watercolors by Canadian artist Ray Dirks. Most depict scenes of life in contemporary Africa, particularly Ethiopia and Sudan. They are cheerful, if less than compelling. Workers said other exhibitions would replace this one, but they didn't know when that might be. The Casa Oswaldo Guayasamín, which is possibly most impressive for its finely worked iron railings, a marble staircase, graceful arches and other architectural features, is open 10:30 am to 5:30 pm Tuesday to Saturday, 9:30 am to 12:30 pm Sunday. Admission costs US$1.

Next door to the House of Guayasamín, at Obrapía No 107, is the **Casa del Abanico** (House of Fans), where you can buy painted, collapsible handmade fans. Most are junk. The store is mentioned here only because you will likely see many tourists milling about the place and think you're missing something. The tourists are there only because – nine times out of 10 – they were led there by a local guide who presumably gets a kickback on purchases he initiates.

South on Oficios, at Amargura, is the domed **Lonja del Comercio** (Market House), a former commodities market erected in 1909. In 1996 the building was completely renovated to provide office space for foreign companies with joint ventures in Cuba. Enter the building to admire its central dome with a possible likeness of the god Mercury in bronze at the top. The Lonja faces the north side of the Plaza de San Francisco de Asís, which is notable for the white marble **Fuente de los Leones** (Fountain of Lions) carved by the Italian sculptor Giuseppe Gaginni in 1836. The south side of the square is taken up by the impressive **Iglesia y Monasterio de San Francisco de Asís**, which has the tallest belltower in Havana. Originally constructed in 1608 and rebuilt in the baroque style from 1719 to 1738, San Francisco de Asís was taken over by the Spanish state in 1841 as part of a political move against the all-powerful religious orders of the day. It ceased to be a consecrated church at that time, and later served as a warehouse and post office. During its years as a church, Saint Francis Solano briefly lived there. Out of the public eye are three former cloisters, spacious courtyards and more than 100 tiny apartments for members of the convent who once lived there. The nave of the church, which was beautifully restored during the early 1990s, fortunately is open to the public.

Today the church serves as a concert hall, and off to one side of the nave a small museum of religious paintings, silverware, woodcarvings and ceramics has been set up in the two large cloisters. There's a crypt on the premises that was a popular burial place for local 17th- and 18th-century aristocrats. The nave is open 9:30 am to 7 pm daily. Admission costs US$2, photos an extra US$2, video cameras an extra US$10, plus US$1 to climb the tower.

Return to Oficios and continue south to Brasil. Go west one block to La Habana Vieja's third historic square, the **Plaza Vieja** (Old Square), which dates from the 16th century and was completely restored in 2000. In that same year, most of the buildings surrounding the square – one-time mansions belonging to Havana's wealthiest merchants, replete with elegant porticoes, wide balconies and tiled roofs – were also being revitalized, including several of the buildings mentioned here. By 2002, all of the work around the square is expected to be finished. Even during restoration, the square is a beautiful sight to behold. Historically, the plaza dates from the mid-16th century, when it was called Plaza Nueva (New

Square). Initially it was a public square and a popular gathering place used for military exercises. It served as an open-air marketplace until 1835, when the market moved and the square again became a popular place to gather and discuss the day's events. More recently, the Batista regime constructed an ugly underground parking lot beneath the square that engineers demolished in 1996. Several historic buildings surround the restored square, including San Ignacio No 352, an art gallery, and Mercaderes No 307, the Fototeca de Cuba, which is a free photo gallery presenting exhibitions 10 am to 5 pm Tuesday to Friday, 9 am to noon Saturday.

The **Casa de los Condes de Jaruco**, Muralla No 107 at San Ignacio, has a covered gallery typical of aristocratic homes built around 1737. It contains various shops and art galleries belonging to the Fondo Cubano de Bienes Culturales. It's open 10 am to 5 pm weekdays, 10 am to 2 pm Saturday. Admission is free. Although named after the counts of Jaruco, the house's most famous resident was likely María Mercedes de Santa Cruz y Cárdenas, a famous countess of Merlín, who was born in the mansion and went on to become one of the city's early literary greats. Nearby, at the corner of San Ignacio and Muralla, is the oldest traffic sign in Havana. The sign dates from the time Muralla was called Calle de Ricla in honor

of a count who went by that name and lived in the neighborhood during the mid-18th century. Among other things, the fanciful sign reads: 'Calle de Ricla, in memory of his Excellency the Count of Ricla, sent by His Majesty to restore this city. Year 1763.'

Continue west on Muralla one block and then south on Cuba another block into the poorer southern section of Old Havana. While the area already described falls within what might aptly be called the realm of international tourism, what follows is squarely the realm of predominantly unrestored Havana, where life is often a struggle. Here, the street sweepers don't pass with quite the regularity of street sweepers in the plazas mentioned in preceding pages. Here, the flocks of tourists virtually vanish and police presence isn't nearly as apparent. At night, these streets are dimly lit and the vibes they give off are threatening, even if the danger is mostly imaginary. In short, if you want to see this side of Havana, you'll want to do it when you're not carrying all of your money on you and when you're not wearing jewelry or a watch with a metal band. Everyone will see at a glance that you're a tourist, but you should still try to not look like an easy mark. Avoid this area after dark as there's no reason to be in it then, and your ability to see possible dangers is much smaller in the night. This same warning applies to Centro Habana west of Paseo de Martí and north of San Rafael.

The **Iglesia y Convento de Santa Clara** (1638–1643), Cuba No 610, stopped being a convent in 1920. Later it was the Ministry of Public Works, and today the team in charge of the restoration of colonial Havana is based there. You can visit the large cloister and nun's cemetery between 9 am and 4 pm weekdays for US$2 admission. This site is notable for being the first nunnery in Havana, and it was founded by nuns from Cartagena de Indias. Pay particular attention to the marvelous beamed ceiling in the nave and the handsome columns and pleasing arches in the main cloister. The grounds are somewhat sprawling, covering four city blocks, and among the other sites of particular interest and oftentimes open to the public is the Casa del Marino (Sailor's House), in the second cloister. According to records, this house (the current residence of academics) was built by a pirate-turned-respectable-shipowner who gave the building to his devout daughter. She refused to leave the convent despite all the wealth her father could lavish on her, but he did what he could while she was still in the convent.

Heading south again to the corner of Cuba and Acosta, you'll find Havana's oldest surviving church, the **Iglesia Parroquial del Espíritu Santo** (first completed in 1640), with many burials in the crypt. It was originally built by an odd mix of freed blacks and slaves as a chapel, beginning in 1638. In 1674, it was extensively altered and declared a parish church. What will likely first capture your attention is the exquisite baroque wooden lattice gate. But inside are the true masterpieces – a modern sculpture by Alfredo Lozano and a large painting by Cuban Arístides Fernández. The finely carved ceiling also deserves your attention. On both sides of the nave run catacombs supported by the stumps of buried trees. Be sure to enter the vault that runs beneath the chapel. If you brought a flashlight along with you on your trip, you'll want it here; if you glance into a niche and the light is right, you can make out bones and paintings of skeletons believed to be performing a dance of death. Yes, this might not be the best place to take a child, but it certainly brings out a childlike fear in most of its visitors – that dreaded chill that something just awful involving the living dead is about to happen to you. And this surely is the place of ghosts, if ever there were any. Among the rich history of this church is this tidbit: A royal decree issued by King Charles III of Spain gave the right of asylum to anyone fleeing the law for any offense once they set foot in the church. One can only imagine the terrified souls who sought shelter from the authorities, knowing that the moment they left the church they would likely be whisked off to prison for a very long stay. The church is open 8 am to noon and 3 to 6 pm daily.

The **Iglesia y Convento de Nuestra Señora de la Merced** (construction began in 1775), Cuba No 806 at Merced, was years in the making. Its construction was completed by monks in 1867. It is the favorite site for weddings in Havana, due to its stunningly beautiful interior. This was the church the city's elite attended during much of the 19th century. Its nave, filled with lights that illuminate colorful trompe l'oeil frescoes, elaborate dome paintings and a magnificent altar, is wonderful to enter any time but it's particularly special on September 24, feast day of the Virgin of the Merced. On this day, Catholic and African beliefs come together at the altar as some followers come forward to bow before an image of the Virgin Mary, while others come forward to bow before an image of Obatalá, the Yoruba goddess of the Earth. It's the same image – a statue of the virgin sporting a flowing white robe – but who she *is* depends on the religion to which one adheres. This church is generally open from 8 am to noon and 3 to 5:30 pm daily.

Continue one block farther south on Cuba, go right on Leonor Pérez, and walk five blocks west to the seldom-visited **Museo-Casa Natal de José Martí** at No 314. The apostle of Cuban independence was born in this humble, two-story dwelling on January 28, 1853, and the museum on the edge of Old Havana displays letters, manuscripts, photos, books and other mementos of his life. It's open 10 am to 5 pm Tuesday to Saturday, 9 am to 1 pm Sunday. Admission costs US$1, photos US$2, video cameras US$10. Nearby, to the west across Av de Bélgica, is the longest remaining stretch of the old city wall. The idea of walling the city was first considered in 1558, after French pirate Jacques de Sores plundered Havana. However, as the city didn't have the resources and Spain wasn't yet willing to provide them, no wall was then erected. Instead, Spain sent more troops to guard Havana, and beginning in 1589 the mouth of the nearby harbor was fortified to prevent pirates from sailing in. Another 80 years would pass before the king of Spain would consider allocating money for a wall around Havana, this time in response to increasing attacks on Cuba by an increasingly powerful British navy. On February 3, 1674, engineer Juan de Síscaras of Spain laid the first of millions of stones that would be used in the 1.5m thick, 10m high, 5km long wall. Needless to say, the wall didn't exactly go up overnight. In fact, it took almost a century of daily work on it before the wall was completed in 1740. A bronze map at the remnants of the wall shows the outline of the original layout. Among the defenses erected along the wall were nine bastions, each with sentry boxes staffed night and day, and some 180 big guns aimed toward the sea were also installed. The only way in and out of the city, from 1740 until demolition of the wall began on August 8, 1863, was through 11 highly guarded gates that closed every night and opened every morning at the sound of a solitary gunshot. Many of the stones used to pave Havana's streets and construct the city's buildings were pulled from the monstrous wall, much of which still stood five decades after its demolition began.

To the right of the wall fragment is Havana's huge Estación Central de Ferrocarril (Central Train Station) where *La Junta*, the steam locomotive that inaugurated the line to Matanzas in 1843, is on display. Built in 1840, it is the oldest locomotive in Cuba. The station also isn't without glory. Built upon the ruins of an old Spanish shipyard, it opened its doors to business in 1912. The spacious waiting rooms and wide platforms have seen few alterations in 90 years. Cuba, incidentally, was the first country in Latin America to have a railway. The first train to make a move on Cuban soil did so way back in 1837 – years before Spain had lain its first train track.

If you're continuing the walking tour into Centro Habana, take Agramonte from the park on the north side of the train station north five blocks. Turn left on Máximo Gómez, and from the next corner you'll see the Fuente de la India in the center of a major boulevard.

CENTRO HABANA (MAP 2)

Central Havana borders La Habana Vieja, which from a visitor's point of view is the city's chief offering. But Centro Habana isn't without its fair share of attractions. This neighborhood, which developed when burgeoning Havana could no longer fit within its defensive walls, is home to several must-see sites, including the Capitolio Nacional, the Palacio de Bellas Artes and the Museo de la Revolución. It's home to considerably more hotels, restaurants and bars than is Old Havana, and its central location puts it within easy striking distance of La Habana Vieja and Vedado, the popular neighborhood immediately to the west.

Whereas most of Old Havana seems to have a tourist attraction in every direction, Centro Habana is the commercial heart of Cuba's capital, with many stores and even a few US-style shopping centers. Yet this neighborhood is also home to more than 200,000 people. Away from the main boulevards, there's little more to see than block after block of tall houses, most in need of a good paint job. The busiest and best section of Centro Habana for a tourist is Parque Central, which though named many decades ago, is still Havana's Central Park. Ringing it, at all times of the day, are taxis ready to take you anywhere you want to be.

Like Old Havana, Centro Habana is a culturally and historically rich neighborhood best explored in a walking tour. If you're wondering whether you should stay in Centro Habana or in the colonial district next door, the answer is you're better off staying in La Habana Vieja – if you can afford it. The hotels there tend to be more expensive than those found in Centro Habana, but they are all in or near the heart of the restored section of Old Havana. To see the best Havana has to offer the tourist, you need only exit your hotel if you're staying in La Habana Vieja.

Centro Habana Walking Tour

Begin this walk at the **Fuente de la India**, which is east of Parque de la Fraternidad, between Máximo Gómez and Dragones. This white Carrara marble fountain, carved by Giuseppe Gaginni in 1837 for the Count of Villanueva, portrays a regal Indian woman adorned with a crown of eagle's feathers and seated on a throne surrounded by four gargoylesque dolphins. The woman's face and everything about her demeanor conveys pride and confidence. In one hand she holds a horn-shaped basket filled with fruit, in the other she holds a shield bearing the city's coat of arms. The coat of arms consists of three distinct symbols, the first of which features a golden key between two mountains and a sun over the sea. It represents Cuba's geographic position relative to North and South America. Another symbol contains three stripes on white background and represents the three departments Cuba was administratively divided into during colonial days. The remaining symbol, a royal palm looking ever so stately, represents the unyielding nature of the Cuban people.

Across the street to the west is **Parque de la Fraternidad** (Fraternity Park), originally a Spanish military parade ground. The park was established in 1892 to commemorate the fourth centenary of the Spanish landing in the Americas. In 1927, it was remodeled and renamed to mark a Pan-American Conference held in Havana that year. The name was meant to signify American brotherhood and include all peoples in the Western Hemisphere. The ceiba tree presently protected by a high iron fence was planted in a mixture of soil from all the countries of the Americas, and busts of prominent Latin and North Americans were set up around the park. Ceiba trees, giants of disappearing jungles and savannas, have been revered throughout Latin America, from the ancient

Inca to contemporary Maya, as life givers. Today the park is the terminus of numerous city bus routes, and you'll see many photogenic old American cars now used as collective taxis parked in the middle of the streets.

The huge white marble building north of the park is the Capitolio Nacional. Before visiting it, have a look at the **Real Fábrica de Tabacos Partagás**, Industria No 520, on the west side of the Capitolio. One of Havana's oldest cigar factories and certainly its most famous, this Havana landmark was founded in 1845 by a Spaniard named Jaime Partagás, and today some 400 workers roll such famous cigars as Lusitanias and Churchills. Factory tours take place at 10 am and 1 pm weekdays, except for two weeks of holidays in January and July. During the tour, visitors get to see bushels of tobacco leaves handled on the ground floor, with sorting, rolling, pressing, ringing, boxing, box decoration and so on taking place on upper floors. Admission costs US$10, which is probably worth the price of being able to boast that you've toured the facility. As far as factory tours go, this isn't a BMW assembly plant or the production center for jet fighters. About the most exciting thing happening at this or any cigar factory is some terribly underpaid worker brainlessly rolling another cigar that he can't afford to smoke on a week's salary. And seeing row after row of workers doing this doesn't somehow raise the excitement level to the nth degree. Occasionally individual visitors are simply added to boorish tour groups, so if you see large tourist buses parked outside it's better to come back some other time. Otherwise just have a look around the salesroom, with its comprehensive display of Havana cigars and demonstration roller; entrance is free 9 am to 7 pm weekdays, 9 am to 5 pm Saturday. There's also a bar where you can sample a cigar.

Dominating this entire area is the magnificent **Capitolio Nacional**. It's similar to the US Capitol Building in Washington, DC, but much richer in detail. Initiated by the US-backed dictator Gerardo Machado in 1929, the Capitolio took 5000 workers three years, two months and 20 days to build at a cost of US$17 million. It was the seat of the

Cuban Congress until 1959 and now houses the Cuban Academy of Sciences and the National Library of Science and Technology. Visually, the structure is divine. The exterior is notable mostly for the sense of power and steadfastness it exudes, qualities conveyed by the dominant use of severe architectural lines, cold white Capellanía limestone and block granite, softened only a little by six rounded Doric columns atop the staircase leading to the main entrance, on the east side of the building. A stone cupola rising 62m and topped with a replica of 16th-century Florentine sculptor Giambologna's bronze statue of Mercury in the Palazzo de Bargello continues to dominate Havana's skyline. Directly below the dome is a copy of a 24-carat diamond set in the floor. Highway distances between Havana and all sites in Cuba are calculated from this point.

The entryway opens up into the Salon de los Pasos Perdidos (Room of the Lost Steps, so named because of the room's unusual acoustics), at the center of which is the statue of the republic, an enormous bronze woman standing 11m tall and symbolizing the mythic Guardian of Virtue and Work. In size, it's smaller only than the gold Buddha in Nava, Japan, and the Lincoln Monument in Washington, DC, in the US. The 120m-long room is perhaps the most impressive of the former capitol's many impressive rooms, with its pilasters of modern green marble on gilt bronze bases, and a floor comprising a virtual field of Portoco marble cut and laid in intricate designs and waxed to perfection daily. Dozens of sculptured panels in Roman style and giant French doors add to the beauty of the room's walls, while overhead 32 candelabras in Italian Renaissance style and an arched ceiling decorated in rows of friezes add to the splendor of the room. Huge copper lamps resting on carved pedestals of glittering copper, finely decorated doors and 20 marble benches imported from Italy only make visitors wonder why the capitol isn't still used by the country's decision makers. Two long lateral galleries lead from the Salon de los Pasos Perdidos, off which are dozens of rooms that

once served as congressional offices. Though not as large as the big room, these are every bit as carefully detailed, and the former chambers of the Senate and House of Representatives are just as grand. A small book could be written on all the architectural details found in the Capitolio Nacional. No visit to Havana would be complete without a tour of this extraordinary building. Comprehensive guided tours in Spanish are offered 9 am to 7:30 pm daily. Admission costs US$3, plus US$1 for the tour.

On the north side of the Capitolio is the ornate neobaroque **Centro Gallego**, Paseo de Martí and San Rafael, erected as a Galician social club between 1907 and 1914. The center, which contains myriad arcades, columns, balconies and sculptures, was built around the existing Teatro Tacón, which opened in 1838 with five masked Carnival dances. This history is the basis of claims by the present 2000-seat **Gran Teatro de La Habana** that it's the oldest operating theater in the Western Hemisphere. The National Ballet of Cuba and the State Opera are based here. Guided tours of the theater (☎ 61-3078), with a glimpse behind the scenes, are offered 9 am to 6 pm daily. Admission costs US$2.

Parque Central, across Paseo de Martí from the Centro Gallego, has long been a popular meeting point between old and new areas of Havana. The park was expanded to its present size after the city walls were knocked down in the late 19th century, and the marble statue of José Martí (1905) at its center was the first statue of the poet to be erected in Cuba. The monument to Martí went up on the tenth anniversary of his death. You may notice a group of men engrossed in an animated discussion a bit over from the statue toward the Capitolio. This is the famous *esquina caliente* (hot corner), where baseball fans avidly debate their favorite sport. One of Havana's finest grand hotels, the **Hotel Inglaterra**, faces the west side of the square. At a banquet here in 1879, José Martí made a speech advocating independence, and much later US journalists covering the so-called Spanish-American War stayed at this hotel. Bar La

Sevillana just inside the Inglaterra is a nice place for a break, as is the hotel's sidewalk terrace. However, for air-conditioning and ice cream, try the Pasteleria Francesa, between the Inglaterra and the **Hotel Telegrafico**. The Inglaterra, incidentally, is the oldest hotel in Cuba, its doors having opened to business in 1856. **Calle San Rafael**, the street between the Inglaterra and Gran Teatro, is Centro Habana's main pedestrian precinct for Cubans, if you're interested in a detour.

The most memorable section of **Paseo de Martí** (also called the Paseo del Prado) is to the north of Parque Central. Construction of this stately boulevard began outside the city walls in 1770, and the work was completed in the mid-1830s during the term of Captain General Miguel Tacón, who ruled from 1834 to 1838. He also constructed the original Parque Central. The idea behind Paseo del Prado was to create in Havana a boulevard as splendid as any found in Paris, Florence or Madrid at the time. Tacón achieved his objective, but unfortunately Paseo del Prado is in great need of restoration. It remains to be seen whether the city will restore it to its original splendor, or simply make do with contemporary improvements. Regardless, it's unlikely the government will allow its broken lights, cracked marble and deep ruts to remain for long since it's making sincere efforts to renovate so much of the rest of the city. Incidentally, the bronze lions along the promenade are a relatively late addition, joining the promenade in 1928. At Paseo de Martí No 302, at the corner of Ánimas, is the neo-Renaissance **Palacio de los Matrimonios**, the former Casino Español dating from 1914. On Saturday morning passersby can see many couples getting married here.

A block north on Paseo de Martí is the sumptuous old **Hotel Sevilla**, Trocadero No 55, the former Sevilla-Biltmore (erected 1908) where Enrico Caruso stayed when he came to perform in Havana in 1920. Graham Greene had one of his characters staying in room No 510. Enter to view the historic photos posted at the Paseo de Martí end of the lobby. One of Cuba's most famous cocktails, the Mary Pickford (rum, pineapple juice and grenadine), was invented at this hotel's bar. Also on Trocadero, just east across Agramonte, is the **Museo Nacional Palacio de Bellas Artes**, which was thoroughly renovated in 1999 and 2000. This gallery, erected in 1956 on the site of a former marketplace, houses Cuba's most important fine-arts collection, with original European painting downstairs (including works by Goya, Murillo, Zurbarán, Rubens, Velásquez, Hans Memling and Sorolla) and Cuban painters from the 17th through the 20th centuries. Also on display is a fine collection of Roman, Greek and Egyptian statuary (the museum claims it is the largest public collection of classical antiquities in Latin America).

Since 1976, the square in front of the Palacio de Bellas Artes has accommodated the **Pavillón Granma**, housing the yacht *Granma* that carried Fidel Castro and 81 other revolutionaries from Tuxpán, Mexico, to Cuba in 1956. Today this glass-encased memorial is one of the holiest shrines of Cuban communism, the equivalent of Mao's mausoleum in Beijing. Today, when Castro wants to make a political statement denouncing US immigration policy toward Cuba or whatever, he often has his minions organize a 'spontaneous' mass demonstration in the square. If you're in the area and notice buses unloading children in front of

---

Not Exactly Fidel's *Granma*

The 12m cabin cruiser, *Granma*, that carried Fidel Castro and 81 other revolutionaries from Mexico to Cuba in 1956 is now the namesake of a Cuban province and the official newspaper of the Cuban government. So, the yacht, the province and the newspaper are named after Castro's dearly beloved grandmother, right? Wrong. The yacht (and, hence, Cuba's leading newspaper and one of its provinces) was christened by its original owner, an American, in honor of *his* grandma.

¡ABSOLUTAMENTE NINGUN MIEDO!

the square and Cuban TV crews slowly unloading their equipment, you can bet you're witnessing the beginning of a political rally. (If you ever wondered about news articles citing tens of thousands of Cubans attending a demonstration, don't question the numbers. Fact is, under Castro the government of Cuba has gotten very adept at bussing people to protest sites from schools, urban worksites and fields. Refusing to participate in such a demonstration would be viewed as anti-revolution and would result in some form of disciplinary action.) The pavilion is surrounded by other vehicles associated with the revolution and is accessible from the Museo de la Revolución (read on).

Walk up Agramonte on the west side of the *Granma* to Refugio, where you'll find the **Real Fábrica de Tabacos La Corona**, founded in 1842. During the weekday tours, at 10:30 am and 1:30 pm, you'll see hundreds of workers busy hand-rolling such famous cigars as Romeo y Julieta, Montecristo and Cohiba (Castro's favorite brand until he gave up smoking; Cohiba is also widely regarded as Cuba's finest smoke). The factory salesroom just inside to the left is worth a look. It's open 9 am to 5 pm Monday to Saturday. You can even buy a single cigar of your choice and smoke it at the bar. The tour costs US$10, and the factory salesroom is free. If you toured the Partagás factory, you wouldn't see here anything more than you saw there, and vice versa. One Cuban cigar factory varies little from another.

The **Museo de la Revolución**, opposite La Corona at Refugio No 1, is housed in the former Presidential Palace, constructed between 1913 and 1920. The world-famous Tiffany's of New York decorated the interior, which tells you something about its beauty. The Salón de los Espejos (Room of Mirrors), where ceremonies of induction were held, was designed to resemble the room of the same name at the Palace of Versailles and is equally impressive. Such rooms abound here, although the Capitolio Nacional takes the cake for pure opulence. You might recall that this palace was the site of an unsuccessful assassination attempt against Fulgencio Batista in January 1957

(see History in the Facts about Havana chapter for details). The exhibits inside the former palace's many rooms provide a complete documentary and photographic account of the Cuban Revolution, and it's a must-see for anyone with a taste for Cuban history. Americans are generally amazed by the plethora of alleged terrorist activities against Cuba carried out by the CIA; many of the allegations have, in fact, been documented by American scholars. Most of the labels are in English and Spanish. In front of the building is a fragment of the former city wall as well as an SAU-100 tank used by Castro during the 1961 Battle of the Bay of Pigs. The museum is open 10 am to 6 pm Tuesday, 10 am to 5 pm Wednesday to Sunday. Admission costs US$3, photos US$3, video cameras US$5 and a guided tour US$1; compulsory cloakroom.

On the east side of this museum, up narrow Cuarteles into La Habana Vieja, is the **Iglesia del Santo Angel Custodio**, originally built in 1695, pounded by a ferocious hurricane in 1846 and entirely rebuilt in neo-Gothic style in 1871. This handsome church has hosted many literary and historical moments due to the famous people who have passed through its doors, including Cirilo Villaverde, who set the main scene of his novel *Cecilia Valdés* in the church, and José Martí, who was baptized here in 1853.

Continue east on Cuarteles another block, and then head north on Habana through a picturesque corner of La Habana Vieja to the **Museo Nacional de la Música**, Capdevila No 1. Its collection of Cuban musical instruments is exhibited in the eclectic residence (completed in 1905) of a wealthy Havana merchant. Vintage pianos, many bongo drums, captivating photos of Cuban musicians of yesteryear, lots of old guitars, maracas, claves, kettle drums, guiros, flutes and string instruments from Asia, maribas from Mexico, a xylophone from Laos, castañuelas from Spain – it seems there's a little of everything musical here. Still, it's not a must-see unless looking at musical instruments in glass cases really makes your pipes chime. The museum shop near the entrance sells recordings of Cuban music and concerts take place in the music room a couple of nights a week (check the showcase in front of the museum for schedules of events). It's open 9 am to 4:45 pm Monday to Saturday. Admission costs US$2.

From here walk west on Capdevila, keeping the entrance to the harbor tunnel and the tall **equestrian statue of General Máximo Gómez (1935)** on your right. It was created by Italian artist Aldo Gamba. On the corner of Capdevila and Agramonte is the art nouveau **Palacio Velasco** (1912), the present Spanish Embassy, easily distinguished by the yellow-and-red flag out front. Just beyond, in Parque de los Enamorados, is a surviving section of the colonial **Cárcel** (1838) where many Cuban patriots, including José Martí, were imprisoned. On the opposite side of Av de los Estudiantes is a fragment of wall encased in marble where eight Cuban medical students, chosen at random, were shot by Spanish troops in 1871. Their deaths were a reprisal for their allegedly desecrating the tomb of a Spanish journalist, locally famous for his anti-Cuban sentiments (it was later proven that none of the students had anything to do with the desecration).

Across the street is the **Castillo de San Salvador de la Punta**, designed by the Italian military engineer Giovanni Bautista Antonelli and built between 1589 and 1600. During the colonial era, a chain was stretched 250m to the castle of El Morro every night to close the harbor mouth to shipping. This castle, closed for many years, reopened to the public in late 2000. Inside you'll find a museum devoted to the fort's history (carpenters will drool when they see the museum's lovely beamed ceiling) and a restaurant that was under construction at the time this book went to press.

EASTERN FORTS

The **Castillo de los Tres Santos Reyes Magnos del Morro** was erected between 1589 and 1630 on an abrupt limestone headland to protect the entrance to the harbor in response to the sacking of Havana by French buccaneer Jacques de Sores. As forts go, this one's a beauty. Its layout follows the irregular lay of the land, with the sea slapping at the foot of several sides of the polygonal fortress and a deep moat with high, sloping walls defending the remaining sides. Erected on the broken backs of hundreds of slaves, El Morro served as Havana's lead line of defense until the completion of neighboring **Fortaleza de San Carlos de la Cabaña** in 1774. For more than a century, the fort withstood numerous attacks by French, Dutch and English privateers. But in 1762, after a bloody siege that lasted 44 days, a British force led by Admiral George Peacock and comprised of 173 ships carrying no fewer than 14,000 infantrymen and several thousand slaves captured El Morro by attacking from the landward side and digging a tunnel under the walls. The castle's gallant Spanish commander, Don Luís de Velasco, was killed in the battle, and the British buried him with full military honors.

El Túnel de la Bahía

The tunnel under the mouth of Havana Harbor, connecting La Habana Vieja and La Habana del Este, opened on May 20, 1958, after three years of work by a French company, the Société des Grands Travaux de Marseille. During the four decades that followed, the tunnel became an integral part of life in the capital. Some 25,000 vehicles a day cover the 733m from La Habana Vieja to La Habana del Este in just 44 seconds at the allowable speed of 60km per hour, thereby avoiding a 20km detour via Guanabacoa along narrow, traffic-clogged roads. In 2000, engineers from the French Ministry of Transport were back in Havana doing renovation work that may take several years. Each of the tunnel's two-lane sections will be closed in turn, so that sealant can be injected into the tunnel's roof to ensure that it survives well into the 21st century. The lighting, ventilation, drainage and safety systems are being modernized, with energy savings of 30% predicted.

– David Stanley

¡ABSOLUTAMENTE NINGUN MIEDO!

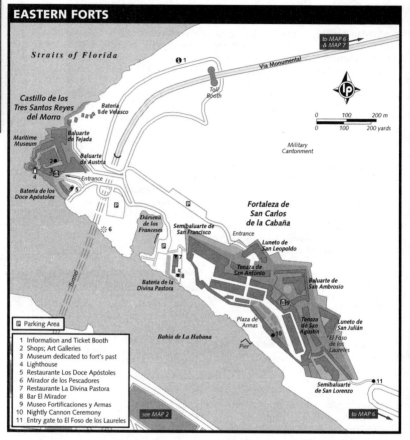

EASTERN FORTS

Straits of Florida

to MAP 6 & MAP 7

Via Monumental

Toll Booth

Castillo de los Tres Santos Reyes del Morro

Batería de Velasco

Military Cantonment

Maritime Museum

Baluarte de Tejada

Baluarte de Austria

Entrance

Batería de los Doce Apóstoles

Dársena de los Franceses

Semibaluarte de San Francisco

Entrance

Fortaleza de San Carlos de la Cabaña

Luneto de San Leopoldo

Tenaza de San Antonio

Baluarte de San Ambrosio

Batería de la Divina Pastora

Plaza de Armas

Tenaza de San Agustín

Luneto de San Julián

El Foso de los Laureles

Bahía de La Habana

Pier

Semibaluarte de San Lorenzo

see MAP 2

to MAP 6

| P | Parking Area |

1 Information and Ticket Booth
2 Shops; Art Galleries
3 Museum dedicated to fort's past
4 Lighthouse
5 Restaurante Los Doce Apóstoles
6 Mirador de los Pescadores
7 Restaurante La Divina Pastora
8 Bar El Mirador
9 Museo Fortificaciones y Armas
10 Nightly Cannon Ceremony
11 Entry gate to El Foso de los Laureles

0   100   200 m
0   100   200 yards

The interior of the fort is marked by two levels connected by multiple staircases. From the entryway, a wide path winds to the right and left. As you walk the path, you'll see many rooms that share a wall with the exterior of the fortress. Today, many remain empty. The occupied ones contain a small museum devoted to the fort's history; there are also two art galleries and a couple souvenir shops. Plans call for the empty rooms to house restaurants and other tourist services. An island of rooms in one enormous building fills the area ringed by the circular path (picture a donut, where the path is the dough and the structure fills the hole). The rooms originally served as barracks, storage rooms for provisions, weapons and ammunition, and as a church, meal room, a store, a hospital, officers quarters and offices. Today, there's a bar-restaurant that serves expensive, decent food in one of the rooms and the rest are off-limits to the public. In 1845 a lighthouse was added to the castle, the first in Cuba. The fort is open 8 am to 8 pm daily. Admission costs US$2, another US$2 for photos, and US$1 more for the guided tour.

The **Fortaleza de San Carlos de la Cabaña** was built between 1763 and 1774 to deny the long ridge overlooking Havana to attackers. It is the largest Spanish colonial fortress in the Americas, built by the Spanish King Charles III after Spain regained control of Cuba through a treaty with England. Legend has it that the king tried to spy the fort through a telescope; it cost so much money (14 million *duros*, as the currency was then called) that His Majesty was sure it must be visible from Madrid! Just how big is this fort? From one end to the other, it's a whopping 700m. It covers an area of 10 hectares (25 acres), much of which contained storehouses and barracks. During the mid-19th century, more than 1300 troops lived at the fortress, with another 4500 in the area and ready to defend the fort in a moment's notice. Among their powerful weapons were 120 bronze cannons, many of which can still be petted.

The fort was so awesome that no one ever dared to attack it. Which isn't to say there was never blood shed at the fortress, which to this day bears the name of the king who ordered its construction. During the 19th century Cuban patriots faced firing squads in the Foso de los Laureles outside La Cabaña's southeast wall. Dictators Machado and Batista used the fortress as a military prison, and immediately after the revolution Che Guevara set up his headquarters there and many of Batista's officers were tried and condemned there. Later it served as a military academy, and only in recent years have visitors been allowed inside to see the collection of armaments at the Museo Fortificaciones y Armas near the center of the fort (most of the weapons are from Asia, the 'coolest' of them being a catapult). The fort's rooms also contain bars, over-priced restaurants, art galleries, souvenir shops, a room containing exhibits offering evidence of the success of the revolution, and even a candy store. If you're fortunate, the mango trees on the premises will be bearing fruit during your visit. The trees are on a large grassy square lined with benches; the square lends itself very well to picnics.

There are public restrooms here and at El Morro. The fort is open 10 am to 10 pm daily. Admission costs US$3 until 6 pm and US$5 thereafter, photos US$2 and video cameras US$5. Nightly at 8:45 pm a cannon is fired on the harbor side of La Cabaña by a squad attired in 19th-century uniforms, a holdover from Spanish times when such a shot signaled that the city gates were about to close. The ceremony begins at 8:30 pm. Just outside the main entrance of the fort is a military zone containing several missiles pointed at the USA and reportedly at the ready – a dubious allegation given the amount of rust on them.

Surprisingly few tourists visit La Cabaña, while El Morro is usually jammed. This is because the tour buses unload their masses at El Morro but rarely provide time for La Cabaña, even though it's a much larger fortress. Around mid-morning it's especially chaotic at El Morro, as the tour buses from Varadero stop there on their way to Havana. If you're on your own and arrive at this time, first tour La Cabaña in relative peace and then head to El Morro. Beware that a US$1 per person fee is charged if you only wish to visit the park, but this is waived if you buy a ticket to either of the castles.

See the Places to Eat chapter for descriptions of the better restaurants and bars around the forts.

Getting There & Away

To get to the fortresses from Centro Havana, take the CicloBus through the tunnel from Dragones and Águila near the Hotel New York. This bus without seats is accessible via small ramps that lead to the doors. Cyclists are obliged to use it to get to La Habana del Este as riding a bicycle through the tunnel is prohibited. If you don't have a bicycle, you can walk to the head of the line and get on the first bus (ask the person selling bus tickets). Get off at the first stop after the tunnel; it's only a 10-minute walk back to either fortress. You can get there on the M-1 Metro Bus too, from which you'll also alight at the first stop after the tunnel, but make sure you're near an exit as very few people will get out there. Otherwise, a metered tourist taxi from La Habana Vieja should cost only a couple of dollars.

An interesting way to return to Havana is via the Casablanca ferry. From the entrance to La Cabaña, go down into the moat and follow it around to a gate just below the huge Christ statue.

If you're driving to the fortress, note that the parking attendants at the three parking areas charge US$1.

VEDADO (MAP 3)

Vedado translates to 'forest reserve'; during the colonial era, cutting down trees was forbidden here. That changed at the conclusion of the 'Spanish-American' War in 1898, when a peace treaty between Spain and the United States placed Cuba under US military occupation. With US troops in control of the island nation, Americans felt more comfortable than ever investing in Havana, and they saw the undeveloped rolling hills of Vedado, immediately west of Centro Habana, as a good place to do it.

The US intervention endowed Cuba with a series of weak, corrupt and dependent governments. In this climate, wealthy American companies found they could have their way in Cuba; by the 1920s they owned two-thirds of the country's farmland and most of its mines. Tourism from the United States to Havana (reached by ferry from Miami) also rose to new heights during the 1920s and early '30s as the prohibition of alcohol in the USA advanced the Yankee view that Havana was a haven for legal drinking, gambling and prostitution. Within a few years, Vedado was thick with high-rise hotels, restaurants, nightclubs and other businesses.

Indeed, the skyline of present-day Vedado was shaped during the Machado and Batista years, when American Mafia bosses Meyer Lansky, Lucky Luciano and Santo Trafficante built multiple-story casino-hotels in the neighborhood and counted on the corrupt leaders to put down any opposition to their endeavors. The mobsters' government aid was secure but it didn't come without cost: The amount of payola they doled out to Machado cannot be accurately reported, but Batista's ill-gotten gain is said to have included US$250,000 up-front for a gambling license and 10% of all gaming profits thereafter.

Batista exacted a heavy price from the casino operators but he rewarded them richly. Among the assistance he provided the racketeers: He waived visa requirements to make it easy for Americans to visit Cuba; he expanded the Cuban airline industry to facilitate travel to the island; and he permitted 24-hour gambling with no limits on wagers. Government supervision of the gaming rooms was minimal or nonexistent. Cubans who complained that the rich got richer while the poor grew poorer were dealt with brutally.

Batista's favors to the Mob were many, and they were not without political repercussions. The blatant abuses of power fueled dissent among the Cuban masses and spurred support for the rebels in the mountains to the south. Batista and the Mob underestimated the threat the rebels posed, but there was no denying their strength on January 1, 1959 – the day the *barbudos* battled their way from the Sierra Maestra and seized control of Havana. Within days, Fidel Castro and other leaders of the revolution set up headquarters on the 22nd floor of the Havana Hilton, the biggest hotel-casino in town, and aptly renamed it the Hotel Habana Libre.

Today, Vedado is a mostly residential neighborhood with a population of 175,000, although it has a lively commercial area and is home to the Universidad de La Habana, the oldest and largest of Cuba's institutions of higher learning. Vedado is often referred to locally as 'modern Havana,' to distinguish it from the older neighborhoods of La Habana Vieja and Centro Habana. For the visitor, it's a neighborhood with more than a few attractions, a wide selection of restaurants and numerous hotel choices (thanks to the Mafia bosses of the 1930s, '40s and '50s). Most sites of interest to the visitor are within easy walking distance of one another.

Vedado Walking Tour

An ideal place to begin a stroll is the neocolonial-style **Hotel Nacional** (1930) on Calle 21 near Calle O. In August 1933, the

US-backed dictator Gerardo Machado was overthrown during a popular uprising, and a month later army sergeant Fulgencio Batista seized power. On October 2, 1933, some 300 army officers displaced by Batista's coup sought refuge in the newly opened Hotel Nacional, where the US ambassador Sumner Wells was staying. Aware that the reins of power had changed hands, Wells found urgent business elsewhere and Batista's troops attacked the officers, many of whom were shot after surrendering. The Nacional manages to convey the atmosphere of a bygone era and it's well worth a look around. From the main entrance, stroll straight ahead through the lobby and out into the gardens behind the hotel. Several huge naval guns set up by the Spanish during the late 19th century still point out to sea from this cliff-top park where enormous peacocks have free range.

As you leave the Nacional, keep straight ahead on Calle 21 three blocks to the **Coppelia** ice cream parlor in the middle of a park on your left. Erected in the 1960s in a cheerfully open egalitarian style, the Coppelia brand of ice cream has faced hard times due to declining milk production, but it still manages to keep open this Havana landmark and serve tasty ice cream to hordes of Habaneros daily. The scene at the parlor, especially in the evening when people have left work, is somewhat shocking. Huge queues of peso-paying Cubans line the sidewalks around the park awaiting their chance to purchase scoops of ice cream. Security guards let groups of 20 people or so in to the center of the park, where the ice cream parlor is, to prevent unruly behavior in the parlor. The same security guards typically direct foreigners toward a pricey dollar section with no lines. If you want to pay the lower amount, just stay in the line with the locals.

Cine Yara, at the corner of Calles 23 and L, is the heart of Vedado, with famous 'La Rampa' sloping down to the sea. The cinema is one of the city's cleanest, and therefore one of its most popular. Cross over to the towering **Hotel Habana Libre**, where a 670 sq meter Venetian tile mural by Amelia Peláez is splashed across the front of the hotel facing Calle L. In the lobby is Alfredo Sosa Bravo's *Carro de la Revolución* made from

RICHARD I'ANSON

Hotel Nacional, where Winston Churchill, Frank Sinatra and Ava Gardner checked in (not together)

525 ceramic pieces, plus some of Havana's top visitor facilities, including a major bank, travel agencies, airline offices, an immigration desk, shops, restaurants, bars and nightclubs. Go on in and have a look.

Walk three blocks southeast on Calle L to the **Monumento a Julio Antonio Mella**, the student leader who founded the first Cuban Communist Party in 1925. In 1929 the dictator Machado sent an assassin to Mexico City and Mella was murdered. Across the street is the monumental central stairway of the **Universidad de La Habana**, founded by Dominican monks in 1728 after the reforming Bourbon kings assumed the Spanish throne. In 1842 the university, which is commonly referred to as La Colina, was secularized. The present neoclassical complex dates from the second quarter of the 20th century, and today some 30,000 students (2000 of them foreigners), taught by 1700 professors, follow courses in the social sciences, humanities, natural sciences, mathematics and economics.

Go up the stairway and through the monumental gateway into Plaza Ignacio Agramonte, the university's central square. In this square, in the shade of a large tree, you'll see a tank that was captured by the rebels in 1958. In front of you will be the **Biblioteca** (library) and to your left the Edificio Felipe Poey, with two unusual museums. The **Museo de Historia Natural**, downstairs, is the oldest museum in Cuba, founded in 1874 by the Royal Academy of Medical, Physical and Natural Sciences. Many of the stuffed specimens of Cuban flora and fauna date from the 19th century. Upstairs is the **Museo Antropológico Montané**, established in 1903, with a rich collection of pre-Columbian Indian artifacts. The most important objects are the wooden 10th-century Ídolo del Tobaco, discovered in Guantánamo Province, and the stone Ídolo de Bayamo. The exhibits are color-coded to indicate the three periods of Indo-American civilization in Cuba: Pre-Ceramic (red), Proto-Ceramic (green) and Ceramic (yellow). Both museums are open 9 am to noon and 1 to 4 pm weekdays; both are closed in August. Admission costs US$1 each.

Go down through the park on the north side of the Edificio Felipe Poey and exit the university compound via a small gate to reach the **Museo Napoleónico**, San Miguel No 1159 at Ronda. The four-story Italianstyle mansion (1928) contains 7000 objects associated with Napoleon Bonaparte, amassed by Cuban sugar baron and great admirer of Napoleon Julio Lobo and by politician Orestes Ferrera. The collection of objects, mostly from Napoleon's period of exile on St Helena, includes one of several bronze Napoleonic death masks made two days after the emperor's death by his personal physician, Dr Francisco Antommarchi, who later lived in Cuba. No, Napoleon never lived in or visited the mansion (many people ask this question of museum staff). The museum is open 10 am to 5:30 pm Tuesday to Sunday. Admission costs US$5, including a guided tour. The 10,000-seat **Estadio Universitario Juan Abrahantes**, where student teams play soccer and baseball, is just up the hill from this museum.

If you wish to continue on this walking tour, go south on Av de la Universidad alongside the stadium to Av Salvador Allende and follow the course described in the next section, titled Plaza de la Revolución. Anyone pressed for time should catch a taxi straight to the Memorial José Martí.

Other Vedado Sites

A good distance from the Vedado walking tour but worth a visit is the **Museo de Artes Decorativas**, Calle 17 No 502, between Calles D and E, a cheap taxi ride from anywhere in Vedado. The sumptuous rooms of this stately mansion (completed in 1927), formerly owned by the Countess of Revilla de Camargo, are decorated in various styles: rococó, Regency, neoclassical, Empire, English, Asian and art deco. As befits a stately mansion, the rooms are filled with gorgeous furniture, most of it European from the 18th and 19th centuries, and fine displays of porcelain from Msissen, Chantilly and Sevres. There is also a fine exhibit of Chinese porcelains. The museum is open 11 am to 6:30 pm Tuesday to Saturday. Admission costs US$2.

Four blocks away is another somewhat isolated museum that's worth the cost of cab fare. It's the **Museo de la Danza**, corner Calle G and Linea, which claims to be the only museum in the Western Hemisphere devoted entirely to dance. Here you'll find exhibits portraying Cuban ballerinas as well as dancers from Russia, Spain and Mexico. There are well-displayed photos of ballet companies, theater troupes and individual stars. There are also prints of programs, lots of paintings and sketches of dancers, posters advertising shows of yesteryear, dance medals bestowed by Fidel Castro and lots of text (some in English) of the history of dance worldwide and in Cuba. The museum is housed in a beautiful colonial-style two-story building. It's open 11 am to 7:30 pm Tuesday through Saturday. Admission here costs US$2.

Also in Vedado is the **Castillo del Principe** (1767–1779), an irregularly shaped fortress constructed to protect nearby valleys. It is said to contain moats, underground passage-ways, vaulted galleries, cisterns and all sorts of other intriguing stuff, but today it serves as police headquarters and is very off-limits to tourists.

Plaza de la Revolución

Known as the Civil Square until 1959, the Plaza de la Revolución is a Soviet-era, heavy-on-gray-concrete square ringed by the seat of government, various ministry buildings and an enormous memorial to José Martí. Most visitors to Havana first see the spacious plaza from the window of a taxi as they make their way into Havana from José Martí International Airport. It's easily identified by the multistory bronze-and-neon mural of Che Guevara that runs up the side of the building housing the Ministry of the Interior.

If you're short on time, there's little reason to pass this way again. With the exception of the memorial to José Martí, which houses a museum dedicated to the man, there's little of interest to the tourist here. The memorial, made from concrete and covered in a thin veneer of gray marble, is the tallest structure in Havana, rising 138.5m

above sea level. Because the plaza and the sites near it are within a short walk of each other, they are described in a walking tour. This tour picks up where the Vedado tour ends, at the Museo Napoleónico.

Plaza de la Revolución Walking Tour Beginning at the Museo Napoleónico (see earlier), walk south on Av de la Universidad. To the left, off Av Salvador Allende beyond the stadium, is the **Quinta de los Molinos**, a former residence of General Máximo Gómez and now a mediocre museum devoted to the man and set in the university's former botanical gardens. It's open 9 am to 5 pm Tuesday to Saturday, 9 am to noon Sunday. Admission costs US$1. The shabby park with its shady benches and lovely old trees is free. It's a favorite place for young musicians to practice their instruments, but there are no trails under the mature trees and the ground is littered with broken branches.

If time is short, skip the Quinta and continue south on Av de la Independencia past Havana's lively **bus station**, which you should enter to see the colorful mural *Alboradas de la Revolución* by Orlando S Suárez, a student of Mexican muralist Diego Rivera. It's intriguing to walk around Cuba's largest bus station, and there's a pharmacy, bookstore, post office, snack bars and public toilets (which you might need by then). Two blocks south of the bus station on Av de la Independencia is the **Biblioteca Nacional José Martí** (1957), with a photo exhibit in the lobby. It's open 8 am to 5:45 pm Monday to Saturday. Admission is free.

You are now on **Plaza de la Revolución**. Although this gigantic square has come to symbolize the Cuban Revolution, due to the huge political rallies held here during the '60s, most of the buildings date from the Batista era. On important occasions, Castro and other leaders have addressed hundreds of thousands of assembled Cubans from the podium in front of the star-shaped, 138.5m-high **Memorial a José Martí** and big events usually take place here on the afternoons of May 1 and July 26. The 17m marble statue of a seated Martí in front of the memorial is the work of Juan José Sicre. In 1996 the memorial was renovated and is open to the public 9 am to 5 pm Monday to Saturday. Admission to the museum dedicated to José Martí, at the base of the memorial, costs US$3, and if you'd like to take the elevator up to the enclosed 129m viewpoint, it's US$5 total (photos free).

Castro's office is in the long building behind the memorial, the heavily guarded **Comité Central del Partido Comunista de Cuba**, once the Ministry of Justice. The Ministry of the Interior on the north side of the square is easily identifiable for its huge

Ernesto 'Che' Guevara mural and the slogan 'Hasta la Victoria Siempre.' West of it is the **Teatro Nacional de Cuba**, which opened on March 16, 1960, with the show 'The Respectful Hooker' and the attendance of its famous author, Jean Paul Sartre. The theater is the venue of jazz, theater and ballet festivals and a host of other cultural activities. There's a popular café and a piano bar on the premises.

From the Teatro Nacional de Cuba, walk five blocks northwest on Paseo to Calzada de Zapata, and then another six blocks southwest on Zapata to Calle 12 and the

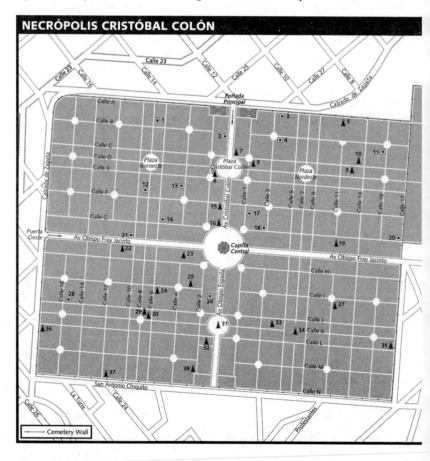

NECRÓPOLIS CRISTÓBAL COLÓN

Necrópolis Cristóbal Colón, Cuba's most important cemetery.

Necrópolis Cristóbal Colón

Laid out like a little city of the dead, with numbered streets and avenues on a rectangular grid, the Necrópolis accommodates the graves of just fewer than a million people interred here between 1868 and the present. Many of the graves have impressive marble tombstones, making this the largest sculpture park in the country. At the center of the cemetery is the Capilla Central (Central Chapel), which was com-

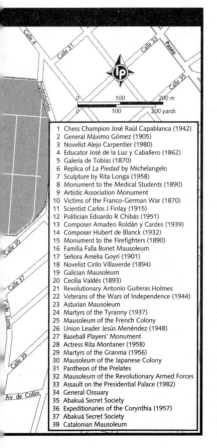

1 Chess Champion José Raúl Capablanca (1942)
2 General Máximo Gómez (1905)
3 Novelist Alejo Carpentier (1980)
4 Educator José de la Luz y Caballero (1862)
5 Galería de Tobías (1870)
6 Replica of *La Piedad* by Michelangelo
7 Sculpture by Rita Longa (1958)
8 Monument to the Medical Students (1890)
9 Artistic Association Monument
10 Victims of the Franco-German War (1870)
11 Scientist Carlos J Finlay (1915)
12 Politician Eduardo R Chibás (1951)
13 Composer Amadeo Roldán y Cardes (1939)
14 Composer Hubert de Blanck (1932)
15 Monument to the Firefighters (1890)
16 Familia Falla Bonet Mausoleum
17 Señora Amelia Goyri (1901)
18 Novelist Cirilo Villaverde (1894)
19 Galician Mausoleum
20 Cecilia Valdés (1893)
21 Revolutionary Antonio Guiteras Holmes
22 Veterans of the Wars of Independence (1944)
23 Asturian Mausoleum
24 Martyrs of the Tyranny (1937)
25 Mausoleum of the French Colony
26 Union Leader Jesús Menéndez (1948)
27 Baseball Players' Monument
28 Actress Rita Montaner (1958)
29 Martyrs of the *Granma* (1956)
30 Mausoleum of the Japanese Colony
31 Pantheon of the Prelates
32 Mausoleum of the Revolutionary Armed Forces
33 Assault on the Presidential Palace (1982)
34 General Ossuary
35 Abakuá Secret Society
36 Expeditionaries of the Corynthia (1957)
37 Abakuá Secret Society
38 Catalonian Mausoleum

pleted in 1886 and is the most regal of the chapels on the premises. The chapel is peach-colored, Romanesque in style and has an octagonal base. Inside you'll find stained-glass windows from Switzerland and an impressive fresco over the altar of the Last Judgment. The cemetery is a must-see and it is best appreciated with the aid of a little guidebook, devoted solely to the grand graveyard, which comes with a large fold-out map of the grounds. The book is a bargain at US$5. It's written in Spanish and English and is for sale at the entrance of the cemetery. If you have a near-vampire fascination with cemeteries, you'll want to purchase the 160-page, 180-photograph 'Guide to the Cristóbal Colón Necrópolis in Havana' guidebook, published in English and available in bookstores throughout Havana. The cemetery is open 9 am to 5 pm daily. Admission costs US$1.

Soon after entering through the neo-Romanesque northern gateway (1870), you'll find the tomb of independence leader General Máximo Gómez (built in 1905) on the right (look for the bronze face in a circular medallion). Farther along past the first circle, and also on the right, are the monument to the firefighters (1890); the Familia Falla Bonet mausoleum (of artistic interest); and the Capilla Central (see above). Just northeast of this chapel, at the corner of Calles 1 and F, is the tomb of Señora Amelia Goyri, who died while giving birth on May 3, 1901. The marble figure of a woman holding a large cross with the baby in her arms is easy to find, due to the many flowers piled on the tomb and the local devotees in attendance. When the bodies were exhumed, the baby was in her arms. Señora Amelia is the focus of a miraculous cult, and its followers never turn their backs on her.

Also worth seeking out is the tomb of Orthodox Party leader Eduardo R Chibás, on Calle 8, between Calles E and F. During the '40s and early '50s Chibás was a relentless crusader against the political corruption of his time, and as a personal protest he committed suicide during a radio broadcast in 1951. At his burial ceremony, a young Orthodox activist named Fidel Castro jumped on top of Chibás' grave and made a fiery speech denouncing the old establishment. The event marked the political debut of the most influential Cuban of the 20th century.

A bronze plaque at the corner of Calles 23 and 12, one block from the cemetery entrance, marks the spot where Fidel proclaimed the socialist nature of the Cuban Revolution on April 16, 1961, at a funeral service for all those killed during a counter-revolutionary raid on a Havana air base the previous day.

Several art galleries, cinemas, shops and cafeterias now grace this lively corner of Vedado. From the corner of Calles 23 and 12, any northbound Metro Bus will take you straight back to La Rampa (two stops).

Along the Malecón

Aside from investigating wonderful Old Havana, there's no better way to pass time in the Cuban capital than strolling the sweeping boulevard that hugs the Atlantic from the Castillo de San Salvador de la Punta in Centro Habana to the Hotel Nacional in Vedado. This boulevard is properly called Avenida de Maceo, but everyone in Havana knows it simply as Malecón (Sea Wall) in reference to the stone wall that skirts the northern edge of the boulevard and protects seaside Havana from hurricane-whipped breakers.

The Malecón was constructed during the American administration in 1901, and for a brief time there were actually some small structures built on the north side of the sea wall. The appeal of being close to the water is nothing new, but in this case Mother Nature wouldn't hear of it. Not a year passed before swells from a mighty summer storm toppled the buildings. Today it's still possible to see their foundations, between the Hotel Deauville and the Castillo de San Salvador de la Punta. Nothing else of the structures remains.

From the Castillo de San Salvador de la Punta, the Malecón extends along the coast 8km west to Castillo de Santa Dorotea de la Luna da la Chorrera, a fortress at the mouth of the Río Almendares. Here two one-way tunnels dive under the river, and the main

thoroughfare continues southwest through Miramar as Avenida 5 (hereafter called 'Av 5'), eventually becoming the *autopista* (freeway) to Mariel.

If you're in terrific shape, consider walking – or jogging! – the entire length of the Malecón. And here's a tip that'll ensure you the ultimate Malecón stroll: No matter where you begin your walk along the Malecón, head east from your starting point (walk toward La Habana Vieja, not away from it). That way you'll have the magnificent Castillo de los Tres Santos Reyes Magnos del Morro in front of you most of the way, providing an excellent backdrop to the lovely scenes that appear before you as you journey on.

Be advised that the nicest strip for walking along Avenida de Maceo begins below the Hotel Nacional and continues to the castle on the point. But if that's a bit much for you, consider taking a bicycle taxi the entire route *or* start your walk at the Parque Maceo, near the intersection of Malecón and Calle Padre Varela. In 2000, nearly all of the colonial-era homes fronting the Malecón from Padre Varela to the fort were renovated, and the wide concrete sidewalk on the sea side of Avenida de Maceo was re-poured. Unless a big hurricane hammers Havana between the time these pages were penned and the time you read them, the walk between the park and the fort will be a very pleasant one.

The following walking tour describes not only sites directly along the Malecón, but also those very close to it.

Malecón Walking Tour Although **Castillo de Santa Dorotea de la Luna de la Chorrera** (completed in 1643), at the mouth of Río Almendares, is called a 'castle' now, it was never more than a fortified tower built to defend the territory west of the city and to watch for warships and pirates' vessels sailing toward the Bahía de la Habana. The two-story tower contained little more than sentry posts, artillery emplacements, barracks and storage rooms during its years of military service. Records indicate that it rarely housed more than 100 troops. The tower was designed by engineer Juan Bautista Antonelli, who also designed a similar tower in Cojímar, east of town, and was completed during the administration of Álvaro de Luna y Sarmiento, after whom La Chorrera tower was named.

As a lookout post and defender of the city, La Chorrera was a two-time loser in June 1762. It was on the 6th of that month that the British fleet appeared on the horizon, its mission to sack Havana. Sentries at the tower reported to the governor of Havana that there were more than 100 ships off the coast, but there didn't seem to be any warships among them and only a handful were bigger than standard merchant ships. Based on the sentries' observations, the governor wrote in his diary that day: 'Only six or eight large vessels could be recognized. The rest were small vessels sailing from different parts and they numbered 140. We came to the conclusion that it was the British merchant fleet that every year sails in front of this port in the present season.'

Indeed, the sentries had given the governor bad information. There were no fewer than 28 warships among a fleet of support ships, and they hadn't come that great distance to shop. The British had quite expected a naval response from the city to meet them on the open sea, but since the Spanish authorities mistook the flotilla of destruction as a fleet of traders, the British decided to send ships east and west of the city and surprise-attack its fortifications on foot. The first defensive positions to come under attack were the fortified towers of La Chorrera and Cojímar, both taken within a matter of hours. The main body of the British force then assaulted the Castillo de los Tres Santos Reyes Magnos del Morro, which they captured after a 45-day siege that left 349 Spanish soldiers dead, 300 wounded and 373 taken prisoner. After securing El Morro, the British then used the 342 iron and bronze cannons, tons of gunpowder and 4157 shoulder weapons captured at El Morro against La Punta and La Fuerza castles. Troops at both castles surrendered soon after. Today, it's possible to tour La Chorrera and even eat there; a restaurant and a snack stand are on site. The fortress is open 10 am to 2 am daily. Admission costs US$2.

Continue northeast along the Malecón toward the 22-story **Hotel Meliá Cohiba** (completed in 1994) at the west end of Paseo. The Meliá Cohiba is one of the most luxurious hotels in Cuba, and it's worth a stop to see its gorgeous marble-rich lobby (which is always air-conditioned – something to keep in mind if you're overheating). Behind the Spanish-operated Meliá Cohiba is the **Hotel Riviera** (completed in 1957), once a playground for US gangsters. Indeed, the hotel was built on the order of Meyer Lansky, one of the top American Mafia bosses at the time. Notice the large circular hall on the right as you enter the lobby; it was a gambling casino until Castro shut it down. Gambling has not been permitted in Havana since Batista left town.

Continuing east on the Malecón five more blocks, you'll come to a large outdoor **flea market** at the corner of Malecón and Calle D. The market consists of tables, on a searing asphalt parking lot, on which are mostly wooden sculptures, leather goods, papier-mâché cars, low-quality ceramic figurines and percussion instruments. It's open daily except Monday. For a wider selection and higher quality goods, visit the handicraft market on Calle Tacón in Old Havana.

Walk 10 minutes east along the Malecón. At Calle G you'll see the **Monumento a Calixto García** (erected 1959), a Cuban general who is honored for his deeds to unseat the Spanish during the late 19th century. Twenty-four bronze plaques around the equestrian statue provide a history of García's 30-year struggle for Cuban independence. In what could be described as a mean feat, the US military leaders prevented Calixto García and all other Cuban rebels from attending the Spanish surrender in 1898 despite the aid they provided the Americans.

On Calle G a short walk from the monument is the **Casa de las Américas**, a major cultural institution sponsoring literary and artistic seminars, conferences and exhibitions.

It's also home to one of Cuba's largest publishing houses. Inside there's a small bookstore, as well as an art gallery featuring more than 6000 pieces by Latin American artists. The facility is open 10 am to 4:30 pm Tuesday to Saturday, 9 am to 1 pm Sunday. Admission to the gallery costs US$2.

Two blocks south of the Casa de las Américas on Calle G (Av de los Presidentes) is the 10-story, 144-room **Hotel Presidente** (completed in 1928). This art deco hotel, fully restored in 2000 to its original splendor, has been a favorite haunt of foreign entertainers playing in town for years. In the middle of the avenue next to the hotel is a former monument to Cuba's first president, Tomás Estrada Palma, who is now looked upon as a US puppet. His statue was toppled and all that remains of the monument are his shoes. On the other side of Calle G is the neobaroque **Ministerio de Relaciones Exteriores** (Ministry of Foreign Affairs).

East toward the Hotel Nacional is a stretch of the Malecón known as Av Washington because the former US Embassy was here. In the center of the boulevard is the neoclassical-style **Monumento a las Víctimas del *Maine*** (inaugurated in 1925), which had an American eagle on top until the 1959 revolution. The current inscription on the side of the monument alludes to a Cuban theory that US agents deliberately blew up their own ship to create a pretext for declaring war on Spain: '*A las víctimas de el* Maine *que fueron sacrificados por la voracidad imperialista en su afán de apoderarse de la Isla de Cuba*' (To the victims of the *Maine* who were sacrificed by voracious imperialism in its desire to gain control of the island of Cuba). You might recall that the *Maine* sank near the mouth of Havana Bay following an explosion of unknown origin on February 15, 1898. Two hundred and sixty-six sailors and two officers died in the destruction of the military ship. The US accused Spain of blowing up the *Maine* and used the incident as a pretext for declaring war on Spain. Soon thereafter, Spain lost many of her colonies, including Cuba. The rectangular, seven-story building at the western end

of this square was the US Embassy and now houses the US Interests Office. Facing this building, a bit back toward the *Maine* monument, is the famous billboard: '*Señores Imperialistas ¡No les tenemos absolutamente ningún miedo!*' (Dear Imperialists: We are not the least bit afraid of you!). Of course, the feeling is mutual.

The next site you'll come to as you proceed east on the Malecón is the 18th-century **Torreón de San Lázaro**, a watchtower built by the Spanish. Like La Chorrera fortified tower, the San Lázaro tower was not designed to stave off a major assault, and it too fell quickly to British troops during the invasion of 1762. Nearby is a 1916 bronze **Monumento a Antonio Maceo**; Maceo was the general who cut a blazing trail across the entire length of Cuba during the 1895 War of Independence. The monument, created by Italian Domenico Boni, shows the lieutenant general on horseback with his sword (a common sugarcane machete) held high. The rear of the horse faces what had been the US Embassy and is today the US Interests Office. Many Habaneros see the position of the statue as yet another Cuban gesture of defiance aimed at the USA.

Behind the Parque Maceo is the 24-story **Hospital Nacional Hermanos Ameijeiras** (completed in 1980), the tallest occupied building in Centro Habana (the Memorial a José Martí, an obelisk that rises some 138.5m above sea level, is the tallest structure in Havana). Some of the clinics inside the hospital specialize in treating foreigners (see Emergencies in the Facts for the Visitor chapter).

Head into Centro Habana, and just before you reach the Castillo de San Salvador de la Punta you'll come to the **Centro Cultural de España** (Spanish Cultural Center), where you'll find a ground-floor room devoted to paintings and sketches by renowned Spanish artists and a 2nd-floor gallery devoted to Cuban artwork. The exhibits in both galleries tend to change every 10 to 12 weeks. Generally there are between 75 and 100 artworks on display. The center is open 10 am to 5 pm weekdays. Closed weekends. Admission is free.

When you've reached the **Castillo de San Salvador de la Punta**, you will have come to the end of this walking tour. See the Centro Habana section, earlier, for information on the castle.

PLAYA & MARIANAO (MAP 4)

The municipality of Playa, west of Vedado across the Río Almendares, includes the prestigious residential neighborhoods of Miramar, Cubanacán, Náutico, Flores, Siboney, Atabey, Barlovento and Santa Fé. To the south is the more proletarian municipality of Marianao.

Many of Havana's foreign embassies are in Miramar and business travelers could consider staying at one of the large resort hotels there to have easy access to the many facilities originally created to serve the diplomatic community. Those interested primarily in sightseeing and entertainment, however, will find commuting to Vedado, Centro Habana and La Habana Vieja a continual nuisance and expense.

Many of Havana's business or scientific fairs and conventions take place at Cubanacán, where there are also several specialized medical institutes. Despite the austerity of the *período especial*, vast resources have been plowed into biotechnological and pharmaceutical research institutes in this area.

Yachties, anglers and scuba divers will find themselves using the Marina Hemingway at Playa's west end. Marianao is noted mostly for the Tropicana Nightclub, Cuba's most famous cabaret.

Miramar

Immense banyan trees stand in the park on Av 5 between Calles 24 and 26. Nearby, at Calle 28 No 113, between Avs 1 and 3, is the **Pabellón para la Maqueta de la Capital**. It's an ultramodern pavilion containing a huge 1:1000 scale model of Havana originally created for urban planning purposes and now a tourist attraction. The model is fun to look at, but unless you're in town for a long time you're better off visiting real sites instead of looking at tiny replicas of them. There's little else of interest to the tourist in

the pavilion, which is open 9:30 am to 5:15 pm Tuesday to Saturday. Admission costs US$3, students US$1.

Sixteen blocks southwest, near the Hotel Copacabana, is the **Acuario Nacional** (☎ 23-6401), Av 1 No 6002, at Calle 60. Saltwater fish are the specialty of this aquarium, which is home to more than 300 species of marine life. Expect to see sharks, hawksbill turtles, lots of colorful tropical fish and a fair amount of coral. Dolphin performances (the highlight of the aquarium) take place several times a day, but the posted hours are not to be trusted. Likewise, shark feeding is featured here, but at the time this was penned the hours fluctuated. Your best bet if you're in the area is to ask the ticket seller to tell you the current show times, or to call. The aquarium is in a constant state of renovation, with a new display case or pool replacing a small, cruel one every couple of months. The aquarium is open 6 to 11 pm Monday, 10 am to 6 pm Tuesday to Sunday, until 11 pm Friday; adults US$5, children US$4. The admission fee includes a dolphin show, so you may as well be there for one.

The strikingly ugly **Russian Embassy**, Av 5 No 6402, between Calles 62 and 66, has a smaller tower rising from the building's main tower. Together they resemble one gray block of concrete placed atop a tall skinny one. Be warned that Russians generally are viewed as vulgar people in Cuba. If you're in a taxi in the vicinity of the embassy and make mention of it, expect to hear some strong unfriendly remarks about Russians from the driver. It's ironic that after years of financial aid from Russia, Cubans today hold them in such low regard. Why? Cubans generally give one of three reasons, with the reason given varying on whom you talk to: They are bad tippers (waiters, taxi drivers, bartenders, etc); they are messy and vulgar (hotel staff who clean their rooms and bartenders who pour them vodka); and their construction standards are sub-par, such that many buildings built in Havana under Russian supervision are now falling apart despite the fact many are less than two decades old (people who live or work in such structures).

While in the area you'll no doubt spy the domed **Iglesia Jesús de Miramar**, Av 5 at Calle 82, a gigantic neo-Romanesque church. This church has little historic significance and, despite its size, is eminently passable.

Marianao

The former Cuartel Colombia military airfield at Marianao is now a school complex called **Ciudad Libertad**. You may enter to visit the **Museo de la Alfabetización**, which describes the 1961 literacy campaign, when 100,000 *brigadistas* ages 12 to 18 spread out across Cuba to teach reading and writing to farmers, workers and the aged. The museum is open 8 am to noon and 1 to 4:30 pm weekdays, 8 am to noon Saturday. Admission is free. In the center of the traffic circle, opposite the entrance to the complex, is a tower in the form of a syringe in memory of Carlos Juan Finlay, who discovered the cause of yellow fever in 1881.

Cubanacán

Cuba's leading art academy is the **Instituto Superior de Arte**, Calle 120 No 1110, off Av 9 (accessible only from the northwest). An art school was established in the former Havana Country Club here in 1961, and in 1976 it was elevated to the status of institute. The Faculty of Music occupies the original country-club building, and after the revolution a number of other facilities were erected on the site of the former 18-hole championship golf course. The most striking of these is the Faculty of Plastic Arts (opened in 1961), designed by Ricardo Porro, with long curving passageways and domed halls in the shape of a reclining woman. Across a small stream from the main building is the Faculty of Theater and Dance. Some 800 students study here and it offers courses for foreigners.

The **Palacio de las Convenciones**, or Havana Convention Center, Calle 146 between Avs 11 and 13, is one of Cuba's most dramatic modern buildings. Built for the Nonaligned Conference in 1979, the four interconnecting halls contain an auditorium with 2101 seats, and there are 11 smaller

halls. The 589-member National Assembly meets here twice a year.

Pabexpo, Av 17 and Calle 180, just two blocks off Av 5, opened in 1987. Pabexpo's 20,000 sq m of exhibition space in four interconnecting pavilions are filled with about 15 business or scientific shows a year. The Tourism Fair in May is worth trying to attend if you happen to be in Havana at the time.

The ultramodern **Centro de Ingenería Genética y Biotecnología**, Av 31 and Calle 190, 1km south of the Palacio de las Convenciones, is the focus of Cuba's genetic engineering and biotechnology research. Cuba first became involved in biotechnology in 1981, and this center opened in 1986 after an initial investment of US$140 million. Since then the 400 Cuban scientists employed in this enormous complex have developed a number of unique methods of medical treatment and several new vaccines. It's the largest of its kind in Latin America.

Two blocks away is the **Centro Nacional de Investigaciones Científicas**, Av 25 and Calle 158, where the anticholesterol wonder drug Ateromixol, or PPG, was created. This remarkable work has been conducted without foreign assistance, and it possibly holds the key to a world-class pharmaceutical industry of the future.

The substantial **Museo del Aire** on Calle 212 between Avs 29 and 31, La Coronela, has 22 planes and helicopters on display, most of them ex-military aircraft. Don't miss Che Guevara's personal Cessna 310, or the space suit used by Cuba's first cosmonaut. The museum is open 9 am to 4 pm Tuesday to Sunday. Admission costs US$2, a guided tour US$1 and photos US$2.

Activities

Deep-sea fishing can be arranged at the Marlin office next to Papa's Restaurant-Bar at the Marina Hemingway (☎ 24-1150), 20km west of central Havana. It's on the 2nd floor of the only two-story building in the vicinity of the restaurant. If the office is unoccupied (as it often is), try the one-story building 50m to the east with the sign out front that reads, 'Puerto Marina Hemingway.' This building is air-conditioned, so the fishing folks can often be found staffing a small desk just inside the entrance. Four hours of deep-sea fishing, for as many as four persons, costs US$285 minimum, with prices ranging upward depending on how far away from shore you want the captain to take you and the size of the boat used. Rates for six hours start at US$395 and for eight hours at US$440. Included are a captain, a sailor and tackle. May through July is the best time to catch white marlin and black marlin. August, September and October are blue-marlin months. Don't expect to find many sail fish in the waters around Cuba. The same office offers water-skiing or jet-ski rentals for US$17 for 15 minutes. Hotel tour desks should also be able to arrange these things.

La Aguja Centro de Buceo (La Aguja Dive Center; ☎ 24-5088), between Papa's Restaurant and the shopping center, offers scuba diving for US$33/49 for one/two dives, plus US$5 for gear. They go out at 10:30 am and return at 2 pm every day, weather permitting. There are 14 good dive spots in the area, and they take tourists to the ones that are most promising. English is spoken and a reservation is not required but a passport is. Call ahead if you are a big group (more than five). A diving excursion to Varadero or Playa Girón costs US$70. Reader reviews have been favorable.

For information on the Ernest Hemingway International Marlin Fishing Tournament held here in May, see the boxed text, 'Fishermen Ahoy.'

Getting There & Away

To get to Playa from La Habana Vieja, take bus No 264 from Desamparados, between Picota and Compostela, near the old city wall southeast of the Estación Central de Ferrocarril. Otherwise try bus No 132 or 232 from Dragones and Industria beside the Capitolio in Centro Habana. For Marianao, take bus No 34 from Dragones and Industria.

To reach the Marina Hemingway, take bus No 9 or 420 from near the tunnel under the Río Almendares in Miramar.

The Marina Hemingway (☎ 24-1150, fax 24-1149), Av 5 and Calle 248, in Santa Fé, 20km west of central Havana, has four channels, each 15m wide, 4.5m deep and 1km long. Each channel has berths capable of accommodating 100 cruisers or yachts. Several restaurants, a shopping center, grocery store, telecommunications center, Servimed Pharmacy (beside Restaurante Fiesta) and various upscale hotels are at Marina Hemingway. The port office is near Papa's Restaurant, but cruising yachts clear customs at a wharf near Villa Paraíso, 2km west of Marina Hemingway. You can call the marina over channels 16 or 72 (VHF). Cruising yachts are not allowed to stay in Havana Harbor itself.

Visiting American yachties should visit the marina office to get a letter from the port officials stating that you were there as a guest of the marina, and that all visa and docking fees were paid by the marina as a goodwill gesture. This will prove that no money was spent in Cuba in violation of US laws, whether any sum of money was spent or not.

Getting Around

Havanautos (☎ 24-0646, 24-0647) is on the third floor of the Sierra Maestra Building, Av 1 and Calle 0, Miramar. Panautos (☎ 22-7684), at La Copa Service Station, Calle 42 and Av 3, near Hotel Copacabana, rents only luxury cars. Cubacar (☎ 24-1707) has an office across the street from Hotel El Viejo y El Mar at the Marina Hemingway.

There are Servi-Cupet gas stations at Av 31, between Calles 18 and 20 in Miramar; Calle 72 and Av 41 in Marianao (near the Tropicana); and on the traffic circle at Av 5 and Calle 112 in Cubanacán. Oro Negro is at Av 5 and Calle 120, Cubanacán. All are open 24 hours a day.

Many of the old American automobiles cruising up and down Línea and Av 3 between Vedado and Miramar are collective taxis charging 10 pesos per person per ride.

PARQUE LENIN AREA (MAP 5)

The city's largest recreational area is Parque Lenin, off the Calzada de Bejucal in Arroyo

Naranjo, 20km southeast of central Havana. Set aside between 1969 and 1972, this is one of the few developments in Havana from that era. These 670 hectares of parkland and beautiful old trees surround an artificial lake, the Embalse Paso Sequito, just west of the much larger Embalse Ejército Rebelde, which was formed by the damming of the Río Almendares.

The main things to see are south of the Embalse Paso Sequito, including the Galería de Arte Amelia Peláez (admission US$1). Opposite is the Bosque Martiano, with a small library under a bridge. Up the hill there's a dramatic white marble monument (1984) to Lenin by the Soviet sculptor LE Kerbel, and west along the lake is an overgrown amphitheater and an aquarium with freshwater fish and crocodiles (admission US$1). The bronze monument (erected in 1985) to the late Celia Sánchez, a longtime associate of Fidel Castro who was instrumental in having Parque Lenin built, is rather hidden beyond the aquarium. A ceramics workshop is nearby.

Most of these attractions are open 9 am to 5 pm Wednesday to Sunday, and admission to the park itself is free. You can rent a rowboat on the Embalse Paso Sequito from a dock behind the Rodeo Nacional. A 9km narrow-gauge children's railway with four stops operates inside the park from 10 am to 3 pm Wednesday to Sunday.

A visit to Parque Lenin can be combined with a trip to **ExpoCuba**, at Calabazar on the Carretera del Rocío in Arroyo Naranjo, 3km south of Las Ruinas restaurant. Opened in 1989, this large permanent exhibition showcases Cuba's economic and scientific achievements in 25 pavilions based on themes such as sugar, farming, apiculture, animal science, fishing, transportation, construction, food, geology, sports and defense. The Pabellón Central, opposite Gate A, presents the products and public facilities of Cuba's 14 provinces and one special region. Cubans visiting ExpoCuba flock to the amusement park at the center of the complex, bypassing the rather dry propaganda displays. A revolving restaurant is atop a tower, with a long queue at the elevator. The Feria Internacional de La Habana, Cuba's largest trade fair, is held at ExpoCuba the first week of November. Despite the rather impressive sound of all this, ExpoCuba is poorly maintained. The exhibits consist mostly of large photos of equipment or people in fields using equipment and aren't very interesting. The vast majority of the facility's visitors are schoolchildren who arrive by the busload and spend little if any time in the exhibit halls. Instead, they seem rather addicted to the swing sets at the center of the complex. ExpoCuba is open 9 am to 5 pm Wednesday to Sunday. Admission costs US$1. Parking is available for US$1 at Gate E at the south end of the complex.

Directly across the highway from ExpoCuba is the 600-hectare **Jardín Botánico Nacional**, which is open 8:30 am to 4:30 pm Wednesday to Sunday. Admission costs US$0.60. The Pabellones de Exposición (opened in 1987), near the entry gate, is a series of greenhouses with cacti and plants native to Cuba. The highlight here is the Japanese Garden (1992), which was the brainchild of Japanese designer Yoshikuni Arake, who tried to achieve 'harmonious serenity' with his creation. Unless you see it on an unbearably hot day, you'll likely feel the designer achieved his objective. This portion of the National Botanical Garden was a gift from Japan's government in 1989 as a token of friendship to the people of Cuba. You can join 'ecotourists' off a tour bus for an organic, vegetarian buffet lunch in Restaurante El Bambú for US$14. The tractor train ride around the park departs four times a day and costs US$3, gardens admission included. Parking costs US$2.

The extensive **Parque Zoológico Nacional**, off Calzada de Bejucal, on Av Zoo-Lenin in Rancho Boyeros, chiefly consists of a bus ride through an African park where visitors see giraffes, hippos, zebra and other African wildlife. For most of the zoo's animals, there are no bars to be seen, simply many hectares of grasslands ringed by tall walls. However, there is a hyena compound (none smiling in their cage); they aren't released into the open area because they'd eventually eat most of the other live exhibits. There's also a rather impressive lion den. A series of gates allows the tour bus to drive right into the lion compound, past a group of lounging lions and then drive out. It's not a good idea to wave at the lions, as any one of them would have little difficulty jumping into your window. If you're lucky, an elephant will come up to your bus and stick his trunk in (it happens occasionally). There's also a walk-through area housing leopards, tigers, monkeys and many other species in cruelly cramped cages. The zoo is open 9 am to 3:15 pm Wednesday to Sunday. Admission costs US$3/2 adult/child, US$5 for a vehicle and all of its occupants (no taxis are allowed). The bus ride through the zoo costs US$0.40 and is worth every cent.

In the northwestern corner of Parque Lenin, behind Motel La Herradura, is the **Club Hípico Iberoamericano** (☎ 44-1058). Horseback riding through the park on a horse rented from the club costs US$12 an hour, although it's much cheaper to rent horses from boys at the nearby amusement park. The club's Escuela de Equitación offers riding classes for US$12 an hour. The club is open 9 am to 5 pm daily.

The **Club de Golf La Habana** (☎ 45-4578), Carretera de Vento, kilometer 8, Reparto Capdevila in Boyeros, lies between Vedado and the airport. It's a bit hard to find the first time as the signposting is poor and the course itself is on a back road not visible from the nearby highways. It's also called the 'Diplo Golf Club,' but most Cubans know it as 'golfito' (ask directions frequently). Originally titled the Rover's Athletic Club, it was established by a group of British diplomats in 1948. Nowadays the course is open 8 am to 8 pm daily, and starting time reservations are not usually necessary. There are nine holes with 18 tees to allow 18-hole rounds. Green fees are US$20/30 for nine holes/18 holes, clubs and cart US$10, caddie US$10. In addition, the club has five tennis courts (US$2) and a bowling alley (open noon to 11 pm daily). Nonmembers can use the club's swimming pool for US$2, or pay US$5 to use the pool with a drink and light meal included. This par-35 course is patronized mostly by diplomats and resident businesspeople, making it a good place to make contacts.

Getting There & Around

The easiest way to get to Parque Lenin is by train from Cristina Station (☎ 78-4971), Av de México and Arroyo, Cuatro Caminos in Havana, to the Estación Galápago de Oro on the northwest side of the park. It runs four times a day. Bus No 88 from Víbora and No 113 from Marianao run right through the park; otherwise, there's bus No 31 to Galápago de Oro and bus No 473 to El Globo, just south of the park.

Access to ExpoCuba is also easy. A three-wagon railcar departs the Estación 19 de Noviembre, on Calle Tulipán in Nuevo Vedado, Thursday to Sunday for the exhibition at 9 am, and leaves ExpoCuba for Cristina Station at 10:48 am. It departs Cristina for ExpoCuba at 12:36 pm, and leaves ExpoCuba for Tulipán at 5 pm (one peso each way). Additionally, bus No 88 serves ExpoCuba.

There's a Servi-Cupet gas station at Av de la Independencia and Calle 271 in Boyeros, near the Hospital Psiquiátrico north of the airport. It's accessible only from the northbound lane and is open 24 hours a day.

ACTIVITIES
Diving

Scuba diving is offered at the Marina Hemingway. For details, see the Activities section under Playa & Marianoa, earlier in this chapter. Tours for scuba divers are the specialty of Marsub SA (☎ 7-33-3055, fax 7-33-3481, marsub@ceniai.inf.cu), Calle B No 310, between Calles 13 and 15 in Vedado. It has scuba packages based at Havana, María La Gorda, Varadero, Playa Larga (Bay of Pigs), Cienfuegos, and Villa Covarrubias (Las Tunas), plus dive cruises from Trinidad to Jardines de la Reina.

Boating

The main cruising season for yachts is winter (December to April) when the weather is mild, the winds are reliable and hurricanes are unknown. The season begins with the

Merry Christmas in Havana Yachting Regatta in late December and culminates with the Havana Cup International Yachting Regatta in May, both held annually at Havana's Marina Hemingway. For information, contact the marina (☎ 24-1150, fax 24-1149) or see Tourist Offices near the beginning of the Facts for the Visitor chapter. Cubanacán offices worldwide will have information about these too.

Golf & Fishing

There are only two golf courses on all of Cuba, one of which is the nine-hole Club de Golf La Habana in Parque Lenin. For details, see the Parque Lenin Area, earlier in this chapter.

Cuba's finest deep-sea fishing is along the northwest coast, where the fast-moving Gulf Stream has created a prime game fishing area. For details, see Activities in the Playa & Marianao section, earlier.

COURSES
Language

An excellent way to justify an extended stay in Cuba while acquiring skills and learning Spanish is to take a course. The largest organization offering study visits for foreigners is Mercadú SA (☎ 33-3893, fax 33-3028, mercadu@ceniai.inf.cu), Calle 13 No 951, at the corner of Calle 8, Vedado, Havana 23, Cuba 12300. Mercadú can arrange regular study and working holidays at any of Cuba's universities or at the many higher education or research institutes around Cuba. Its catalog lists numerous programs, including study tours, research visits, participation at scientific events, regular academic study, extended research trips and organized encounters with professionals in selected fields. Since 1991 Mercadú has operated a summer school in July and August that includes about 150 courses at universities in Havana, Matanzas and Pinar del Río and various institutes in the fields of agriculture, communication, economics, education, medicine, science, sociology, sports and technology.

Mercadú also arranges registration at specialized symposiums, conferences, seminars and workshops throughout the year.

Fishermen Ahoy!

Every May an Ernest Hemingway Marlin Fishing Tournament is held at Havana's Marina Hemingway. In 1950 Hemingway himself donated the cup and helped draft the original rules and regulations of this contest, which has been held annually ever since. Registration costs US$500/600 for teams of three/four anglers for four days of fishing using 30lb line. Fully equipped boats can be hired at US$250 to US$500 a day with two weeks' prior notice. Visas and prior reservations are not required of competitors arriving on their own boats. To take home the Ernest Hemingway Cup, an angler must have won three times, not necessarily in consecutive years. For further information, contact Marina Hemingway (☎ 24-1150, fax 24-1149).

One-week tours are organized for professionals in fields such as education, health, law, music, architecture, theater, art, sports, agriculture and forestry. Most tours have a 10-person minimum, so they're mostly of interest to those trying to put together a creative tour package for a group of students or colleagues.

Of special interest are Mercadú's intensive courses in the Spanish language and Cuban culture at Havana University, varying from two weeks to four months with three levels of participation. A placement test is given at the university at 9 am on the first Monday of every month. Classes of three to 10 students receive four hours of instruction daily from weekdays. A two-week course costs US$200 tuition; four weeks is US$250; four months is US$800. A participation certificate is issued. You can sign up in person at the Mercadú office in the Edificio Varona at the university, or contact them in advance (☎ 70-4667, fax 33-5842). Mercadú has 17 branch offices at various universities throughout Cuba, all providing the same services.

Something similar is offered by the Centro de Idiomas y Computación José Martí

(☎ 22-9338, fax 24-4846, ice@ceniai.inf.cu), Calle 90 No 531, Miramar, Havana. The courses usually involve four hours of classes a day, five days a week, and are at four different levels. A diploma is issued to those who complete the advanced courses. These are marketed abroad by Cubamar Viajes (www.cubamar.cubaweb.cu). You can also sign up on the spot by giving one week's notice. The tuition is US$130/200/300/330 for one/two/three/four weeks of intensive lessons.

From the United States, Global Exchange (☎ 415-255-7296, fax 415-255-7498, www .globalexchange.org) organizes Spanish language instruction in Cuba for US$850 to US$1750 for eight days to one month, including airfare from Cancún, room and board, visas and instruction. Music lessons are also offered.

Art & Film

Courses for foreigners can be arranged throughout the year by the Oficina de Relaciones Internacionales of the Instituto Superior de Arte (☎ 21-6075, fax 33-6633, isa@ reduniv.edu.cu), at Calle 120 No 1110, Cubanacán, Playa, Havana 11600. Courses in percussion and dance are available almost any time, but other subjects, such as the visual arts, music, theater and aesthetics, are offered when professors are available.

The courses usually involve four hours of classes a week at US$10 an hour (US$15 an hour for postgraduate studies). Prospective students must apply two months in advance. The school is closed for holidays in July and August, but courses for groups are still possible at that time with advance notice. Anyone bringing a group of at least 15 students to Cuba for such a course is eligible for free tuition and board. The institute also accepts graduate students for its regular winter courses, and an entire year of study here (beginning in September) as part of a regular five-year program will cost US$2500. Successful students will be granted a diploma or certificate. Accommodations in student dormitories can be arranged for US$15 a day including breakfast and dinner, for the first 30 days, and US$9 a day for subsequent days.

The Centro Nacional de Conservación, Restauración y Museología (☎ 61-5043, fax 33-5696), Calle Cuba No 610, 10100 Havana, offers courses in the fields of artistic and architectural restoration. Numerous two-week courses are offered in March and November, with others in February, May and October. Tuition ranges from US$150 to US$350 per course.

The Taller Experimental de Gráfica (☎ 62-0979, fax 24-0391), Callejón del Chorro No 6, Plaza de la Catedral, Havana, offers instruction in the art of engraving. During a one-month course (US$250) the student will prepare an engraving with 15 copies, while the three-month course (US$500) teaches students more advanced techniques.

Places to Stay

In selecting your Havana hotel, bear in mind that most of the sights you'll want to see are in La Habana Vieja and Centro Habana. You'll no doubt note a relatively large number of hotels in the Vedado neighborhood and might assume that *that's* where you want to be. After all, who would build many large hotels there if there wasn't a lot to see and do there?

The answer to that question is: The Mafia built them. Gangsters from the USA built casinos in Vedado during the 1930s, '40s and '50s. Of course, for scores of out-of-town visitors to patronize your casinos there's got to be accommodations for them, so the mafiosi built big hotels to go with their casinos. The Habana Libre, the Riviera, the Nacional and many other hotels all were under the control of organized crime figures until Fidel Castro came to power.

The casinos are now closed (have been for 40-plus years), and with them Vedado's key attractions disappeared. So the abundance of hotels in any particular neighborhood clearly should not be a major consideration when deciding where to stay in Cuba's capital city. Bottom line: With all that it has to offer, the most desirable neighborhood in which to stay is Old Havana. Not surprisingly, there are no budget hotels in the old section of Havana. However, there are a few in nearby Centro Habana, so if you're frugal you'd be wise to consider a hotel there.

Generally, Havana's hotel prices are high by Latin American standards. The Cuban government relies heavily on tourist dollars to boost its flagging economy, and since the government owns and controls most of Havana's hotels, it charges accordingly. Also, much of the year hotel rooms are in short supply, which drives up room rates but also increases the visitor's need to arrive with a hotel reservation. If you arrive without one, expect to search the city before finding a modestly priced room (if you're willing to spend US$150 a night on a room, this warning doesn't apply to you).

There's an official requirement that all arriving tourists have three nights accommodations prebooked, which is a ploy intended to induce visitors to buy a package tour or book rooms at state-owned hotels. Immigration officials at the airport may ask to see your hotel voucher if they suspect you don't have a reservation. Since most visitors come on package tours, the officials don't bother checking hotel vouchers all the time, but they may do so if it's obvious you don't have a booking because of what you wrote or didn't write on your tourist card (always fill in the 'address in Cuba' line). If you don't have anything to show, they're entitled to hang on to your passport until you book and prepay your room at the airport tour desk, and you could end up being forced to stay at an inconveniently located or very expensive place.

Fortunately, Horizontes, Cuba's largest medium-priced hotel chain, has a website (www.horizontes.cu) that provides detailed information on all of their properties and explains how to prebook a room (fax 33-4361, crh@horizontes.hor.cma.net). Any type of written confirmation from Hori-

Mob legacy: Vedado hotels

140

It's Tough Renting a Private Room in Havana

Since 1993, when it became legal for Cubans to have dollars, a booming market in private accommodations has emerged, and visitors now have the option of renting rooms in Cuban homes in most towns and some beach areas.

But the government, which owns and operates virtually all of Cuba's hotels, resorts and holiday camps, hasn't welcomed this development, and Decree No 171 of July 1997 imposed stiff licensing fees on these *casas particulares* to collect considerable revenue while making them less competitive with the state hotels.

Homeowners must now pay a monthly licensing fee of between US$100 and US$250 per room, depending on the area, whether they have any guests or not. It costs the operator another US$45 per month to post a sign outside the house advertising the availability of rooms, and an additional fee must be paid if off-street parking is provided. Considerable paperwork is involved, and the personal details of each foreign guest must be reported to the authorities. Inspectors visit the houses regularly to check the books. If the owner decides to suspend the license temporarily, there are extra costs and various bureaucratic barriers to starting up again.

This sector receives nothing from the government in return for the high taxes it pays. State-run travel agencies, such as Cubatur, Havanatur and Rumbos, will not reserve private rooms. All advertising and promotion must be done by the operators themselves.

If you're planning to stay at one of these places, don't tell the immigration officer at the airport, as you'll be taken aside and forced to pay up front for a government hotel. This despite the fact that the tax paid monthly on one private room may be more than the official earns in a year!

SEÑORES IMPERIALISTAS ¡NO LES TENEMOS ABSOLUTAMENTE NINGÚN MIEDO!

PLACES TO STAY

zontes should be sufficient to get you out of the airport, and a Horizontes hotel is highly recommended for your first night or two. Horizontes also offers fly/drive packages, which include a car and a hotel room (from US$100 a night double), but in practice the participating hotels tend to give their worst rooms to those on such packages.

Otherwise, ask the person who sells you your plane ticket if they can reserve a room for your first night. Foreign tour operators affiliated with the Cuban travel agency Havanatur can usually do this for you, often with a three-night minimum booking; see the Getting There & Away chapter. Cubana offices act as booking agents for deluxe hotels belonging to the Sol Meliá chain. Marsub (☎ 33-3055, fax 33-3481, marsub@ceniai.inf.cu), Calle B No 310, between Calles 13 and 15 in Vedado, can book individualized itineraries for scuba divers.

Another option is to phone personally or fax your hotel of choice a day or two before you fly to Cuba to check prices and availability. If you reserve verbally, be sure to write down the name of the person you're talking to, both to have something to tell the immigration officer and in case you arrive to find the hotel full. All of the required phone numbers are provided in this book.

Private rooms are readily available in Centro Habana and Vedado, but very few are in La Habana Vieja. You'll pay anywhere from US$15 to US$35 per room, with those in Vedado usually of better quality and more expensive than those in Centro Habana. In general, private rooms aren't very nice, and many a visitor has wasted valuable touring time, going from one residence with a room to rent to another, searching for a decent place to bed down. Since your time is better spent seeing sites, private rooms aren't recommended here.

Lastly – and this cannot be overstated – the hotel prices here are not scripture. They could be considerably less than what you encounter. That's because in late 2000 when this book was being penned, the government was making improvements to most of its hotels. In some cases, the changes meant little more than new paint and carpeting. In other places, such as the Hotel Deauville, even the elevators were being replaced.

Needless to say, the government likely wasn't investing heavily in its already popular hotels with the intention of leaving prices the same. Play it safe: Add 25% or more to the prices shown here when budgeting your trip. If the rates are lower than you calculated, you'll be sitting pretty. The price categories used in this book are hard to pin down, but are loosely defined as Budget (less than US$50/night), Mid-Range (US$50 to US$80/night); and Top End (more than US$80/night).

LA HABANA VIEJA (MAP 2)

If you can afford it, this is the neighborhood you'll want to call home during your Havana stay. It's here, more than in any other part of the city, that you can really feel Havana's rich history. While there are many Spanish colonial buildings in Centro Habana, in Old Havana it seems every building, every street and every plaza was designed when the Spanish ruled the country, and indeed most of them were.

Adding to La Habana Vieja's appeal are its many bars, restaurants, museums and cafés. Music simultaneously drifting from a dozen venues into the streets of Old Havana isn't uncommon, and stopping in on some of these places between explorations of the neighborhood's many historic sites is a terrific way to enliven your time in Cuba's wonder-packed capital.

Unfortunately, the privilege of staying in La Habana Vieja doesn't come cheap. With the exception of a few rooms at the Hostal Valencia, room rates here in late 2000 started above US$50 per day. If you visit mid-December through January, or if you're reading this book in 2002 or 2003, expect to pay significantly more for a hotel room in Old Havana.

Mid-Range

The *Hostal Valencia (Habaguanex; ☎ 57-1037, fax 33-5628, Oficios No 53)*, at Obrapía, offers 12 rooms with cold showers in a mid-18th-century colonial mansion for US$46/60/75 single/double/triple year-round. The rooms tend to be noisy due to the use of shutters instead of glass windows. It's under Spanish management, which explains why the hotel restaurant, which is open noon to 11 pm daily, specializes in paella. There's a good cigar shop here and the Valencia's courtyard is charming.

Top End

During his stays in Havana during the 1930s, author Ernest Hemingway put up at the five-story, pastel pink *Hotel Ambos Mundos (Habaguanex; ☎ 60-9529, fax 60-9532, Obispo No 153)*, at Mercaderes. The 52 rooms (some without windows) cost US$65/90 single/double. The hotel was built in 1922 and there's a popular piano bar on the ground floor that's occasionally the haunt of Hemingway impersonators. The open-sided bar atop the hotel is a terrific find, particularly in the evening when it's not blasted by the unforgiving tropical sun. Massage of the Swedish variety (as opposed to the Thai variety) is available in your room. Transtur has a desk here.

The *Hostal Condes de Villanueva (Habaguanex; ☎ 62-9293, fax 62-9682, hconde@villanueva.ohch.cu, Mercaderes No 202)*, at Lamparilla, near Plaza de San Francisco de Asís, reopened in 1999 after a complete rebuild. Also known as El Hostal del Habano, it caters primarily to cigar aficionados with a cigar shop, cigar club and cigar storage facilities. Each of the nine rooms bears the name of a different tobacco growing area, and prices range from US$68/95 to US$115/175, depending on the category.

The 25-room *Hotel Florida (Habaguanex; ☎ 62-4127, fax 62-4117, Obispo No 252)*, at Cuba, is a three-story building in the purest colonial style, with arches and pillars around the central courtyard. Constructed in 1836 as the residence of a wealthy merchant, the building later served as a bank and was subsequently divided into residential housing. In 1999 it underwent a thorough renovation. Regular rooms are US$75/90 low season, US$75/105 high season, while a suite will set you back US$125/150 low season, US$150/175 high season. This stately old hotel also has a very elegant café with some of the plushest seating in the city, recommended for a splurge even if you're sleeping cheap elsewhere.

Havana's finest hotel may be the *Hotel Santa Isabel (Habaguanex; ☎ 33-8201, fax 33-8391, Baratillo No 9)*, on the east side of the Plaza de Armas. Originally the Palacio de los Condes de Santovenia, the building became a hotel in 1867 when the last family member to live here, General Domingo Santovenia, was exiled by the Spanish for ineptitude. In 1996 this three-story edifice was upgraded to five-star standards. The 17 regular rooms are US$110/150, while the 10 spacious suites with balconies facing the square go for US$135/190, all including breakfast, use of the safe in the room and parking. The location is splendid and the staff amenable.

The venerable *Aparthotel Santo Ángel*, Brasil and San Ignacio, on the north side of Plaza Vieja, was still under renovation at press time. Other classic hotels that will be renovated by Habaguanex at least until 2002 include the 100-room *Hotel Saratoga* and the 144-room *Gran Hotel* near Parque de la Fraternidad. All three hotels warrant investigation when they reopen to the public.

In late 2000, the *Hostal San Miguel* on Calle Tacón was in the process of being constructed from the decrepit shell of the Palacio San Miguel, which was built in 1915. When the run-down former residence (never an actual palace) opens as a hotel in 2001 or 2002, it will reportedly consist of 10 guest rooms, a lobby, a bar and a viewing room that faces the harbor. Although 'hostal' generally means *inexpensive* in backpacker lingua, this place will likely be posh and priced accordingly.

CENTRO HABANA (MAP 2)

This is the city's bustling business center. The streets in Centro Habana always seem to be filled with people on their way to something special. And perhaps they are; there's no shortage of prominent buildings, factories and museums here, including the fantastic Capitolio Nacional, the Museo de la Rev-

olución, a pridefully restored castle, two famous cigar factories and numerous former palaces.

And because Centro Habana abuts La Habana Vieja, you needn't go far to find yourself within the extents of the city's original boundaries and all the ambiance and history found there. Today, little remains of the wall that once separated Centro Habana from La Habana Vieja. To travel between the two neighborhoods, you need only walk along one of the many roads that they share. And because there is a wide range of hotel rates here, Centro Habana is a fine neighborhood to focus your hotel search.

Budget

Hotel New York (Islazul; ☎ 62-6300, Dragones No 156) stands beside the monumental Chinese gate (erected in 1999) at the entrance to the Barrio Chino, just off Parque de la Fraternidad. The 94 rooms in this old five-story hotel are US$13/16 with bath (cold water only), fan and worn mattress. The whole place is in need of fumigation. The New York is patronized mostly by Cubans from the interior, who are allowed to rent rooms for one week maximum. You may meet a few characters in the lobby trying to push various scams. The New York's cafeteria serves cheap plates of spaghetti, and a beer garden is beside the building.

The *Hotel Lido (Horizontes; ☎ 33-8814, Consulado No 210)*, between Ánimas and Trocadero in the rather seedy Colón district, is one of the cheapest Havana hotels regularly catering to foreigners. Its 65 rooms with cold shower cost US$16/25 low season, US$26/35 high season. The rooms with balconies are nicer. You can lock your valuables in a safety deposit box at the reception for US$2 a day (don't leave valuables unattended in your room). The cafeteria (open 7 am to 9:30 pm) off the lobby serves a reasonable breakfast, as does a stand-up peso place around the corner at Trocadero No 107 (open weekdays only). The Lido's fifth-floor roof bar rustles up a good meal of pork, veggies and chips for US$6. It's open 4 pm to 4 am daily. The Lido staff can arrange inexpensive taxis.

The **Casa del Científico** (☎ 62-4511, 63-8103, Paseo de Martí No 212), at Trocadero, offers rooms in an elegant old building with grand stairways, marble columns, courtyards, and terraces overlooking the promenade. The six rooms with shared cold-water bath on the 2nd floor are US$25/31, while the six with private warm-water baths on the 3rd floor are US$45/55. The rooms are rather ordinary but adequate. Several restaurants are here but the food doesn't match the setting (one reader observed the old 'fill the mineral-water bottle from the tap and pretend to open it as you approach the table' trick). This hotel is generally full December through March.

Hotel Lincoln (Islazul; ☎ 33-8209), on Av de Italia between Virtudes and Ánimas, has 84 air-conditioned rooms with hot-water bath and TV for US$35/45, breakfast included. This nine-story hotel was the second-tallest building in Havana at the time of construction in 1926. A nightclub with a show is on the roof, and although most of the guests are Cuban, you'll also be welcome.

Until 2000, the cheapest regular hotel in Havana was the four-story **Hotel Isla de Cuba** (Islazul; ☎ 57-1129, Máximo Gómez No 169). It was being restored at the time of writing and a handful of workers on scene anticipated it wouldn't reopen until 2003. If it's open, check it out. Erected in the 1880s, elegant wrought-iron railings highlight this often-overlooked hotel. Prior to renovation, mostly Cubans stayed here. Most likely it will be beyond their means when it reopens.

Mid-Range

The five-story **Hotel Caribbean** (Horizontes; ☎ 60-8241, fax 66-9479, Paseo de Martí No 164), between Colón and Refugio, underwent a complete renovation in 1998. The 35 rooms go for US$36/54 single/double. The price includes the use of the safe in the room. This hotel is usually fully booked December through March (indeed, a clerk admitted that the hotel often overbooks to ensure that it's full).

Since the 1970s, individual tourists on something of a budget have been sent to the

14-story **Hotel Deauville** (Horizontes; ☎ 33-8813, fax 33-8148), Av de Italia and Malecón. The 144 rooms with balcony, hot shower and air-conditioning are US$42/46. The buffet breakfast is US$5 extra. Facilities include a swimming pool (closed until 10 am) and a cafeteria with a view of Havana on the roof of the six-story section, a poor restaurant (off the lobby), a souvenir shop (upstairs), a disco (in the basement) and a Transtur car rental desk (in the lobby). The hotel was being renovated in 2000.

Top End

The neoclassical **Hotel Inglaterra** (Gran Caribe; ☎ 60-8593, fax 60-8254, Paseo de Martí No 416), at San Rafael opposite Parque Central, was erected in 1875. In recent years the Inglaterra has been overshadowed by new competitors and it's no longer the prime place to stay, as it once was. The 83 rooms are US$80/100 single/double and petty theft has been reported. The rooftop La Terraza bar offers entertainment several nights a week, and the noise can be heard throughout the building (the hotel generator is also noisy). The mojitos served at the streetside bar are among the best in town; just don't order any food there. The Inglaterra's US$15 city sightseeing tour, with daily departures at 9:30 am and 2:30 pm, is a major waste of time and money. A Transtur car rental desk is here.

The yellow-colored **Hotel Plaza** (Gran Caribe; ☎ 60-8583, fax 60-8591, Agramonte No 267), at Neptuno, is an elegant four-story hotel erected in 1908 with Spanish touches such as tile floors and neoclassical columns. The 188 rooms are US$80/120 and you can't beat the location for Centro Habana. Many of the guests will have arrived on some kind of cheap package tour. The piano bar at the Plaza is open 24 hours. There's a lovely rooftop terrace for guests only. A Transtur car rental office is on the premises.

The **Hotel Sevilla** (Gran Caribe; ☎ 60-8560, fax 60-8582, 33-8582, Trocadero No 55), between Paseo de Martí and Agramonte, is a colonial-style hotel that lives up to the Old World aura of its name. In a city brimming with unique hotels, this 1908 structure, managed by the French Accor chain, is another of the greats. The 188 smallish rooms are US$100/130/140 single/double/triple. There's a sauna and fitness club, and the Sevilla's swimming pool is open to nonguests upon payment of US$5 at the rear entrance at Paseo de Martí and Ánimas. Its Patio Sevillano café off the lobby is open 24 hours a day, and the hotel restaurant near the front door lays out a breakfast buffet 7 am to 10 am daily for US$10. The 9th-floor rooftop restaurant/bar offers lovely views. Havanautos, Transtur, Havanatur and Cubatur are also here.

The majestic, eight-story **Hotel Golden Tulip Parque Central** (Cubanacán; ☎ 66-6627, fax 66-6630), next to the Hotel Plaza on the north side of Parque Central, just opened in 1998. The 281 rooms are US$130/180, or US$250 for a suite. Two rooms can accommodate disabled guests. The full-service business center and conference rooms suggest the Golden Tulip's target clientele. A swimming pool, fitness center and Jacuzzi are on the roof. There's also an elegant bar with occasional mariachis and an overpriced restaurant on the ground floor. Guests and nonguests can place calls from booths next to the reception desk.

VEDADO (MAP 3)

This section of Havana was *the* place to be in all of Cuba during the 1940s and '50s, when casinos in Vedado's finest hotels attracted large crowds night and day and the action was fast and furious. Elsewhere, beautiful women and athletic young men performed at cabarets, while smaller but no less enthusiastic audiences attended sex shows featuring men such as El Toro (the Bull), who lived up to their nicknames.

Castro closed the casinos as soon as he seized power, and El Toro was put out to pasture. There are still plenty of cabarets in Vedado and plenty of restaurants and bars, but the neighborhood, which mostly dates from the 20th century, doesn't have nearly

PLACES TO STAY

The Hotel Inglaterra, a good place to stay and a great place for a *mojito*

the appeal of either La Habana Vieja or Centro Habana. Instead of feeling like a place where time stood still, it feels like many commercial neighborhoods in Latin America that could do with some sprucing up.

Also, whereas Old Havana and Centro Habana are mostly flat, Vedado is very hilly. Some people tire rather quickly of walking up and down its hills. Vedado shouldn't be your first choice for hotel accommodations, even though it offers rooms spanning all three price categories (as does Centro Habana). If, however, you're taking advantage of a very appealing travel package that includes staying in Vedado during your time in Havana, don't fret; La Habana Vieja is only a 10-minute taxi ride away.

Budget & Mid-Range

Persons waiting to catch a bus out of town often stay at the **Hotel Bruzón** *(Islazul;* ☎ *57-5682, Bruzón No 217)*, between Pozos Dulces and Av de la Independencia, next to the bus station. This four-story hotel has 46 rooms with bath for US$18/24 single/double. Avoid the wretched basement restaurant.

The four-story **Hotel Universitario** *(☎ 33-3403, fax 33-3128)*, on Calle 17 at Calle L opposite the Servi-Cupet gas station, has 21 rooms for US$25/34. The ambiance here is dreadful. There's a cafeteria and a more substantial restaurant on premises, but they are not inviting.

Near the university is the six-story **Hotel Colina** *(Horizontes;* ☎ *33-4071, fax 33-4104)*, Calles L and 27, with 79 rooms for US$50/64. The rooms are not particularly comfortable. Here, you're paying for its proximity to the university. It runs a 24-hour snack bar.

The eight-story **Hotel Vedado** *(Horizontes;* ☎ *33-4072, fax 33-4186, Calle O No 244)*, between Calles 23 and 25, is more of a package-tour place. It has an older section next to the Hotel St John's and a newer wing, sometimes called 'Hotel Flamingo,' around the corner off Calle 25, both costing about US$44/58 low season, US$55/70 high season, breakfast included. The 192 rooms are a reasonable value, there's a swimming pool and Cabaret El Cortijo offers a fla-

menco show at 10 pm nightly (US$5 and a one-drink minimum). The hotel's cafeteria, a pleasantly remodeled one, is open 24 hours.

The 13-story **Hotel St John's** *(Horizontes;* ☎ *33-3561, Calle O No 216)*, between Calles 23 and 25, was fully renovated in 1999 and offers comfortable rooms with air-conditioning. The 96 rooms are US$65/80 with breakfast. The 14th-floor Pico Blanco nightclub is a local institution. Half of it is a swimming pool, half of it is a lounge with windows on three sides. There's a cabaret show nightly 10 pm until 3 am. The show is a bargain at US$10. Food is US$5.

Top End

The 17-story **Hotel Capri** *(Horizontes;* ☎ *33-3747, fax 33-3750)*, on Calle 21 at Calle N, retains the flavor of the '50s even though the gambling casino closed in 1959 and Mafia notables no longer frequent the rooftop swimming pool or the Salón Rojo. The Capri was the site of a bombing in July 1997 that left one man dead. The lobby is attractive, but the rooms are dingy and the entire hotel is in need of a face-lift. The 215 rooms are US$65/80 single/double in low season, US$78/94 high season. The breakfast buffet is US$5 extra. One reader recommended the food, service and view in La Terraza Florentina restaurant on the top floor. The main Transtur car rental office is next door.

The five-story **Hotel Victoria** *(Gran Caribe;* ☎ *33-3510, fax 33-3109)*, Calles M and 19, has 31 rooms for US$80/100 year-round. This mini deluxe hotel, erected in 1928, caters to business travelers. There's a small swimming pool, a bar and a store on premises.

The 17-story **Hotel Riviera** *(Gran Caribe;* ☎ *33-4051, fax 33-4228)*, at Paseo and Malecón, was built in 1957 by US Mafia boss Meyer Lansky. The 354 rooms are US$72/96 low season and US$80/110 high season, including breakfast. Some of the rooms have good sea views, and two have been laid out for disabled guests. There are lots of facilities, including a spacious lobby, swimming pool, buffet restaurant (downstairs), coffee shop (near the pool), Havanautos and Transtur car rental desks and Cubatur and Cabanacán tour desks. The exchange office gives cash advances on Visa and MasterCard. It's open 9 am to 7 pm daily. Top salsa orchestras play in the Riviera's Palacio de la Salsa, and several good theaters are in this area. You'll have to use taxis to get to the Vedado tourist district and old Havana.

Since 1930 the **Hotel Nacional** (Gran Caribe; ☎ 33-3564, fax 33-5171), at Calles 21 and O, has been Havana's flagship hotel in a commanding location overlooking the Malecón. Famous former guests include Winston Churchill, Ava Gardner and Frank Sinatra (who attended a Mafia reunion at the Nacional in 1946). Canadian Prime Minister Jean Chrétien stayed here during his April 1998 official visit. This huge eight-story landmark edifice has 442 surprisingly plain rooms for US$120/170 low season, US$150/200 high season. The presidential suite is US$1000. Cheap package tours can decimate these rates, and one must be prepared for the variable service of a Cuban-run hotel. The 6th floor has been designated the executive floor with its own reception, telex, fax, meeting rooms and secretarial staff for business travelers. Among the Nacional's many facilities are two swimming pools, tennis courts, pharmacy, barber shop, business desk, Havanautos and Transtur car rental agencies, guarded parking lot, taxi stand and the Cabaret Parisién (see the Entertainment chapter). The hotel's exchange office will give cash advances on Visa and MasterCard. Nonguests willing to post a US$15 food and drink credit may use the hotel's large outdoor pool from 10 am to 5 pm.

Havana's largest hotel, the **Hotel Habana Libre** (Gran Caribe; ☎ 33-4011, fax 33-3141), at Calles L and 23, opened in March 1958 just prior to the 1959 revolution. Once part of the Hilton chain, it's now efficiently managed by Spain's Tryp Hotels. The 574 rooms with balcony cost US$140/160, breakfast included. Even if you don't stay here, this hotel is useful for its many facilities, including a telephone center, Photo Service

branch, shops, Havanautos office and taxi stand. Also here are a 2nd-floor swimming pool and the Cabaret Turquino on the 25th floor (nightly show 10:30 pm until 4:30 am). Foreign journalists and Europeans often stay here.

Overlooking the Riviera is the soaring 22-story **Hotel Meliá Cohiba** (Cubanacán; ☎ 33-3636, fax 33-3949), Paseo, between Calles 1 and 3, which is managed by the Spanish Sol Meliá hotel chain. Opened in 1994, the hotel has 462 rooms beginning at US$165/215/280 single/double/junior suite, year-round. Rooms on the executive (20th) floor are US$215/265/330. Two rooms are accessible to disabled guests and 59 have Jacuzzis. Facilities include a swimming pool, fitness center, sauna, business center, conference rooms, shopping arcade, art gallery, the Havana Café, bars and restaurants. The hotel's Habana Café is home to a cabaret show nightly starting at 9 pm; admission costs US$11. This hotel is overpriced.

The 10-story **Hotel Presidente** (Gran Caribe; ☎ 33-3753, fax 33-3753), Calzada and Calle G, wouldn't be out of place on a street just off Times Square in New York. Built in 1928, just before the Great Depression hit Cuba, it has 160 rooms. The Presidente has a swimming pool and 10th-floor bar. In 2000, it was closed for renovations but should be open in early or mid 2001.

PLAYA & MARIANAO (MAP 4)

In these neighborhoods it's possible to find not only some very reasonably priced accommodations, but also some of Havana's top hotels. The Hotel Meliá Habana, for example, wouldn't look out of place among the very finest of Cancún's beach resorts. There are also some recommended restaurants here. But there's relatively little to see and do in these neighborhoods, and traveling between them and La Habana Vieja and Centro Habana gets stale pretty quickly.

As for ambiance, these are the neighborhoods where rich American gamblers and marlin fishermen built their homes-away-from-home during Havana's wild years leading up to the revolution. Whereas the other three neighborhoods previously mentioned are a mix of residential and commercial real estate, Playa and Marianao contain mostly wide streets lined with palms and once-fine homes that are now showing their age. For most visitors, these neighborhoods seem a bit removed from the Havana they came to experience.

Budget

The **Motel Las Olas** (☎ 29-4531, fax 22-3960), where Calle 32 meets the sea, offers six rooms with air-conditioning and a fan, a safety box, TV, an inviting pool and a restaurant. This place is very popular with Cubans and is a superb budget value at US$21/32/46 single/double/triple. Its downside: It can be difficult at times hailing a taxi in this area.

The **Residencia Universitaria Ispjae** (☎ 23-5370), Av 1 at Calle 22, is another excellent-value place that is with 12 air-conditioned rooms with baths and cable TV for US$27/44. These twin two-story buildings face the ocean; the reception is in the bar inside. There's a pool on the premises. Meals are available for US$3 for a bread-and-cheese breakfast, or US$5 for lunch or dinner. Secure parking is available.

The **Hostal Icemar** (Ministerio de Educación Superior; ☎ 23-6130, fax 23-7735, Calle 16 No 104) has 50 air-conditioned rooms with TV for US$30/48 single/double, including breakfast. This three-story student residence is in a nice area and has a pool, but it's not the value of the Motel Las Olas.

Villa Costa (☎ 29-2250, 29-0558, fax 24-4104), Av 1 between Calles 34 and 36, has seven air-conditioned rooms with baths and fridge for US$27/44, including breakfast. It's right on the breezy coast and has a swimming pool. Run by the National Protocol Office, it's a very good deal. Be sure to call ahead to reserve a room.

The Ministerio de Educación Superior also operates the **Hostal Costa Sol** (☎ 29-0828), Av 3A and Calle 60. The 11 air-conditioned rooms cost US$25/48 and are well priced at that. The hotel restaurant has an inexpensive menu, which makes the Costa Sol worth a visit in any case. From Av 5, it's easy to catch a bus or taxi. A bus ride

into Vedado from here will set you back only US$0.40.

Mid-Range

The **Hotel Mirazul** (☎ 24-0088, ☎/fax 24-0045, Av 5 No 3603), between Calles 36 and 40, is an elegant old mansion now operated as a hotel by the Ministerio de Educación Superior. The eight air-conditioned rooms with baths and TVs cost US$45 to US$60 single or double, depending on the room size. A restaurant/bar is available, but there's no pool. It's an excellent value and usually full.

The **Hotel El Bosque** (Gaviota; ☎ 24-9232, fax 24-5637), Calle 28A between Avs 49A and 49B, offers clean and comfortable air-conditioned rooms (54 in all), plus a pool table, a swimming pool, a bar, restaurant, beauty shop and a business center. The rates of US$49/64 are very reasonable. The drawback is the distance of the hotel from major attractions, but taxis are always out front.

The upscale **Hotel Kohly** (Gaviota; ☎ 24-0240), at Av 49 and Calle 36A, has 136 air-conditioned rooms (same quality as the rooms at El Bosque), a tennis court, a gym, bars, restaurants, a swimming pool, a bowling alley, massage, dancing lessons and a beauty parlor. It's very popular with wealthy Cubans, but because it too is fairly isolated, it is not popular with international visitors. However, there are usually two or three taxis out front at all hours and the rates of US$54/68 are very reasonable.

A couple of kilometers out of the way, the four-story **Hotel Biocaribe** (Cubanacán; ☎ 33-6487), at Av 31 and Calle 158, is in a poorly marked location next to the huge Centro de Ingenería Genética y Biotecnología. The 120 rooms are used by foreigners undergoing treatment at the nearby medical facilities. This inconvenient hotel is far from the beach, but the pool is inviting, there's a bar and even a guy rolling cigars. Rates are US$45/64 most of the year, and US$57/81 December through March and July and August.

Top End

The **Complejo Neptuno-Tritón** (Gran Caribe; ☎ 24-1606, fax 24-0042), on the coast at Av 3 and Calle 70, features twin 22-floor hotel towers originally built in 1979 and fully renovated in 1999 (although a year later it already looked worn). Each identical tower has its own reception area and 266 rooms, and both charge US$55/70 single/double low season, US$70/90 high season. The Tritón has Havanatur, Rumbos and Havanautos desks, while the Neptuno has Transtur, Cubana de Aviación, Cubatur and Havanatur booking offices in the reception area. A large swimming pool stands beside the rocky shore. This place is poorly maintained and depressing.

Hotel El Viejo y El Mar *(Cubanacán;* ☎ *24-6336, fax 24-6823)*, or 'The Old Man and the Sea,' is at the Marina Hemingway, Av 1 and Calle 248, 20km west of colonial Havana. This boring six-story coastal hotel, managed by Mexico's Qualton hotel chain, has 140 rooms in the main building for US$68/95, plus 46 rooms in a long row of two-story units called 'cabañas' for US$60/74. The rooms are only fair but the food is good. There's a swimming pool. This hotel and its neighbors are recommended only for travelers whose main interest is yachting, deep-sea fishing or scuba diving, as they make poor bases from which to tour Havana.

Prices at El Viejo y El Mar have come down since the 1996 opening of the **Hotel Acuario** *(Cubanacán;* ☎ *24-7628, fax 24-4379)*, also known as El Jardín del Edén in the center of the marina, down the road from Restaurante Fiesta. The 314 rooms cost US$60/80 low season, US$70/90 high season, in a series of three- and four-story blocks between the marina channels. There's a much-needed shuttle service here, a few taxis and the rooms are comfortable.

Hotel El Comodoro *(Cubanacán;* ☎ *24-5551, fax 24-2028)*, at Av 1 and Calle 84, is right on the coast, about 15km west of La Habana Vieja. The 134 rooms in the main four-story building date from before the revolution and cost US$65/90 low season, US$80/110 high season. Another 10 rooms in a two-story cabaña block facing the ocean cost the same. In 1990 the 163 two-story, tile-roof units of Bungalows Alborada

were completed, complemented in 1996 by a further 165 units at Bungalows Pleamar directly opposite (the hotel and bungalows share a reception desk). These two complexes have their own swimming pools. At either place, a unit with sitting room, TV, kitchenette and fridge will cost US$89/118 low season, US$98/137 high season for a one bedroom, or US$153/180 low/high season for a two bedroom. The new units are much larger and more comfortable than the old hotel rooms, if 20% more expensive. The hotel's small sandy beach is protected from the waves by a large iron seawall, and the Comodoro is a good choice for anyone looking for real resort atmosphere within a taxi ride of the city. There are lots of facilities, including a tennis court, shopping mall, and the Havana Club disco. A beer at the hotel bar will run you US$3. Cubacar has a car rental office here.

Hotel Palco *(Cubanacán;* ☎ *24-7235, fax 24-7236)*, Calle 146, between Avs 11 and 13, attached to the Palacio de las Convenciones, is a top business hotel with 180 rooms for US$74/94 low season, US$91/111 high season. The Palco has a business center, a pool, two restaurants, two bars and a cigar shop. It's a fine hotel in the center of Havana's most fashionable neighborhood.

The five-story **Hotel Copacabana** *(Gran Caribe;* ☎ *24-1037, fax 24-2846)*, at Av 1 and Calle 44, is a 168-room hotel complex charging US$85/136 year-round. It's right on the coast, and although there's no beach, a seawall creates a protected pool. The hotel also features a regular swimming pool, tennis courts and scuba diving, and aquascooters can be hired to explore the coast. The Ipanema Disco and a Transtur car rental agency are also on the premises.

The **Hotel Chateau Miramar** *(Cubanacán;* ☎ *24-1952, fax 24-0224, reservas@ chateau.cha.cyt.cu)*, on Av 1 between Calles 62 and 64, is a stylish five-story hotel. The 50 rooms with mini-fridges cost US$95/120 year-round. There's a post office at the reception and a swimming pool next to the sea. This small hotel has a more intimate feel than its neighbors, and the service here is superior.

In 1999 the Gaviota/Accor chain built the six-story ***Novotel Miramar*** *(☎ 24-3584, fax 24-3583)* on Av 5 at Calle 74. The Novotel offers 427 rooms with all the amenities for US$100/135; add US$13 for breakfast. It's a big place that's a couple of blocks from the coast and although it has several restaurants and a large pool, it's nothing special.

Residencial Turístico Marina Hemingway *(Cubanacán; ☎ 24-6768, fax 24-1149)* has 68 rooms in a variety of bungalows along the channel starting at US$130 single or double. The same reception (down the road past Chan Chan) controls 22 houses at ***Villa Paraíso*** in a nicer (though more remote) location along the seawall, 2km beyond El Viejo y El Mar. These cost US$140 for a one bedroom, US$200 for a two bedroom and US$250 for a three bedroom. There's a swimming pool. You'd need to rent a car to stay here, as it's seldom visited by taxis.

Next to the Neptuno-Tritón is the gorgeous ***Hotel Meliá Habana*** *(Cubanacán; ☎ 24-8500, fax 24-8505)*, on Av 3 between Calles 76 and 80, which opened in 1998. The 409 rooms in this 11-story hotel start at US$165/215 year-round. Four rooms are accessible to disabled persons. You realize you're in a hotel run by private professionals rather than government functionaries as soon as you request some service. There's a business center, 14 conference rooms and an impressive lobby (marble everywhere, rattan furniture, enormous ferns, cascading vines, canals of clean-flowing water, the works). Cuba's largest and most beautiful swimming pool stands next to a desolate, rocky shore.

PARQUE LENIN AREA (MAP 5)

There's really no good reason to stay so far from Havana's top attractions, but if something (fear of others, perhaps) compels you to situate in the Parque Lenin area you'll want to know what's available. And so, without further ado, a description of the accommodations offered in the Parque Lenin area:

The ***Motel Rodeo Nacional*** *(☎ 44-3026 ext 242)*, directly below the rodeo grandstand (on the side facing the lake), has four rooms for US$10 single or double (or US$5 for four hours).

Nicer is the ***Motel La Herradura*** *(☎ 44-2819)*, next to the riding school in the northwest corner of Parque Lenin, 6km from the international airport, with a single-story block of rooms with mini-fridges for US$17 for one bed and twice that for two. There are five rooms in all, each with air-conditioning, color TV and hot bath. Parking costs US$1. The Estación Galápago de Oro is adjacent to the motel. A terrace bar serving pizza is opposite the motel. The motel is often full.

Places to Eat

In general, the food served in Havana's restaurants is not high quality or particularly tasty. That's because the vast majority of the restaurants are state controlled, which means that the entity that does a spotty job of stocking Havana's markets is the same one tasked with delivering fresh meats, fish, produce and spices to Havana's restaurants. As a result, the food in the Cuban capital generally isn't very good, and shortages of beef and fish are common.

Likewise, because most of Havana's restaurants are state-run, the service they provide is usually no better than the quality of their food. That's due to the fact that the waiters have little incentive to provide superior service. Ninety-nine times out of a hundred, the tips customers leave for waiters are reluctantly handed over to managers. In communist Cuba, even waiters' tips go into a collective money pool administered by the government.

So, if you're staying at one of Havana's best hotels, spending US$150 or more each night for a room, and you're wondering why the hotel's restaurant is so lousy, now you know. In Havana, don't assume that a pricey hotel restaurant is any better than an independent restaurant. Generally, hotel-based restaurants are simply more expensive than others. Assuming *you get what you pay for* is the wrong approach to dining in Havana.

Cuban restaurant menus are usually in Spanish only (see Food in the Language section at the back of this book for help reading menus). What you get depends on the provisions delivered to the chef that day. Some days the selection is good, others it's pitiful. Most of the time you won't be told whether an item is available until you've asked for it. Your success in ordering will increase if you pick the simplest thing on the menu, such as chicken or pork. Any dish with the word *criollo* (Creole) in it is usually

---

Havana's Private Restaurants

The government's approval of *paladares* in 1995 improved the dining situation in Havana considerably. Paladares are family-run restaurants, several of which are quite good. To limit competition with state-run restaurants, a paladar is limited to 12 seats and to meals consisting of pork, chicken or fish. They can't legally offer beef, shrimp or lobster. In practice, paladares usually offer items that aren't listed on the menu. Ask for the specials.

Some paladares have written menus and some don't. Some accept pesos, but all prefer dollars. If there's a menu, check how much a beer costs, and if it's more than $10 the menu is written in pesos. It always works out cheaper to pay in pesos, but exchanging a major currency to pesos and back again usually isn't worth the hassle of the meager restaurant savings. If a paladar's menu doesn't show prices, always ask the cost of a meal before ordering it to prevent being overcharged.

Many paladares have two or three menus listing the same dishes but with different prices, depending on how much they think you might be willing to pay. Don't hesitate to walk out if you sense a scam. Also, beware that the price you paid once may be quite different a few days (or even hours) later; you should check the menu every time. And don't let a hustler lead you to a restaurant unless you're willing to cover his commission.

To allow you (a wise Lonely Planet reader) to quickly distinguish between private and state-run restaurants, we identify all privately operated restaurants as 'paladares,' even if the sign outside says 'restaurant.' Whenever this book mentions a 'restaurant' it's referring to a government-operated place.

SEÑORES IMPERIALISTAS INO LES TENEMOS ABSOLUTAMENTE NINGUN MIEDO i

Cuba's Creole Cuisine

Cuban cuisine consists chiefly of food from the *cocina criolla* (Creole kitchen). It has its origins in Spain and Africa, and its heavy, fatty dishes are generally ill-suited for life in the American tropics. The typical Cuban meal is pork or chicken, rice and beans. After a large portion of pork, rice and beans on a hot day, you won't feel like doing much of anything.

Many people assume Cuban food will be tasty in the way of food from other hot spots – high in flavor, low in weight. The spicy food of Thailand, for example, is filling and tasty but doesn't slow you down like a heavy plate of beans and pork will. Yet hot spices and chili peppers are not used in Cuban cooking; instead, the dishes here are seasoned with garlic and onions.

Cubans are avid meat eaters, and many tourists are disappointed to find so little fish available in Havana. Fresh vegetables are scarce, even at the luxury hotels, but fruit is usually offered. Vegetarians are generally frustrated in Havana because a chronic shortage of vegetable oil means that vegetables are usually cooked in lard. Salads here generally contain meat.

The most common dish offered at Cuban restaurants is *carne asada* (roasted meat), usually *puerco asado* (roasted pork), or *carne de cerdo* (pork). State-run restaurants should also have *carne de res* (beef), *picadillo* (ground beef) and *arroz con pollo* (chicken and rice). *Filete Uruguayo* is steak stuffed with ham and cheese.

Lobster is an endangered species in Cuba, the result of so many being slaughtered for tourist plates or exported for hard currency. Still, it's usually available at government-run restaurants for a large chunk of change.

Ajiaco is a typical meat, garlic and vegetable stew. *Congrí oriental* (rice cooked with red kidney beans) was introduced by French coffee planters from Haiti during the 19th century. In eastern Cuba it's called *moros y cristianos* (rice with black beans), a dish that has often been compared to the racial mix on the island itself. *Fufú* (boiled green bananas mashed into a paste and seasoned with salt) is usually eaten with meat.

SEÑORES IMPERIALISTAS ¡NO LES TENEMOS ABSOLUTAMENTE NINGÚN MIEDO !

a safe bet, as the ingredients should be readily available.

Also, many places now add a service charge to the bill, and more often than not this 10% or 15% fee is not mentioned on the menu. Be sure to check your bill before leaving a tip to ensure that you don't tip twice. Look for '10%,' '15%' or 'servicio' on your bill. If you don't see one of these clues don't hesitate to ask, *¿servicio está incluido en la cuenta?'* (Is service included in the check?).

If you're very happy with the service you received and want to reward the server, leave a small tip on the table and *very discreetly* slip a significant tip to the waiter. Assume that the restaurant manager is watching the server while they're at your table (supervision of tip money is one of the manager's official duties). If the manager doesn't see the waiter receive a tip, he'll assume the small tip on the table was the only one left.

The lengths of the following restaurant write-ups are generally indicative of the quality of the establishments described. Most of the restaurants that receive a lot of ink here are top-notch by local standards; the exceptions are places likely recommended to you by other guidebooks or by locals, but that really are best avoided. All of those restaurants that receive short write-ups here deserve mention, but they aren't likely places you'd eat at twice in your home town. Unfortunately, Havana's restaurants don't currently warrant many lengthy write-ups. Also shown are various self-catering establishments for you do-it-yourselfers.

The price categories used in this book are Budget (US$3 to US$7), Mid-Range (US$8 to US$15), and Top End (US$16 and up). Prices are per meal. Often, one high-end dish can result in misleading reporting, so these ranges should be viewed as approximates. Otherwise, virtually all restaurants in Havana offering lobster would fall into the Top End category, even though all other dishes on the menu might be solidly Mid-Range or even Budget. In the write-ups that follow, the author describes many meals and their prices to give you, Lonely Planet's wise, worldly and wonderful readers, an accurate presentation of Havana's restaurant scene.

Generally, within each price category the places to eat mentioned here appear in order of quality. Some restaurants appear where they do due to a particular specialty, while others score high marks (and receive top billing) for their terrific ambiance. If you're choosy about where and what you eat, you'd be wise to read at least those write-ups within your price range. Since none of the restaurants discussed here is grossly overpriced, it's likely worth your while to read (or at least skim) all the write-ups.

LA HABANA VIEJA (MAP 2)
Self Catering
Fresh loaves of bread are sold at ***Panadería San José*** *(Obispo No 161)*, which is open 24 hours.

La Lluvia de Oro *(Obispo No 314)* also has freshly baked bread and some groceries. It's open 9 am to 9 pm daily.

Try the ***Mercado El Cristo*** *(Brasil No 461)*, one of the best-stocked markets in Centro Habana. It's basically a small department store (selling items such as make-up, toys and TVs) and a grocery store (selling soups, pasta and other kitchen goods). It's open 9 am to 11 pm daily.

Harris Brothers *(O'Reilly No 526)*, just off Parque Central, stocks a fair amount of groceries and houses a small café.

Budget
Cafe París *(Obispo No 202)*, at San Ignacio, has the feel of a pub, only brighter and without British airs. Living up to its name, the waiters aren't the chattiest in town. The París serves light, inexpensive chicken meals, but most people come to drink and

enjoy the buoyant live music. Filling slices of pizza (US$0.50) are dispensed from a takeout window on the side of the building. It's open 24 hours.

The fan-cooled and pleasantly set ***Restaurante Hanoi***, at the corner of Brasil and Bernaza, serves typical Cuban dishes with a Vietnamese flavor. The Hanoi is not promoted as a tourist restaurant; complete meals are available for less than US$3 and national cocktails (basically, those that are rum-based) are only US$1 each while beers are US$0.85 for Cuban brands and US$1 or US$1.50 for imports. This excellent find for budget travelers usually offers six combination meals to choose from. The *ropa vieja* (shredded beef stew served with white rice and black beans) is the tastiest of the combination plates. Mariachis often wander in, play a few songs and wander out. The Hanoi doesn't discriminate against prostitutes, which occasionally means that men eating by themselves will be propositioned mid-meal. It's an asspain, but a firm *No, gracias* generally puts an end to the come-ons. It's open noon to 11 pm daily.

La Lluvia de Oro, on Obispo at Habana, has a good selection of inexpensive light meals, including pizza, chicken and sandwiches. The atmosphere is nice, with a long wooden bar, overhead fans and live music every night. The booze is locally priced (as opposed to tourist priced), which allows for both locals and tourists to hang out here.

Service charges are a tip for the government, not for your server

There's a public toilet at the rear of the restaurant. It's open 24 hours.

The *Café Taberna*, at the corner of Mercaderes and Brasil facing the stately Plaza Vieja, is popular with wealthy Cubans (there are a few of them around) for its fine food and very attractive setting. The restaurant is on the ground floor of a building erected in 1772, and the decor – from the elegant old mahogany bar to the brass ceiling fans and crown moldings – is well done. The menu features sandwiches (US$3 or thereabouts), appetizers ranging from US$2.50 for a fruit cocktail to US$8 for a seafood salad, and main courses in the US$5 to US$7 price range. This is a classy place without upscale prices. The writer forgot to note the hours. Sorry about that.

Perfect for those on a tight budget, *Cafetería Torre La Vega* (*Obrapía No 114a*), next to the Casa de México, serves large bowls of spaghetti for about US$1 at a high

Cuba's Copious Cocktails

The official bartender's guide produced by Havana Club includes the recipes of 100 Cuban cocktails, including 10 'Cuban classics,' five 'imaginative' drinks, 10 winter cocktails, 20 long drinks and 55 short drinks.

The most famous of the classic cocktails are the Cuba Libre (rum, cola and ice, stirred), invented to toast Cuban independence in 1902, and the daiquirí (rum, lemon juice, sugar, maraschino and crushed ice, shaken). The daiquirí was created in Oriente, Cuba, around the turn of the 20th century, and was improved during the 1920s with the introduction of the electric blender at Havana's El Floridita bar. The daiquirí can also be made with a variety of fruits.

Another local favorite is the mojito (rum, lemon juice, sugar, soda, mint leaf and ice, stirred), a refreshing drink on a hot afternoon. The presidente (rum, red vermouth, grenadine and ice, stirred) is named for President Mario García Menocal, whose love of drink was surpassed only by his fondness for dipping into the public purse.

The roaring '20s witnessed the birth of many cocktails: the ron collins (rum, sugar, lemon juice, soda and ice, stirred), the Havana special (rum, pineapple juice, maraschino and ice, shaken), the Mary Pickford (rum, pineapple juice, grenadine and ice, shaken), and the Isla de Pinos (rum, grapefruit juice and ice, stirred). During the 1940s Cuban bartenders came up with the mulata (rum, lemon juice, cacao liqueur and ice, shaken) and the saoco (rum, water of a green coconut, and ice, stirred).

After you've tried the 10 classics, Cuban bartenders still have plenty to offer. On a sizzling summer day order a planter's punch (similar to the daiquirí but larger and containing tropical fruit) or a piña colada (rum, pineapple juice, coconut cream and crushed ice, shaken). In Cuba a Bloody Mary is made with rum and called a Cubanito (rum, tomato juice, lemon juice, Worcestershire sauce, Tabasco sauce, salt and ice, stirred).

Other popular drinks are the Cuban Manhattan (rum, angostura, red vermouth and ice, stirred), the highball (rum, water, soda or ginger ale, and ice, stirred), the Cuba bella (daiquirí with grenadine, chocolate syrup and crème de menthe), the stinger (rum and crème de menthe, shaken), and the zombie (three types of rum with lemon juice, pineapple or orange juice, grenadine, tropical fruit and ice).

Whenever a cold front moves in, drown your troubles in grog (rum, hot water, lemon juice and sugar, stirred). Other winter drinks include ron toddy (rum, hot water, sugar and spices, shaken) and hot buttered rum (rum, butter, sugar and spices, boiled). A shot of rum in a cup of tea, coffee or hot chocolate is also very good.

– David Stanley

SEÑORES IMPERIALISTAS ¡NO LES TENEMOS ABSOLUTAMENTE NINGÚN MIEDO!

wooden bar. *Bistec de cerdo* (pork steak, US$3), *ropa vieja* (beef stew, US$2.40) and *pollo frito* (fried chicken, US$3) are among some of the restaurant's other offerings. The food's only mediocre, same with the ambiance, but this seldom-visited establishment is good if your primary interest is putting some food in your system. It's open 9 am to 9 pm daily.

The menu at the popular **Restaurante El Castillo de Farnés** *(Av de Bélgica No 361)*, at Obrapía, changes frequently, but expect to find most dishes in the US$4 to US$7 price range. The food here is mostly Cuban, and the clientele is generally a mix of Havana cigar hustlers and foreigners. This is one of the best places in town to buy a sandwich (US$3 to US$5), and Cuba Libres and mojitos are a reasonable US$1.50 (domestic beer runs US$1, Heineken for US$1.50). Music from the very popular Monserrate Bar drifts in. Farnés is open noon to midnight daily; look for the small door beside the bar of the same name.

Restaurante Puerto de Sagua *(Av de Bélgica No 603)*, at Acosta opposite the Palacio de Balboa, serves mostly seafood at reasonable prices and has a long Havana bar. Menu items include: lobster enchilada (US$6.50), grilled chicken (US$3.50), lobster pizza (US$3.50), paella (US$10, minimum two persons), calamari served in its ink (US$3.50), seafood cocktail (US$1.50). This is a somewhat elegant place, with clothed tables and waiters in black jackets providing excellent service. The romantic establishment is even air-conditioned, which makes the prices all the more reasonable. It's open noon to midnight daily.

The **Bar-Restaurante Cabaña**, at the north end of Calle Tacón around the corner from the Museo Nacional de la Música, is a pleasing, open-sided restaurant and bar with lovely views of the harbor and the eastern forts. The food is good here, and the specialties include chicken stuffed with ham and cheese, roast pork in its own juice, and a baked half chicken (all cost US$7). The dishes come with rice, black beans, salad, coffee and dessert. The national drinks are reasonably priced at US$1.50 each, and

there's a surprising selection of European and Cuban wines, though most appeared to be low-end brands. It's open 24 hours and a very good place to remember if you're in the area late at night.

Cafetería La Primera de Aguacate *(Aguacate No 12)*, just north of Tejadillo and not far from the Museo de la Revolución, is famous for its *cajitas*. It's open noon to 10 pm daily.

If you happen to be shopping at the handicrafts market on Calle Tacón and need to get a bite to eat or use a restroom, **La Torre de Oro**, at the corner of Tacón and Empedrado, is a good place to keep in mind. It's nothing special, just an uncovered corner square with a few tables and public restrooms. It's open 24 hours.

Mid-Range

Restaurante El Patio *(San Ignacio No 54)*, at Empedrado, occupies the romantic inner courtyard of an old colonial palace on the Plaza de la Catedral and is possibly the most popular restaurant in Havana due to its excellent location, inviting and shaded plaza-facing tables and live music 24 hours a day (three bands rotate eight-hour shifts around the clock). Menu items include *pollo a la naranja* (chicken in orange juice, US$9), *pierna de cerdo asada* (roasted pork leg, US$9) and some fairly tasty and well-priced appetizers, including *coctel de frutas tropicales* (tropical fruit cocktail, US$3) and *gazpacho de la casa* (US$4.50). Also available is a large selection of cocktails (most around US$3), beers (US$2.50 domestic, US$3 imported) and pretty good sangría (US$3). Note: El Patio uses only 3-year-old Havana Club rum in its Cuba Libres (US$3); they are quite possibly the best in Havana. If you have one here and one at Café de O'Reilly, which uses a rum that makes paint thinner taste good by comparison, you'll know the difference between a good Cuba Libre and a dreadful, vengeful one. The restaurant is open noon to midnight daily; the terrace is open all the time. Bathrooms in the courtyard are open to the general public and cleaned hourly (tips welcome).

Cuba's Top Rums

Cuba is famous for its *ron* (rum), a crude variety of which has been made on the island since the 16th century. However, it wasn't until the sugar boom of the mid-19th century that modern distilleries appeared on Cuba to produce large quantities of quality rum for export.

Bacardí rum was first brewed in Santiago de Cuba in 1878, and although the Bacardí trademark departed for Puerto Rico in 1960, the original factory is still in Santiago de Cuba, producing Caney rum and other brands. The quality remains excellent.

Cuba's most famous brand is Havana Club, which was founded at Cárdenas in 1878 but now has its main factory at Santa Cruz del Norte, east of Havana. The figure of the Giraldilla statue from Havana's Castillo Real de la Fuerza appears on every bottle of Havana Club.

Cuba's smoothest rum is widely regarded to be Matusalem Añejo Superior, brewed in Santiago de Cuba since 1872. Other top brands are Varadero and Caribbean Club. The rums mentioned here are generally available in bars throughout Havana.

¡ABSOLUTAMENTE NINGUN MIEDO !

One of Havana's most celebrated bar-restaurants is *La Bodeguita del Medio (Empedrado No 207)*, off Plaza de la Catedral (for a description of La B del M's bar, see the Entertainment chapter). Restaurant-wise, the food here is mediocre at best. Many tourists taking a lead from other guidebooks enter La B del M with high expectations. After all, the place is full of Hemingway lore and 'Papa' wouldn't patronize a crummy place, would he? Perhaps La B del M *was* a fine bar-restaurant – 50-plus years ago, when the author is known to have had a couple of drinks here. The specialty of the house is leg of pork (US$10.50) and it's improperly prepared. The shredded jerked beef (US$8.20) and the roasted chicken with salsa (US$8.90) are equally bad. Despite the hype, you're wiser spending your money

elsewhere. La Bodeguita is open noon until midnight daily.

El Café Mercurio, in the Lonja del Comercio on Plaza de San Francisco de Asís, is an elegant indoor-outdoor café-restaurant with cappuccino and espresso machines, air conditioning, intimate booths, live music most of the time, a full bar, waiters in black ties, and marble everywhere. Meal offerings include grilled fish (US$8), grilled lobster for two served with garlic and wine sauce (US$25), steak tartar (US$9), a combo plate of pork, shrimp, lobster and beef scallops (US$18), a variety of salads (US$4 for a 'panaché' of tropical fruit, for example, ranging to US$9 for a chef salad). There are even burgers (US$5.50) and a selection of sandwiches (most around US$5) on the Mercurio's long menu. If you're in need of a little pampering, this is a good place to find it. The Mercurio is open 24 hours.

Directly opposite the Mercurio is the Viennese-style *Café del Oriente*, at Oficios and Amargura, with a marble floor, an ornate plaster ceiling, mahogany paneling, huge mirrors, VIP service, a pianist or string quartet and air conditioning, all for the price of a coffee (a cappuccino, no less). Of course, you're also able to order off the café's upscale lunch menu (tropical fruit bowl for US$5, sandwiches for US$7, etc) or its dinner menu (seafood from US$14 to US$29, meats from US$12 to US$30, etc). The food's fine, but overpriced by international standards. There's also seating outdoors facing a lovely plaza. The Oriente is open noon until 1 am daily.

Facing the Plaza de Armas, *La Mina (Obispo No 109)*, between Oficios and Mercaderes, is a popular place to sit on the terrace and sip drinks while enjoying live music and a passing parade of foreigners and Habaneros separated from you by only a thin wall of planter boxes filled with tropical plants. La Mina offers a host of national dishes, most in the US$8 to US$11 range. The chef recommendations include the Caribbean Combination (chicken, shrimp, pork and fruit, cooked in 'a secret sauce,' US$14.50). The food's only OK despite the tantalizing descriptions of the dishes, but it's the ambiance you come here for. Often in the evenings as many as three bands will be playing simultaneously in this expansive establishment, with two dining areas out front on a shaded section of cobblestone streets and a more intimate dining area inside a lovely courtyard, away from the prying eyes of passersby. La Mina is open 24 hours.

Two comfortable restaurants near the Plaza de Armas specialize in Asian cuisine. *La Torre de Marfil (Mercaderes No 111)*, between Obispo and Obrapía, offers Cantonese and Cuban cuisine. Most dishes cost between US$4 and US$10. It's open noon to 10 pm Monday through Thursday, and noon until midnight the rest of the week. *Al Medina (Oficios No 12)*, between Obrapía and Obispo, upstairs, serves Lebanese lamb and mutton dishes. Reader reports on Al Medina have been favorable. It's open noon to 11 pm daily.

Established in 1830, *La Zaragozana*, on Av de Bélgica between Obispo and Obrapía, serves international cuisine and seafood amid air-conditioned splendor. Expect to spend around US$9 for a combination plate. It's open noon to midnight daily. Flamenco dancing is performed here Thursday and Saturday at 10:30 pm (no cover charge). La Zaragozana is next door to the celebrated El Floridita of Hemingway fame, and is less snobbish.

The *Paladar El Rincón de Eleguá (Aguacate No 257)*, off Obispo, has complete meals for US$10, or lobster for US$15. It's open noon to midnight daily.

The 2nd-floor *Restaurante D'Giovanni (Tacón No 4)*, at Empedrado, is in the Moorish-style ex-Casa de Aróstegui, erected in 1759. The menu consists mostly of Italian dishes starting around US$5, plus meat dishes (US$6 on up) and seafood (starting at US$9.25). Watch the price of the side salad. A 10% service charge is added to the bill. The strength of this place is the few tables, large enough only for two, that overlook the busy handicrafts market on Calle Tacón and the harbor beyond. Unfortunately, this isn't the kind of place that will allow you to occupy one of these tables for drinks only. The food is totally forgettable, the service a bit pushy and seemingly desperate. It's open noon to midnight.

Top End

Havana's finest Italian restaurant may be *Restaurante La Dominica (O'Reilly No 108)*, at Mercaderes, a block from Hotel Ambos Mundos. The menu ranges from pasta (US$6 to US$10.50) to meat and seafood dishes (US$8.50 to US$24). The decor is elegant, but few tourists patronize this place due to the somewhat elevated prices. That's a bit unfortunate as the food and service are above par due to the foreign management. It's open noon to midnight.

The *Restaurante La Paella*, in Hostal Valencia at Oficios and Obrapía, offers eight paella dishes (from US$8 to US$15 per person, two person minimum), shrimp (US$10), grilled lobster (US$23) and salmon (US$10). There are other, less expensive dishes. La Paella is open noon to 11 pm daily. There's often a band performing here, adding to the establishment's cheerful ambiance. Occasionally patrons have to wait a little while to be seated.

El Floridita (Obispo No 557), at Av de Bélgica, is a rather elegant restaurant serving good food, although most of it is grossly overpriced. Here you can order standard sandwiches (US$4 to US$7), a shrimp cocktail (US$15!), a lobster cocktail (US$15!) and the special house sandwich containing lobster, shrimp, salmon, vegetables, catsup and tartar sauce (it's actually better than it sounds, US$10). There are other high-end meals. El Floridita is open 11 am to midnight daily; see the Entertainment chapter for the scoop on the bar at El Floridita.

CENTRO HABANA (MAP 2)
Self Catering

The main public market is the *Mercado Agropecuario Egido*, on Av de Bélgica between Corrales and Apodaca. The action is over by 2 pm. A stand at Av de Bélgica No 568, next to the market, sells glasses of *guarapo* (sugar cane juice) for less than a peso.

PLACES TO EAT

World's Finest Daiquirís

Just as the debate over who invented the margarita continues, the origin of the daiquirí is as clear as gin. But unlike the margarita's many storied histories, the daiquirí has only two.

According to one history, the drink was born at the start of the 20th century, its parents two engineers at a mine named Daiquirí outside Santiago de Cuba. On a scorching day the men combined their provisions – some rum, lemons and sugar – and drank it all up. So pleased were they with the taste of the beverage that they named it, fittingly, after the name of the mine.

According to another history, a general named William Rufus Shafter led US troops who disembarked on the outskirts of Santiago de Cuba during the Spanish-American-Cuban War. And, indeed, there *is* a Playa Daiquirí near the city. The general learned Cuban soldiers were fond of drinking a mixture of rum, sugar and lemon juice. He decided to try it with a little ice. The American was so taken with the concoction that he gave it a name – daiquirí, after the local beach.

Whether the drink takes its name from two engineers and a mine or a general and a beach is very hard to say. You might want to give it some thought over a drink. But there's no disputing how the cocktail became world famous. It was served at the Venus Hotel in Santiago de Cuba about the time of WWI. From there it made its way to El Floridita in Havana, which at the time had already existed for many years.

Long before the classy Centro Habana bar became a haunt of Ernest Hemingway, it had caught the attention of European writers such as André Demaisen, who in Les Nouvelles Littéraires described the boisterous ambiance of El Floridita, 'where the best drinks in the world were on offer, and amongst them the unforgettable daiquirí, prepared with white rum.'

With Hemingway's frequent visits, beginning in 1940, the bar and its primiere drink became legendary. 'Papa' would read newspapers at the Floridita while sipping daiquirís topped off with grapefruit juice. Celebrities anxious to socialize with the great writer – Jean-Paul Sartre, Gene Tunney, Gary Cooper, Ava Gardner, Tennessee Williams and many others – paid him visits at the bar, which fueled more travel literature on the Floridita and its popular drink.

Today there are no fewer than 17 different daiquirís served at El Floridita. All contain ice and one of two labels of Havana Club rum (one-year-old White or three-year-old Gold), but the fruit used in each varies from banana and mango to coconut and kiwi. Even if you don't drink, El Floridita is a good place to cool your feet after a day of walking. The bar, Havana's oldest (dating from 1817) is always air-conditioned, its chairs are comfortable and its ambiance cheerful.

SEÑORES IMPERIALISTAS ¡NO LES TENEMOS ABSOLUTAMENTE NINGÚN MIEDO!

The **Supermercado Isla de Cuba**, Máximo Gómez and Factoría, on the south side of Parque de la Fraternidad, is a full-blown supermarket – perhaps the best in Havana in terms of selection. It's open 10 am to 6 pm Monday to Saturday, 9 am to 1 pm Sunday.

Caracol El Cristal, in the middle of Manzana de Gómez off Parque Central, sells only alcohol and basic groceries. It's open 9 am to 7 pm daily.

Mercado Los Fornos (Neptuno No 162), between Consulado and Industria off Parque Central, sells groceries and bread most hours of the day and night.

For a decent supermarket, try **Almacenes Ultra** (Av Simón Bolívar No 109), at the corner of Rayo near Av de Italia. It's open 9 am to 6 pm Monday to Saturday, 9 am to 1 pm Sunday.

La Época, Av de Italia and Neptuno, is a hard-currency department store with a supermarket in the basement. Prior to entry you must check your handbags in an adjacent *guardaropa*. It's open 9:30 am to 9:30 pm Monday to Saturday, 9 am to 1 pm Sunday.

Farther west is **Supermercado Amistad** (San Lázaro No 1109), just below Infante.

It's open 10 am to 6 pm weekdays, 9 am to 1 pm Saturday.

Las Terrazas de Prado, at the corner of Paseo de Martí and Genios, is a corner courtyard containing a snack stand, a shop selling butter, margarine and other cooking aids, and two small stores selling beverages and liquors to go. It's open 10 am to 10 pm daily.

Adjacent to the Hotel Inglaterra and facing the Parque Central is the easy-to-overlook *Pastelería Francesa*, which would be a shame to overlook on a hot day if you're in the area and searching for something cool. Here it's possible to buy ice cream sundaes, baguettes, Cuban sandwiches and lots of pastries, with few items more than a dollar or two. There's seating in an air-conditioned dining area until about 8 pm or so, then the pastries are moved to a stand outside. Food is available here 8 am until 11 pm, unless there's a run on the snack stand and it sells out of goodies, in which case it will close early. The *trés gracias* sundae, for US$1.80, comes with a split banana and, occasionally, a little syrup. Men: The pretty Cuban girls coming on to you here are probably prostitutes.

Budget

Several Spanish social clubs around Havana have excellent, inexpensive restaurants open to the public. For example, the *Asociación Canaria de Cuba (Av de las Misiones No 258)*, between Neptuno and Ánimas, behind Hotel Plaza, has a restaurant open noon to 8:30 pm Wednesday to Sunday. This place is a bit hard to find, but definitely worth the effort. First, find the entrance of the Asociación. Then, proceed up the flight of stairs immediately on the left. At the top of the stairs proceed straight ahead and you'll find yourself in a simple, fan-cooled restaurant with high-backed wooden chairs, white tablecloths and responsive waiters. Grilled lobster is a bargain at US$6.50, shrimp enchiladas are US$5, beef stew or pork steak is US$1.95 and fruit cocktail is US$0.50...you get the picture. The prices here are so low the establishment can't make change for big bills; you've been

warned. The lobster arrives in large chunks smothered in a delicious white cheese; if you don't want the cheese, just remove it or say *No queso, por favor* when you order the lobster. If you believe the author is high on this place, you're right!

Another Spanish social club with a restaurant, the *Centro Andaluz (Paseo de Martí No 104)* serves reasonable meals, including *canciller* (swordfish with ham and cheese). You can see flamenco dancing here Saturday at 9 pm and Sunday at 6 pm. It's closed Monday.

The *Café del Prado*, Paseo de Martí and Colón, attached to the Hotel Caribbean, is a popular corner restaurant-bar offering a wide selection of beverages, egg dishes, sandwiches, spaghettis and pizzas, plus roasted chicken, fried pork chunks and beef steaks. Few items cost more than US$4, and many are under US$2. It's open 7 am to 3 am.

Between Neptuno and Virtudes, *Paladar Las Delicias de Consulado (Consulado No 309)*, upstairs, has pork dishes for US$6 and there's a nice terrace overlooking the street. It's open 9 am to 1 am daily.

Paladar Doña Blanquita (Paseo de Martí No 158), between Colón and Refugio, near Hotel Caribbean, has been recommended by tourists. You'll be handed a proper typewritten menu listing main plates in the US$5 to US$9 range ('large portions, no trickery'). You can dine in the elegant salón or on the pleasant terrace overlooking the promenade. It's open noon to midnight daily.

Arabian cuisine was once offered at the *Restaurante Oasis (Paseo de Martí No 256)* in the Centro Cultural Cubano Arabe. The menu now consists mostly of snack food like hot dogs (Do you dare eat a Cuban hot dog???), though it's possible to order half a chicken with fries and a salad for US$3.50. There's a floor show Saturday at 9 pm. A shop at the entrance sells bread. This is a place to grab a beer or a soda; open 2 pm to 3 am daily.

The *Restaurante El Baturro*, on Av de Bélgica a couple of blocks from the Estación Central de Ferrocarril, features Spanish food at very reasonable prices in a pleasing setting with a trio of musicians performing most of the time. Indeed, it's one of the best restaurants around. Meals offered include *fricase de ternera* (a beef stew served with boiled potatoes and vegetables; a little salty but delicious, US$3.50), *fabada a la asturiana* (a large bowl of delicious white beans with chunks of pork tossed in for flavor, US$4.85), and *pulpo al tomate y ajos en aciete y cebollas* (octopus with tomatoes in olive oil and onions, US$4.30). Drinks are locally priced. Open for lunch and dinner.

Paladar Amistad de Lanzarote (☎ 63-6172, *Amistad No 211*), between Neptuno and San Miguel, charges US$6 for most meals. The portions are large and the staff speaks English. It's open noon to midnight daily. **Paladar Bellamar** (*Virtudes No 169*), near Amistad, offers chicken, pork and fish dishes at US$6 a plate. It's open noon to 10 pm daily.

Open noon to 11 pm. **Feria Los Fornos**, on Neptuno between Paseo de Martí and Consulado, grills meats (US$2 to US$6) in an open courtyard. It's only decent and the service isn't terrific, but the place is open 24 hours and it's cheap. **Cafetería Rumbos**, beside the Parque Central, has chicken, snacks and drinks, which you can consume in a stuffy inside dining area or, better yet, take with you. It's open 24 hours.

Mid-Range

Part of the film *Fresa y Chocolate* was shot at **Paladar La Guarida** (☎ 62-4940, 63-7351, *Concordia No 418*), between Gervasio and Escobar. Now it's a trendy restaurant, although still inexpensive (the specialty is *cherna caimanero*, or red snapper, for US$8). Manager Carye del Valles will show you photos of the many Hollywood stars who have dined here, including Jack Nicholson. It's open 7 pm to midnight; reservations are recommended. If you can't get in, try Paladar Sagitario (see later).

According to the menu at **Restaurante Tien-Tan** (*Calle Cuchillo No 17*), between Zanja and San Nicolás, 'Tien-Tan' means Temple of Heaven, and you might leave this establishment a believer. Tien-Tan expands its English-Spanish-Chinese menu

every couple of years. At the time of writing, there were no fewer than 176 items from which to choose. Among the better ones: fried chicken breast in lemon sauce (US$10 for a very large portion, half that for an individual size), and filet of fish with salsa (this is a large fish, nicely fileted and smothered in a delicious salsa (US$10). Prices are in pesos, but you can pay in dollars (request your change in dollars or expect to be burdened with pesos). Expect a 20% service charge to be added to your bill (not mentioned on the menu). It's open 11 am to 11 pm daily.

It's a difficult call, but perhaps the **Restaurante Guang Zhou**, at the opposite end of the short pedestrian street Calle Cuchillo, is a better value than the Tien-Tan. It also offers a menu in English and Spanish and on the lengthy menu you'll find prices quoted in dollars (at Tien-Tan, it's a good idea to ask the price *in dollars* before you order, as the dollar-peso exchange rate could pose surprises when the bill arrives). The prices at Guang Zhou are considerably more down to earth than at the Temple of Heaven. Vegetarians will find lots of meatless dishes from which to choose, many for less than US$2. If you're very hungry and it's very late, this is a terrific place to satisfy your stomach. Open 24 hours.

The nearby **El Pacífico** (*San Nicolás No 518*), at Cuchillo, serves authentic Chinese food in the heart of Havana's small but lively Chinatown. The food here is good, but not as good as at either Tien-Tan or Guang Zhou. It's west of the Capitolio, off Zanja, two blocks west of Av de Italia. It's open noon to 7 pm Tuesday to Sunday.

A fellow who goes by the great name of Omar runs **Paladar Torressón** (☎ 61-7476, *Malecón No 27*), upstairs. Complete meals should cost US$10 to US$15, but the bread and side vegetables might unexpectedly be added to your bill. You get a good sea view from the terrace here. It's open noon to midnight.

Inside the Capitolio Nacional, on a terrace overlooking Paseo de Martí, is the very peaceful **Restaurante Los Escudos** (Coat of Arms Restaurant). From the

RICHARD I'ANSON

BRENT WINEBRENNER

Distance filters out the city's hustle and bustle.

BRENDA TURNNIDGE

The sands of Playas del Este are a perfect place to take the kids…

RICK GERHARTER

…or to take a quiet getaway from them.

An abundance of politics and literature inspires artists as well as activism (clockwise from left: Parque Lenin, Cojímar's Ernest Hemingway monument and Hotel Habana Libre).

CHARLOTTE HINDLE

MARK NEWMAN

RICHARD I'ANSON

Arts, crafts and music express the many moods of Havana.

breezy, marble-floored terrace it's very pleasant to enjoy a beverage or a meal while watching lots of street action below. The best-value items are on the lower end of the price range: Havana-style chopped meat (tasty, US$5.50), lemon chicken (delicious, US$8) and sandwiches for US$3. It's open the same hours as the capitol (9 am to 7:30 pm daily). Be sure to tell the ticket taker at the entrance of the Capitolio Nacional that you're here for lunch or dinner, so you can avoid the entrance fee.

Paladar Sagitario (☎ 78-3205, *Virtudes No 619*), between Gervasio and Escobar, doesn't have a printed menu, so clarify prices (usually around US$8 to US$10) when ordering.

EASTERN FORTS

There are a few dining establishments worthy of comment here in the shadow of El Morro, the largest Spanish colonial fort in the Americas. See the Eastern Forts map in Things to See & Do for locations.

In addition to the restaurants and bars inside the forts, there are several just below them and facing Old Havana. Below El Morro, the *Restaurante Los Doce Após-toles*, so named for the battery of 12 cannons atop its ramparts, serves *comida criolla*. It's a better than average government-run kitchen, and the prices are reasonable. It's open 12:30 to 11 pm daily. *Bar El Polvorín*, just beyond Los Doce Apóstoles, offers drinks and light snacks at tourist prices. Also, the music here is generally too loud and the heat (El Morro steals the bar's sea breeze) can be atrocious. It's open 10 am to 4 am daily.

Below La Cabaña, just beyond the Dársena de los Franceses, is another battery of huge 18th-century cannons. The upscale *Restaurante La Divina Pastora*, behind the guns, offers upscale seafood and is very popular with groups bused in from Club Med and other resorts. Here, grilled filet of fish costs US$10, stuffed shrimp smothered in white sauce goes for US$15, lobster Thermidor runs US$25, and a combo plate of squid, crab, oysters, fish, lobster and shrimp costs US$25. If you've got a sweet tooth, consider following your meal with a glass of watermelon liqueur served over ice. Open noon until 11 pm daily, it's a terrific place to chow down if you don't mind paying higher-than-average prices.

Just around the corner and considerably more intimate is the *Bar El Mirador*, served by the same kitchen that prepares food for La Divina Pastora. The offerings and prices are very different, however. The house special here is a combination plate of veal filet, shrimp and chicken, served with a mushroom sauce, potatoes and onions. Other items include grilled pork chops (US$8) and a skewer of grilled veal and seafood (US$18). You might want to consider having your food with a pitcher of sangría (US$7, fills four glasses). Most afternoons a band performs at the breezy, open-sided bar that overlooks the harbor and Old Havana. Open noon until midnight daily, it can be reached by taxi, and there are usually taxis out front to take you back (if you don't see any, ask your driver to wait for you or to come back for you).

VEDADO (MAP 3)
Self Catering

One of the great finds in all of Vedado is the *Pain de París* (*Calle 25 No 164*), near the intersection with Calle O. Here it's possible to purchase lots of delicious pastries, including croissants, eclairs and tarts, most for less than US$1. Also available are baguettes, sandwiches and a variety of coffee and fruit drinks, all at low prices. Although it's practically across the street from popular Hotel Vedado, few tourists notice it and even fewer enter it. Their loss. The Pain de París, which is cool but tiny with only three or four tables, is open 24 hours.

You'll find a *supermercado* below the Edificio Focsa, Calle 17 at Calle N. It's open 9 am to 6 pm Monday to Saturday, 9 am to 1 pm Sunday.

The *Mercado Agropecuario*, Calles 19 and B, has fresh fruits, vegetables and meats at local prices. Some stalls sell peso snacks.

Supermercado Meridiano is in Galerías de Paseo, across the street from the Hotel Meliá Cohiba. It's open 10 am to 5 pm weekdays, 10 am to 2 pm Sunday.

'Coffee, Tea or Cuba?'

Thirty years ago, when international hijackers were finding refuge in Cuba, that question was a joke occasionally uttered by US flight attendants in lieu of the more traditional 'Coffee, tea or juice?'

Today, a common question heard *in* Cuba is 'Coffee or tea?' (or, more precisely, ¿Café o té?). This is particularly true in Havana, where many Habaneros can't get through the day without the caffeine rushes these beverages bring.

Habaneros usually take their coffee strong and black in a small cup loaded with sugar. It's an energy hit called a *cafecito* or *café cubano*. A morning favorite is *café con leche*, a mixture of strong black coffee and hot milk in a large cup. *Café americano* is weak coffee in a large cup. Coffee is almost never offered after dinner at restaurants.

Té (tea) or *yerba buena* (a local name for tea) is often taken with *limón* (lemon). Some hotels don't serve tea, but they will always be happy to give you a pot of hot water *(cafetera de agua caliente)* if you bring your own tea bags with you.

Coffee aficionados should visit the Café Habana, at the corner of Amargura and Mercaderes, when in La Habana Vieja. This corner café serves Habaneros almost exclusively. Don't let the puzzled looks of the regulars upset you. They're simply not used to seeing foreigners in their humble coffee house with worn bar stools and a menu that consists of café espreso (US$0.90), artificial orange juice (US$0.50) and little else.

Budget

Cubans waiting to buy ice cream with pesos line the sidewalk outside **Coppelia**, Calle 23 at Calle L, in the park diagonally opposite the Hotel Habana Libre. If you wish to join them, ask for *el último*, but try to not look like a tourist. A certain number of people from the line are admitted in groups every 30 minutes. The security guards on duty here direct foreigners to a dollar section without any line, where ice cream sells for US$0.01 a gram, plus US$0.20 cover. Coppelia is open 11 am to 11 pm daily.

Likewise, if you've got a hankering for ice cream and you find yourself in the vicinity of the Malecón near the Hotel Nacional, you'll want to know about **Bim Bom**, at the corner of Infanta and Calle 23. Bim Bom serves only ice cream and it's priced for Habaneros. You get a view of the ocean and the cascades that tumble down a steep embankment on the north side of Hotel Nacional. Bim Bom is open 10 am to midnight daily.

When price is all that matters, consider the **Rumbos Cafetería** at Calles 23 and P. The Rumbos serves the worst food imaginable from a nutritionist's perspective, but accountants have to love its prices: disgusting premade sandwiches and Frisbee-tough individual pizzas for around US$2, fatpacked cheeseburgers for US$1, slices of sugar cake for US$0.30, vintage hot dogs wrapped in bacon for US$0.80. If immediate medical service is needed, you'll be glad to know the light in the Rumbos is bright fluorescent – perfect light in which to find a vein if you're trying to administer in IV. It's always open.

Beside the flea market on the Malecón, where Calle E meets the sea, there's a **Ditú MiConuco**. This establishment consists of several upscale snack stands, each with its open dining areas (in this case, tables under open-sided thatch-roof palapas). Ditú MiConuco caters to locals, offering decent food cheap. Typically there are three meals to choose from, each with one entrée (such as chicken, pork or beef) and several side orders. The cost of these combination plates rarely exceeds US$4. Food can also be ordered à la carte – pizza with chicken (US$1.50), cheeseburgers (US$1.35), and so on. Open noon until midnight daily.

El Conejito *(Calle M No 206)*, at the corner of Calle 17, is *the* place in Havana to taste rabbit, and most dishes cost less than US$8. Other dishes here include beef for US$4, chicken for US$3.50, pasta for less than US$4, grilled fish for US$6.25, and lobster for US$8. If you can't handle the somber Tudor decor, check out the cheap beer garden behind the restaurant. It's open noon to midnight daily.

The **Restaurante Bulerías**, Calle L, between Calles 23 and 25, opposite the Hotel Habana Libre, has Spanish cuisine illustrated in a pictorial menu. A ham-and-cheese sandwich or a hamburger will set you back only US$1. Pricier items such as baked chicken are available, but few are more than US$3. There are tables outside near the sidewalk as well as in the basement ('subterranean dining room,' if you prefer). It's open 24 hours a day. There's a lively disco here most days 10 pm to 4 am (US$5 cover, US$1 for a beer).

On the corner of Calles 23 and O are two places, one atop the other. In the basement is **La Taberna**, which is usually cool and damp-smelling and always cheap: continental breakfast for US$1.40, ham sandwiches for US$1, roasted pork or fried chicken for US$1.80. Just above it is the **Cafetería Sofía**, which has lots of people-watching potential and the same menu as La Taberna but charges more for its food. Hence, tourists tend to eat here while locals tend to favor the subterranean restaurant. Neither has air conditioning. Whereas La Taberna is open late, the Sofía is open 24 hours.

Paladar Los Helechos de Trinidad (Calle 25 No 361), between Calles K and L, is one block south of the Hotel Habana Libre. Most dishes are US$5. It's open noon to midnight daily. **Paladar Los Amigos** (Calle M No 253), in the back, at Calle 19 near Hotel Victoria, serves good meals for US$10, including side plates. It's open noon to midnight. **Paladar Gringo Viejo** (☎ 32-6150, Calle 21 No 454), between Calles E and F, offers a good atmosphere and large portions of invariably brilliant food. A detailed menu in pesos is provided, with nothing more than US$10 (you can pay in dollars). It's open 1 to 11 pm Monday to Saturday.

On the corner of Calles 21 and N is a place few tourists tend to enter that can be quite the Cuban cultural scene on any given day. It's the **Restaurante Caribeno**, open since the earliest days of the revolution and popular with many civic groups, such as the local club of grandfathers. These groups usually fill most of the restaurant when they're happening, and old favorites keyed by a pianist and accompanied by outbreaks of singing and dancing are staples of such gatherings. The food here is secondary, but not bad. Entrées include fried chicken (US$4.50) and smoked ham (US$4.50). Bummer: The French fries are among the oiliest on Earth. Open noon until midnight daily.

Paladar Los Tres Mosqueteros (☎ 61-4734, Calle 23 No 607), between Calles E and F, offers the chance to dine on an upstairs balcony. The owner, Roberto, doesn't furnish a menu, but dishes range from US$4 for chicken to US$8 for lobster. It's open 11 am to 8 pm daily. **Paladar Yiyo's** (☎ 32-8977, Calle L No 256), between Calles 17 and 19, Apt 202 (2nd floor), is friendly and dishes are reasonable at US$5 to US$6.

Paladar La Última Instancia (Calle D No 557), between Calles 23 and 25, on Parque Mariana Grajales, upstairs, is open noon to midnight. **Paladar Amor** (Calle 23 No 759), between Calles B and C, 3rd floor, is not far from La Última Instancia. The *pollo el amor* is good, if you haven't already had enough chicken. You may have to wait in the elegant drawing room until a table becomes free. It's open noon to midnight daily.

Farther afield is **Paladar El Helecho** (Calle 6 No 203), between Calle 11 and Línea.

Mid-Range

The **Paladar El Hurón Azul** (☎ 79-1691, Humboldt No 153), at Calle P, is possibly the best private restaurant in Havana. It serves a dozen or so authentic Cuban dishes, among them a filling combination plate called La Guajira that consists of a large, thin pork steak nicely seasoned, a corn tamale stuffed with pork, fried sweet bananas and fried green plantains, black beans mixed with white rice, and a salad (all for US$9). Other entrées include baked chicken, grilled fish and smoked pig served with pineapple salsa. There's no beef or lobster served here, due to government restrictions on private

PLACES TO EAT

restaurants. The decor here is quite soothing: white walls beautified with colorful paintings, flower-filled vases here and there, air-conditioning and cloth-covered tables. All dishes are priced from US$7 to US$9. A 10% service charge is added to every bill. It's worth waiting if all the tables are full. The Blue Ferret (El Hurón Azul in English) is open noon to midnight daily.

Several other reasonably priced restaurants are near the Hotel St John's. **Restaurante Wakamba**, on Calle O between Calles 23 and 25, serves half a chicken stuffed with ham, chorizo, olives and cheese (US$7.50); a grilled pork steak (US$3.15); a ham steak (US$2.30); and smoked pig (US$3.50), among a long list of offerings. Wakamba is the name of a Kenyan tribe and art from the tribe decorates the walls. If your waiter, to inflate your bill, brings you a side salad you didn't order, send it back. It's open noon until midnight four nights a week and until 2 am Thursday, Friday and Saturday. An adjacent cafeteria with hot dogs and other snacks is open 24 hours.

Across the street below Hotel St John's is **Cafetería Marakas**, which is similar to Wakamba (air-conditioning, similar prices, casual attire) and also has breakfast specials, plus pork, fish and chicken dishes for around US$3. However, this is perhaps a better place to come for a drink as there is a bigger and better selection, starting with fresh-squeezed orange juice (US$1.20 a glass). A variety of coffee drinks are available for around US$1 a cup. The Marakas is open 7 am to 3 am daily.

Café Concerto Gato Tuerto (☎ 66-2224, Calle O No 14), between Calles 17 and 19, is a chic cafe and bar with live music Friday and Saturday at 11 pm for a US$5 cover charge. The onion soup here is good and reasonably priced, as is the ropa vieja. Chef Miguel Magraner's langosta Magraner consists of lobster fried in butter with a little sweet-and-sour sauce (US$19).

Adjacent to the Hotel Habana Libre is **La Rampa Cafetería**, at the corner of Calles 23 and L, which gets more than its fair share of foreign visitors due to its proximity to the major hotel. The chef's special here is spaghetti al gamberi, which is spaghetti with shrimp and olive oil and garlic, for US$6. Only slightly better is the roasted chicken (US$7) and a burger (US$4 to US$6, depending on toppings). The high

Helpful Food Phrases

A short menu decoder appears at the back of this book, in the Language chapter. Here are some phrases you might find useful when dining out:

¿Puedo ver la carta, por favor?	Can I see the menu, please?
¿Tiene una carta en inglés?	Do you have a menu in English?
¿Qué es esto?	What is that?
¿Viene con ensalada?	Does it come with salad?
¿Cuál es la especialidad de este restaurante?	What is the specialty here?
¿Qué me recomienda?	What do you recommend?
¿Qué están comiendo ellos?	What are they eating?
¿Qué ingredientes tiene este plato?	What ingredients are in this dish?
No pedí esto.	I didn't order this.
Quiero algo para beber.	I'd like something to drink.
¿Tienen una sillita para el bebé?	Do you have a highchair for the baby?
Muchas gracias, estaba buenísimo.	Thank you very much, that was delicious.
¿El servicio está incluido en la cuenta?	Is service included in the check?
La cuenta, por favor.	The check, please.

SEÑORES IMPERIALISTAS ¡NO LES TENEMOS ABSOLUTAMENTE NINGÚN MIEDO!

point of this place is the air-conditioning. It's also open 24 hours.

Top End

One of the author's favorite escapes is the **Restaurante-Bar Polinesio** on Calle 23 between Calles L and M. The Polinesio provides patrons with an air-conditioned setting in wonderfully overdone Polynesian decor. The restaurant is Havana's finest in terms of ethnic themes, from the decor to the Polynesian-flavored food. This place isn't cheap (entrees start at US$10) but it's worth it. Also, if you're watching your budget, consider ordering just the chicken fried rice (US$4.50); it's a filling meal in itself and very good. Be sure to request a window-side table. Open noon to 3:30 pm and 7:30 to 11 pm daily.

Across the street from the Restaurante-Bar Polinesio is the **Restaurante Mandarín**, which makes little effort to mimic the appearance of anything Chinese. But the food here is good and a step down in price from the Polinesio. The tasty specialties of the house include lobster chop suey (US$9), 'crumby lobster in a sweet-and-sour sauce' (US$9.25) and shrimp chop suey (US$6.60). There's also special fried rice for US$4.25 that includes diced ham, bacon, carrots, egg, sprouts and scallions; one portion will fill the average person. Unfortunately, the television in the bar here is usually turned up louder than most people would appreciate. Open noon until 4 am daily (a good place to keep in mind after midnight).

Until the mid-1990s, the air-conditioned **Restaurante Monseigneur**, at the corner of Calles 21 and O, was a bit dreary. But as the '90s wound down the subterranean restaurant prettied itself up. Today, the decor is elegant (ignoring the faux-marble wallpaper) and dining is by candlelight. Men in black ties serve filet mignon with mushrooms (US$9), shrimp enchiladas (US$11.50), grilled chicken (US$6) and *mar y tierra* (chicken, roast beef and 'rings of lobster,' US$20), and there's usually a pianist playing American classics. Most of the dishes come with potatoes and vegetables. The catch of the day is always a good choice here

and usually costs around US$8. Consider the baked Alaska or ice cream with fruit for dessert. Open for lunch and dinner.

The ever-popular **Restaurante El Cortijo**, Calles O and 25 at Hotel Vedado, is a fairly good Spanish restaurant with dishes in the US$7 to US$13 range. It's open noon to 10 pm daily; after closing it becomes a cabaret.

Restaurante La Torre *(Calle 17 No 55)*, at the corner of Calle M, is on the top floor of the Edificio Focsa, 125m above the city. This 36-story apartment building – the highest in Cuba – once housed Soviet technicians. You'll get your best view of Havana from here, which makes the leisurely service bearable. La Torre's French-style menu consists of pricey lobster, fish and chicken dishes. Appetizers run US$5 to US$12, entrées from US$17 to US$28, desserts are US$5ish. This swank restaurant faces the city, while the bar faces the sunset. La Torre is open noon to midnight daily; the bar 11:30 am to 2 am daily.

Not far from the Riviera and Meliá Cohiba hotels is the **Centro Vasco**, at the corner of Calles 3 and 4, serving reasonably priced Spanish dishes 24 hours a day.

Also in this part of town is **Restaurante 1830** *(Calzada No 1252)*, near the Almendares tunnels, one of Havana's most elegant restaurants (though it's not very good). It's open noon to 10 pm daily. After 10 pm there's live music and salsa dancing in the garden behind the restaurant (don't come on a windy night). The **Mesón La Chorrera** is in the old tower nearby. It's open noon to 2 am daily.

In the Hotel Habana Libre you'll find two restaurants, the less fancy of the two being **El Barracon**. Here traditional Cuban dishes range in price from US$4 for black bean stew to US$14 for Creole roasted pork with onion sauce. Most dishes, including the *pollo asado a la guajiro* (roasted chicken in a bitter orange sauce) cost US$10. Seafood specialties start at US$15.50. The Barracon is open 1 to 4 pm and 8 pm to 2 am daily.

For a more formal setting, try the Habana Libre's **Restaurante Sierra Maestra**, which offers lemon chicken breast (US$9.50),

PLACES TO EAT

grilled salmon filet (US$13), beef and chicken kabobs (US$14), filet of pepper steak (US$15) and a host of other entrées in a waiters-in-black-tie setting. Open 7 pm to 1 am daily.

PLAYA & MARIANAO (MAP 4)
Self-Catering

Buy groceries at *Supermercado* in the shopping complex opposite the Sierra Maestra building, Av 1 and Calle 0. It's open 9 am to 6 pm Monday to Saturday, 9 am to 1 pm Sunday.

The *Panadería Doña Neli* kiosk, at Av 5A and Calle 42, sells hard-currency bread. It's open 7 am to 6 pm Monday to Saturday, 7 am to 1 pm Sunday.

Supermercado Flores, Calle 176 between Avs 1 and 3, in Flores, sells bread. It's open 10 am to 6 pm Monday to Saturday, 10 am to 1 pm Sunday. The cafeteria at the end of the building has cheap snacks.

Budget

There are a few paladares to try in Miramar, including *Paladar La Familia* (*Calle 6 No 302*), at Av 3 (open noon to midnight daily), and *Paladar Calle 10* (☎ 29-6702, Calle 10 No 314), between Avs 3 and 5 (open noon to midnight), run by a guy named Emilio. Insist on a printed menu.

At Marina Hemingway, next to Papa's Restaurant-Bar, there's a snack bar and nightly show at the *Cabaret Marina*, where you can get light fare off a barbecue during daylight hours.

Mid-Range

One of Havana's most famous private restaurants is *Paladar Los Cactus de 33* (☎ 23-5139, Av 33 No 3405), between Calles 34 and 36 in Playa, which has been reviewed in several international lifestyle magazines; TV specials have been filmed here. The printed menu lists fish, poultry and pork dishes for US$8 to US$12, including garnish. It's open 10 am to midnight daily.

El Aljibe, on Av 7 between Calles 24 and 26, is a Havana institution. The specialty here is rotisserie chicken, and you'd be making a mistake ordering anything else.

For US$12 plus 10%, your meal arrives on three large plates: One contains a half chicken, cooked to perfection. Another is filled with black beans and white rice. Yet a third large plate is packed with French fries and hot fried sweet bananas. If you manage to empty either of the last two plates, someone comes around with a couple of pots and fills them up again. As you might suspect, the decor is not subtle, either. Everything's muscular, from the stout wooden chairs to the thick wood cloth-covered tables to the powerful ceiling fans to the jungly foliage that rings this upscale, thatch-roof, open-sided eatery. For what it's worth, *Cigar Aficionado* magazine gives El Aljibe its highest rating for Cuban food. Open 12 to 12 daily.

Nearby is *Dos Gardenias*, on Av 7 at Calle 28, an upscale complex with several restaurants, bars and shops. You'll have a choice of pizza and Chinese food here. Dos Gardenias is also called El Rincón del Bolero for the nightly shows beginning at 9 pm (US$10 cover). The complex is open noon to midnight daily.

The *Paladar Vistamar* (☎ 23-8328), on Av 1 between Calles 22 and 24, is in the 2nd-floor family-room-turned-restaurant of a private residence that faces the sea. With six tables (one large enough to accommodate a party of eight), it's oversize by paladar standards, which is good because the Vistamar has become so popular that the extra seating is needed. The food here is delicious, but it's not cheap. Most entrées run US$11 with salad. A large lobster with salad sets you back US$18. It's open 11 am to midnight daily.

Restaurante El Pavo Real, at Av 7A and Calle 4, close to the bicycle bridge over the river between Miramar and Vedado, has an extensive medium-priced Chinese menu. It's open noon to midnight daily.

La Casa de Quinta y 16 (also known as Restaurante El Ranchón), Av 5 at Calle 16, is an upscale garden restaurant with an elegant façade. However, this place can be incredibly humid and is best avoided on an uncomfortably warm evening. The food is good and reasonably priced. Most chicken, beef, pork and fish dishes cost less than US$10. It's open noon to 10:30 pm.

El Tocororo, at Calle 18 and Av 3, like El Aljibe, is a Havana institution, but it's overpriced, featuring seafood ranging from fried fish (US$15) to lobster tail (US$24). There's no written menu – rather, a waiter tells you the food of the day in English or Spanish – and not being able to read a menu bothers some people. Everything, even the bread and rice, is à la carte, and 10% is added on top. It's one of Havana's top restaurants, with candlelit tables and an elegant garden atmosphere. It's open noon to midnight daily.

A better value is *Don Cangrejo (Av 1 No 1606)*, between Calles 16 and 18, another seafood specialist. Here, the fresh fish comes with a sea view and air-conditioning. The restaurant, a favorite with wealthy Cubans, is known for its crabs (US$15), and they arrive at your table with a bib, a mallet and a butcher block. Hammer away! A fine alternative is grilled fish of the day (usually sole), served with a slight coat of olive oil and garlic, and a side of (greasy) fries and peas for US$6. If you're feeling fancy, try the crabmeat flambéed with rum and dressed up with mushrooms, tomatoes, peppers and onion and served with white rice (US$12). Don Cangrejo is open noon to midnight daily.

If you're looking for a place that Cubans find intimate and pleasant in the vicinity of Marina Hemingway, look no farther than *Restaurante El Laurel (Av 5 No 26002)*. This is not a fancy place and the odor coming off the marina isn't always fresh. What's nice about it, besides that it overlooks the marina, is its size and layout – basically a half-dozen small tables under individual palapas in what could be someone's backyard. Specialties include the catch of the day (US$8), a slice of smoked ham (US$6 to US$10), and chicken smothered in mozzarella (US$6.50). Open daily noon until 11 pm.

Out on the marina and in view of the Restaurante El Laurel is *Papa's Restaurant-Bar*, an air-conditioned place on the waterfront that specializes in seafood. The ambiance isn't terrific (although the management tries for elegance, with black ties and an occasional violinist) but the food is very good. Among the more popular dishes are: garlic shrimp (US$10), shrimp with chili sauce (US$11), lobster (US$18), chicken (US$5) and filet mignon (US$12). Open 2 pm to 2 am daily. The violinist generally arrives around 8 pm.

Top End

The following restaurants cater mostly to diplomats and businesspeople on expense accounts, and most are very good. But if you came to Havana dressed like a backpacker and didn't bring so much as one nice outfit, you'd likely feel out of place at any of the following restaurants.

El Rancho Palco, Av 19 and Calle 140, is in a forest near the Palacio de las Convenciones. The Cuban cooking is served under one of the finest thatched roofs you'll likely ever see. This place has terrific ambiance all the time but particularly at night, when live salsa music fills the air. Only fans cool the place, but most of the time they're all that's needed. Beef is the specialty here, with filets ranging from US$14 to US$36. Fish dishes (mostly US$14), chicken dishes (mostly US$8) and shrimp dishes (mostly US$18) are also offered. This romantic restaurant is open noon to 11 pm daily.

Another memorable restaurant is *La Ferminia (Av 5 No 18207)*, at Calle 184, which surely is one of Havana's top dining establishments. The setting: An elegant converted colonial mansion along one of Havana's finest residential boulevards. The house special, served by waiters in black ties, consists of a combination plate of lobster, shrimp, fish filet, chicken, beef scallops, sausage, vegetables and potatoes (US$28). Most everything else is priced around US$12, including shrimp Thermidor and grilled filet of fish with lemon sauce. There's a cigar shop on the premises. It's possible that here you'll get better food, overall, than at El Rancho Palco. It's open noon to 11 pm.

La Cecilia (Av 5 No 11010), between Calles 110 and 112, opposite Servi-Cupet, is an upscale garden restaurant featuring

Cuban cuisine, especially steak and lobster. Prices mostly run US$10 to US$16. There's no live music here. Instead, you listen to large parrots make noises in a spacious cage. Sound boring? Nah. This place is fairly romantic, with lots of tables under wooden roofs and amid gardens. The chief drawback: It does get humid here. La Cecilia is open noon to midnight daily.

PARQUE LENIN AREA (MAP 5)

One of Havana's most celebrated restaurants is **Las Ruinas**, on Cortina de la Presa on the southeast side of Parque Lenin. It's a striking combination: ruined walls of an old sugar mill engulfed in modern architecture highlighted by René Portocarrero's stained-glass windows. The antique furnishings enhance the elegant atmosphere. The menu includes grilled filet of fish (US$11), beef rolled with ham and bacon (US$10), Caribbean queen lobster grilled with butter (US$20), lobster cocktail (US$8), pizzas (US$4.50 to US$7) and grilled chicken with potatoes (US$5). Unfortunately, the food doesn't live up to its surroundings. Las Ruinas is open 11 am to midnight Tuesday to Sunday.

There are four other restaurants of substance in the area, the only one really worth mentioning being the **Restaurante El Bambú**, in the Jardín Botanico. It offers good vegetarian food cheap, as well as sodas, ice cream and other snack food. The Bambú is open for lunch only, noon to 3 pm Wednesday through Sunday. The remaining three restaurants appear on the map entitled Parque Lenin Area and are on there not so much as recommendations, but rather as places to grab a quick bite if you're in the area and starving. Otherwise, you're best off waiting until you return to town.

Entertainment

Havana presents a smorgasbord of live entertainment – and most of it's free. If you stroll around La Habana Vieja any afternoon, you'll hear music pouring into the streets from many restaurants and bars. There's no better way to tap into the Cuban music scene than to settle into a chair at any of these places, listen to the music and watch locals and visitors rejoice together. If you love to dance, don't hesitate.

A holdover from the '50s, Havana also presents numerous gala floor shows with big bands, leggy dancers, smooth singers, jugglers, acrobats and loads of glamour and excitement. The most famous cabaret show is presented outdoors at Havana's Tropicana nightclub. But the Nacional, Capri, Havana Libre and Riviera Hotels have fine cabarets as well.

Many of Havana's hotels also contain discos that open at about 10 pm and stay open four or more hours. Discos intended mainly for Cubans (ie, those outside hotels) often have a 'couples only' rule, but it rarely applies to foreigners. Regardless, there are usually many willing female partners waiting at the door (you're expected to pay your partner's entrance fee). The rule is intended to curb prostitution, but the profession flourishes at discos anyway; the prostitutes pose outside as wannabe dance partners and change their proposition once you've escorted them in.

There are several theaters in Havana where Spanish-language plays are presented, but the only way to obtain reliable information about programming is to go to the theater beforehand and buy advance tickets, if possible. Often, the ticket booth is occupied only an hour or so before the drama begins.

There is no shortage of cinemas in Havana and some of the better ones are mentioned here. Unlike some venues, these are intended specifically for Cuban use and are priced accordingly – a small amount of change and you're in. Most foreign films are shown in their original language with Spanish subtitles. Many cinemas actually show videos on television-size screens. If a sign out front says *pantalla grande*, it means you'll see the film on a big screen.

Just Come On In!

The best way to appreciate Havana's music scene is also the least expensive. It's roaming the historic streets of La Habana Vieja during the afternoon and slipping into those bars, cafés and restaurants where the music is live and the rhythms infectious. The sounds of music generally last until dark, when most tourists retreat to their hotels overly fearful of what the night might bring. At some places, the music lasts well into the witching hours. At Restaurante El Patio, it never stops.

If you're game for an afternoon devoted to hearing Havana's music for the masses – Habaneros as well as foreigners – you might want to begin your journey in the Plaza de la Catedral and head south, following the suggested walking tour. Along the route, live music can often be heard at La Bodeguita del Medio, Restaurante El Patio, Café O'Reilly, O'Reilly's, Café París, La Mina, Restaurante La Paella, El Café Mercurio, Bar La Marina and Café Taberna.

If you intend to have a drink at most of these places, start at Café Taberna and head north. When it's time to find a taxi to take you back to your hotel, it's much easier near the Plaza de la Catedral than it is near the Plaza Vieja (where Café Taberna is). There are always taxis parked at the intersection of Calles Tacón and Empedrado, a short walk from Plaza de la Catedral. If you're up for it, forgo the motorized taxi for a bicycle taxi. They can be found at the same intersection.

ENTERTAINMENT

¡ABSOLUTAMENTE NINGUN MIEDO!

BARS
La Habana Vieja &
Centro Habana (Map 2)

Bars are heading up the entertainment chapter? Yes, sir/ma'am. In Old Havana, few bars aren't also music venues, where talented local musicians unite most afternoons and play predominantly Cuban classics. This is the *real* Havana, where money doesn't separate the island's residents from its visitors. Most of the bars mentioned here are frequented by mariachis or host a house band. There's never a fee to enter them.

Old Havana's most celebrated bar is *La Bodeguita del Medio (Empedrado No 207)*, off Plaza de la Catedral, which Ernest Hemingway is known to have visited at least twice during the 1930s. The management has billed La B del M as a Hemingway haunt ever since, earning millions of dollars over the years on the sale of *mojitos* it claims the great author fancied here. A big sign on one wall, apparently in Hemingway's handwriting, says he preferred to drink his mojitos here and his daiquirís at El Floridita. The latter is definitely true. However, there's no evidence the great author ever frequented La B del M, which incidentally makes mojitos that are among the city's worst with watered-down rum and

Hot Off the Presses

The free *Cartelera* entertainment newspaper published every Thursday and usually available at hotel reception and/or tour desks contains comprehensive listings of cinema programs, theatrical presentations, musical events, TV schedules, art galleries, museums, hotels, restaurants, bars and nightclubs. If you have trouble finding a *Cartelera*, consider visiting the newspaper's headquarters at Calle 15 No 602, at the corner of Calle C in Vedado. Beware, the office is closed on weekends. If you're in Vedado on a Friday, you might want to look for posters in front of the Cine Yara advertising rock concerts around town during the coming weekend.

charges US$4 apiece for them. In decades past, notables including Salvador Allende, Harry Belafonte and Nat King Cole left their autographs on the wall. It's hard to imagine anyone of their stature spending time in this tourist trap now. The bar opens around 11 am and closes around midnight.

O'Reilly's, on the corner of San Ignacio and O'Reilly, is a small open-air bar and café with a dozen tables under a shade tree. It's recommended for people-watching, as seemingly every tourist strolling through Old Havana passes by this pleasant place. Although most patrons only sip drinks here, a few snacks are available. It opens around 9 am and stays open late daily.

A stone's throw away is *Café de O'Reilly (O'Reilly No 203)*, between Cuba and San Ignacio, which is considerably more barlike than O'Reilly's. There's a bar on both floors of this two-story open-sided joint that's a bit run down. Beware, only the lowest-quality liquors are used here. Snacks as well as booze are available 11 am to 3 am. A band performs most nights on the 2nd floor (reached by a rickety, narrow circular staircase), where you'll find caged birds and loud music all day. The bathrooms here are disgusting; even if you're in need, pass this place by.

Like La Bodeguita del Medio, *El Floridita (Obispo No 557)*, at Av de Bélgica, cashes in on the Hemingway legend as best it can (the bar-restaurant contains numerous photos of the man, taken four to six decades ago). A bartender named Constante Ribalaigua assured El Floridita's place in Cuban drinking history when he began using shaved ice to make frozen daiquirís here in the 1920s. A decade later Hemingway arrived and the Papa Hemingway Special (basically, a daiquirí made with grapefruit juice) was created in his honor. If you'd like to order a daiquirí (there are now 17 on the drink menu), they're US$6 apiece (and worth every cent). El Floridita is open 11 am to midnight daily.

After you've had one daiquirí at El Floridita in Hemingway's honor, head south on Av de Bélgica one block to Obrapía, where you can have a daiquirí at the *Monserrate*

Meeting Gays & Lesbians in Havana

As you would expect in a city as cosmopolitan and international as Havana, the gay, lesbian, bisexual and transgender community is large, if not readily visible. Consequently, the challenge for the visitor is connecting with that community in order to enjoy its activities and members. However, once you're connected to this extensive but very discreet community, your experience and knowledge of the city will be immeasurably deepened.

Homosexuality is legal in Cuba and most people seem to have a live and let live attitude, especially in Havana. Gay bashing is very rare, although police harassment does occur, more often directed at Cubans than at foreigners. One should also be alert to *jineteros* or *pingueros* and take common sense precautions.

There are no overtly gay bars or discos, and the location of the frequent private and semi-private parties throughout Havana changes continuously. But a little bit of questioning (speaking Spanish is decidedly helpful here), combined with Cubans' eagerness to meet foreigners, should enable a visitor to connect with the gay scene without too much difficulty.

The best location for keying in to what is happening is in front of the Cine Yara at Calle 23 and Calle L in Vedado. This is a busy area, across from the Hotel Habana Libre and Coppelia (the ice cream shop that opened the Cuban *Fresa y Chocolate*, a must-see movie if you want to understand contemporary Cuban views toward gays and lesbians) and full of tourists and Cubans alike. At night, the crowd in front of the theater becomes very gay. A few conversations often lead to an invitation to a *fiesta de diez pesos* (semi-private party), sometimes held in large colonial homes. Admission is usually US$1 and the crowds are often mixed men and women. Expect to see a drag show as part of the entertainment.

Other locations to meet gays and lesbians have included El Café Mercurio in the Lonja del Comercio on Plaza de San Francisco de Asís in La Habana Vieja, and the Cubalse cafeteria next to the Fiat showroom on the Malecón (at Marina) in Vedado. Also try the Castropol, a cabaret, near the corner of Malecón and Av de Italia, operated by a Spanish foundation that presents drag shows and a disco on Monday, Tuesday, Wednesday and Thursday nights. Try Joker, at Linea and Calle 10, or Ecodisco, at Linea and Calle E, bar-discos in Vedado that attract a mixed crowd. Ask Cuban acquaintances for other suggestions.

Semi-regular discos that attract a friendly crowd include Periquiton de Mantilla on Saturday, Rosalia de Castro near the Capitolio in Centro Habana, or Fiestas de Papito and Fiesta de H y 21. Discreetly inquire among the people in front of the Cine Yara as to the dates and whereabouts of these or other locales.

Some semi-private parties are held with a predominantly lesbian clientele. Once again, inquire among the Cuban gays you meet, as the location and dates change frequently.

Beaches in Havana that are popular with gays include El Chivo just through the tunnel under the harbor to East Havana or a more pleasant one at Avs 16 and 1 in Miramar. Both beaches are rocky and difficult for swimming. A much, much nicer beach, pleasant for swimming, is Mi Cayito, in Santa María del Mar in the Playas del Este, about 20km east of Havana.

– Rick Gerharter

SEÑORES IMPERIALISTAS ¡NO LES TENEMOS ABSOLUTAMENTE NINGÚN MIEDO!

Bar for a third of the price quoted by the red-coated waiters in El Floridita. The food at the Monserrate is cheap but not tasty. Monserrate has a stage and on it seem to play the best bands in Havana. This is a super place to plant yourself in the late afternoon.

Across the street from the Monserrate Bar, *El Castillo de Farnés* offers patrons a smaller, quieter environment. The band at Monserrate can be heard very well at El Castillo de Farnés. The presence of hustlers at these places might cause foreign women to feel uncomfortable, in which case the terrace of the nearby Hotel Inglaterra is an excellent alternative.

El Caserón del Tango (*Jústiz No 21*), off Oficios (down the street beside the Museo del Automóvil), has a nice, untouristy bar where you can get sandwiches and drinks for pesos. On Wednesday and Friday at 5 pm there's a special program of tango singing and dancing, and tango lessons can be arranged. The Casa de la Comédia across the street sometimes presents live theater in Spanish.

Havana's best, and least expensive, music

Bar La Marina, Oficios and Brasil, offers an agreeable corner courtyard shaded by an impressively large mass of vines that serve as a ceiling and a roof (don't come here if it's raining, as the rain comes right in!). A Cuban band plays most afternoons and evenings, and the friendly atmosphere is most agreeable. La Marina is a fine place in which to rest your feet for awhile and possibly enjoy an inexpensive snack after visiting the Monasterio de San Francisco de Asís. The bar is open until 11 pm daily.

Bar Dos Hermanos (*San Pedro No 304*), at Sol near Muelle Luz, was a favorite Havana hangout of Spanish poet Federico García Lorca during his three months in Cuba in 1930. Pub snacks such as oyster cocktails, meatballs, hamburgers and chicken go well with the drinks. The salty atmosphere adds to the flavor, but this is a rather seedy area late at night. It's open 24 hours.

Though not a bar by name, the ***Café París***, at the corner of Obispo and San Ignacio, serves booze and indeed most of the people who patronize it don't order food. That's because they are there more to listen to the music, and the management doesn't mind if you take a table but order only drinks; taking a table when the café is full and not ordering anything at all is another matter. At the time of writing, Café París generally had an even mix of patrons – about 50% Habaneros and 50% international visitors. Open 24 hours, it is a good place to remember.

Other places to hear music for free in Old Havana are mentioned in the boxed text,

'Just Come On In!' and don't warrant further description. However, it should be mentioned here that the bars, cafés and restaurants in or near the Plaza de la Catedral and the Plaza de Armas tend to stay open later than those south of Calle Obrapía because there are more tourists near them after dark. At the time of writing, the areas directly west and south of Plaza Vieja felt unsafe at night.

In Centro Habana, ***Restaurante Prado 264*** (*Paseo de Martí No 264*), open noon to 10:30 pm daily, has a long wooden bar in the back. Eating here, however, is dicey – you might pay dollar prices for peso food.

Vedado (Map 3) & Playa & Marianao (Map 4)

There's no shortage of bars in Vedado, the most popular of which are in hotels. The bars inside the Hotel Habana Libre and the Hotel Nacional are favorites with people who come to Havana regularly on business.

There are lots of bars in Playa and Marianao, most found inside the larger hotels. One of the best of the independent bars there is ***La Maison*** (☎ *24-0126, Calle 16 No 701*), at Av 7, a very tasteful piano bar that opens at 10 pm daily except Sunday. There's a US$2 minimum charge per person.

FOLK DANCE & MUSIC
La Habana Vieja & Centro Habana (Map 2)

In Old Havana, the ***Casa de la Cultura de La Habana Vieja*** (☎ *63-4860, Aguiar No 509*), in an old convent between Amargura and Brasil, presents Afro-Cuban dancing, rumba dancing or folk singing at 7 or 9 pm nightly. The program varies every week (and it could be canceled if it's raining), but count on things beginning an hour late in any case. Admission to dances where drinks are sold is five pesos; most other events are free. The staff can arrange Cuban dance lessons for you.

Bands such as the locally popular Los Izquierdos, El Casino, Los Bocucus, and El Prisma rehearse at the **Salón de Ensayo Benny Moré** (☎ 78-8827, Neptuno No 960). You're welcome to observe them playing

Havana's Hookers

Prostitution is not legal in Cuba, although a visitor to Havana might wrongly get the impression that it is. That's because, despite a crackdown on prostitution in recent years, there are many prostitutes plying the streets, bars and dance clubs of Havana.

Prior to 1996, when the government started rounding up prostitutes, the women literally lined up outside tourist haunts, such as the Restaurante El Patio in La Habana Vieja. Back then the prostitutes would *pssst* prospects and interested men would respond with a *hello* in whichever language they spoke (mostly German). The cost, then and now, runs US$50 to US$100, as a matter of interest.

Today, prostitutes can still be found at El Patio and just about every other tourist haunt in town, only they are a lot more discreet, offering their availability with a mere glance and a smile. Interested men continue to reply with *Hallo!* or whatever, but now they take a stroll with their new acquaintance and talk business elsewhere.

Sex for money in Havana isn't the scandalous, shame-ridden thing it is in the USA and elsewhere. Prostitution is generally viewed by locals as a means of putting food on the table in a country where getting enough to eat is a major occupation. Often, the sex occurs at home, with mama preparing the bed and offering her daughter's companions something to drink.

boleros (ballads), danzón, guaracha, or whatever, 9:30 am to noon and 2 to 5 pm Tuesday to Saturday. For information, ask for Pedro next door at No 958.

In Centro Habana, traditional folk music is played on Thursday, Friday and Saturday 7 pm until midnight at the **Casa de la Trova** (☎ 79-3373, San Lázaro No 661), near Parque Maceo. Admission is free. This is real *son*, and fans of Ry Cooder's *Buena Vista Social Club* will be overjoyed at what's on offer.

Vedado (Map 3)

Saturday 9 pm to 2 am, authentic Cuban boleros are performed in an open-air setting at **El Hurón Azul** (☎ 32-4551), the social club of the Unión Nacional de Escritores y Artistas de Cuba (UNEAC), Calles 17 and H, for US$5. Numerous Cuban intellectuals associated with UNEAC are usually in attendance. Wednesday at 5 pm there's a *peña* with Afro-Cuban dances (also US$5).

The **Conjunto Folklórico Nacional**, founded in 1962, specializes in Afro-Cuban dancing (all of the drummers are *santeros*). See them perform during the Sábado de Rumba every other Saturday at 3 pm at El Gran Palenque, Calle 4 No 103, between Calzada and Calle 5, in Vedado. Admission costs US$5. This group also performs at Teatro Mella. During the second half of January, a major festival, FolkCuba, unfolds here.

CABARET
Centro Habana (Map 2) & Vedado (Map 3)

The **Cabaret Nacional** (☎ 63-2361), in La Habana Vieja at San Rafael and Paseo de Martí below the Gran Teatro de La Habana, is open 10 pm to 3 am nightly, with a show at 11:30 pm if enough patrons are present (admission US$3). Don't plan your evening around this place, as the schedules are erratic. As at all the cabarets, minimum dress regulations apply: definitely no shorts or t-shirts, and preferably a button-down shirt and pants other than jeans. You'd be wise to bring at least one dressy outfit with you to Havana.

The Show Only Gets Better

Thought the first half of the cabaret show was impressive? Wait 'til the second half. To quell the short attention spans of most humans, all of Havana's gala floor shows are arranged with the most spectacular numbers placed in the second half. If you're growing tired and thinking of leaving at intermission, don't. You'll be glad you stayed for the second half of the show.

!ABSOLUTAMENTE NINGUN MIEDO!

The following venues are in Vedado:

The **Palacio de la Salsa** in the Hotel Riviera (☎ 33-4051), Paseo and Malecón, is patronized mostly by foreigners and Cuban nouveaux riches. To get a table, you'll have to arrive early or make a reservation in person. Though touristy and expensive, top salsa musicians such as Los Van Van and Isaac Delgado perform regularly at the Palacio, and it's a must if you're into this kind of thing. It's open 10 pm to 4 am daily. Admission costs US$10 to US$20, depending on the performers.

Nearby, the **Havana Café** (☎ 33-3636), at the Hotel Meliá Cohiba, Paseo, between Calles 1 and 3, is open nightly with a show at 9:30 pm. It charges US$5/10 minimum at bar/table. The layout is cabaret style, with tables and chairs surrounding a stage and dance floor. American 1950s memorabilia, including old cars, motorcycles and gas pumps, constitutes the decoration. Most people come to have dinner and dance, as it's hip and trendy.

Cabaret Turquino, on the 25th floor in the Hotel Habana Libre, Calles 23 and L, opens nightly at 10:30 pm and stays open until 4:30 am. The popular band Lady Salsa performs Thursday, Friday and Saturday, and the 12-piece band Ataché Havana performs Monday and Tuesday. Magician Omar Ferret and the band Carta Blanca perform Wednesday and Sunday. Admission costs US$5 for hotel guests, US$11 for all others. The nighttime view of Havana is superb, and you can order dinner here.

Cabaret Parisién, in the Hotel Nacional, Calles 21 and O, hosts a nightly cabaret show. The doors typically open at 9:10 pm with dinner at 9:30 followed by the show. The shows here are the next best to those at the Tropicana. If you're unable to buy a ticket to see a Tropicana show (usually you need to buy them at least a day in advance), consider seeing a show here. If you really dislike smoke, avoid the Parisién; it fills with cigarette and cigar smoke early on and doesn't air out until the next day. Cost with dinner is US$55. After midnight the Parisién becomes a disco.

The **Cabaret Salón Rojo** (☎ 33-3747), at the Hotel Capri, Calle 21, between Calles N and O, opens at 10 pm, with a floor show at 11:30 pm. There's a large stage in front of a huge dance floor, and the clientele is largely Cuban. That's because the price of admission is more affordable, and because the dance floor allows audience members to become part of the show, as it were. This appeals a lot to Cubans, who generally aren't shy folks (as opposed to the tourists, who generally aren't familiar with the music and aren't sure how to dance to it). The atmosphere at the Red Room Cabaret is usually raw, vibrant and hot. It's closed Monday. Admission costs US$15.

Playa & Marianao (Map 4)

Cuba's most famous nightclub is the **Tropicana** (☎ 27-0110, Calle 72 No 4504), at Av 43, in Marianao (closed Monday). Since the Tropicana opened in 1939, famous artists such as Benny Moré, Nat King Cole and Maurice Chevalier have performed here. Over 200 dancers perform during Tropicana's 1950s-style cabaret show 'Paradise Under the Stars.' The doors open at 8:30 pm and the show begins at 10 pm. Admission including one drink is around US$85 per person, depending on the table. Tropicana bookings can be made through any hotel tour desk, with hotel transfers included. The on-site ticket office is open 10 am to 4 pm daily, and although booking in person is no cheaper than booking through a hotel, you'll be able to choose your own table. Bar seats are sometimes available for US$35 on nights when bookings are light, but these cannot be reserved in advance. You just show up at 8:30 pm and ask.

To avoid struggling to get the attention of the server during the show, small groups could consider ordering a bottle of rum and a selection of mix. The dress code here requires that men wear long pants and shoes (important to remember if you'll be arriving by tour bus straight from a long day of sightseeing). The Tropicana is an open-air locale and the show is canceled on rainy nights. If the rain begins before the show starts, a full refund will be given. If it starts to rain before the show is half over, refunds are proportionate to how much of the show was presented before the performance is suspended. An after-hours club called *Arcos de Cristal* is on the same premises as the Tropicana, and it has a show that starts after the one at the Tropicana finishes.

DANCE CLUBS
Centro Habana (Map 2) & Vedado (Map 3)

Palermo (☎ 61-9745), at San Miguel and Amistad, is a Centro Habana disco with live music. It opens at 10 pm Thursday to Sunday and there's a US$2 cover charge. There's also *Discoteca Ribera Azul* (☎ 33-8813), downstairs from the lobby of the Hotel Deauville, Av de Italia and Malecón. It's closed Tuesday. Admission costs US$5 per couple.

The following venues are in Vedado:

Cabaret Las Vegas (☎ 70-7939, *Infanta No 104*), between Calles 25 and 27, presents dance music and a show at midnight (assuming the musicians show up). It's a rough place with plenty of prostitutes and is not set up for tourists. It's open 10 pm to 4 am daily; admission costs US$5 per person.

The *Pico Blanco* (☎ 33-4187), on the 14th floor of the Hotel St John's on Calle O between Calles 23 and 25, opens nightly at 9 pm (US$5 cover). Around midnight some rather famous Cuban musicians often put in an appearance, including César Portillo de la Luz, who wrote *Contigo en la Distancia* and other Cuban classics.

Other Vedado clubs include *Club La Red* (☎ 32-5415), Calles 19 and L, and *Karachi*

Club, Calles 17 and K, which is open 10 pm to 5 am daily with a US$5 cover. They're busiest after 11:30 pm on Friday and Saturday. One reader reported seeing rumba dancing at Karachi on a Saturday afternoon.

Two local discos west of here are *Discoteca Amanecer* (☎ 32-9075), Calle 15, between Calles N and O (open 10 pm to 4 am daily, US$3 per person), and *Club Tropical*, Línea and Calle F (open 9 pm to 2 am daily).

The *Discoteca* (☎ 57-5682, *Bruzón No 217*), at Hotel Bruzón near the Plaza de la Revolución, draws many locals. It's open 10 pm to 3 am daily except Monday. Admission costs US$4 per couple on Saturday night, US$2 other nights.

The *Café Cantante* (☎ 33-5713), below the Teatro Nacional de Cuba at Paseo and Calle 39 (side entrance), is a disco with live salsa music and dancing. Just a few minutes' walk from a half dozen ministries around Plaza de la Revolución, it's said to be a hangout for 'yummies' (young urban Marxist managers). The type of tourist and the local women they favor are also very much in evidence. No shorts, T-shirts or hats may be worn inside, there's no entry for those under 18, and no photos are allowed. It's open 9 pm to 5 am Tuesday to Saturday. Admission costs US$10. A peso matinee for Cubans takes place here 4 to 7 pm some days, with around 40 old ladies in line for a seat before 4 pm.

Playa & Marianao (Map 4)

The *Havana Club Disco* (☎ 22-7712), behind Hotel El Comodoro, Av 1 and Calle 86, Miramar, is one of Havana's largest video discos, with a seating capacity of more than 400. It's open 10 pm to 3 am Monday to Saturday. Admission costs US$10. Drink prices aren't posted and the bartenders won't tell. Guests are given a card on which each purchase is punched and you pay as you leave: Be prepared for a shock. The crowd consists mostly of elegantly dressed young *jineteras* and male tourists over 50, although a quota of young Cuban couples is allowed in free after waiting in line for a very long time (the drinks come in plastic cups). It's serious business for the ladies of the night, and US$100 isn't much to them. On Sunday there's a matinee 2 to 7 pm for persons aged 16 to 30 only and identification is carefully checked (admission US$3). Readers report a discreet gay presence at the matinee. A large electronic sign inside the disco urges patrons to dance for anti-imperialist solidarity, even as American pop tunes are played.

The *Río Club* (☎ 29-3389, *Calle A No 314*), between Avs 3 and 3A, La Puntilla, in Miramar, opens at 10 pm. This disco claims to offer *el sonida más duro de la ciudad* (the hardest sound in town). Beware: Some of the Río's drink prices are sky high. Be wise and ask the price before ordering.

CINEMAS

There are about 200 cinemas in Havana. Some have a 5 pm screening and most have a screening at 8 pm. Sadly, the classic Cuban films you'd love to see seldom play at these venues, where Hollywood of yesteryear is the standard fare.

Centro Habana (Map 2)

Cine Payret (*Paseo de Martí No 505*), opposite the Capitolio Nacional, presents six showings daily in the largest and most luxurious cinema in Centro Habana, erected in 1878 (it was scheduled to undergo renovation in 2001). On the opposite side of the capitol from the Payret is *Cine El Mégano*, Industria and San Martín. *Cinecito*, San Rafael and Consulado, behind the Hotel Inglaterra, shows films for children.

Also try *Cine Actualidades* (*Av de Bélgica No 262*), behind the Hotel Plaza.

Vedado (Map 3)

Film festivals are often held at *Cine La Rampa* (*Calle 23 No 111*), at Calle O. Havana's most famous cinema, *Cine Yara*, at Calles 23 and L, opens at noon and offers seven showings daily in three halls. Farther afield is *Cine Riviera* (*Calle 23 No 507*), near Calle G.

Cine Charles Chaplin (*Calle 23 No 1157*), between Calles 10 and 12, is a venue for previews and special screenings at 5 and 8 pm

daily except Tuesday. Nearby, try *Cine 23 y 12* at Calles 23 and 12. It's open 2 to 9 pm daily.

If you're staying at the Riviera, Meliá Cohiba, Morro or Presidente hotels, you could check *Cine Trianón* (*Línea No 706*), between Paseo and Calle A. You can also see live theater (in Spanish) here Friday and Saturday at 8:30 pm, Sunday at 5 pm.

THEATER
Centro Habana (Map 2)

The *Gran Teatro de La Habana* (☎ 61-3078), Paseo de Martí and San Rafael, is the seat of the acclaimed Ballet Nacional de Cuba, founded in 1948 by Alicia Alonso. The National Opera performs here occasionally. The building also contains the Teatro García Lorca and several smaller concert halls where art films are sometimes shown. You can count on some type of live musical event every Friday, Saturday and Sunday (check the notices posted outside the theater). The ticket office is open 9 am to 6 pm Tuesday to Saturday and 9 am to 3 pm Sunday, remaining open until the performance begins on days when something is scheduled. Concert tickets average US$10, and you can request a backstage tour of the theater throughout the day for US$2.

Lighter fare is presented at *Teatro Fausto* (*Paseo de Martí No 201*) at Colón. The humorous programs Friday and Saturday at 8:30 pm and Sunday at 5 pm are great fun.

Well-known performers such as Leo Montesino often appear in the vaudeville variety shows at *Teatro América* (☎ 62-5416, *Av de Italia No 253*), between Concordia and Neptuno. They're usually staged Saturday at 8:30 pm and Sunday at 5 pm (tickets are sold on the day of the performance).

Vedado (Map 3)

Important foreign troupes usually appear at the *Teatro Nacional de Cuba* (☎ 79-6011), Paseo and Calle 39, on the Plaza de la Revolución. The National Symphony Orchestra sometimes plays in the main hall, the Sala Avellaneda, or the smaller Sala Covarrubias on the back side of the building. The Ballet Nacional de Cuba also performs here from

CHARLOTTE HINDLE

See ballet, opera or film at the Gran Teatro de La Habana.

time to time. The ticket office is at the far end of a separate single-story building that's beside the main theater. It's open 10 am to 6 pm Tuesday to Thursday, 3 to 9 pm Friday to Sunday. Programs are Friday and Saturday at 8:30 pm and Sunday at 5 pm. The best seats cost US$10.

If you understand Spanish, it's well worth attending a performance of the Grupo Teatro Rita Montaner in the **Sala Teatro El Sótano** (☎ 32-0630), Calle K between Calles 25 and 27, not far from the Habana Libre. Contemporary Cuban theater is often presented here on Friday and Saturday at 8:30 pm, Sunday at 5 pm. The box office is open 5 to 8:30 pm Friday and Saturday, 3 to 5 pm Sunday.

The **Teatro Nacional de Guiñol** (☎ 32-6262), Calle M between Calles 17 and 19, near Hotel Victoria, presents puppet shows for children Saturday at 5 pm and Sunday at 10:30 am and 5 pm.

Also check **Café Teatro Brecht**, Calle 13 at Calle I, where varied performances often take place on Saturday at 8:30 pm and Sunday at 5 pm. Tickets go on sale one hour before the performance.

Teatro Mella (☎ 3-8696, Línea No 657), between Calles A and B, is noted for its Cuban contemporary theater and dance. Other times there are guest performances and the Conjunto Folklórico Nacional performs here occasionally. If you have kids, come to the children's show Sunday at 11 am.

Sala-Teatro Hubert de Blanck (☎ 3-5962, Calzada No 657), between Calles A and B, is named for the founder of Havana's first conservatory of music (1885). The Teatro Estudio, based here, is Cuba's leading theater company. You can usually see plays in Spanish Saturday at 8:30 pm and Sunday at 7 pm; admission costs US$5. Tickets are sold just prior to the performance.

ROCK

Patio de María (Map 3; Calle 37 No 262), between Paseo and Calle 2 in Vedado, near the Teatro Nacional de Cuba, is a local youth hangout run by María Gattorno. Here you'll find Disco Mix (live salsa music) on Friday and Sunday 9 pm to 2 am and rock concerts by well-known groups, including Zeus, most Saturdays 6 pm to midnight.

ENTERTAINMENT

Dancing lessons can be arranged. This unpretentious counterculture venue has received considerable media coverage in Cuba and abroad, partly due to Gattorno's AIDS-prevention educational work.

JAZZ

Vedado's *Jazz Club La Zorra y El Cuervo (Map 3; ☎ 66-2402)*, Calles 23 and O, opens nightly at 10 pm. Admission costs US$5. The house band is good, and their free-style jazz is a nice change from salsa. Thursday is blues night.

The *Casa de la Música (Map 4; ☎ 24-0447)*, Av 35 and Calle 20 in Miramar, is one of Havana's top venues, launched with a concert by renowned jazz pianist Chucho Valdés in 1994. It's run by the recording company Egrem and the programs are generally a lot more authentic than the cabaret entertainment you see at the hotels. Salsa concerts begin at 10 pm Tuesday to Saturday. There is a US$10 to US$20 cover charge and drinks are available.

CLASSICAL

The *Teatro Amadeo Roldán (Map 3; ☎ 32-1168)*, Calzada and Calle D in Vedado, presents concerts by the Orquesta Sinfónica Nacional in the 886-seat Sala Amadeo Roldán, while soloists and small groups play in the 276-seat Sala Caturla. Built in 1922, this magnificent building was destroyed by an arsonist in 1977 and only reopened in 1999 after a careful restoration.

SPECTATOR SPORTS

From October to March, baseball games take place Tuesday, Wednesday and Thursday at 7:30 pm, Saturday at 1:30 and 7:30 pm, and Sunday at 1:30 pm at the 58,000-seat *Estadio Latinoamericano* (Map 3), Patria and Pedro Pérez, in Vedado just south of Centro Habana. Entry costs three pesos. Havana has two national teams, Industriales and Metropolitanos.

Friday at 7 pm, boxing matches sometimes occur at *Kid Chocolate* (Map 2), Paseo de Martí, next to Cine Payret, directly opposite the Capitolio Nacional.

Volleyball and basketball matches are held at the *Sala Polivalente Ramón Fonst* (Map 3), opposite the main bus station, on Av de la Independencia, in Vedado.

You can usually watch soccer matches on weekends at 3 pm at the 15,000-seat *Estadio Pedro Marrero* (Map 4), Av 41 and Calle 46, near Hotel Kohly in Playa. The Cristal Brewery, directly behind the field, does not give tours.

Shopping

Havana's strong suits are its colonial-era buildings, plazas and objects, such as the cannons protruding from her forts and the roads made of rock that continue to serve Old Havana well. Leisure shopping, a pastime of the bourgeoisie in countries that have an affluent middle class, isn't one of Havana's strengths.

Dollar shops at hotels sell the predictable tourist fodder – cheap dolls and woodcarvings, junky jewelry, low-quality leather goods, Che Guevara posters, 'Cuba' t-shirts and Cuban cigars. *Guayaberas*, those pleated men's tropical shirts most often associated with Mexico, are also available. All hotel shops have bottles of rum and many sell bags of ground Cuban coffee. Cuba's state recording company, Egrem, produces quality compact discs and cassettes of Cuban music.

Unless you're an American traveling illegally in Cuba, it's a good idea to hang onto the receipts whenever you purchase goods with dollars at a hotel shop, as these give you the right to export the items duty-free without question. This is especially true in the case of cigars: Cubans on the street often sell foreigners contraband cigars, and these will raise questions if found by Cuban customs upon departure. In practice, however, the Cuban authorities are unlikely to open your checked luggage as you're leaving Cuba.

It's worth knowing that the goods (including alcohol) sold for dollars at Intur and Caracol tourist shops in the hotels are tax-free and similar in price to what is sold in the duty-free shops at the airports. There's no big monetary advantage to waiting until the last minute to do all your shopping. The main advantage of buying goods at the airport is that you don't need to lug them around as much.

Paintings by Cuban artists are widely available in Havana. If you buy an original painting, print or sculpture, be sure to ask for a receipt to prove you bought it at an official sales outlet; otherwise, it will be confiscated by customs upon departure. Original works of art purchased in the street or directly from the artist require an export permit that costs from US$10 to US$30 and is valid for up to five paintings. The artist or vendor should be able to obtain the permit for you (pay only a deposit until they do); otherwise, don't buy anything that won't fit into your luggage. This situation also applies to paintings sold at street markets. Tourist art is not supposed to require a permit, but the Cuban customs officers often have difficulty distinguishing kitsch from Cuban national treasures, and you should assume that any artwork too large to hide will be confiscated unless you have an official receipt or export permit.

To preserve the natural environment, visitors should refrain from purchasing souvenirs made from wild plants, animals, birds, seashells or coral. Without an official receipt, conch shells and coral will be confiscated by Cuban customs. For security reasons, all luggage is X-rayed between the check-in counter and the aircraft, and any pieces with suspicious profiles (such as those displayed by shells and corals) are separated and held for identification by the owner. In these cases a thorough search is carried out. International customs regulations intended to protect endangered species also prohibit the import/export of items containing turtle shell, black coral, some butterflies and many reptiles.

WHAT TO BUY

The premier item for export, as far as most tourists are concerned, is the Cuban cigar. Though cigars made from Cuban tobacco but grown on other Caribbean islands have now surpassed the quality of cigars sold in Cuba, they remain the top-selling tourist take-home. Alternatives include the usual kitschy tourist stuff mentioned earlier that'll usually placate the friends or relatives, as well as some quality paintings, ceramics and woodcarvings.

Cigars

All genuine Cuban cigars are hand-rolled and packed in tightly sealed cedar boxes. There are 42 different types and sizes of Havana cigars, classified as fine, medium or thick. Thickness is measured in sixty-fourths of an inch, from 26 to 52 sixty-fourths, while the length can vary from 100 to 240mm. A single brand can come in several different sizes, and the same size category can refer to various types of cigars of other brands. The most common types are Mareva (129mm), Corona (142mm) and Julieta (178mm), available in most brands.

Cuba's flagship brand is Cohiba, created in 1966 for diplomatic use and available to the general public only since 1982. It's named for the original Taíno word for tobacco and comes in 11 medium to strong flavors. The H Upmann company founded in 1844 produces the five numbered varieties of Montecristo, some of Cuba's most popular cigars. Before he gave up smoking in 1989, President Castro's favorites were Corona Grande Montecristo and Cohiba Espléndidos. Medium-flavored Punch cigars were designed for export to the United Kingdom as far back as 1840. Another classic is the stronger Partagás type, rolled in Havana since 1845. Beginning in 1901, the strength of the Bolívar cigar has mirrored the personality of the liberator of South America. The milder Romeo y Julieta was invented in 1903 by a Cuban who had traveled widely in Europe. Other mild brands include Quintero and Rafael González. Sample prices per sealed box of 25 cigars are as follows:

Bolívar Corona Robusto	US$105
Cohiba Coronas Especiales	US$266
Cohiba Espléndidos	US$383
Diplomáticos No 3	US$88
Diplomáticos No 4	US$75
Larrañaga	US$25
Montecristo No 3	US$93
Montecristo No 4	US$75

Partagás 1898	US$143
Partagás Habanero	US$37
Partagás Lusitano	US$169
Punch Coronation	US$60
Romeo y Julieta Churchill	US$137
Romeo y Julieta No 1	US$63
Romeo y Julieta Panetelas	US$39

Black-market cigars sold on the street are often of dubious quality and even sealed boxes may have been tampered with. If saving money is more important than getting the real thing, at least examine the individual cigars to make sure they're tightly rolled without any tiny air pockets or protuberances. The cigar should be soft when squeezed gently between your fingers. The covering should be smooth as silk and all cigars in the box should have a uniform color and shape. If the tobacco doesn't have a deep robust smell, it's probably a low-quality fake of little value. Some counterfeit cigars made from waste tobacco swept from factory floors have no draw and are impossible to smoke.

Unless you know cigars well, pay a bit more to be sure of what you're getting, and get an official sales receipt from a hotel shop to eliminate the possibility of problems with Cuban customs. Some marketeers offer fake receipts but customs officers can easily spot them. Tourists are allowed to export US$2000 worth of documented cigars per person. Amounts in excess of this, or black-market cigars without receipts, will be confiscated (Cuban customs seize more than 500,000 undocumented cigars a year). Of course, you can buy additional cigars in the airport departure lounge after you've passed Cuban customs, but the 50 cigar tax-free limit applies in most countries. Mexican customs in Cancún, Tijuana and Monterrey conduct rigorous cigar searches. Cuban cigars are prohibited entry into the US and will be seized by US customs if found.

Humidors

Humidors are wooden cases designed for storing cigars in which the air within is kept properly humidified so the tobacco doesn't lose its flavor. In Havana, it's possible to purchase some beautifully carved humidors, most usually no larger than a boot box and, therefore, easy to pack in a large suitcase – *if* you anticipated making purchases in Havana and you set aside space in your luggage. Some of the humidors found around town have scenes of Havana or the Cuban countryside carved on their lids. Many simply have 'Havana' or the name of a famous cigar factory carved on them. The boxes make for lovely gifts and they don't have to be used for storing cigars. They can, for example, be used as fancy containers for pens, staplers, tape dispensers and other desk-related items. If you're considering purchasing a memento, consider a humidor; it'll last much longer than a box of cigars – and no one's gotten throat or tongue cancer from a humidor.

Artwork

It's possible to purchase paintings by Cuba's classic artists – Wilfredo Lam, Victor Manuel, Amelia Peláez and Mariano Rodríguez among them – as well as some of the country's up-and-coming stars, such as Manuel Mendive, Tomás Sanchez and Zaida del Rio. Unless you're an investor, don't buy on the basis of a name, but rather on the way in which a piece moves you. Generally, the finest paintings for sale will be found in galleries, but you might find a painting that captures the essence of Havana and gives you a warm and fuzzy feeling all over at an open-air market. It might even be cheap. If it isn't, negotiate. Prices for art in Cuba are not set in stone.

One kind of art that Cuba produces with real gusto and creative flair is political poster art. The best of these exhibit little or no text but communicate a message in a bold and clever way. Likewise, you'll come across ceramics that beautifully depict the façades of Spanish colonial homes, and you'll come across lots of crummy ceramic figurines of dumpy Cuban mamas smoking

---

Exporting Artwork

When buying art at an official outlet always ask for an official receipt to show Cuban customs, especially if the object won't fit in your suitcase and will be obvious. To discourage private trading, officials often confiscate undocumented artwork at the airport. It should be possible to export art objects legally purchased at state-run art galleries (but not street markets) duty-free when validated by receipts, although there's always the chance that the airport official may consider your sales receipt not good enough.

Certificates to export artwork are issued by the Registro Nacional de Bienes Culturales, Calle 17 No 1009, between Calles 10 and 12, Vedado. It's open 8:30 to 11:30 am weekdays. To obtain an export certificate you must bring the objects here for inspection; fill in a form; queue for two hours; pay a fee of US$10 to US$30, which covers from one to five pieces of artwork; and return 24 hours later to pick up the certificate. Some artists will offer to obtain the permit for you upon payment of a deposit. However, the only way to be sure that your paintings won't be confiscated at the airport is to obtain the permit yourself in person.

¡ABSOLUTMENTE NINGUN MIEDO!

---

fat cigars. Cuban sculpture can be quite attractive as well, although most of it is junk. The big names on the Cuban ceramics scene are Roberto Fernández Martinez, Teresita Gómez, Antonia Eiriz, Carballo Moreno, Alfredo Sosabravo, Jacqueline Maggi and Amelia Peláez.

WHERE TO SHOP
La Habana Vieja (Map 2)

The Palacio de la Artesanía, Cuba No 64, at Tacón, is where the Varadero tour buses drop off groups to buy souvenirs, crafts, musical instruments, compact discs, clothing and jewelry at fixed prices. One shop stocks Cuban liqueurs in a variety of flavors, including coffee, mint and banana. This building is the former Palacio de Pedroso, erected by Havana Major Mateo Pedroso in 1780. In the mid-19th century it was Havana's high court and later police headquarters. The Palacio de la Artesanía is open 10 am to 7 pm daily.

You can haggle for paintings and other items at the nearby open-air handicraft market on Calle Tacón, between the cathedral and the harbor, daily except Sunday. This is the largest and best of Havana's three open-air handicrafts markets, and it's a pleasure to wander. Buy only those paintings you can conceal in your suitcase; otherwise your purchases could be confiscated if the airport customs officials judge them to be Cuban national treasures (see the introduction to this chapter for discussion of customs and bringing home your souvenirs). This is not a joke: Lonely Planet has received many letters from irate tourists who were relieved of their souvenirs by Cuban customs officials waiting in the security area after immigration.

The state-owned Fondo Cubano de Bienes Culturales, Muralla and San Ignacio at Plaza Vieja, sells original handicrafts and works of art (with receipts that should allow their export). It's open 10 am to 5 pm weekdays, 10 am to 2 pm Saturday.

Longina Música, Obispo No 362, has a good selection of compact discs, plus musical instruments such as bongos (US$75), guitars (US$75), maracas (US$5), güiros (US$13) and tumbadoras (US$700). It's open 10 am to 7 pm Monday to Saturday, 10 am to 1 pm Sunday.

Galería Victor Manuel, on Plaza de la Catedral, is perhaps *the* place in Havana for high-end shopping. Here you'll find beautiful humidors, captivating paintings by various artists, Tiffany-style glass lamps, fantastic wooden figurines, lots of fine silver jewelry and leather goods, and plenty of ceramics as well. Open 9 to 9 daily.

Galería Manos, Obispo No 411, between Aguacate and Compostela, is a craft outlet with dolls, masks and other handmade souvenirs. It's open 10 am to 6 pm weekdays, 10 am to 5 pm Saturday. Habana 1791, at the corner of Obrapía and Mercaderes, sells perfume made from tropical flowers. The date 1791 was selected at random, according to a clerk; the shop opened in the late 1990s. Hours are 9:30 am to 6 pm.

If you've been looking for a hand fan, look no farther than Casa del Abanico, on Obrapía between Mercaderes and Oficios, which sells painted fans. Most are not fine quality. Colección Habana, on Mercaderes between Empedrado and O'Reilly, offers some quality souvenirs, including classy ashtrays with scenes of Cuba contained in them.

Bottle collectors will want to check out Droguería Johnson, at the corner of Calles Obispo and Aguiar. This antique pharmacy dates from 1850 and was thoroughly renovated in mid-2000. When it reopened then, its exquisite wooden cabinets and mile-long counter contained lots of wonderful little bottles that were hot sellers.

The Taller Experimental de Gráfica, on Callejón del Chorro off Plaza de la Catedral, sells engravings and prints that you can see made on the premises (US$15 to US$800). It's open 10 am to 4 pm weekdays. The Galería Víctor Manuel is on the corner nearby.

Two important art galleries are opposite the Monasterio de San Francisco de Asís. The Galería de Carmen Montilla, Oficios No 164, features a huge ceramic mural by Sosa Bravo in the rear courtyard. It's open 9:30 am to 5 pm Monday to Saturday. The Estudio Galería Los Oficios, Oficios No 166, presents the works of Nelson Domínguez, whose workshop is directly upstairs. It's open 10 am to 5:30 pm Monday to Saturday.

Galería Roberto Diago, Muralla No 107, at San Ignacio, on Plaza Vieja, specializes in naïve paintings. It's open 10 am to 5 pm weekdays, 9 am to 2 pm Saturday. The Taller de Serigrafía René Portocarrero, Cuba No 513, between Brasil and Muralla, has paintings and prints by young Cuban artists in the US$30 to US$150 range. You can see the artists at work here. It's open 9 am to 4 pm weekdays.

Centro Habana (Map 2)

La Manzana de Gómez, near Agramonte and San Rafael off Parque Central, is an elegant European-style covered shopping mall built in 1910 that awaits restoration. La Exposición, in a downstairs corner of La Manzana, sells reproductions of works of famous Cuban painters for US$3 to US$10 each. Shipping tubes are available.

The Area de Vendedores por Cuenta Propia, Máximo Gómez No 259, at Suárez, is a permanent flea market where you can pick up Santería beads, old books, leather belts and so on. Look for the building with 'La Nueva Isla Ropa y Sedería' painted on the side; the market's inside. It's open 9 am to 5 pm Monday to Saturday, 9 am to 1 pm Sunday. Much more of the same is available at the large open-air market at the corner of Av Simón Bolívar and Aguila (daily).

The main shopping streets for Cubans are San Rafael and Av de Italia. Variadades Galiano, at San Rafael and Av de Italia, is a former Woolworths, as you could guess from the lunch counters inside. They sell old records and you can pay for everything in Cuban pesos. It's open 10 am to 6 pm Monday to Saturday, 9 am to 1 pm Sunday. Several similar stores are north along Av de Italia.

Galería Orígenes, in the Gran Teatro de La Habana on Paseo de Martí, opposite Parque Central, exhibits paintings and sculpture for sale. It's open 9 am to 6 pm daily.

Galería La Acacia, San Martín No 114, between Industria and Consulado, behind the Gran Teatro de La Habana, has paintings by leading artists and antiques. Export permits are arranged. It's open 10 am to 3:30 pm weekdays, 10 am to noon Saturday. Also have a look at the paintings and sculpture at Galería Galiano, Av de Italia No 258, at Concordia, opposite Teatro América. If you see something you like, you must negotiate a price directly with the artist. It's open 10 am to 6 pm Tuesday to Saturday.

Vedado (Map 3)

La Habana Sí, opposite the Hotel Habana Libre at the corner of Calles L and 23, has a good selection of compact discs, cassettes, books, crafts and postcards. It's open 10 am to 10 pm Monday to Saturday, 10 am to 7 pm Sunday. The shop promotes Cuban artists and writers, but it's mostly a music store. The Librería Fernando Ortíz, on Calle M opposite the Hotel Colina, contains one of the largest offerings of books in Spanish and English on Cuba or written by Cubans. It's open 9 am to 9 pm weekdays, and 9 am to 7 pm Saturday.

Meñique Ropa de Niños, at the Hotel Habana Libre, sells quality mountain bikes for US$150.

An open-air Crafts Market is on Calle 23 between Calles M and N. It's worth browsing to see the sort of things Cubans think tourists want to buy.

Galerías de Paseo, across the street from the Hotel Meliá Cohiba, is a surprisingly upscale shopping center selling designer clothes and consumer items to affluent Cubans.

Plaza Carlos III, on Av Salvador Allende between Arbol Seco and Retiro, is a modern shopping mall where Cubans spend their dollars on shiny consumer goods. If you need a dress or tennis shoes, a portable radio or a bicycle, this is the place to come. Open 10 am to 7 pm Monday through Saturday, and 10 am to 2 pm Sunday.

Galería Ciudades del Mundo, Calle 25 at Calle L, presents expositions on Havana and other cities of the world. It's open 8:30 am to 5 pm weekdays. The Centro de Prensa Internacional, Calle 23 at Calle O, often mounts poster exhibitions.

The Centro de Arte 23 y 12, Calle 12 at Calle 23, features contemporary Cuban art. It's open 10 am to 5 pm Tuesday to Saturday. Other art galleries are at the Casa de las Américas, Calles 3 and G, open 10 am to 4:30 pm Tuesday to Saturday, 9 am to 1 pm Sunday (admission US$2); at Galería Haydee Santamaría, on Calle G, next to the Casa de las Américas, 10 am to 5 pm Tuesday to Saturday, 9 am to 1 pm Sunday (admission US$2); and at the Unión Nacional de Escritores y Artistas de Cuba (UNEAC), Calles 17 and H.

Since 1990 a local painter named Salvador González Escalona has converted Callejón de Hamel, between Aramburu and Hospital, off San Lázaro, into an open-air art center with vivid murals on the walls and sculpture in the street. Salvador has a studio at No 1054 (☎ 78-1661) where his paintings may be viewed (and purchased), and the studio organizes free cultural activities on the street outside, such as folkloric dancing after 11 am on Sunday, children's theater at 10 am on the third Saturday of each month, and street theater at 7 pm on the fourth Thursday of the month. The studio is open 10 am to 6 pm daily.

Playa & Marianao (Map 4)

La Maison, Calle 16 No 701, at Av 7, is Havana's center for high fashion, with a large boutique selling designer clothing, shoes, handbags, jewelry, cosmetics and sou-venirs. Models strut the catwalk here in outlandish costumes nightly at 10 pm (US$10 admission). La Maison's upscale hairdresser works noon to 7 pm (closed Sunday).

La Casa del Tabaco, Av 5 and Calle 16, includes an upscale cigar salesroom, a smoking room where you can purchase individual cigars, and a small bar where you can light up. It's arguably Havana's top cigar store. It's open 10 am to 6 pm Monday to Saturday, 10 am to 1 pm Sunday.

Egrem Tienda de Música, Calle 18 No 103, at Av 1, specializes in compact discs and is open 9 am to 6 pm Monday to Saturday. The Casa de la Música, Av 35 and Calle 20, also has a good selection of compact discs. It's open 10 am to 10 pm daily.

Excursions

With all there is to see and do in La Habana Vieja, Centro Habana and Vedado, you likely won't have the time to take side trips from the throbbing heart of Havana. But if you do, Ernest Hemingway's Cuban retreat, the gorgeous salt-and-pepper beaches east of town, and four communities on the other side of Bahía de la Habana make for fine day trips.

MUSEO HEMINGWAY

In 1939 the great US novelist rented the villa Finca la Vigía (Watchtower Farm) on a hill at San Francisco de Paula, 15km southeast of central Havana (see Map 1). A year later he bought the white house, a lovely farm house erected in 1888 with a view of the distant sea, and lived there for much of the next 20 years, dividing his time between Cuba (mostly for the marlin fishing), Spain (mostly for the bullfights) and the United States (mostly to hunt birds in Ketchum, Idaho, where he is buried in the town cemetery beneath a plain horizontal gravestone).

Each morning Hemingway would rise at dawn in the home with pool and watchtower he bought for US$18,000 and spend six hours writing, standing in oversized moccasins before a typewriter he kept atop a wooden bookcase. After working, he'd often drive to Cojímar, on the ocean east of Havana, where he kept his fishing boat *El Pilar*, and he'd spend the afternoon fishing in the Gulf Stream. Other days, he'd head into town, generally to El Floridita for a daiquirí, the newspaper and conversation. In the evening he'd receive personal friends in his living room or scandalize the neighbors by swimming nude in his pool.

The villa's interior has remained unchanged since the day Hemingway left it in 1959. Many of his personal possessions are on casual display, just out of arm's reach. Here you see his shoes, glasses, books, hunting trophies, his boat, his Nobel Prize medallion, heads of antelope mounted in every room (except, perhaps, the bathroom),

knives, rifle bullets, carved animal figurines from Africa and badges and patches including one that reads 'War Correspondent.' Upon his desk, under a plane of glass, are photos of one of his wives and his children. Off the living room is a library filled with books from floor to ceiling; lion skulls and a stuffed cheetah and a large desk made from dark wood add to the home's African ambiance. Here is the living room where he romanced young Italian countess Adriana Ivancich under the pained glare of Mary, his fourth and last wife. Penciled diary entries record his morning weight. In the bathroom off the master bedroom there's a jar containing a pickled lizard; the reptile was killed by one of Hemingway's cats, but the author was so impressed with its bravery that he felt the need to immortalize it. All around the one-story white-washed home are the overgrown grounds on which he once instructed his gardener: 'Your job will be not to cut, not to prune.' The rule, too, seems not to have changed. The mango trees here bear delicious fruit in April and May, and you would not be the first person to take home a Hemingway mango and try to grow a tree from it.

The Museo Hemingway is open 9 am to 4 pm Monday to Saturday, 9 am to 12:30 pm Sunday. Admission costs US$3, photos US$1. To prevent the pilfering of objects, visitors are not allowed inside the house, but much can be seen through the open windows and doorways. On rainy days the windows of the house are kept closed to protect the furnishings from moisture, and one may tour only the garden (admission is reduced to US$1 at these times). Even then it's still worth coming to see Hemingway's hacienda from the driveway, his fishing boat, the graves of four of his dogs, and the pool where actress Ava Gardner, following Papa's lead, once swam naked. There's now a store (with restrooms) on the premises where you can purchase Hemingway books and lots of souvenirs. It might interest you

Ernest 'Papa' Hemingway

American journalist, novelist and short-story writer Ernest Hemingway (1899–1961) spent the better part of 20 years in Cuba, and you can follow a 'Hemingway Trail' around Havana. Hemingway first visited Cuba in 1928, and during the 1930s he often stayed in room No 511 at the Hotel Ambos Mundos (Both Worlds) in La Habana Vieja. Graffiti he supposedly wrote on the wall of La Bodeguita del Medio near the cathedral – *mi mojito en La Bodeguita, mi daiquirí en El Floridita* – put both those places squarely on the list of the world's 'great' bars.

After covering the Spanish Civil War, Hemingway returned to Havana, and in 1939 he purchased an estate called Finca la Vigía just outside the city. Here he lived and wrote until his departure for Idaho in 1960. Before leaving, Hemingway donated his estate to the Cuban people, and since 1962 it has housed the Museo Hemingway. Everything has been carefully preserved exactly the way the writer left it, as if the owner were only temporarily absent.

Ever the sportsman, Hemingway kept his fishing boat, *El Pilar*, at Cojímar, and he himself named a 6km stretch of sea off Havana 'Hemingway's Mile.' Hemingway's *The Old Man and the Sea* (1952), based on the life of a fisherman from Cojímar, won him the Nobel Prize for Literature in 1954. His *Islands in the Stream*, three stories about life in wartime Havana and the hunt for German U-boats off Cuba, was published posthumously in 1970. In 1950 Hemingway donated the cup that is still awarded at the annual fishing tournament held every May at Havana's Marina Hemingway. In 1960 Fidel Castro caught the biggest fish and was photographed shaking hands with the writer. The two rarely passed words; the photo is one of the very few ever taken of the two men together.

Hemingway's relationship with the revolution is a matter of controversy, and although he did denounce Batista's brutality, Hemingway took no part in the events unfolding around him. It's rather ironic that this world-class traveler and adventurer should have had so little to say about the revolution. He left Cuba voluntarily, first for what would be his last stay in Spain, to return to Ketchum, Idaho, a town he'd visited frequently, usually to hunt birds or drink with friends at the Ram Bar in nearby Sun Valley. On July 21, 1961, old beyond his years and unable to recover from electric shock therapy prescribed for depression and a deteriorating mental condition, Hemingway ate his last meal at Ketchum's Christiana Restaurant. At home the next morning, he committed suicide with a shotgun. He was 62.

SEÑORES IMPERIALISTAS ¡NO LES TENEMOS ABSOLUTAMENTE NINGUN MIEDO!

to know that prior to moving to Havana, the author spent much of his time on the north side of the Gulf Straight, in Key West, Florida, where he lived in a two-story house with his second wife, Pauline, and their several six-toed cats. That home, which he abandoned in 1939, is also now a museum devoted to 'Papa,' and living on the grounds are more than 50 descendants of their several cats. There is no Hemingway museum in Ketchum, incidentally.

To reach San Francisco de Paula, take Metro Bus M-7 (Cotorro) from Industria, between Dragones and Av Simón Bolívar, on Parque de la Fraternidad, in Centro Habana. Or take a taxi and expect to pay around

US$20 or so for the roundtrip, depending on the amount of time spent at the site, the type of taxi taken and your negotiating skills (try to reach a price beforehand).

REGLA (MAP 6)

The old town of Regla, just across the harbor from La Habana Vieja, is a center of Afro-Cuban religions, including the all-male secret society Abakúa, members of which are known as *ñáñigos*. Several *babalawo* (Santería priests) reside in Regla, and it's not hard to find one if you're in need of advice (in Spanish). You'll probably be presented with protective beads, in which case it's customary to leave a donation on the altar in the living room. One famous Regla babalawo is Eberardo Marero, Ñico López No 60, between Coyola and Camilo Cienfuegos, and others live nearby.

Long before the success of the revolution, Regla was known as the Sierra Chiquita (Little Sierra, after the Sierra Maestra) for its revolutionary traditions. This working-class neighborhood is also notable for a large thermoelectric power plant and shipyard. Regla is almost free of tourist trappings, and you'll see lots of little peso food items for sale along Martí as you stroll up to the main square, Parque Guaicanamar, at Martí and Céspedes. It's well worth taking the short ferry ride across the harbor to see this untouristy part of Havana and to visit Regla's revered image of the Virgin.

During the 1950s, when the nightclubs, casinos and prostitutes of Vedado appealed to many Americans, Regla was known mostly for a gang of professional pirates who lived there and made their living stealing items from American yachts anchored in the harbor. Ernest Hemingway, who occasionally anchored *El Pilar* in the harbor at night, instructed his watchmen to shoot the pirates in the legs but to be careful not to shoot any holes in his boat. Though it was against the law, Hemingway kept a pistol on board. It doesn't appear the weapon was ever needed.

Regla is easily accessible on the regular passenger ferry that departs every 10 minutes (10 centavos) from Muelle Luz, San Pedro and Santa Clara, in La Habana Vieja. Bicycles are readily accepted on the ferry via a separate line that enters first.

Things to See & Do

Beyond a huge ceiba tree on Santuario, in front of you as you get off the ferry, is the **Iglesia de Nuestra Señora de Regla** with La Santísima Virgen de Regla on the main altar. This black Madonna is associated with Yemayá, the *orisha* (spirit) of the ocean and patron of sailors (represented by a blue color). Legend claims the image was carved by St Augustine, 'the African,' in the 5th century, and that in the year 453 AD a disciple brought the statue to Spain to safeguard it from barbarians. The small vessel in which the image was traveling survived a storm in the Strait of Gibraltar, so the figure was recognized as the patron of sailors. These days, rafters attempting to reach the US from Cuba also evoke the protection of the Black Virgin.

In the early 17th century a hut was built at Regla to shelter a copy of the image, and when this was destroyed during a hurricane, a new Virgen de Regla was brought from Spain in 1664. In 1714 Nuestra Señora de Regla was proclaimed patron of Bahía de La Habana. A pilgrimage is celebrated here on September 7, when the image is taken out for a procession through the streets. The church is open 7:30 am to 6 pm daily. Mass is held at 8 am Tuesday, Wednesday, Friday, Saturday and Sunday, and on Sunday a second Mass is held at 5 pm. A branch of the Museo Municipal de Regla is next to the church.

The main section of the **Museo Municipal de Regla** is at Martí No 158. A couple of blocks straight up the main street from the ferry, this museum records the history of Regla and its Afro-Cuban religions. Don't miss the small exhibit on Remigio Herrero, first babalawo of Regla, complete with his shackles of slavery and *elegguá* (idol). An Observatorio Astronómico was established in the museum building in 1921. The museum is open 9:30 am to 6 pm Monday to Saturday, 9 am to 1 pm Sunday. Admission costs US$2 to all sections.

From the museum head straight (east) on Martí past Parque Guaicanamar, and turn left on Albuquerque and right on 24 de Febrero, the road to Guanabacoa. About 1.5km from the ferry you'll see a high metal stairway that gives access to **Colina Lenin**. In 1924 Antonio Bosch, the socialist mayor of Regla, created a monument to mark the death of Lenin, one of the first of its kind outside the USSR. The olive tree that Bosch planted at the top of the hill is surrounded by seven figures and a huge image of Lenin is below. A small exhibition on the history of Colina Lenin is in a pavilion on the back side of the hill, and although it's usually closed, much is visible through the windows. When it's open, Colina Lenin accepts the ticket from the Museo Municipal de Regla for entry. Colina Lenin offers a good view of the harbor. Also, cemetery buffs can find some interesting headstones, many dating to the 19th century, in the nearby Cemeterio de Regla.

GUANABACOA (MAP 6)

In the 1540s the Spanish conquerors concentrated the few surviving native Indians at Guanabacoa, 5km east of central Havana. A town was founded here in 1607, to later become a center of the slave trade. In 1762 the British occupied Guanabacoa, but not without a fight from its mayor, José Antonio Gómez Bulones, better known as Pepe Antonio, who attained almost legendary status by conducting a guerrilla campaign behind the lines of the victorious British.

Guanabacoa today is a lively, colorful town well worth a wander around. (Guanabacoa is also the name of the municipality that surrounds the town.) There are no hotels here, access on public transportation is not easy, and the town is surrounded by ugly industrial suburbs, but it's still worth making the effort if you have time.

Things to See & Do

The **Iglesia de Guanabacoa**, also known as the Iglesia de Nuestra Señora de la Asunción, Pepe Antonio, at Adolfo del Castillo Cadenas, on Parque Martí in the center of town, was designed by Lorenzo Camacho and built between 1721 and 1748. The gilded main altar and nine lateral altars are worth a look, and a painting of the Assumption of the Virgin is at the back. Notice the Moorish-influenced wooden ceiling. If the main doors are closed (as they usually are), try getting in through the parochial office on Enrique Guiral, on the back side of the church (open 8 to 11 am and 2 to 5 pm). The **Galería de Arte Concha Ferrant** is at Martí No 8A, across Parque Martí from the church. It's open 9 am to 5 pm Tuesday to Saturday, 10 am to 2 pm Sunday. Admission is free. The Administración Municipal building also faces the park.

The town's main sight is the **Museo Municipal de Guanabacoa**, Martí No 108, two blocks west of Parque Martí. Founded in 1964, most of the exhibits relate to the history of Cuba during the 18th and 19th centuries. The museum is most famous for its rooms on Afro-Cuban culture, but these are often closed and if they're the main reason for your visit, you might ask before paying your US$2. The museum is open 10:30 am to 6 pm Monday and Wednesday to Saturday, 9 am to 1 pm Sunday. It was closed for renovations in 2000 but was expected to reopen in early 2001. The **Casa de la Trova** (☎ 97-7687) across the street at Martí No 111 is a popular venue for local folksingers.

The **Bazar de Reproducciones**, Martí No 175, two blocks west of the museum, sells artwork with Afro-Cuban themes, including orishas, dolls, collars, ceramics, metalwork, textiles, papier-mâché objects and graphics. While the Museo Municipal is closed (see above), part of its collection is being displayed here. Hours are 10 am to 6 pm Monday to Saturday.

Conspicuous for its Moorish arch, the eclectic **Teatro Carral**, at Pepe Antonio No 364, off Parque Martí, now houses a cinema. From here, go north one block on Pepe Antonio to Rafael de Cárdenas and then head east three blocks to the **Convento de Santo Domingo** (1748). This former Franciscan monastery is the second most important church in Guanabacoa, and its eight altars, wooden ceiling and adjacent cloister are worth seeing, but it's often closed.

Among the more somber sites in all of Cuba is the **United Hebrew Congregation Cemetery**, on Av Martí, where stands a Holocaust memorial with the text: 'Buried in this place are several cakes of soap made from Hebrew human fat, a fraction of the six million victims of Nazi savagery in the 20th century. May their remains rest in piece.'

Getting There & Away

Bus No 3 to Guanabacoa leaves from Máximo Gómez and Aponte near the Hotel Isla de Cuba (being renovated) in Centro Habana. Bus No 5 begins its run to Guanabacoa from the park across the street from Havana's main bus station. You can also get here on bus Nos 195 and 295 from Vedado. Bus No 29 arrives from Regla. Be aware that bus Nos 5 and 29 stop right in front of the church in the center of Guanabacoa, while Nos 3, 195 and 295 pass a few blocks away (you should ask when to get off for Parque Martí). You can walk downhill from Guanabacoa to Regla and the Havana ferry in about 45 minutes, passing Colina Lenin on the way.

CASABLANCA (MAP 6)

Casablanca, just across the harbor from La Habana Vieja, is best known for its towering white marble **Estatua de Cristo**, created in 1958 by well-known Cuban sculptor Jilma Madera. As you disembark the harbor ferry, keep straight up the stairway in front of you. Follow the road on the left to the rather grotesque 15m statue – an easy 10-minute walk. There's a splendid view of Havana from the statue and a 24-hour snack bar at its base. It's possible to reach the fortress of La Cabaña from this side via a red gate at the switchback in the road on your way up to the statue. Behind the statue is the **Observatorio Nacional** (not open to tourists).

The Hospital Naval (☎ 62-6825), off the Vía Monumental in La Habana del Este, northeast of Casablanca, has a recompression chamber accessible 24 hours a day.

Passenger ferries to Casablanca depart Muelle Luz, San Pedro and Santa Clara, in La Habana Vieja, about every 15 minutes (10 centavos). Bicycles are welcome.

The Estación Casablanca (☎ 62-4888), next to the ferry wharf, is the western terminus of the only electric railway in Cuba. In 1917 the Hershey Chocolate Company of the US state of Pennsylvania built this line to Matanzas, and trains still depart for Matanzas five times a day (currently at 4:10 and 8:32 am, and 12:30, 4:22 and 9 pm). The 8:32 am service is an 'express.' You'll travel via Guanabo (25km, $0.80), Hershey (46km, $1.45), Jibacoa (54km, $1.65) and Canasí (65km, $1.95) to Matanzas (90km, $2.80). The train usually leaves Casablanca on time but often arrives an hour late. Bicycles aren't allowed on this train.

COJÍMAR AREA (MAP 6)

Cojímar was founded in the 17th century at the mouth of the Río Cojímar. In 1762 an invading British force landed here and quickly overran a watchtower that had been erected specifically to keep a lookout for invading forces.

During the 1940s and '50s Ernest Hemingway kept his boat, *El Pilar*, in the harbor of this little village, 10km east of Havana, and Cojímar became the prototype of the fishing village in Hemingway's novel *The Old Man and the Sea*, which won him a Nobel Prize for Literature in 1954. The novel is about an old fisherman in a small boat who manages to catch a huge fish, only to look on helplessly as sharks devour the fish before he can bring it back to his village.

In 1994 Cojímar was a departure point for thousands of 'rafters' lured to Florida by US radio broadcasts and promises of political asylum.

Overlooking the harbor is the **Torreón de Cojímar**, the overrun Spanish watchtower presently occupied by the Cuban coast guard. Next to this tower and framed by a neoclassical archway is a gilded bust of Ernest Hemingway erected by the residents of Cojímar in 1962.

EXCURSIONS

Gregorio Fuentes, after whom Hemingway is thought to have modeled the protagonist in his novel *The Old Man and the Sea*, still lives in Cojímar. His home is the green and white house at Calle 98 No 209, at the corner of 3D, five blocks up the hill from Restaurante La Terraza (see below). Gregorio is almost a century old, and he makes a living by charging visitors US$10 for conversations concerning Hemingway (hey, he's not exactly pulling down a generous pension from Castro & Co).

East across the river from Cojímar is Alamar, a large housing estate of prefabricated five-story apartment blocks built by *microbrigadas* beginning in 1971.

A definite tourist attraction and the best place to eat in Cojímar is the upscale *Restaurante La Terraza*, Calle 152 No 161, open noon to 11 pm daily. Seafood is the house specialty and it's served on an enclosed, air-conditioned terrace overlooking the bay. A lobster tail costs US$15, or you can select a live lobster from the tank for US$25, plus 10% service charge. Photos of Hemingway adorn the walls. The bar, which was frequented by the author, opens at 10:30 am.

The huge 55,000-seat **Estadio Panamericano**, on the Vía Monumental between Havana and Cojímar, was built for the 1991 Pan-American Games. On the other side of the highway is the **Complejo Deportivo del Habana del Este**, which is principally a baseball field.

Getting There & Away

Bus No 58 from Av de la Independencia and Bruzón, near Havana's main bus station, reaches Cojímar. In Centro Habana you can pick this bus up at Paseo de Martí No 59, near the Malecón. You can catch it back to Havana from Calle 92 in Cojímar, though it's sometimes full and won't stop.

Alternatively, catch the Metro Bus M-1 (Alamar), at the corner of G and 27 in Vedado, or at Paseo de Martí No 563 opposite the Capitolio in Centro Habana, and get out at the third stop after the tunnel. Cross the highway to the Hotel Panamericano, from which it's around 2km on foot downhill through the village to the Hemingway bust. Bus Nos 195 and 265 from Havana also service the Hotel Panamericano.

PLAYAS DEL ESTE (MAP 7)

The 'Beaches of the East' are magazine-cover salt-and-pepper beaches dotted with coconut trees and blessed with body-surfing-ready white-capped swells that are light blue from shore to 100m out and deep blue from there to the horizon. Inland, the sand gives way to grass and, despite the popularity of the area, private homes and hotels are pleasantly spread out. Although new places are opening all the time, Playas del Este doesn't suffer from the stacking, crowding and overbuilding so common in other parts of Cuba. Here, you feel you're visiting a wonderful place a decade or so before it's ruined by excessive development. And unlike the public beaches of Jamaica, where toughs accost tourists to buy trinkets or drugs, or the Dominican Republic, where gun-toting guards keep locals off 'public' beaches, here the scene is *muy tranquilo*. If anything, you might wish there were a few more coconut trees to provide shade, or you might find yourself having to decide whether or not to have another Cuba Libre or join the hard-bodied types playing a rather serious game of beach volleyball.

Playas del Este, Havana's pine-fringed Riviera, begins in the suburb of Bacuranao, 18km east of central Havana, and continues east through Tarará, El Mégano, Santa María del Mar and Boca Ciega to the town of Guanabo, 27km from the capital. About a dozen large resort hotels are scattered along this 9km stretch of Atlantic sand, with the largest concentration at Santa María del Mar. Most of the facilities for Cubans are in Guanabo, and this is the place to look for a private room if you're into them (such lodgings are prohibited at Boca Ciega and Playa Santa María del Mar). In general you'll find the food and lodging much less expensive at Guanabo than at Santa María del Mar, but you'll find a lovelier strip of beach and better beachside restaurants and bars near Playa El Mégano.

The hotel area of Santa María del Mar is now heavily patrolled by uniformed security guards, and the prostitutes that used to descend on the area like black birds have withdrawn to the west end of El Mégano and to Guanabo. The heavy security presence makes this area safe, but it also eliminates much of the local color, and at times Santa María del Mar can be like a graveyard, albeit a beautiful one. You'll mainly find Cuban families on the beach at Guanabo, Cuban holidaymakers at Boca Ciega, foreign tourists at Santa María del Mar, and men and women in search of each other at the west end of El Mégano. The only clear and present dangers anywhere in Playas del Este, unless you're foolish with your money, are the sun (bring plenty of lotion) and the surf (beware of possible riptides and don't swim far out). Also, you'd be wise to bring some water or another nonalcoholic beverage to keep from dehydrating under the strong sun.

Foodwise, there's no shortage of good places to eat in the vicinity of Playas del Este

(see Map 7 for locations). The author's personal favorite is **Restaurante-Parrillada Costarenas**, a stucco-walled, tile-floored, cloth-covered–tables restaurant with a lovely seaview and an upstairs bar. Here it's easy to watch the waves roll in, and the prices are also appealing: pork steak (US$2.55), beef steak (US$3.55), smoked pork loin (US$4.55), half chicken (US$3.15), filet of fish (US$7.75), pork roll with orange juice and rum sauce (US$3.70). **Parrillada D'Prisa** is a very casual open-sided beachside bar with a few offerings, including filet of fish (US$8), chicken (US$5), hamburger (US$1), shrimp plate (US$12) and lobster (US$15). Its strong suit: The staff will serve you wherever you placed your beach towel. Nearby (and next to a popular volleyball court) is the **Kiosko Playa**, a simple thatch-roofed place with tables on the beach ringed by wooden benches. The kitchen serves individual ham pizzas (US$3.75), chicken (US$4.25), hot dogs, sandwiches and most everything else for US$3 or less. This is a popular spot.

Other likeable dining options in P del E include: **Restaurante Mi Casita de Coral**, a fan-cooled, lovely place with a friendly staff that offers lobster brochettes (US$8.75), grilled filet of fish (US$5), lobster enchilada with chili sauce (US$7.75) and shrimp enchilada (US$6); **Restaurante My Cayito** is on a tiny mangrove island on a lake and consists mostly of a half-dozen palapas with tables and chairs under them, chickens roaming free and a large cage containing birds. This place is very funky and drinkers will appreciate the full bar. Offerings include grilled fish (US$10), shrimp (US$10) and lobster (US$26). There's a show most Saturdays and Sundays at 3 pm. There's also a show at **Cabaret Guanimar**, which is open 9 pm until 2 am Thursday through Sunday (closed the rest of the week). You pay US$2.50 to enter and to see the show and to stick around afterward when the roofless joint becomes a disco; another US$3 will get you a buffet dinner. It's very popular with locals. Most of the other places mentioned here open for lunch and close around 10 pm.

EXCURSIONS

Getting There & Around

Private blue buses (five pesos) from Gloria and Agramonte, near Havana's Estación Central de Ferrocarril, will bring you to Guanabo, though they don't pass through Santa María del Mar.

Bus No 400 to Guanabo leaves every hour or so from Taya Piedra, a park two blocks east of Cristina Station in Havana.

A tourist taxi from Playas del Este to Havana will cost around US$20 for the car.

Taxis can be readily hailed along the coastal road until sundown, after which time they become somewhat scarce.

It's easy to get around. You could hail a taxi or you could catch one of the blue-and-white Omnibuses that ply the coastal route all day 30 minutes apart. To catch one, wait beneath one of the blue-and-white concrete palapas at road's edge. They operate 8 am until midnight and cost US$0.50 a ride.

Language

Spanish is the official language of Cuba, and knowledge of it is a great help in traveling around the country on your own. Away from the hotels and tourist centers, few people speak English and then only very poorly. Despite this, many Cubans have some knowledge of English since it's taught in primary school from grade six (age 12). Almost all museum captions in Cuba are in Spanish only. Luckily, Spanish is a phonetic language that is easy to pick up. This section offers pronunciation rules and a list of Spanish words and phrases.

If you speak no Spanish at all, you can always ask directions simply by pointing to the name in this guide. Never hesitate to try out your broken Spanish on Cubans! A Belgian reader sent us this:

Cuba really is a country where you gain a lot by being able to speak Spanish. We visited Honduras and Mexico before, and especially in Honduras, it doesn't make such a difference, as the local people are not interested in telling their views and stories (which is quite normal, I guess, when there has been so much state and military repression and when the average level of education is low). In Cuba, people are highly skilled and they have a point of view and an opinion on almost everything, which makes it extremely interesting to be able to talk to them (and we experienced that most of them were quite willing to talk to us). I think the effort of learning Hindi before going to India might be too great, but I would recommend everybody learn some Spanish before going to Cuba – otherwise you miss the best of the country's culture and complex 'reality.'

Words of Arawak Indian origin that have passed into Spanish and other European languages include *barbacoa* (barbecue), *canoa* (canoe), *cigarro* (cigar), *hamaca* (hammock), *huracán* (hurricane), *maíz* (maize), *patata* (potato) and *tabaco* (tobacco). The only commonly used words of African origin are associated with the Afro-Cuban religions, but Afro-Cuban speakers have given Cuban Spanish its rhythmic intonation and soft accent.

Phrasebooks & Dictionaries

Lonely Planet's *Latin American Spanish phrasebook* by Sally Steward is a worthwhile introduction to the Spanish language. Another useful resource is a paperback Spanish-English/English-Spanish dictionary. It will also make a nice gift for some friendly Cuban when you're about to leave the country.

Pronunciation

Spanish pronunciation is, in general, consistently phonetic. Speak slowly to avoid getting tongue-tied until you become confident of your ability. To familiarize yourself with the sound of the language, check out a set of Spanish language-learning records or tapes from your local library as you're preparing for the trip.

Vowels Spanish vowels are very consistent and have easy English equivalents.

a   is like 'a' in 'father.'
e   is like 'e' in 'bet.'
i   is like 'ee' in 'feet.'
o   is like 'o' in 'note.'
u   is like 'oo' in 'food.' When modified by an umlaut, as in 'Camagüey,' it is pronounced 'w.'
y   is considered a consonant except when it stands alone or appears at the end of a word, in which case its pronunciation is identical to the Spanish 'i.'

Consonants Spanish consonants generally resemble their English equivalents but there are some major exceptions. Pronunciation of the letters *f, k, l, m, n, p, q, s, t* and the consonant *y* is virtually identical to English. *Ch* and *ñ* are considered separate letters, with separate dictionary entries.

LANGUAGE

b resembles its English equivalent but is indistinguishable from 'v.' To differentiate the two, refer to the former as 'b larga,' the latter as 'b corta.' (The word for the letter itself is pronounced like the English 'bay.')

c is like the 's' in 'see' when it's before e and i, otherwise like English 'k.'

d closely resembles 'th' in 'feather.'

g is as the 'g' in 'gate' before 'a,' 'o' and 'u'; before 'e' or 'i' it is a harsh, breathy sound like the 'h' in 'hit.' Note that when 'g' is followed by 'ue' or 'ui' the 'u' is silent, unless it has an umlaut (ü), in which case it functions much like English 'w.'

h is always silent.

j most closely resembles English 'h,' but is slightly more guttural.

ll is like the 'y' in 'yes.'

ñ is like 'ni' in 'onion.'

r is nearly identical to the English 'r' except at the beginning of a word and after 'l,' 'n' or 's,' when it is often rolled.

rr is very strongly rolled.

v resembles English, but see 'b,' above.

x is like 'x' in 'taxi' except for a very few words, such as Mexico, in which it is pronounced as a Spanish 'j.'

z is like 's' in 'sun.'

Diphthongs A diphthong is one syllable made up of two vowels, each of which conserves its own sound. In Spanish, the formation of a diphthong depends on a combination of 'weak' vowels (*i* and *u*) or 'strong' ones (*a, e* and *o*). Two weak vowels or a strong and a weak vowel make a diphthong, but two strong vowels are pronounced as separate syllables.

Here are some diphthongs in Spanish, and their approximate English pronunciations:

ai as in 'hide'
au as in 'how'
ei as in 'hay'
ia as in 'yard'
ie as in 'yes'
oi as in 'boy'
ua as in 'wash'
ue as in 'well'

Stress Stress, often indicated by visible accents, is very important, since it can change the meaning of words. In general, the second-to-last syllable is stressed if the word ends in 's,' 'n' or a vowel. Those with other endings have stress on the last syllable.

Accents are used primarily to indicate deviations from this rule, in which case the accented syllable is stressed. Thus, *sótano* (basement), *América* and *porción* (portion) each have the stress on different syllables. When counting syllables, remember that diphthongs constitute only one. When words appear in capitals, the written accent may be omitted, but it is still pronounced.

Greetings & Civilities

In their public behavior Cubans are very informal, but when approaching a stranger for information, you should always preface your question with a more formal greeting like *buenos días* or *buenas tardes*. Cubans routinely address one another as *compañero* or *compañera* (comrade), but the traditional *señor* and *señora* are always used with foreigners.

yes	*sí*
no	*no*
Thank you.	*Gracias.*
You're welcome.	*De nada.*
Hello.	*Hola.*
Good morning.	*Buenos días.*
Good afternoon.	*Buenas tardes.*
Good evening/night.	*Buenas noches.*
Goodbye.	*Adiós/chau.*
I understand.	*Entiendo.*
I don't understand.	*No entiendo.*
I don't speak much Spanish.	*Hablo poco español.*

Useful Words & Phrases

and	*y*
to/at	*a*
for	*por, para*
of/from	*de, desde*
in	*en*
with	*con*
without	*sin*
before	*antes*

after	*después*
soon	*pronto*
already	*ya*
now	*ahora*
right away	*en seguida*
here	*aquí*
there	*allá*
Where?	*¿Dónde?*
Where is/are…?	*¿Dónde está/están…?*
When?	*¿Cuándo?*
How?	*¿Cómo?*
How much?	*¿Cuánto?*
How many?	*¿Cuántos?*
How much does it cost?	*¿Cuánto cuesta?*
I would like…	*Me gustaría…*

Getting Around

airplane	*avión*
bicycle	*bicicleta*
bus	*guagua, autobús, ómnibus*
car	*auto*
hitchhike	*hacer botella*
motorcycle	*motocicleta, moto*
ship	*barco, buque*
taxi	*taxi*
train	*tren*
truck	*camión*

I would like a ticket to…
  Quiero un boleto/pasaje a…
What's the fare to…?
  ¿Cuánto cuesta hasta…?
When does the next plane/train/bus leave for…?
  ¿Cuándo sale el próximo avión/tren/ómnibus para…?
first/last/next
  primero/último/próximo
single/return (roundtrip)
  ida/ida y vuelta

Accommodations

hotel	*hotel, villa*
reception	*carpeta*
single room	*habitación para una persona*
double room	*habitación doble*
What does it cost?	*¿Cuánto cuesta?*

per night	*por noche*
all-inclusive	*todo incluído*
shared bath	*baño compartido*
private bath	*baño privado*
too expensive	*demasiado caro*
cheaper	*mas económico*
May I see it?	*¿Puedo verla?*
I don't like it.	*No me gusta.*
the bill	*la cuenta*

Around Town

airport	*aeropuerto*
train station	*estación de ferrocarril*
bus terminal	*terminal de ómnibus*
bathing resort	*balneario*
toilet	*baño*
post office	*correo*
letter	*carta*
postcard	*postal*
airmail	*correo aéreo*
registered mail	*certificado*
stamps	*sellos*

Geographical Expressions

The expressions below are among the most common you will encounter in this book and in Spanish language maps and guides.

archipelago	*archipiélago*
bay	*bahía*
beach	*playa*
bridge	*puente*
cape	*cabo*
cove	*ensenada*
dam	*presa*
highway	*carretera, vía*
hill	*cerro*
lagoon	*laguna*
lake	*lago*
marsh	*estero*
mount	*cerro*
mountain range	*cordillera*
national park	*parque nacional*
pass	*paso*
point	*punta*
reef	*arrecife*
reservoir	*embalse*
river	*río*
swamp	*ciénaga*
waterfall	*cascada, catarata, salto*

LANGUAGE

Food

The words below are alphabetized in Spanish for easy reference when deciphering Cuban restaurant menus, most of which will be in Spanish only.

agua	water
aguacate	avocado
aguja	swordfish
ahumado	smoked
ajiaco	meat stew
ajo	garlic
albóndiga	meatball
almíbar	sweet syrup or juice
apio	celery
aporreado	pounded, beaten
arroz	rice
asado	roasted
atún	tuna
azúcar	sugar
bacalao	cod
batido	milkshake
bebida	drink
bistec	beefsteak
bocadillo	sandwich
boniato	sweet potato
bonito	striped tuna
café	coffee
caldo	soup
camarones	shrimp
cangrejo	crab
carne	meat
cazuela	casserole, stew
cebolla	onion
cerdo	pork
cereza	cherry
cerveza	beer
chatinos	banana chips
cherna	sea-bass
chicharrón	pork rind
chorizo	sausage
chuletas	chops
ciruela	plum
cocido	stew, cooked
cocina	kitchen
col	cabbage
coliflor	cauliflower
conejo	rabbit
congrí	rice with red beans
cordero	lamb
croqueta	deep fried patty
dulce	sweet
enchilado	shellfish stew
ensalada	salad
entremés	hors d'oeuvre
espinacas	spinach
fideos	vermicelli
filete	filet
flan	caramel pudding
fresa	strawberry
fricasé	meat stew
frijoles	beans
frito	fried
fruta	fruit
fruta bomba	papaya
garbanzos	chickpeas
guanábana	soursop
guayaba	guava
guineos	small bananas
guisado	stew
guisantes	peas
hamburgesa	hamburger
helado	ice cream
hervido	boiled
hielo	ice
huevo	egg
jamón	ham
jugo	juice
langosta	lobster
leche	milk
lechón	suckling pig
lechuga	lettuce
legumbres	vegetables
limón	lemon
maíz	corn
malanga	taro
mantequilla	butter
manzana	apple
mariscos	seafood
merluza	hake
mermelada	jam
moros y cristianos	rice with black beans
mortadella	sausage
ñame	yam
naranja	orange
natilla	caramel pudding
oca	goose
ostiones	oysters
paella	seafood and rice casserole
palomilla	doveling

pan	bread
papas	potatoes
pargo	red snapper
pepino	cucumber
pera	pear
pescado	fish
picadillo	mincemeat
pimienta	pepper
piña	pineapple
plátano	banana
pollo	chicken
potaje	thick soup
puerco	pork
puré	mashed potatoes
queso	cheese
remolacha	beet
res	beef
revoltillo	scrambled eggs
revuelto	scrambled
ron	rum
rosbif	roast beef
sal	salt
salchicha	sausage
salsa	sauce
sopa	soup
tajada	slice
tasajo	jerked beef
té	tea
ternera	veal
tiburón	shark
tocino	bacon
tomates	tomatoes
toronja	grapefruit
tortilla	omelet
tortuga	turtle
tostada	toasted
tostones	banana chips
vegetariano	vegetarian
vino	wine
yuca	manioc, cassava
zanahoria	carrot

Days of the Week

Monday	lunes
Tuesday	martes
Wednesday	miércoles
Thursday	jueves
Friday	viernes
Saturday	sábado
Sunday	domingo

Time

Telling time is fairly straightforward. Eight o'clock is *las ocho*, while 8:30 is *las ocho y treinta* (literally, eight and thirty) or *las ocho y media* (eight and a half). However, 7:45 is *las ocho menos quince* (literally, eight minus fifteen) or *las ocho menos cuarto* (eight minus one quarter). Times are modified by morning *(de la mañana)* or afternoon *(de la tarde)*. It's also common to use the 24-hour clock, especially with transportation schedules.

Numbers

1	uno
2	dos
3	tres
4	cuatro
5	cinco
6	seis
7	siete
8	ocho
9	nueve
10	diez
11	once
12	doce
13	trece
14	catorce
15	quince
16	dieciseis
17	diecisiete
18	dieciocho
19	diecinueve
20	veinte
21	veintiuno
22	veintidós
30	treinta
31	treinta y uno
40	cuarenta
50	cincuenta
60	sesenta
70	setenta
80	ochenta
90	noventa
100	cien
101	ciento uno
102	ciento dos
110	ciento diez
120	ciento veinte
130	ciento treinta
200	doscientos

300	*trescientos*	1100	*mil cien*
400	*cuatrocientos*	1200	*mil doscientos*
500	*quinientos*	2000	*dos mil*
600	*seiscientos*	5000	*cinco mil*
700	*setecientos*	10,000	*diez mil*
800	*ochocientos*	50,000	*cincuenta mil*
900	*novecientos*	100,000	*cien mil*
1000	*mil*	1,000,000	*un millón*

Glossary

aguardiente – cane brandy
americano – in Cuba, this means a citizen of any country in the Western Hemisphere (from Canada to Argentina); a citizen of the USA is called either a *norteamericano* or *estadounidense*
apagón – an electricity blackout
Arawak – linguistically related Indian tribes that inhabited most of the Caribbean islands and northern South America
arroba – an antiquated measurement representing about 25 Spanish pounds
audiencia – a court representing the Spanish crown in colonial times

babalawo – a Santería priest; also *babalao*
batey – originally an open space in the center of an Indian village; later adopted to refer to a group of service buildings around a sugar mill
bohío – thatched hut

caballería – an antiquated Spanish measurement representing about 13.4 hectares
cabildo – a town council during the colonial era
cacique – chief; originally used to describe an Indian chief and today used to designate a petty tyrant
camarera – housekeeper (the Spanish term *criada*, which also means 'brought up,' is considered offensive in revolutionary Cuba)
carpeta – a hotel reception area
cayo – a coral key
CDR – Comités de Defensa de la Revolución; neighborhood watch bodies originally formed in 1960 to consolidate grassroots support for the revolution. They now play a decisive role in health, education, social and voluntary labor campaigns.
central – a modern sugar mill
chequeré – a gourd covered with beads to form a rattle
cimarrón – a runaway slave
claves – rhythm sticks that are used by Cuban musicians
cola – line, queue

Cubanacán – soon after landing in Cuba, Columbus visited a Taíno village called Cubanacán, meaning 'in the center of the island.' Now a large Cuban tourism company uses the name.
criollo – Creole; Spaniard born in the Americas

daiquirí – a rum cocktail made with crushed ice and other ingredients, named for the Río Daiquirí, near Santiago de Cuba, where it was invented in 1899
divisas – hard currency

encomienda – land with an indigenous workforce, entrusted to an individual by the Spanish crown during the early colonial era

flota – the Spanish treasure fleet
FMC – Federación de Mujeres Cubanas; Federation of Cuban Women, founded in 1960 and active in local and national politics

Granma – the yacht *Granma* carried Fidel and his companions from Mexico to Cuba in 1956 to launch the revolution; in 1975 the name was adopted for the province where the *Granma* arrived
guagua – a local bus
guajiro – a country person
guaracha – a satirical song for a single voice backed by a chorus
guarapo – fresh sugarcane juice
guayabera – a pleated, buttoned men's shirt

imperio, el – 'the empire'; a term used in the official Cuban media to refer to the USA, which is led by *imperialistas*
ingenio – an antiquated term for a sugar mill

jinetera – a female prostitute
jinetero – a male tout who hustles tourists
joder – to mess up or spoil

lenguaje chavacán – a type of slang used by young people
libreta – a ration book

M-26-7 – the '26th of July Movement,' Fidel Castro's revolutionary organization, named for his abortive assault on the Moncada army barracks in Santiago de Cuba on July 26, 1953

machetero – one who cuts sugarcane using a machete

mambí – a 19th-century rebel fighting Spain (plural: *mambises)*

máquina – an old North American car

maraca – a rattle used by Cuban musicians

mogote – a limestone monolith found at Viñales

mojito – a stirred drink made of rum, lemon juice, sugar, soda, mint leaf and ice

Moncada – a former army barracks in Santiago de Cuba named for General Guillermo Moncada (1848–1895), a hero of the wars of independence

moneda nacional – Cuban pesos

Oriente – the region comprised of Las Tunas, Holguín, Granma, Santiago de Cuba and Guantánamo Provinces

orisha – a Santería deity

package(d) tourists – in Cuba it's easy to spot them; they're required to wear color-coded plastic wristbands to allow resort security personnel to pick out non-guests

paladar – a privately owned restaurant

palenque – a hiding place for runaway slaves during the colonial era

parada – bus stop

PCC – Partido Comunista de Cuba; Cuba's only political party, which was formed in October 1965 by merging cadres from the Partido Socialista Popular (the pre-1959 Communist Party) and veterans of the guerrilla campaign

peninsular – a Spaniard born in Spain but living in the Americas

quintal – an antiquated measurement representing 100 Spanish pounds

rancheador – one who hunted down fugitive slaves during the colonial period

reconcentración – a tactic of forcibly concentrating rural populations, used in Cuba by the Spaniards during the Second War of Independence

rumba – an Afro-Cuban dance form that originated among plantation slaves during the 19th century. During the '20s and '30s, the term 'rumba' was adopted in North America and Europe for a ballroom dance in 4/4 time. In Cuba today, to *rumba* simply means 'to party.'

salsa – a catchall designation used for Cuban music based on *son*

Santería – an Afro-Cuban religion

santero – a priest of Santería

sello – stamp (in a passport or on a letter)

SIDA – *síndrome de inmunodeficiencia adquirida* ('AIDS' in English)

son – Cuba's basic form of popular music that jelled from African and Spanish elements in the late 19th century

Taíno – a settled, Arawak-speaking tribe that inhabited much of Cuba prior to the Spanish conquest; the word itself means 'we the good people'

trago – an alcoholic drink

UNEAC – Unión Nacional de Escritores y Artistas de Cuba (National Union of Cuban Writers and Artists)

UJC – Unión de Jóvenes Comunistas; a student group active in politics

vara – an antiquated Spanish measurement representing about 36 inches

VIH – *virus de inmunodeficiencia humana* ('HIV' in English)

Yoruba – an Afro-Cuban religion originating in Nigeria

zafra – sugarcane harvest

zambo – a person of mixed black and Indian race

zarzuela – operetta

zenus – spirits worshipped by the Indians

LONELY PLANET

You already know that Lonely Planet produces more than this one guidebook, but you might not be aware of the other products we have on this region. Here is a selection of titles which you may want to check out as well:

Cuba
ISBN 0 86442 750 6
US$19.99 • UK£11.99 • 139FF

Jamaica
ISBN 0 86442 780 8
US$17.95 • UK£11.99 • 140FF

Diving & Snorkeling Cuba
ISBN 1 86450 136 7
US$16.95 • UK£10.99 • 130FF

Latin American Spanish Phrasebook
ISBN 0 86442 558 9
US$6.95 • UK£4.50 • 50FF

Available wherever books are sold.

Index

Text

A

accommodations (general)
140–50
  costs 66, 140, 141–2
  phrases 195
  prebooking 140–1
  private rooms 96, 141
accommodations (specific)
  Aparthotel Santo Ángel
  143
  Casa del Cientifico 144
  Complejo Neptuno-Tritón
  148–9
  Gran Hotel 143
  Hostal Condes de
  Villanueva 142
  Hostal Costa Sol 148
  Hostal Icemar 148
  Hostal San Miguel 143
  Hostal Valencia 142
  Hotel Acuario 149
  Hotel Ambos Mundos
  112, 142
  Hotel Biocaribe 148
  Hotel Bruzón 146
  Hotel Capri 146
  Hotel Caribbean 144–5
  Hotel Chateau Miramar
  149
  Hotel Colina 146
  Hotel Copacabana 149
  Hotel Deauville 145
  Hotel El Bosque 148
  Hotel El Comodoro 149
  Hotel El Viejo y El Mar
  149
  Hotel Florida 142–3
  Hotel Golden Tulip Parque
  Central 145
  Hotel Habana Libre 125–6,
  147
  Hotel Inglaterra 119, 145
  Hotel Isla de Cuba 144
  Hotel Kohly 148
  Hotel Lido 144
  Hotel Lincoln 144

  Hotel Meliá Cohiba 131,
  147
  Hotel Meliá Habana 150
  Hotel Mirazul 148
  Hotel Nacional 124–5, 147
  Hotel New York 144
  Hotel Palco 149
  Hotel Plaza 145
  Hotel Presidente 132, 147
  Hotel Riviera 131, 146–7
  Hotel Santa Isabel 143
  Hotel Saratoga 143
  Hotel Sevilla 119, 145
  Hotel St John's 146
  Hotel Universitario 146
  Hotel Vedado 146
  Hotel Victoria 146
  Motel La Herradura 150
  Motel Las Olas 148
  Motel Rodeo Nacional 150
  Novotel Miramar 150
  Residencia Universitaria
  Ispjae 148
  Residencial Turístico
  Marina Hemingway 150
  Villa Costa 148
  Villa Paraíso 150
Acuario Nacional 133
agriculture 34–5
AIDS 79
air travel 86–92
  glossary 87
  Internet bookings 89
airlines 56–7, 91
airport 75, 96–7
Alarcón, Ricardo 32
alcohol. See drinks
Almeida, Juan 20
Álvarez, Santiago 48
animals, treatment of 50
aquarium 133
Arawak 47
architecture 47–8
art courses 139
art galleries 109, 114, 182–3,
  188

artwork 46–7, 179, 181
ATMs 65

B

Bahía de Cochinos. See Bay
  of Pigs
banks 64–5
bars 170–2
Batista, Fulgencio 19–20, 22,
  74, 124, 186
Bay of Pigs 23–4
beaches 190–2
Biblioteca Nacional José
  Martí 127
Biblioteca Pública Provincial
  Rubén M Villena 111
bicycling 101–2
birds 30–1
blacks 36–7, 82–3
boats 62, 93, 102, 137–8
Bolívar, Simón 15, 112
books 70–2. See also literature
bribes 66–7
Buena Vista Social Club 44, 45
buses 91–2, 97–8
business hours 83–4

C

cabaret 173–5
Cánovas, Antonio 17
Capitolio Nacional 118
Cárcel 121
Carpentier, Alejo 45–6, 106,
  107–8
cars 98–101
  driver's license 61
  insurance 100
  renting 99–101
  road rules 99
Casa de África 112
Casa de la Obra Pía 112
Casa de las Américas 131–2
Casa de Lombillo 108
Casa de los Árabes 111
Casa de los Condes de Jaruco
  114

Casa de México Benito Juárez 112
Casa Oswaldo Guayasamín 112–3
Casablanca 189, **Map 6**
Castillo de la Real Fuerza 110
Castillo de los Tres Santos Reyes Magnos del Morro 121
Castillo de San Salvador de la Punta 121, 133
Castillo de Santa Dorotea de la Luna de la Chorrera 130–1
Castillo del Principe 127
Castro, Fidel
    as revolutionary 20–2, 124, 129–30
    as political leader 9, 22–6, 31–2, 119–20, 127–8
    books about 71
    cigars & 180
    Ernest Hemingway & 186
Castro, Raúl 20, 32
Catedral de San Cristóbal de La Habana 106–7
Catholicism 50
CD ROM 72
CDs 44–5
Centro Cultural de España 132
Centro de Arte Contemporáneo Wilfredo Lam 108
Centro de Ingenería Genética y Biotecnología 134
Centro Gallego 118
Centro Habana 116–21, **Map 2**
    accommodations 143–5
    entertainment 170–4, 175, 176
    restaurants & food 157–61
    shopping 182–3
    walking tour 116–21
Centro Nacional de Investigaciones Científicas 134
Céspedes, Carlos Manuel de 16, 109
Chibás, Eduardo 20, 129–30

Chijona, Gerardo 49
children, traveling with 81
Cienfuegos, Camilo 20, 22
cigars 82, 117–8, 120, 180
cinemas 176. *See also* films
Ciudad Libertad 134
classical music 42, 178
climate 27–8, 53
Club de Golf La Habana 137
Club Hípico Iberoamericano 137
cock fighting 50
coffee 162
Cojímar area 189–90, **Map 6**
Colina Lenin 188
Columbus, Christopher 11, 13, 110
Comité Central del Partido Comunista de Cuba 128
Concepción Valdés, Gabriel de la 45
conduct 49–50
consulates 62–3
cookbooks 72
Coppelia 125
coral reefs 28
costs 66
courses 138–9
credit cards 65
crime 80, 82
cruises 93. *See also* yachting
Cuban Missile Crisis 24
Cuban Revolution 20–2
Cubana de Aviación 56–7
Cubanacán offices 56, 134
Cugat, Xavier 42–3
cultural centers 81–2
currency 64
customs 63–4
cycling. *See* bicycling

D

daiquirís 158
dance 40, 127
dance clubs 175–6
danzón 40
diarrhea 78
Díaz Torres, Daniel 49
disabled travelers 80–1
discrimination 37, 82–3
diseases 78–9

diving & snorkeling 70, 135, 137
documents 57–62
Dorticós, Osvaldo 22
drinks
    cocktails 154
    coffee & tea 162
    daiquirís 158
    rum 156
    water 77
driving. *See* cars

E

Eastern Forts 121–4, 161, **122**
Echeverría, José Antonio 20
economy 32–6
education 37–8
Eisenhower, Dwight 22, 23
El Floridita 157, 158, 170
El Templete 110–1
El Túnel de la Bahía 121
electricity 76
email 68–9
embassies 62–3
emergencies 83
employment 85
entertainment 169–78
    bars 170–2
    cabaret 173–5
    cinemas 176
    dance clubs 175–6
    music 169, 177–8
    sports 178
    theater 176–7
    traditional 172–3
entry permits 58–9
environmental issues 28
Escalera, José Nicolás de la 46
Escobar, Vicente 46
Estadio Panamericano 190
Estadio Universitario Juan Abrahantes 126
Estrada Palma, Tomás 19, 132
etiquette 49
excursions 185–92
ExpoCuba 136

F

Farmacia Taquechel 112
fauna 30–1

Bold indicates maps.

ferries 102
films 48–9, 72, 139. *See also* cinemas
fishing 134–5, 138
flea market 131
flora 28–30
food. *See* restaurants & food
Fortaleza de San Carlos de la Cabaña 121–3
Fuente de la India 116–7
Fundación Alejo Carpentier 107–8

G

Galería Victor Manuel 109, 182
García, Calixto 131
García Espinosa, Julio 49
gay & lesbian travelers 80, 171
geography 26–7
golf 137, 138
Gómez, José Miguel 19
Gómez, Manuel Octavio 48
Gómez, Máximo 16, 17, 18, 121, 127, 129
Gómez Yera, Sara 48–9
González, Celina 44
González Escalona, Salvador 47
government 31–2
Goyri, Amelia 129
Gran Teatro de La Habana 118
Granma 73, 117, 119–20
Grau San Martín, Ramón 20
Grillo, Frank 'Machito' 43
Guanabacoa 188–9, **Map 6**
Guantánamo US Naval Base 25
Guayasamín, Oswaldo 112–3
Guevara, Ernesto 'Che' 20, 21, 22, 24, 25, 71, 111, 128
guidebooks 70
Guillén, Nicolás 45
Gutiérrez Alea, Tomás 48

H

habanera 40
health issues 76–9. *See also* public health

climatic considerations 78
diseases 78–9
food & water 77–8
medical kit 77
treatment 83
vaccinations 61–2, 77
women's 79
heat, effects of 78
Helms–Burton Law 59
Hemingway, Ernest 107, 112, 138, 158, 170, 185–7, 189–90
hepatitis 78
Heredia y Heredia, José María de 45
Hernández, Melba 20
highlights 104
history 11–26, 71
HIV 79
holidays 84
horseback riding 137
Hospital Nacional Hermanos Ameijeiras 132
hotels. *See* accommodations
housing 37
human rights 39
humidors 181
hurricanes 27–8

I

Iglesia de Guanabacoa 188
Iglesia de Nuestra Señora de Regla 187
Iglesia del Santo Angel Custodio 120
Iglesia Jesús de Miramar 134
Iglesia Parroquial del Espíritu Santo 115
Iglesia y Convento de Nuestra Señora de la Merced 115
Iglesia y Convento de Santa Clara 114–5
Iglesia y Monasterio de San Francisco de Asís 113
immunizations 61–2, 77
Instituto Cubano del Arte e Industria Cinematográficos (ICAIC) 48
Instituto Superior de Arte 134

insurance
car 100
travel 61
international transfers 66
Internet
resources 69–70
ticket sales 89

J

Jardín Botánico Nacional 136
jazz 44, 178

K

Kennedy, John F 23, 24, 25
Khrushchev, Nikita 23, 24

L

La Giraldilla 110
La Habana Vieja 105–16, **Map 2**
accommodations 142–3
entertainment 170–3
restaurants & food 153–7
shopping 181–2
walking tour 105–16
Lage, Carlos 32
Lam, Wilfredo 47, 108
language 52, 164, 193–8
language courses 138–9
laundry 76
lesbians. *See* gay & lesbian travelers
libraries 81, 111, 127
licenses 59–61
literature 27–8. *See also* books
López, Narciso 45
luggage storage 76

M

Maceo, Antonio 16, 17, 132
Machado y Morales, Gerardo 19, 118, 124, 125, 126
Mafia 124, 140
magazines 73–4
Magoon, Charles 19
mail 67
Maine 17, 19, 132
Malecón 130–3
maps 54
Marianao. *See* Playa & Marianao

Martí, José 17, 18, 42, 45, 115–6, 119, 120, 121, 127–8
Martínez, Raúl 47
McKinley, William 19
measurements 76
medical kit 77
Mella, Julio Antonio 126
Mendive, Manuel 47
Mexican tourist cards 59
Ministerio de Relaciones Exteriores 132
Miramar 133–4
money 64–7
Moré, Benny 43
movies. See cinemas; films
municipalities 27, 32, **26**
museums
Casa de Lombillo 108
Casa de los Árabes 111
Casa de México Benito Juárez 112
Memorial a José Martí 127–8
Museo Antropológico Montané 126
Museo de Arte Colonial 109
Museo de Artes Decorativas 126
Museo de Historia Natural 126
Museo de la Alfabetización 134
Museo de la Cerámica Artística Cubana 110
Museo de la Ciudad 109–10
Museo de la Ciudad No 2 111
Museo de la Danza 127
Museo de la Revolución 120
Museo de Simón Bolívar 112
Museo del Aire 134
Museo del Automóvil 111
Museo Hemingway 185–7

Museo Municipal de Guanabacoa 188
Museo Municipal de Regla 187
Museo Nacional de Historia Natural 111
Museo Nacional de la Música 120–1
Museo Nacional Palacio de Bellas Artes 119
Museo Napoleónico 126
Museo Numismático 111
Museo-Casa Natal de José Martí 115–6
Quinta de los Molinos 127
music 40–2, 169, 177–8

N

Napoleon 126
native peoples 11–3, 47
Necrópolis Cristóbal Colón 129–30, **128–9**
newspapers 73–4, 170
Nixon, Richard 22
Noche Plaza 106
nueva trova 42

O

Ochoa Sánchez, Arnaldo 25
overfishing 28

P

Pabellón para la Maqueta de la Capital 133
Pabexpo 134
Padrón, Juan 49
painting 46. See also art galleries; artwork
País, Frank 20, 22
Palacio de las Convenciones 134
Palacio de los Capitanes Generales 109
Palacio de los Condes de Santovenia 111
Palacio de los Marqueses de Aguas Claras 107
Palacio de los Matrimonios 119
Palacio del Marqués de Arcos 108

Palacio del Segundo Cabo 110
Palacio Velasco 121
Parque Central 118–9
Parque de la Fraternidad 117
Parque Lenin area 135–7, **Map 5**
accommodations 150
restaurants & food 168
transportation 137
Parque Zoológico Nacional 136–7
Paseo de Martí 119
passports 57–8
Pavillón Granma 119–20
Pérez Roque, Felipe 32
phones 67–8
photography 75
plants. See flora
Playa & Marianao 133–5, **Map 4**
accommodations 147–50
entertainment 172, 174–6
restaurants & food 166–8
shopping 184
Playas del Este 190–2, **Map 7**
Plaza de Armas 109
Plaza de la Revolución 127–9
Plaza Vieja 113–4
politics 31–2, 71
pollution 28
population 36–9
postal services 67
Prado, Dámaso Pérez 43
Prío Socarrás, Carlos 20
private rooms.
See accommodations
prostitution 82, 173
public health 38–9

Q

Quinta de los Molinos 127

R

radio 74–5
ration cards 33
Real Fábrica de Tabacos La Corona 120
Real Fábrica de Tabacos Partagás 117–8
refunds 67

Bold indicates maps.

Regla 187–8, **Map 6**
religion 50–1
Remington, Frederick 17
restaurants & food (general)
151–68. *See also* drinks
cookbooks 72
costs 66
cuisine 152
paladares 151
safety 77–8
words & phrases 164, 196–7
restaurants & food (specific)
Al Medina 157
Almacenes Ultra 158
Asociación Canaria de
Cuba 159
Bar El Mirador 161
Bar El Polvorín 161
Bar-Restaurante Cabaña
155
Bim Bom 162
Cabaret Guanimar 191
Cabaret Marina 166
Café Concerto Gato
Tuerto 164
Café del Oriente 156
Café del Prado 159
Cafe París 153
Café Taberna 154
Cafetería La Primera de
Aguacate 155
Cafetería Rumbos 160
Cafetería Sofía 163
Cafetería Torre La Vega
154–5
Caracol El Cristal 158
Centro Andaluz 159
Centro Vasco 165
Coppelia 162
Ditú MiConuco 162
Don Cangrejo 167
Dos Gardenias 166
El Aljibe 166
El Barracon 165
El Café Mercurio 156
El Conejito 162–3
El Floridita 157, 158, 170
El Pacífico 160
El Rancho Palco 167
El Tocororo 167
Feria Los Fornos 160

Harris Brothers 153
Kiosko Playa 191
La Bodeguita del Medio
156
La Casa de Quinta y 16
166–7
La Cecilia 167–8
La Época 158
La Ferminia 167
La Lluvia de Oro 153–4
La Mina 156–7
La Rampa Cafetería
164–5
La Taberna 163
La Torre de Marfil 157
La Torre de Oro 155
La Zaragozana 157
Las Ruinas 168
Las Terrazas de Prado 159
Mercado Agropecuario
161
Mercado Agropecuario
Egido 157
Mercado El Cristo 153
Mercado Los Fornos 158
Mesón La Chorrera 165
Pain de París 161
Paladar Amistad de
Lanzarote 160
Paladar Amor 163
Paladar Bellamar 160
Paladar Calle 10 166
Paladar Doña Blanquita
159
Paladar El Helecho 163
Paladar El Hurón Azul
163–4
Paladar El Rincón de
Elegguá 157
Paladar Gringo Viejo 163
Paladar La Familia 166
Paladar La Guarida 160
Paladar La Última Instancia
163
Paladar Las Delicias de
Consulado 159
Paladar Los Amigos 163
Paladar Los Cactus de 33
166
Paladar Los Helechos de
Trinidad 163

Paladar Los Tres
Mosqueteros 163
Paladar Sagitario 161
Paladar Torressón 160
Paladar Vistamar 166
Paladar Yiyo's 163
Panadería Doña Neli 166
Panadería San José 153
Papa's Restaurant-Bar 167
Parrillada D'Prisa 191
Pasteleria Francesa 159
Restaurante Bulerías 163
Restaurante Caribeno 163
Restaurante D'Giovanni
157
Restaurante 1830 165
Restaurante El Bambú 168
Restaurante El Baturro
159–60
Restaurante El Castillo de
Farnés 155
Restaurante El Cortijo 165
Restaurante El Laurel 167
Restaurante El Patio 155
Restaurante El Pavo Real
166
Restaurante Guang Zhou
160
Restaurante Hanoi 153
Restaurante La Divina
Pastora 161
Restaurante La Dominica
157
Restaurante La Paella 157
Restaurante La Terraza
190
Restaurante La Torre 165
Restaurante Los Doce
Apóstoles 161
Restaurante Los Escudos
160–1
Restaurante Mandarin 165
Restaurante Mi Casita de
Coral 191
Restaurante Monseigneur
165
Restaurante My Cayito
191
Restaurante Oasis 159
Restaurante Puerto de
Sagua 155

Restaurante Sierra Maestra 165–6
Restaurante Tien-Tan 160
Restaurante Wakamba 164
Restaurante-Bar Polinesio 165
Restaurante-Parrillada Costarenas 191
Rumbos Cafetería 162
Supermercado Amistad 158–9
Supermercado Flores 166
Supermercado Isla de Cuba 158
Supermercado Meridiano 161
retirement age 39
Robaina, Roberto 32
Roca, Vladimiro 32
rock music 177–8
Rodríguez, Arsenio 42
rum 156
rumba 40, 44
Russian Embassy 133

S

safety issues 80, 82
salsa 42
Sánchez, Celia 20
Santamaría, Abel 20
Santamaría, Haydée 20
Santería 50–1
scuba diving. See diving & snorkeling
seniors' cards 61
sexually transmitted diseases (STDs) 79
shipwrecks 14
shopping 179–84
slavery 15–6, 37, 51
snorkeling. See diving & snorkeling
Solás, Humberto 49
son 41–2, 44
Sores, Jacques de 121
Spanish
conquest 13–4

Bold indicates maps.

language 52, 138–9, 164, 193–8
special events 84–5
sports, spectator 178
STDs 79
student cards 61
sugar industry 14–6, 35
sunburn 78

T

Taínos 11, 13
Taller Experimental de Gráfica 109, 182
taxes 67
taxis 93, 96, 101
tea 162
Teatro Nacional de Cuba 128
telephones 67–8
television 74–5
tetanus 78–9
theater 40, 176–7
tickets, onward 61
time zone 75–6
tipping 66–7
toilets 76
Torreón de Cojímar 189
Torreón de San Lázaro 132
Torricelli Act 25
tourism
industry 35–6
responsible 54
tourist cards 57–8, 59
tourist offices 55–7
tours
organized 93–5, 102
walking 105–16, 116–21, 124–6, 127–9, 130–3
trains 92–3, 98
transportation
air travel 86–92
bicycles 101–2
boats 62, 93, 102
buses 91–2, 97–8
cars 98–101
taxis 93, 96, 101
trains 92–3, 98
walking 101
travel agencies 103
travel books 70–1
travel insurance 61

traveler's checks 65
trees 29, 30
Tropicana 174–5
Túnel de la Bahía 121
turtles 29
TV 74–5
typhoid 78

U

Universidad de La Habana 126
Urrutia, Manuel 22
US
embargo 9, 24, 59
emigration to 39
intervention 17, 19, 124
naval base 25
visitors from 59–61

V

vaccinations 61–2, 77
Vedado 124–7, **Map 3**
accommodations 145–7
entertainment 172, 173–4, 175, 176–7
restaurants & food 161–6
shopping 183–4
walking tour 124–6
Vega, Pastor 49
video 75
Villaverde y de la Paz, Cirilo 45, 120
visas 58
volunteer work 85

W

walking 53, 101. See also tours
water 77
websites 69–70
Weyler, Valeriano 17
wildlife. See fauna
women travelers 79–80
work 85

Y

yachting 62, 70, 137–8
youth cards 61

Z

zoo 136–7

Boxed Text

Afro-Cuban Religions 51
Air Travel Glossary 87
A Break for Turtles 29
A Cobblewood Road? 109
'Coffee, Tea or Cuba?' 162
A Cuban Chronology 12
Cuban Musical Instruments 41
Cuba's Copious Cocktails 154
Cuba's Creole Cuisine 152
Cuba's Top Rums 156
Cuba's Two-Channel Government 74
Don't Call Him 'Loco' 31
El Túnel de la Bahía 121
Ernest 'Papa' Hemingway 186
Exporting Artwork 181
Fishermen Ahoy! 138
Floss It 55
From Doctor to Revolutionary to Hero 21
Havana at Its Best 104
Havana's Hookers 173
Havana's Private Restaurants 151
Helpful Food Phrases 164
Hot Off the Presses 170
Human Rights in Cuba 39
Internet Bookings 89

It's Tough Renting a Private Room in Havana 141
José Martí 18
Just Come On In! 169
Killer Storms 28
Little Loss of Control 34
Medical Kit Check List 77
Meeting Gays & Lesbians in Havana 171
Not Exactly Fidel's Granma 117
Party at the Cathedral 106
Private Rooms Runaround 96
The Ration Card 33
Salvaging Sunken Galleons 14
Should Americans Visit Cuba? 59
The Show Only Gets Better 174
Signing On in Havana 69
The Slave Trade 15
Small Bills Are Best 65
Sugarcane's Story 35
Think Feet! 53
Those Colorful Trees 30
Those Unhelpful Embassies 63
Through Cuba's Door 57
A Tour Best Avoided 102
World's Finest Daiquirís 158

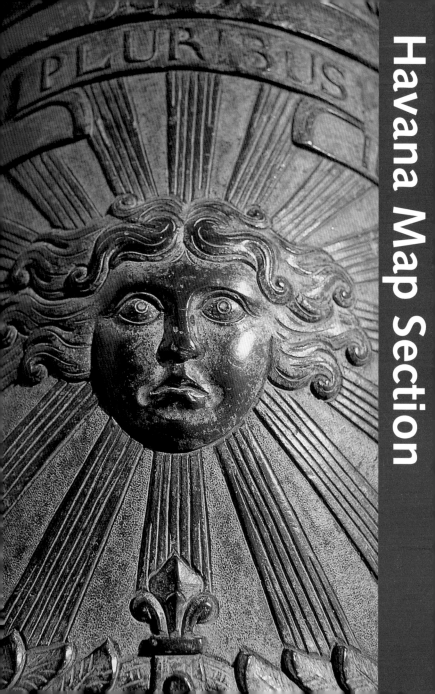

MAP 1 HAVANA

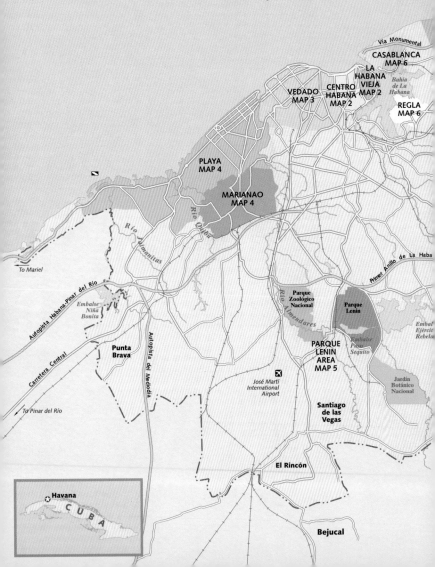

Straits of Florida

Vía Monumental

CASABLANCA
MAP 6

LA
HABANA
VIEJA
MAP 2

Bahía
de La
Habana

VEDADO
MAP 3

CENTRO
HABANA
MAP 2

REGLA
MAP 6

PLAYA
MAP 4

MARIANAO
MAP 4

Río Quibú

Río Jaimanitas

Primer Anillo de La Haba

To Mariel

Río Almendares

Parque
Zoológico
Nacional

Parque
Lenin

Embalse
Niña
Bonita

Embalse
Ejércit
Rebela

Autopista Habana-Pinar del Río

Punta
Brava

Autopista del Mediodía

PARQUE
LENIN
AREA
MAP 5

Embalse
Picao
Sequito

Carretera Central

José Martí
International
Airport

Jardín
Botánico
Nacional

To Pinar del Río

Santiago
de las
Vegas

El Rincón

Bejucal

⭐ **Havana**

C U B A

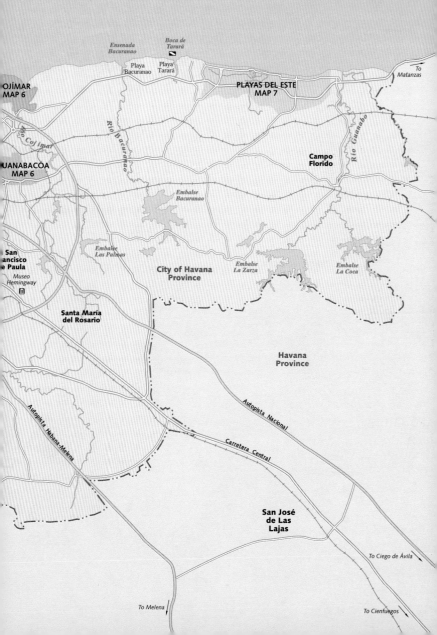

Dive Site

Ensenada Bacuranao

Boca de Tarará

Playa Bacuranao

Playa Tarará

OJÍMAR
MAP 6

**PLAYAS DEL ESTE
MAP 7**

To Matanzas

Río Cojímar

Río Bacuranao

Río Guanabo

GUANABACOA
MAP 6

**Campo
Florido**

*Embalse
Bacuranao*

**San
Francisco
de Paula**

*Museo
Hemingway*

*Embalse
Las Palmas*

**City of Havana
Province**

*Embalse
La Zarza*

*Embalse
La Coca*

**Santa María
del Rosario**

**Havana
Province**

Autopista Habana-Melena

Autopista Nacional

Carretera Central

**San José
de Las
Lajas**

To Ciego de Ávila

To Melena

To Cienfuegos

MAP 2 LA HABANA VIEJA & CENTRO HABANA

to MAP 7

Straits of Florida

0   150   300 m
0   150   300 yards

Malecón ▼4

Av de los Estudiantes

Capdevila

Plaza 13 de Marzo

LA HABANA VIEJA

Malecón

San Lázaro

CENTRO HABANA

Parque de la Fraternidad

Av Simón Bolívar

Capitolio Nacional

to MAP 3 Vedado

ped mall

Estación Central de Ferrocarril

Estación La Coubre

Bahía de La Habana

To Castillo de Atarés (500m)

Fortaleza de
San Carlos
de la Cabaña

see Eastern Forts map

Casablanca

Carretera Casablanca

Carlos Manuel de Céspedes

see inset map

Estación Casablanca

see MAP 6

Bahía de La Habana

Ferry

San Ignacio

Cuba

Oficios

San Pedro

79

Santa Clara

87

Costa

Jesús María

88

Merced

Leonor Pérez

89

San Isidro

Velazco

Desamparados

•••• Walking Tour

0   50   100 m
0   50   100 yards

Castillo Real
de la Fuerza

Catedral de San Cristóbal
de La Habana

97

99

100

Muelle
Luz

96
101 102
105 106
103
104
107
108 109
111
110

Empedrado

Mercaderes

Tacón

112

117

116

118

Plaza
de
Armas

Callejón
del Chorro

Plaza
de la
Catedral

115

O'Reilly

113

123 124
125 127
126
128
129

Justiz

136

Barillo

135

114

Obispo

San Ignacio

119

120

121
122

131
132

134

133

130

137

139
140
142
141

143

144

Carpinetti

Obrapía

138

150

151

152

Lamparilla

146
147
148
149

145

155

Plaza de
San Francisco
de Asís

158

157

159

160

161

Amargura

153

154

156

164

163

Brasil

Aguar

Cuba

162

Plaza
Vieja

Muralla

Oficios

165

Sol

166

San Pedro

PLACES TO STAY
11 Hostal San Miguel
59 Hotel Florida
118 Hotel Santa Isabel; Palacio de los Condes de Santovenia
121 Hotel Ambos Mundos
143 Hostal Valencia; Restaurante La Paella
146 Hostal Condes de Villanueva
154 Aparthotel Santo Ángel

PLACES TO EAT
10 Bar-Restaurante Cabaña
33 Cafetería La Primera de Aguacate
54 Harris Brothers
58 La Lluvia de Oro
64 La Zaragozana; El Floridita
65 Restaurante El Castillo de Farnés
68 Paladar El Rincón de Elegguá
75 Restaurante Hanoi
76 Mercado El Cristo
85 Restaurante Puerto de Sagua
86 Restaurante El Baturro
97 La Torre de Oro
98 Restaurante D'Giovanni
102 Restaurante El Patio; Palacio de los Marqueses de Aguas Claras
111 Restaurante La Dominica
114 Café París
124 La Mina
126 Al Medina
131 La Torre de Marfil
133 Cafetería Torre La Vega
145 Café Habana
149 Café del Oriente
150 El Café Mercurio
155 Café Taberna

ENTERTAINMENT
66 Monserrate Bar
101 La Bodeguita del Medio
110 O'Reilly's
113 Café de O'Reilly
129 Casa de la Comédia
136 El Caserón del Tango

153 Casa de la Cultura de La Habana Vieja
164 Bar La Marina
166 Bar Dos Hermanos

OTHER
9 Museo Nacional de la Música
12 Palacio de Pedroso; Palacio de la Artesanía
13 Police station in colonial-style fortress
14 Seminario de Carlos y San Ambrosio
15 Handicraft Market
24 Iglesia del Santo Angel Custodio
34 Fundación Alejo Carpentier
55 Librería La Internacional
56 Unidad de Filatelia
57 Longina Música
60 Drogería Johnson
67 Lavandería Alaska
77 Drogería Sarrá
79 Iglesia y Convento de Santa Clara
87 Iglesia Parroquial del Espíritu Santo
88 Iglesia y Convento de Nuestra Señora de la Merced
89 Antigua Iglesia de San Francisco de Paula
91 Museo-Casa Natal de José Martí
92 Policía Nacional Revolucionaria
96 Centro de Arte Contemporáneo Wilfredo Lam
99 La Giraldilla
100 Museo de la Cerámica Artística Cubana
103 Casa de Lombillo
104 Mural Artístico-Histórico
105 Taller Experimental de Gráfica
106 Galería Victor Manuel
107 Palacio del Marqués de Arcos
108 Palacio de los Condes de Casa Bayona; Museo de Arte Colonial
109 Colección Habana
112 Palacio del Segundo Cabo; Instituto Cubano del Libro

115 Palacio de los Capitanes Generales; Museo de la Ciudad
116 Statue of Carlos Manuel de Céspedes
117 El Templete
119 Infotur
120 Farmacia Taquechel
122 La Casa del Habano
123 Museo de la Ciudad #2
125 Casa del Obispo; Museo Numismático
127 Museo Nacional de Historia Natural
128 Biblioteca Pública Provincial Rubén M Villena
130 Casa de la Obra Pía
132 Casa de México Benito Juárez
134 Colegio San Ambrosio; Casa de los Árabes
135 Museo del Automóvil
137 Casa de África
138 Museo de Simón Bolívar
139 Habana 1791
140 Statue of Simón Bolívar
141 Casa Oswaldo Guayasamín
142 Casa del Abanico
144 Cadeca
147 Post Office
148 San Cristóbal Agencia de Viajes
151 Lonja del Comercio
152 Sierra Maestra Marine Terminal
156 Banco Financiero Internacional
157 Estudio Galería Los Oficios
158 Galería de Carmen Montilla
159 Post Office
160 Fuente de los Leones
161 Iglesia y Monasterio de San Francisco de Asís
162 Taller de Serigrafía René Portocarrero
163 Fototeca de Cuba
165 Casa de los Condes de Jaruco; Fondo Cubano de Bienes Culturales

MASON FLORENCE

Cigars in factory

CENTRO HABANA

PLACES TO STAY

17 Hotel Deauville;
   Discoteca Ribera Azul
19 Hotel Caribbean; Café del Prado
20 Casa del Científico; Asistur
25 Hotel Lincoln
26 Hotel Lido
30 Hotel Sevilla
41 Hotel Golden Tulip Parque
   Central
42 Hotel Plaza
49 Hotel Telegrafico
51 Hotel Inglaterra
71 Hotel New York
82 Hotel Isla de Cuba

PLACES TO EAT

4 Paladar Torressón
6 Las Terrazas de Prado
7 Centro Andaluz
18 Paladar Doña Blanquita
27 Restaurante Oasis
35 Paladar Sagitario
36 Paladar La Guarida
39 Paladar Bellamar
40 Paladar Las Delicias de
   Consulado
44 Asociación Canaria de Cuba

46 Paladar Amistad de Lanzarote
47 Feria Los Fornos
50 Pasteleria Francesa
52 Cafetería Rumbos
69 Restaurante Guang Zhou
70 Restaurante Tien-Tan
73 Restaurante Los Escudos
81 Supermercado La Isla de Cuba
83 Mercado Agropecuario Egido

ENTERTAINMENT

16 Casa de la Trova
21 Teatro Fausto
28 Restaurante Prado 264
38 Teatro América
43 Cine Actualidades
45 Palermo
48 Cinecito
61 Cine El Mégano
62 Gran Teatro de La Habana;
   Cabaret Nacional;
   Centro Gallego
63 Cine Payret
74 Kid Chocolate

OTHER

1 Castillo de San Salvador de la
   Punta

2 Memorial to the Medical
   Students
3 Centro Cultural de España
5 Statue of General Máximo
   Gómez
8 Palacio Velasco;
   Spanish Embassy
22 Real Fábrica de Tabacos La
   Corona
23 Museo de la Revolución
29 Palacio de los Matrimonios
31 Museo Nacional Palacio de
   Bellas Artes
32 Pavillón Granma
37 Galería Galiano
53 La Manzana de Gómez
72 Real Fábrica de Tabacos
   Partagás
78 Fuente de la India
80 Area de Vendedores por Cuenta
   Propia
84 Blue Buses to Guanabo
90 Lista de Espera Office
93 Old City Wall
94 La Lucha Bicycle Shop
95 Bus No 400 to Guanabo

ALFREDO MAIQUEZ

The Real Fábrica de Tabacos Partagás, Havana's most famous, and one of its oldest, cigar factories

A spectacular view of the city from Restaurante La Torre, 36 stories up

Fabulous cabaret at the renowned Tropicana nightclub

VEDADO

PLACES TO STAY

7 Hotel Presidente
13 Hotel Riviera;
   Palacio de la Salsa
14 Hotel Meliá Cohiba;
   Havana Café
25 Hotel Universitario
31 Hotel Victoria
34 Hotel Capri; Cabaret Salón Rojo
36 Hotel Nacional; Cabaret Parisién
54 Hotel Habana Libre; Cabaret
   Turquino; El Barracon;
   Restaurante Sierra Maestra
60 Hotel St John's; Pico Blanco
62 Hotel Vedado;
   Restaurante El Cortijo
83 Hotel Colina
110 Hotel Bruzón; Discoteca

PLACES TO EAT

5 Ditú MiConuco
24 Paladar Yiyo's
26 El Conejito
27 Restaurante La Torre;
   Edificio Focsa
29 Café Concerto Gato Tuerto
32 Paladar Los Amigos
33 Restaurante Caribeno
35 Restaurante Monseigneur
37 Centro Vasco
46 Coppelia
48 Restaurante Mandarín
51 Bim Bom
53 Restaurante Bulerías
55 La Rampa Cafetería
56 Restaurante-Bar Polinesio
59 La Taberna, Cafetería Sofía
61 Cafetería Marakas
64 Pain de Paris
65 Paladar El Hurón Azul
66 Restaurante Wakamba
68 Rumbos Cafetería
76 Paladar Gringo Viejo
79 Paladar Los Helechos de
   Trinidad
90 Paladar El Helecho
95 Mercado Agropecuario
96 Paladar Amor
98 Paladar La Última Instancia
99 Paladar Los Tres Mosqueteros

103 Mesón La Chorrera; Restaurante
    1830; Castillo de Santa Dorotea
    de la Luna de la Chorrera

ENTERTAINMENT

11 Discoteca Amanecer
17 Teatro Amadeo Roldán
18 Club Tropical
20 Café Teatro Brecht
23 Karachi Club
28 Teatro Nacional de Guiñol
30 Club La Red
38 Conjunto Folklórico Nacional;
   El Gran Palenque
40 Sala-Teatro Hubert de Blanck
41 Cine Trianón
43 Teatro Mella
44 Unión Nacional de Escritores y
   Artistas de Cuba; El Huron Azul
47 Cine Yara
58 Jazz Club La Zorra y El Cuervo
63 Cabaret Las Vegas
67 Cine La Rampa
77 Cine Riviera
78 Sala Teatro El Sótano
105 Cine 23 y 12
106 Cine Charles Chaplin
111 Patio de María
112 Teatro Nacional de Cuba;
    Café Cantante

OTHER

1 Monumento a Calixto García
2 Servi-Cupet
3 US Interests Office
4 Flea Market
6 Casa de las Américas
8 Ministerio de Relaciones
   Exteriores
9 Centro Camilo Cienfuegos
10 Servi-Cupet
12 Monumento a las Victimas del
   Maine
15 Galerías de Paseo
16 Servi-Cupet
19 Museo de la Danza
21 Servi-Cupet
22 Banco Metropolitano
39 DHL Worldwide Express
42 Banco de Crédito y Comercio

45 Alliance Française
49 Centro de Prensa Internacional
50 Airline Building;
   Banco de Crédito
52 La Habana Sí
57 Crafts Market
69 Micar; Cubalse Fiat
70 Torreón de San Lázaro
71 Monumento a Antonio Maceo
72 Hospital Nacional Hermanos
   Ameijeiras
73 German Embassy
74 Marsub
75 Museo de Artes Decorativas
80 Galería Ciudades del Mundo
81 Librería Fernando Ortiz
82 Filatelia Especializada
84 Universidad de La Habana (La
   Colina)
85 Edificio Felipe Poey (Museo de
   Historia Natural; Museo
   Antropológico Montané)
86 Museo Napoleónico
87 Monumento a Julio Antonio
   Mella
88 Callejón de Hamel
89 Casa de la Cultura de Plaza
91 Mercadú SA
92 Cubamar
93 Instituto Cubano de Amistad
   con los Pueblos
94 Cadeca
97 Post Office
100 Monumento a José Miguel
    Gómez
101 Quinta de los Molinos
102 Plaza Carlos III
104 Socialist Revolution Plaque
107 Italian Embassy
108 Sala Polivalente Ramón Fonst
109 Bus Station
113 Ministry of the Interior
114 Museo Postal Cubano;
    Post Office
115 Biblioteca Nacional José Martí
116 Memorial a José Martí
117 Comité Central del Partido
    Comunista de Cuba
118 Chinese Embassy
119 Servi-Cupet

DAVID STANLEY

The Castillo de los Tres Santos Reyes Magnos del Morro, built between 1589 and 1630

MAP 3 VEDADO

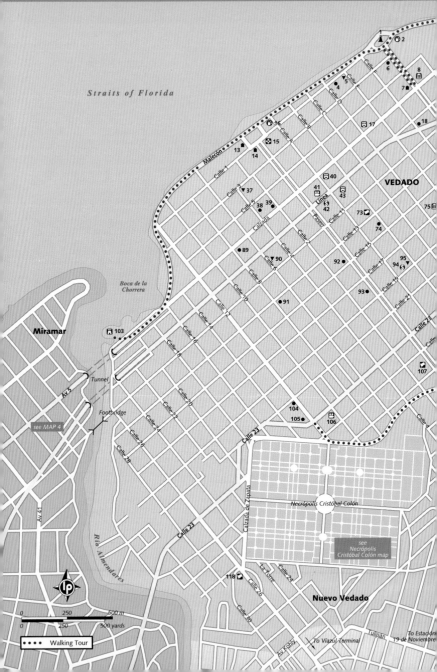

Straits of Florida

VEDADO

Malecón

Calle 1

Calzada

Línea

Paseo

Boca de la
Chorrera

Miramar

Tunnel

Footbridge

Av 5

see MAP 4

Av 41

Río Almendares

Necrópolis Cristóbal Colón

Calzada de Zapata

1ra Torre

Calle 23

Calle 25

*see
Necrópolis
Cristóbal Colón map*

Nuevo Vedado

Av Kohly

Tulipán

To Viazul Terminal

*To Estadión
19 de Noviembre*

0   250   500 m
0   250   500 yards

•••• Walking Tour

Caleta de
San Lázaro

Parque
Maceo

Malecón

San Lázaro

Lagunas

Ánimas

Virtudes

see
MAP 2

Concordia

Neptuno

San Miguel

San Rafael

San Martín

Valle

Salud

Jesús Peregrino

Pocito

Av Salvador Allende

Enrique Barnet

Matoja

Sitio

Peñalver

Desagüe

Benjumeda

Santo Tomás

Clavel

Santa Marta

Arroyo

Estadio Juan
Abrahantes

Castillo
del
Príncipe

Zapata

Bruzón

Calle 19 de Mayo

Plaza de la Revolución

Aranguren

Av 20 de Mayo

Estadio
Latinoamericano

Tombillo

To José Martí
International Airport

Calle 9

Línea

Calle I

Calle H

Tc (Av Por Los Presidentes)

Calle 27

Calle 29

Calle 33

Calle 35

Av Carlos M. de Céspedes

Av de la Independencia

Pozo Dulce

Av de la Universidad

Calle G

Calle J

Calle K

Humboldt

Infanta

Príncipe

Vapor

Jovellar

San Lázaro

San Francisco

Hospital

Aramburu

Soledad

Castillejo

Oquendo

Marqués González

Lucena

Santiago

Zanja

San Carlos

Calzada de Infanta

Calzada del Cerro

Máximo Gómez

MAP 4 PLAYA & MARIANAO

PLACES TO STAY
5 Hostel Icemar
10 Residencia Universitaria Ispjae
13 Motel Las Olas
17 Villa Costa
20 Hotel Mirazul
29 Hotel El Bosque
30 Hotel Chateau Miramar
32 Hotel Copacabana
34 Hostal Costa Sol
40 Hotel Kohly
42 Complejo Neptuno-Tritón
43 Hotel Meliá Habana
44 Hotel El Comodoro
48 Novotel Miramar
56 Villa Paraíso
59 Hotel Acuario
60 Residencial Turístico Marina Hemingway
62 Hotel El Viejo y El Mar
66 Hotel Palco; Palacio de las Convenciones
72 Hotel Biocaribe

PLACES TO EAT
2 Supermercado
4 Don Cangrejo
6 Paladar Calle 10
7 Paladar La Familia
8 Restaurante El Pavo Real
9 Paladar Vistamar
15 El Tocororo
16 La Casa de Quinta y 16; La Casa del Tabaco
22 Dos Gardenias
23 El Aljibe
36 Panadería Doña Neli
38 Paladar Los Cactus de 33
50 La Cecilia
55 Restaurante El Laurel
57 Cabaret Marina; Papa's Restaurant-Bar
63 La Ferminia
64 Supermercado Flores
67 El Rancho Palco

OTHER
1 Sierra Maestra Building
3 Rio Club
11 Banco Financiero Internacional
12 French Embassy
14 Pabellón para la Maqueta de la Capital
18 DHL Express
19 Aster Tintoría y Lavandería
21 Canadian Embassy
24 La Maison
25 Servi-Cupet
26 Farmacia Internacional
27 Casa de la Música
28 Clinica Central Cira Garcia
31 Acuario Nacional
33 Post Office
35 Cadeca
37 British Embassy
39 Estadio Pedro Marrero
41 Russian Embassy
45 Havana Club Disco
46 Cubanacán Express
47 Iglesia Jesús de Miramar
49 Post Office
51 Servi-Cupet
52 Centro de Idiomas y Computación José Martí
53 Servi-Cupet
54 Tropicana Nightclub; Arcos de Cristal
58 La Aguja Centro de Bucco
61 Cubacar
65 Pabexpo
68 Oro Negro
69 Instituto Superior de Arte
70 Museo de la Alfabetización
71 Centro Nacional de Investigaciones Científicas
73 Centro de Ingeniería Genética y Biotecnología
74 Museo del Aire

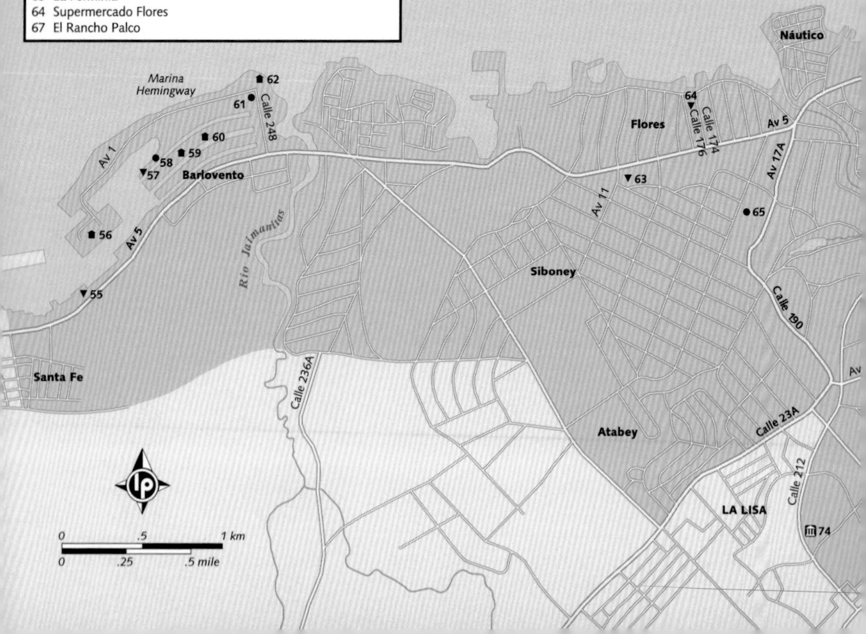

Straits of Florida

Náutico

Marina Hemingway

Flores

Av 5

Av 17A

Calle 248

Calle 174
Calle 176

Barlovento

Av 1

Av 11

63

Av 5

Siboney

65

Calle 180

Santa Fe

Río Jaimanitas

Calle 236A

Atabey

Calle 23A

Calle 212

LA LISA

74

0   .5   1 km
0   .25   .5 mile

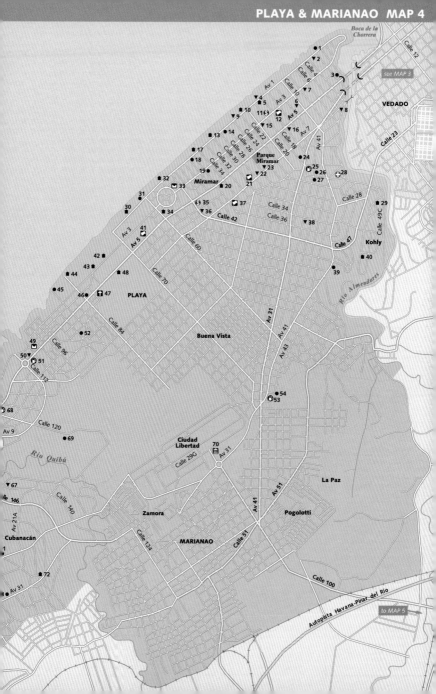

Boca de la Chorrera

see MAP 3

Calle 12

VEDADO

Calle 23

1
2
3
4
5
6
7
8
9
10
11
12
13
14
15
16
17
18
19
20
21
22
23
24
25
26
27
28
29

Av 1
Av 3
Av 5
Av 7
Av 9

Calle 4
Calle 6
Calle 10

Calle 22
Calle 24
Calle 26
Calle 28
Calle 30
Calle 32
Calle 34

Calle 18
Calle 20

Calle 41

Parque Miramar

Miramar

Calle 34
Calle 36

Calle 28
Calle 49C

Kohly

40

39

30
31
32
33
34
35
36
37
38

41
42
43
44
45
46
47
48

Av 3
Av 5

Calle 42

Calle 60

Calle 47

Río Almendares

PLAYA

Calle 70

Calle 84

Buena Vista

52

49
50
51

Calle 96

Calle 112

Av 31
Av 41
Av 43

54
53

68

Calle 120

Av 9

69

Río Quibú

Ciudad Libertad

70

Calle 29G

Av 31

La Paz

67

Calle 140

le 146

Av 21A

Zamora

Calle 124

MARIANAO

Av 41

Av 51

Calle 51

Pogolotti

Cubanacán

1

72

Av 31

Calle 100

Calle 31

Autopista Havana–Pinar del Río

to MAP 5

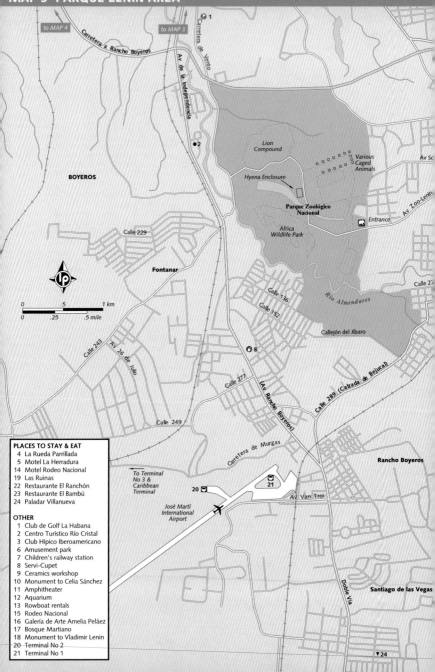

MAP 5 PARQUE LENIN AREA

to MAP 4

to MAP 3

Carretera a Rancho Boyeros

Carretera de Viento

Av de la Independencia

1

BOYEROS

2

Lion Compound

Hyena Enclosure

Various Caged Animals

Av So

Parque Zoológico Nacional

Entrance

Av Zoo-Lenin

Calle 229

Fontanar

Africa Wildlife Park

Río Almendares

Calle 27

Calle 136

Calle 152

Callejón del Jíbaro

Calle 243

Av 26 de Julio

8

Calle 277

(Av Rancho Boyeros)

Calle 289 (Calzada de Bejucal)

Calle 249

Carretera de Murgas

Rancho Boyeros

To Terminal No 3 & Caribbean Terminal

21

20

Av Van Troi

José Martí International Airport

Doble Vía

Santiago de las Vegas

24

PLACES TO STAY & EAT
4 La Rueda Parrillada
5 Motel La Herradura
14 Motel Rodeo Nacional
19 Las Ruinas
22 Restaurante El Ranchón
23 Restaurante El Bambú
24 Paladar Villanueva

OTHER
1 Club de Golf La Habana
2 Centro Turístico Río Cristal
3 Club Hípico Iberoamericano
6 Amusement park
7 Children's railway station
8 Servi-Cupet
9 Ceramics workshop
10 Monument to Celia Sánchez
11 Amphitheater
12 Aquarium
13 Rowboat rentals
15 Rodeo Nacional
16 Galería de Arte Amelia Peláez
17 Bosque Martiano
18 Monument to Vladimir Lenin
20 Terminal No 2
21 Terminal No 1

0   .5   1 km
0   .25   .5 mile

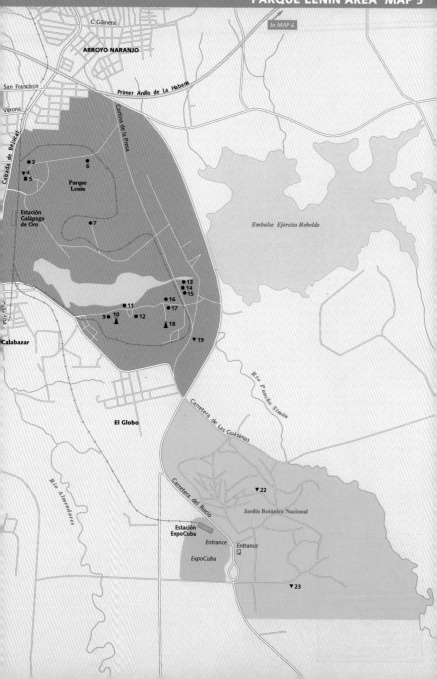

to MAP 6

C Güinera

ARROYO NARANJO

San Francisco

Verona

Primer Anillo de La Habana

Cortina de la Presa

Calzada de Bejucal

● 3
▼ 4
■ 5

● 6

Parque Lenin

Estación Galápago de Oro

● 7

Embalse Ejército Rebelde

● 13
■ 14
● 15

● 16
● 11   ● 17

● 9 ● 10   ● 12
      ▲   ▲ 18

Calle 104

Calabazar

▼ 19

Río Pancho Simón

El Globo

Carretera de Las Guásimas

Río Almendares

Carretera del Rocío

▼ 22

Jardín Botánico Nacional

Estación ExpoCuba

Entrance   *Entrance*
                    P

ExpoCuba

▼ 23

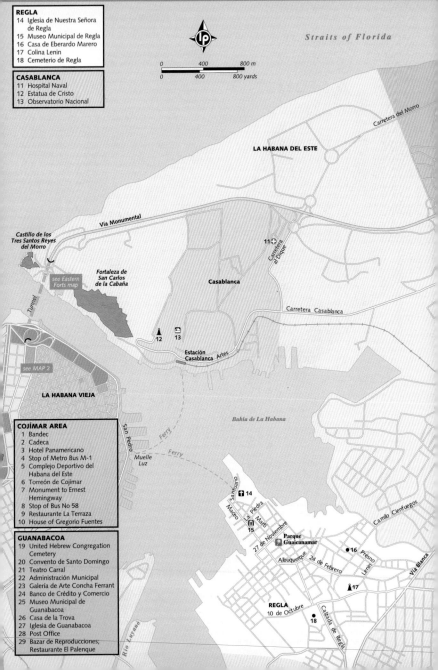

MAP 6 REGLA, GUANABACOA, CASABLANCA & COJÍMAR AREA

REGLA
14 Iglesia de Nuestra Señora de Regla
15 Museo Municipal de Regla
16 Casa de Eberardo Marero
17 Colina Lenin
18 Cemeterio de Regla

CASABLANCA
11 Hospital Naval
12 Estatua de Cristo
13 Observatorio Nacional

COJÍMAR AREA
1 Bandec
2 Cadeca
3 Hotel Panamericano
4 Stop of Metro Bus M-1
5 Complejo Deportivo del Habana del Este
6 Torreón de Cojimar
7 Monument to Ernest Hemingway
8 Stop of Bus No 58
9 Restaurante La Terraza
10 House of Gregorio Fuentes

GUANABACOA
19 United Hebrew Congregation Cemetery
20 Convento de Santo Domingo
21 Teatro Carral
22 Administración Municipal
23 Galería de Arte Concha Ferrant
24 Banco de Crédito y Comercio
25 Museo Municipal de Guanabacoa
26 Casa de la Trova
27 Iglesia de Guanabacoa
28 Post Office
29 Bazar de Reproducciones; Restaurante El Palenque

Straits of Florida

LA HABANA DEL ESTE

Carretera del Morro

Vía Monumental

Castillo de los Tres Santos Reyes del Morro

see Eastern Forts map

Fortaleza de San Carlos de la Cabaña

Casablanca

Carretera al Dique

Carretera Casablanca

Estación Casablanca

see MAP 2

LA HABANA VIEJA

Bahía de La Habana

Ferry

Muelle Luz

San Pedro

REGLA

Parque Guaicanamar

Albuquerque 2a de Febrero

Camilo Cienfuegos

Vía Blanca

10 de Octubre

Calzada de Regla

REGLA, GUANABACOA, CASABLANCA & COJÍMAR AREA   MAP 6

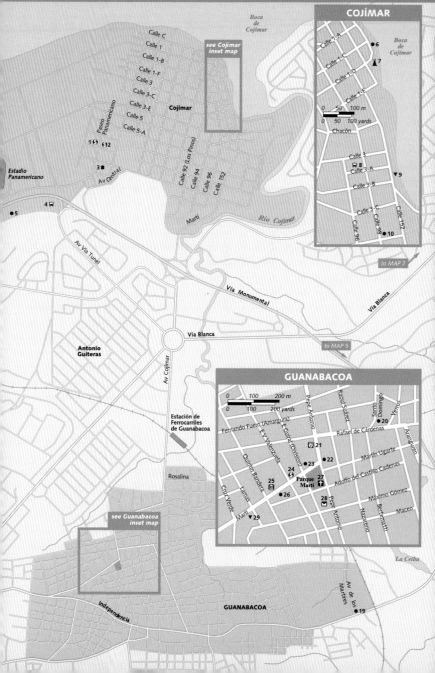

COJÍMAR

Boca
de
Cojímar

Calle 1-A
Calle 1-C
Calle 1-D
Calle 1-E

● 6
▲ 7

0   50   100 m
0   50   100 yards

Chacón

Calle 3
🚌 8
Calle 3-A   ▼ 9
Calle 3-B
Calle 3-C
Calle 96   Calle 98   Calle 152
● 10

to MAP 7

Boca
de
Cojímar

Calle C
Calle 1
Calle 1-B
Calle 1-F
Calle 3
Calle 3-C
Calle 3-E
Calle 5
Calle 5-A

Cojímar

see Cojimar
inset map

Paseo Panamericano

1 ⓘ ⓘ 2

3 ■

Av Central

Estadio
Panamericano

4 🚌

● 5

Calle 92 (Los Pinos)
Calle 94
Calle 96
Calle 152

Martí

Río Cojímar

Av Vía Tunel

Vía Monumental

Vía Blanca

Vía Blanca

to MAP 5

Antonio
Guiteras

Av Cojímar

Estación de
Ferrocarriles
de Guanabacoa

Rosalina

see Guanabacoa
inset map

GUANABACOA

0   100   200 m
0   100   200 yards

Pepe Antonio
Raúl Suárez
Santo Domingo
Venus

Fernando Fuero (Amargura)
F.V. Valenzuela
E.Guiral (División)
Rafael de Cárdenas
● 20

🏛 21
Martín Ugarte
Arangúren

24 ⓘ ● 23   🏛 22
25 🏛   27 ℹ
Quintín Banderas   Parque   Adolfo del Castillo Cadenas
● 26   Martí   28 🏛   Máximo Gómez
Lamas   ▼ 29   Pepe Antonio   Nazareno   Bertematti   Maceo
Cruz Verde   Martí

La Ceiba

Independencia

GUANABACOA

Av de los Mártires

● 19

MAP 7 PLAYAS DEL ESTE

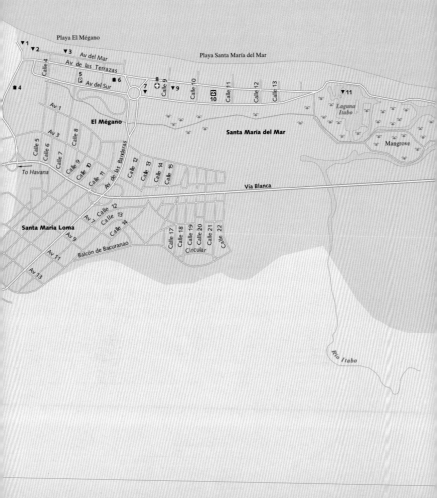

Straits of Florida

Playa El Mégano

Playa Santa María del Mar

▼ 1
▼ 2
▼ 3
Av del Mar
Av de las Terrazas
Calle 4
5
P
6
Av del Sur
8
Calle 9
▼ 9
Calle 10
Calle 11
Calle 12
Calle 13
▼ 11
■ 4
7
▼
10

Laguna
Itabo

Av 1

El Mégano

Santa María del Mar

Mangrove

Calle 5
Calle 6
Calle 7
Av 3
Calle 8
Calle 9
Calle D
Calle 11
Av de las Banderas
Calle 12
Calle 13
Calle 14
Calle 15

To Havana

Vía Blanca

Av 7
Av 9
Calle 12
Calle 13
Calle 14

Santa María Loma

Av 11

Balcón de Bacuranao

Av 13

Calle 17
Calle 18
Calle 19
Calle 20
Calle 21
Calle 22
Circular

Río Itabo

PLACES TO STAY
4 Villa El Mégano
6 Hotel Tropicoco
14 Hotel Gran Via
19 Villa Playa Hermosa

PLACES TO EAT
1 Parrillada D'Prisa
2 Kiosko Playa
3 Restaurante-Parrillada Costarenas
7 Restaurante Mi Casita de Coral
9 Mini-Super Las Terrazas
11 Restaurante My Cayito
12 Mini-Super Caribe Caracol
22 Farmer's Vegetable Market

OTHER
5 Guarded Parking
8 Clinica Internacional Habana del Este
10 Telephone Center
13 Centro Comercial El Dorado
15 Servi-Cupet
16 Cabaret Guanimar
17 Parque de Diveriones
18 Centro Comercial Guanabo
20 Banco Popular de Ahorro
21 Post Office

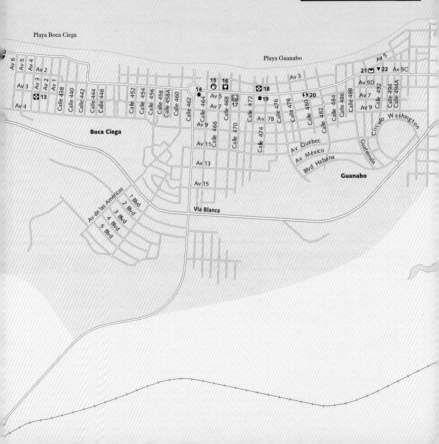

MAP LEGEND

ROUTES

City | Regional
........................Freeway
.....................Toll Freeway
......................Primary Road
................Secondary Road
.................Tertiary Road
.......................Dirt Road

.......................Pedestrian Mall
.................................Steps
...............................Tunnel
................................Trail
..................Walking Tour
...............................Path

TRANSPORTATION

...............Train
...............Metro

...............Bus Route
...............Ferry

HYDROGRAPHY

.......River; Creek
...............Canal
................Lake

...............Spring; Rapids
...............Waterfalls
...............Dry; Salt Lake

BOUNDARIES

...............International
...............State

...............County
...............Disputed

AREAS

...............Beach
...............Building
...............Campus

...............Cemetery
...............Forest
...............Garden; Zoo

...............Golf Course
...............Park
...............Plaza

...............Reservation
...............Sports Field
...............Swamp; Mangrove

POPULATION SYMBOLS

○ **NATIONAL CAPITAL** ...National Capital
◉ **State Capital** ....State Capital

● **Large City** ....Large City
● **Medium City** ....Medium City

● **Small City** ....Small City
○ Town; Village ....Town; Village

MAP SYMBOLS

■ ....Place to Stay
▼ ....Place to Eat
● ....Point of Interest

...............Airfield	...............Church	...............Museum	...............Skiing - Downhill
...............Airport	...............Cinema	...............Observatory	...............Stately Home
...Archeological Site; Ruin	...............Dive Site	...............Park	...............Surfing
...............Bank	...............Embassy; Consulate	...............Parking Area	...............Synagogue
...............Baseball Diamond	...............Footbridge	...............Pass	...............Tao Temple
...............Battlefield	...............Gas Station	...............Picnic Area	...............Taxi
...............Bike Trail	...............Hospital	...............Police Station	...............Telephone
...............Border Crossing	...............Information	...............Pool	...............Theater
...Bus Station; Terminal	...............Internet Café	...............Post Office	...............Toilet - Public
...............Bus Stop	...............Lighthouse	...............Pub; Bar	...............Tomb
...Cable Car; Chairlift	...............Lookout	...............RV Park	...............Trailhead
...............Campground	...............Mine	...............Shelter	...............Tram Stop
...............Castle	...............Mission	...............Shipwreck	...............Transportation
...............Cathedral	...............Monument	...............Shopping Mall	...............Volcano
...............Cave	...............Mountain	...Skiing - Cross Country	...............Winery

Note: not all symbols displayed above appear in this book

LONELY PLANET OFFICES

Australia
Locked Bag 1, Footscray, Victoria 3011
☎ 03 9689 4666 fax 03 9689 6833
email talk2us@lonelyplanet.com.au

USA
150 Linden Street, Oakland, California 94607
☎ 510 893 8555, TOLL FREE 800 275 8555
fax 510 893 8572
email info@lonelyplanet.com

UK
10A Spring Place, London NW5 3BH
☎ 0171 428 4800 fax 0171 428 4828
email go@lonelyplanet.co.uk

France
1 rue du Dahomey, 75011 Paris
☎ 01 55 25 33 00 fax 01 55 25 33 01
www.lonelyplanet.fr

World Wide Web: www.lonelyplanet.com *or* AOL keyword: lp
Lonely Planet Images: lpi@lonelyplanet.com.au